# The Free Human Being

Vladimir Putin opens up the gate to the
Development of the New Age

CW01064972

By

Sandor A Markus, Ph.D., MD., STD.

Lars Helge Swahn, M.Sc.

i

# The Free Human Being

## Vladimir Putin opens up the Gate to the Development of the New Age

In the end of this book there is more specific information about the illustrations in the book.

Because of the dynamic nature of the Internet, any web addresses or links contained in this book may have changed since publication and may no longer be valid.

Rev. Date: 2020-11-22

Address:

www.human-academy.com
www.unifier.se

KDP ISBN: 9798567696187

# Northern Pontifical Academy (NPA)
### The Gnostic Christian Church of the First Christians of Antioch Syrian Orthodox Patriarchate (Apostolically founded in Ecuador thereby in 1968). Government Approved and Registered as a Mystical Order in 1975. No. 1725

The main task of the Nordic Pontifical Academy (NPA) is to work for a Cosmic Community, which is the primary foundation of all Life in the Universe. Through mutual respect, ethical and moral living and the free exercise of philosophical, ideological and scientific belief systems, we can abolish the boundaries between faith and dogma. The NPA works for the elimination of intolerance and sectarianism, which creates division among people and nations and destroys world peace. The NPA works for a Cosmic Community whose foundation is Universal Power, Universal Love and Wisdom.

# Sovereign Imperial Order of Saint Germain

*Know the Truth within you and the Truth will set you free*

*Unifier*

*The real success of a country, a city or a social system is not about its BMP, its wealth, its science, its international status, but rather about its degree of true compassion to caring for all its inhabitants as a human family.*

# The Free Human Being

*There are two realities: the hitherto unknown 5D Matrix, the Soul-related (self) consciousness of reality which is of a higher qualitative cosmic (spiritual) nature.*

*It is Eternal, Infinite and Lasting.*

*... and by the most known, the 3D Matrix reality, which is unreal, temporary, transitory, perishable, an illusion.*

*Whichever of these two realities we choose in our present Age, it will be decisive for our future destiny (life and development) either on earth or on any other galaxy, solar system or planet...*

*The choice is in our hands.*

*Man has unconsciously or consciously allowed himself to be manipulated by the mind and the mind's five lower qualitative qualities, which have caused him sufferings and problems of various kinds.*

*Now is the time to let go and become free from the lower qualitative part of the mind's habitual patterns and attachments and develop the soul (self) related 5D consciousness which we all carry within us.*

*Unifier*

The Free Human Being

*The Sun is always shining, even behind the clouds. Everything is human consciousness, at different levels of creation. Through eons, it is refining to perfection - on its journey in gaining experience through the various realms in nature. The result - a crystal clear shining diamond of consciousness, which is our goal. Through experience it increases in strength and when it begins to approach perfection, the last opponents in creation are seen through, and we become free - we become the Free Human Being.*

*In order to get out of the unreal Matrix in which we have stayed for a long time, we need to raise our vibrations; and this can only be done through the right meditation and focusing in the forehead region "posterior medial frontal cortex", where the soul consciousness and the mind consciousness have their higher qualitative center.*

*We achieve the higher qualitative spiritual consciousness, which is multidimensional and includes the whole of creation.*

*Sandor A Markus - The Unifier*

# Contents

# The Free Human Being

## Russia has already begun the development of the New Age

**Figure 1. The President of the Russian Federation Vladimir Putin is a Reincarnation of Peter the Great who made Russia a Great Power in the 18th century, after the defeat of the Swedish King Charles XII in Poltava, Ukraine on June 28, 1709.**

Vladimir Putin, the President of the Russian Federation, is the only strong and charismatic leader in the world today, who possesses the inner and outer quality, experience and strength required to become a "*World Leader*" for the Earthly Civilization in the New Age, the *Golden Age*, in which our solar system and planet entered the winter solstice on December 21-23, 2012, when many believed that the earth would go under.

The kind of leadership that has hitherto been dominated and ruled by the Illuminati, Cabal (*the deep state*) in the western world, does not conform to the New Age, the Age of Aquarius.

Everything that man has hitherto thought and done belongs to the past, to the previous age, the Age of Pisces, which was predominantly dominated by *emotional will, emotional thinking and emotional action*.

The new age demands "*A New Consciousness in a New Time*" both in the leadership elite and in the earthly population in general. The whole of the earthly civilization, regardless of national and ethnic affiliation, is undergoing a process of change and restructuring, which is now taking place for the first time in the earth's 26,000-year history.

Our solar system and our planet have so far gone through 12 zodiac signs (*ages*) of about 2160 years each. The Age of Pisces was the end of the millennial cosmic cycle, which ended at the winter solstice on December 21-23, 2012, when our solar system and planet crossed the equatorial line in our galaxy and entered a giant photon belt (*light belt*) emanating from the Central Universe, the Central Sun Alcyone in the Pleiadian planetary constellation.

This event symbolizes not only the rebirth of our solar system, our planet, but also the rebirth of the soul (*the self*), the higher qualitative consciousness within man.

All of humanity, without exception, is facing great challenges both individually and collectively. To be able to meet these it requires a different kind of consciousness and leadership based on *Ethics* and *Morality* and not on *selfishness, lust for power* and *materialistic* striving, which has so far dominated most of the leadership elite. Our way of thinking and acting has so far been tainted by *selfishness, lust for power, acquisitiveness, greed, vanity, lust and more*. All this belongs to the animal-human stage of consciousness in the Homo Sapiens, "*The Thinking Human Being*".

It now requires a completely new view of life that turns the human stereotype upside down, the outdated notions of reality upside down, that which Charles Darwin, among other things referred to within his evolutionary teachings.

The previous age, the Age of Phishes, was thus characterized *by emotional thinking, emotional will* and *emotional action*, without any rational thinking. This created the world of *selfishness, materialism, hatred, discord between individuals and nations* in which we find ourselves today.

When it comes to these animal human qualities, we have a good example when it comes to the Swedish leadership elite's view on Russia and on Vladimir Putin.

There is no country in the world that criticizes Russia and Vladimir Putin both as leader and as a private individual as Sweden and the Swedish politicians so far. This may be due to the Jante Act which dominates the Swedish society but also the jealousy that is latent in the Swedish people's subconscious after the cessation of Sweden as a great power, i.e. after the Swedish King Charles XII lost the war in Poltava, Ukraine on June 28, 1709, due to bad strategy.

Sweden is a small country with about 10.4 million inhabitants living on a land area equivalent to about 450,295 km$^2$. The Russian Federation has about 146.8 million inhabitants living on an area that is the largest in the world. This area is about 17,098,242 km$^2$.

Russia is quite sparsely populated due to its enormous land area. The European side is more densely populated than the Russian side. Russia is multicultural and contains many different ethnic groups. The majority, however, are counted as Russians.

The political leadership elite in Sweden are not the right ones to accuse Vladimir Putin of running a dictatorship or to accuse him of being a bad leader for his country. Vladimir Putin has to take into account both a larger population consisting of different ethnic groups, and the sanctions that the US and the EU introduced in 2014 which have been extended until 2021.

Vladimir Putin has inherited a country and leadership that was basically bankrupt when he took over the leadership on August 9, 1999 as Prime Minister of the Russian Federation. Since the March 26, 2000 election, he has been the President of the Russian Federation.

His quick success prompted so-called experts around the world to ask themselves: *who really is Vladimir Putin?*

How many of these experts have figured out who he really is and what his inner qualities are that have been lacking in the other leaders so far?

His background is presented on social media:
*He has a law degree and was recruited as a 23-year-old to the Soviet security service KGB, where he worked with <u>counterintelligence</u> and <u>surveillance of foreign citizens</u> in Leningrad (now St. Petersburg).*

*In 1996, he began working closely with President Boris Yeltsin in Moscow, and was appointed head of the Russian security service FSB.*

If you have insight or knowledge of how a security service such as the KGB or now the GRU or FSB is structured and works, then you know that it consists of different types of activity areas, among other things a psychological section that deals with para-science and parapsychological research activities.

A Security Service such as the GRU and CIA conducts research in para-science. These security services have full control over what happens on earth, but also what concerns the parallel world, the parallel universe.

Communication with alien intelligences, UFOs, etc. are areas that are often incomprehensible to the normal individual to believe in, understand or accept as reality. Every phenomenon and perception of reality that is outside of the human sensory capacity is carefully examined within the psychological section of the security service. That is not the case in Sweden.

The fact that a security service keeps information related to the UFO phenomenon or extraterrestrial beings secret may be due to the fact that the public is not mature from the point of view of consciousness to absorb the kind of information that is beyond the comprehension of her present understanding. This makes her not believe or understand it.

It may also cause anxiety, create fear and insecurity in the majority who discover that extraterrestrial beings do not have to resemble us, have a similar appearance or body as we have. Therefore, all these phenomena since the 1950s have been classified until now.

Thousands of classified documents concerning the so-called paranormal phenomena have been declassified and released and this thanks to Vladimir Putin. He threatened the US to expose the aliens' presence unless the United States announced it. Since then, thousands of different classified information has been published about the presence of aliens and various UFO sightings.

During the present age, man will take part in all hitherto secret information from which man has been shielded from. This both the US and Russian intelligence services, the CIA and the GRU, have kept secret from the public. These disclosures have mainly been about five important areas in addition to the UFO sightings.

Every human being is endowed with a mind ability and seven sensory mind abilities.

Modern man has only knowledge of five sensory mind properties which are *sight, hearing, touch, taste* and *smell.*

The other two mind properties "*Intuition* and *Telepathy*" are not yet developed in most people.

*Intuition* and *Telepathy* include: *Clairvoyance, Precognition* and *Remote Viewing.*

*1) Intuition:* is the Voice of the Higher-Quality Self, the voice of the "Soul", Consciousness. Our intuition is usually best heard when our thoughts are silenced and all that is left is the still ocean of pure consciousness.

Intuition is to know that something is true without there being any logical explanation for how to know it.

Rational thinking wants to be able to see and know how to arrive at a conclusion, but our intuition seems to be reversed in such a way that the conclusion comes first and the explanation comes later.

Within every human being there is a built-in intuitive system that is there to help us read off energies in our environment. Ancient cultures of all times have known about this and used their intuitive and telepathic abilities to communicate with not only other people, but also with nature, animals and the spiritual subtle beings that are constantly around us.

*Mankind has not woven the web of life. We're just a thread in it.*

Whatever we do in the web, we do to ourselves. Everything is intertwined to energy and information and each other. Everything is part of the whole. Nothing is a separate phenomenon.

When we experience with the 5D quantum (unity) consciousness, then we understand that in true reality neither time nor distance exists. Everything happens at the same time. However, in the 3D reality that we live and operate in here and now, both time and distance exist.

This has with our five sensory perceptions of reality to do.

Imagine what would happen if you were born blind, if your visual sense was not functioning. How would you experience the fantastic surroundings consisting of mountains, lakes, forests, plants and animals in different colors and different sizes? You would experience none of these realities at all, although all of this exists.

Imagine if we were to turn off your *sense of touch, sense of smell* and *taste* and leave the sense of hearing intact. What would happen then?

You would not believe any of the information conveyed through the three sensory senses. You would think that everything that is told to you is untrue and unreal and you would consider it a fantasy, because you cannot experience any of this.

If you dive deep enough into the world of atoms in your body, down to the smallest constituents of yourself, then you will find that everything is vibrating energy. That's what our biological body is made of - energy. Nothing else. You would not find any solid matter. You would experience that all you see and experience is energy and information.

What would happen then?

Then you would have an even greater experience of reality than you have experienced so far. You would realize that our 3D world and reality in which we live and dwell is only a limited part (*a fragment*) of a larger reality.

So you understand that both the Russian and American intelligence services GRU and CIA, that their psychological departments for several decades have mapped everything that belongs to the so-called paranormal experiences that we humans can experience through *telepathy* and *intuition*, when we have awaken these abilities.

Through the two tools *Intuition* and *Telepathy* and the refinement of our other five senses we can live in a complete 5D reality. This is a necessity in order to be able to understand the causal connection behind every conceivable situation. We can then communicate with extraterrestrial beings, travel in Spaceships (*UFOs*), socialize with light beings (*so-called spiritual or angelic beings*), which is impossible via our five sensory senses.

The dark negative, destructive forces, the beings that operate through the Illuminati, the Cabal ([1]*the deep state*), want to prevent us from these kinds of experiences and communications. If not, they wouldn't be able to hide from man what they want to hide. They wouldn't be able to manipulate anyone if humans had the ability to see through their plans in advance.

This is exactly what is happening now in the world. This is thanks to the Russian intelligence service GRU and the Pleiadian Federation, who are constantly keeping an eye on these destructive alien creatures and their plans.

Some people confuse *Intuition* with *Instinct*.

*Instinct* controls behaviors that help us survive, while *intuition* describes a more complex human perception.

Intuition is an inner voice that helps us make the right decisions in different situations and to better respond to life's daily challenges.

*2) Telepathy:* involves the transfer of thought from one person's psyche to another's. By telepathy is meant the ability to have direct mental contact with another person without communicating with the help of languages, codes, signs or other physical signal forms, in short thought transfer.

For several decades I have been communicating with extraterrestrial entities (*beings*) who have telepathically transmitted to me about 6,000 pages of information. All this information forms the basis of the New Age man. Since 1993, we have started teaching this through lectures, seminars, workshops, online and through literature.

*3) Clairvoyance:* means clear vision. Examples of clairvoyant forces are not difficult to find. In almost all mythologies and religions, there are examples of people who have experienced visions of different events.

Clairvoyance is a hidden knowledge that exists within all of us which can be awakened, trained. To be able to start training your clairvoyant ability, you must open your higher qualitative part of the mind that has its seat behind the frontal lobe in the "*posterior medial frontal cortex region*" in the brain, the part of the brain that is active in identification and problem solving. We really need to trust that we are all equipped with this ability.

---

[1] In the book when we mention the Cabal (*the deep state*) we mean mostly the destructive negative force in the western world.

The best way to get started and make ourselves receptive is through meditation. Ideally, you should meditate for about 50 minutes daily in a harmonious environment. The focus must be in the forehead region above the root of the nose where the "Third Eye" (*The All-Seeing Eye*) has its center. After some training, this eventually leads to clairvoyant visions.

*4) Precognition:* Precognition means visions and other impressions of future events that could not have been generated otherwise if information about these events were not available even before they took place in reality.

A distinctive feature of precognitions is that they usually have significant importance for the precognitor himself. The events are often about themselves or other relatives. Only a few are about public figures and knowledge of major disasters in advance.

Precognitions are something that, according to the mechanistic worldview, simply cannot exist.

In the 3D mechanistic worldview, time is linear and the future can therefore not exist until it is, so to speak, here. Yet there has always been a belief in all societies that future events can be revealed under certain circumstances, and the examples below show that there is justification for this belief.

Already in the 1990s, I received some information about what the future holds.

*Example 1.* A woman says: "One day I was doing the dishes when I suddenly knew that my son was going to have an accident with his car. But I was sure he would not be injured. I watched the clock and it showed 19.15. My son called me later in the evening to say that he had had an accident with the car, but that neither he nor those who were in the other car were injured. I asked when the accident occurred and he answered at 19.20."

*Example 2.* A woman who had many precognitive experiences tells of one of them: "I was in the sixth month with my second child. I had a vivid dream that the child was born by caesarean section, that it was a boy and that he only lived 18 hours. When he was dead he was lying in a plastic box lined with white flowers. I had a boy who was delivered by caesarean section and he lived for 17 hours and 30 minutes. When the doctor told me he had died I could not cry, so I was brought down so I should see him. He was dressed in a sleeping suit and surrounded by white chrysanthemums and lying in an incubator just as I had dreamed.

*Example 3.* Sometimes a recurring precognition can herald something that is far in the future. This was the case for a woman who tells the following: "From about five to about thirty years of age, I had the same dream at least once every two or three weeks. I was in a field and an airplane crashed or was about to do so and there was parachutes over me. I was always scared and woke up crying. The whole family and all my friends knew about this dream. About ten years ago I was in the field I dreamed of when two jets collided in the air. The parachutes were there and I cried, but it was because my dream had come true and I simply could not believe it. No one was killed. I had absolutely nothing to do with the people in the planes. Since then, the dream has not returned."

*Example 4.* A well-known historical example of a precognitive dream is the one that Bishop Joseph de Lanyi had about the murder of Archduke Ferdinand and his wife Sophie in Sarajevo. "During the night of June 28, 1914, the bishop dreamed that he received a letter from the archduke. In the letterhead was a picture showing how the murder would proceed and in the letter the archbishop announced that he and his wife would be murdered the following day.

In the morning, the bishop told his dream to several people and then held a Mass for the future victims. Later that day, the assassination took place and became the prelude to the First World War. "

Since the 1960s, I have communicated both visually and telepathically with extraterrestrial beings from the Pleiades.

At a later stage, I have also established intuitive and telepathic communication with entities from Arcturus due to my metaphysical, quantum physical interests that are about the quantum medical technology of the future which uses Scalar waves, where the focus is on the causal (*cause-related*) part of the human state of health instead of the very symptoms that medical science has hitherto been devoted to.

We are now establishing the first scientific research center in the Life Sciences in the Nordic countries. The research center is connected to the CelesteMethod® described later in the book.

Our research is primarily focused on the cause behind human mental, emotional (*emotion-related*) and biological (*physical*) problems of various kinds, and secondarily on the symptoms themselves.

My many years of communication with extraterrestrial beings from the Pleiades and later from Arcturus have contributed to my development of the so-called "paranormal, para-psychological" abilities that we are all equipped with and can develop without exception. This is required to reach a "*New Consciousness in a New Time*" and is a necessity to be able to be part of the new civilization, the 5th in order. This will become a reality around the year 2027, when a new generation takes over the development on earth.

Russia has been cooperating with the Pleiadian Federation since 1963, when the first contact was established between President Nikita Khrushchev and the Pleiadian envoy of the Intergalactic Federation Council.

The psychological section within the Russian security service KGB, now GRU, has since conducted research in the so-called paranormal frontiers. This exceeds the comprehension of politicians and heads of state, as well as the normal individual.

Vladimir Putin's consciousness differs markedly from that of the leadership in the United States or Europe, which constantly criticize him for various reasons.

Vladimir Putin possesses a completely different knowledge and consciousness of what concerns the future development of the earth compared to other leaders in the world. Most leaders and heads of state have seized power not out of suitability or experience, but through corruption, lies, manipulation, flattery and false pretensions to the people. None of these rulers will have any significant role during the new age.

Covid-19/20 has been the first test by the Illuminati, CABAL (*the deep state*) to see people's reaction, behavior and how they perceive and react in a completely new situation that they have never experienced before in modern times.

Next in line is SARS-CoV-2 which will appear before the end of the year. This will invoke even greater fear and dread in man when man discovers that nothing will be as it was before, that the world, society does not return to the state that humans believed and hoped for before the beginning of the Covid-19 pandemic.

We have warned about this pandemic already in the 1990s at our seminars and in our literature, and the pandemic has nothing to do with the coronavirus itself, which we mention in this book.

Through the influence of mainstream media (*TV, Radio, Internet, Newspapers*) 24/7, a kind of mental programming and manipulation has been created to invoke anxiety, fear, dread and stress, especially in the older generation. These believe in everything that is said or written by controlled journalists. The Illuminati, Cabal (*the deep state*) knows this.

Through mental influence and radiation from 4G and 5G, the immune system is weakened.

*Through the mobile band's 4G and 5G effects, bacteria, toxic chemicals such as mercury in amalgam fillings in the oral cavity, heavy metals in the body, the organism and cell structure can be activated and turn these toxic substances into weapons that can kill or harm humans. This is not the same as dying from the coronavirus.*

In Sweden, many people who have died from various causes have been counted in the Corona statistics to increase the mortality by the "virus". This has been told by many who have lost one of their relatives due to different kinds of diseases.

If you look in the statistics at the number of people who die annually for various reasons, e.g. flu, medical causes, side effects and malpractices, then the number will be the same. As a percentage, people are now dying in the same numbers as in previous years.

This scenario affects all people around the world no matter they are young or old, rich or poor, famous or non-famous, in power or ordinary citizens. No one escapes unless they have a well-functioning immune system and mental, emotional and biological symbiosis.

When the aforementioned scenario that we have warned about now occurs, the entire current symptom-related healthcare system will collapse. We have warned people about this already in the 1990s.

Synthetic, chemical based medicine will be ineffective and life threatening due to its side effects on the already burdened immune system.

Behind this agenda are the Illuminati, Cabal (*the deep state*), Rothschild, Rockefeller, Soros and the Bilderberg group and their loyal members.

President Vladimir Putin has previously declared that he will help ensure that the agenda of the Illuminati, Cabal (*deep state*) will not be implemented.

All Illuminati, Cabal (*deep state*) led governments, organizations and individuals constantly accuse Vladimir Putin of being a dictator. This is only because he refuses to follow their agenda and submit to their decision to enslave and exterminate humanity.

Vladimir Putin cares for the well-being and development of his own people. He does not want to allow power-mad, manipulative individuals or organizations that have nothing to do with Russia or the Russian people to rule over them.

He believes that the peoples of all countries, in the same way as the organism in the body, should take care of their own development. Imagine if the kidney cells in the kidney community wanted to emigrate or attack the liver community and take over its command.

If instead every organ cell in the organ society could perform its tasks that they have been programmed to, then the human body would never get ill.

Mixing "kidney and liver cells" is exactly what the Illuminati, CABAL (*the deep state*) is doing. To destroy the countries' sovereignty, self-determination-right to live the life they are programmed to do. Otherwise, the world would not have been divided into different countries, different human species in order to individually and together strive for unity consciousness.

This is what President Vladimir Putin has declared, i.e. the nations' sovereignty and mutual cooperation towards unity. His interest is not only about Russia, but about creating peace between countries and people, to abolish crime (*violence*), selfishness, materialism, which contributes to anarchy and the disintegration of society. This is exactly the opposite of what the Illuminati, CABAL advocates.

To get to know Vladimir Putin, *all critics must walk as many steps in his moccasins as he has done himself.* This is an old Native American saying.

Those who criticize or analyze Vladimir Putin, who lacks the experience he has gained over several incarnations on earth, the ability to perceive, see situations from different perspectives, don't get a true picture of his pattern of action. If you are not equipped with similar experiences then you can never understand his behavior and actions.

*To criticize him requires a certain amount of knowledge, but to judge his behavior in different situations requires total knowledge.*

Which of his critics possess similar qualities?

Getting to know Vladimir Putin as a person requires a higher quality multidimensional consciousness. At present, only a few people on earth are equipped with that.

A Russian commentator described Putin like this: "*his political outline was as distinct as the outline of a black cat in a dark room.*"

None of Vladimir Putin's representatives or any other president in the world has succeeded in building a country on his own in principle from the material and economic ruins that Russia and the Russian people have been in since the Russian Revolution of 1917.

If you study the rise and fall of Communism, then you can see that he saved Russia from the chaotic situation that Russia was in for several decades - when Boris Yeltsin handed over the power to Vladimir Putin.

Neither Vladimir Putin's past nor present critics can shoulder his mantle and accomplish what he has done for Russia and for the Russian people.

To be a good leader for a country or for the world, you have to be a very good chess player much like "*Garri Kasparov*".

If a head of state, a leader is not endowed with similar qualities as a world champion in chess, then he cannot become a good leader for the country, society, for his people or for any organization. This all who seek power should think about. But to become a world champion in leadership, the same inner qualities are required as the Russian chess champion Garri Kasparov.

If you are a good and well-known actor, athlete, business leader or speaker, then most people believe that you can become a good leader for the country or the people.

This is not consistent with the truth.

A good leader must think long-term in the same way as a world champion in chess does prior to every move. Every move must be carefully thought through before swinging into action.

*If you make the wrong move then it can be checkmate.*

Critics can make as many mistakes as they like. But if a leader like Vladimir Putin makes the slightest mistake, then he is immediately criticized both in the home country and abroad by his opponents, or by people who usually think short-term.

When it comes to Mainstream Media (MSM), when they interview someone, it is usually about asking all sorts of irrelevant questions that the interviewee cannot give a clearly thought-out answer to.

The person being interviewed is surprised and may think that the interviewer (*journalist*) is disrespectful in his behavior and is just looking for sensation. Or the interviewee is surprised by the question and gives a seemingly ill-considered answer. This creates sensation and fuel for critics and the people who have not understood anything of the interview, but only the incorrect answer given by the interviewee in question.

*After the interview, the vultures arrive to share the prey.*

Man must learn discernment - to distinguish the lie from the truth, the authenticity from the falsehood.

As long as you cannot do that, you cannot see what is true or false, right or wrong in a given situation.

There is a saying that goes: *while the lie has reached to Baghdad, the truth is still looking for its sandals.*

One thing is excite a group of people, create opinion formations, organize demonstrations, rather than come up with constructive solutions that benefit the people as a whole and not just those who criticize. But none of the critics who have come to power so far have in any way ever improved the conditions or situation of their fellow human beings for the better, except for themselves and their families.

If we look at the world today and ask ourselves the question, what has become better in Sweden, France, Germany, England for the people as a whole after they have joined the EU - then it can be stated that socially it has become better in some countries from a material or economic point of view. Technological development has rocketed since the 1990s. Infrastructure has improved markedly in the Western world, while humans have not developed significantly.

The majority of the people viewed from an ethical, moral and acting point of view remain at the primary level on the development scale. Many lack respect, consideration, tolerance, understanding, caring, love for their neighbor, for their surroundings, and without these qualities man cannot move forward on the development spiral.

Most people move around the world with modern technology, mobile phones, modern computers, modern means of communication, which they neither understand nor are interested in knowing how they work, with only a few exceptions. People take it for granted that these technological devices will work.

If you ask the question about how their mobile phone works - then maybe you get the answer that they work well, right?

They have not learned simple basic knowledge in physics - how two individuals can communicate with each other remotely via technical equipment such as transmitters and receivers - what kind of carriers are required to be able to both send and receive information. How can it be possible to send and receive information without delay if one person is in the United States and the other in China?

Man knows nothing about his body or what the word health means in its proper, original context. Man uses his body as a garbage can where they can throw anything in. One day the body doesn't work as it should - then you rush to the nearest health center, pharmacy or doctor's office to get hold of some synthetic-chemical pill to chew on with the hope of the body being restored to its normal state.

Some people train their body for better condition and better appearance, while at the same time considering their head as a kind of ornamental object and not as a hardware that contains a software program which is more comprehensive than NASA's and the Pentagon's software program combined.

Man goes through life with a quantum computer in his head and uses this computer capacity minimally, for non-essentials.

The most intelligent and conscious human being on earth uses about 17% of the total brain capacity consciously according to neuroscience.

The normal individual uses about 6-8% of his brain's total capacity consciously while having access to another 92-94% that is not used consciously.

The total capacity of the human brain can be compared to the world's fastest "Fugaku" supercomputer. "Fugaku" is the world's fastest supercomputer which has been developed by the Riken Institute in Japan. Fugaku has the capacity to deliver 415.5 petaflops, which is 2.8 times faster than the previously American manufactured fastest computer "Summit". Fugaku has sum total 7.3 million processor cores.

It has taken the Riken Institute in Japan 6 years to build the Fugaku supercomputer and it is estimated to have cost around 1 billion dollars to develop.

Fugaku is expected to be brought into operation for real next year but has already started collecting data on the ongoing "covid-19 pandemic". Among other things, it has simulated the spread of the new "corona virus SARS-CoV-2" and has been used to see how effective Japan's infection detection app for the virus has been.

If man is not interested in his human development by using more of his brain computer capacity than hitherto, then he will soon be replaced by an "Artificial Intelligent" robot. What do you do on earth then unless you choose to develop and evolve?

Earth is not meant to be a holiday paradise, a Shangri La for idle people.

Man cannot remain on earth if he doesn't want to evolve or can't do any good.

If you aren't interested in getting to know yourself and your affinity with the whole of creation, then what is your task? The earth survives without man, but man does not survive without the earth.

If we go to the next candidate in the order when it comes to world leadership, then in addition to Vladimir Putin there is only one given candidate.

This is the leader of the People's Republic of China, Xi Jinping.

From a political point of view, Xi Jinping has more experience than Vladimir Putin.

But he is not the world champion in leadership as Vladimir Putin.

*That is what it takes in order to lead a whole world in a whole new spirit.*

"A New Consciousness in A New Time" means that there is nothing left of the past, the past in existence.

The era of selfishness, lust for power, hostility, hatred and exploitation is over.

We must all strive for a unity consciousness that unites us instead of dividing and enslaving us as the Illuminati, CABAL (*the deep state*) strives for.

*/ Unifier*

# Vladimir Putin

Figure 2. The Russian President
Vladimir Putin.

**Vladimir Putin** was born on October 7, 1952 in Leningrad (*St. Petersburg*). He comes from a simple family relationship.

From a young age, Vladimir Putin was interested in sports, especially martial arts such as Judo. During his whole time as a politician he has had an interest in sports.

Vladimir Putin studied law at the Leningrad State University and wrote a doctoral dissertation on the importance of energy policy for future Russian economic success.

After graduating in 1975, he joined the KGB. He participated in the monitoring of foreigners and consular officials in Leningrad.

In August 1981, there was a coup attempt by Communist army commanders with links to the military and the KGB against Mikhail Gorbachev.

On the second day of the coup attempt, Vladimir Putin resigned from the KGB and began a political career.

Vladimir Putin said the decision to resign from the KGB was tough, but he did not support the direction and goals of the coup.

From 1985 to 1990 he was sent to Dresden, East Germany. After the collapse of the East German government, he returned to Leningrad where he became assistant to the rector of Leningrad State University in charge of international relations.

In 1997, Boris Yeltsin appointed him Deputy Chief of Staff. In 1999, he was elected Prime Minister of Russia, with the support of Yeltsin. When Yeltsin unexpectedly resigned a few months later, Vladimir Putin became Russia's president.

On New Year's Eve 1999 when the clock struck 12.00 pm, Boris Yeltsin resigned and Vladimir Putin became the president of the Russian Federation.

*He delivered a speech to the nation, declaring that Russia will never be the same as before.*

*He urged the Russian people to start thinking in new ways and forget everything that have happened so far.*

No one took him seriously.

During the first years of his presidency, Putin received significant popular support because of his tough approach on military issues (such as the war in Chechnya), and supervised a return to economic stability. He cultivated a macho "action-man" image as a fearless leader and athlete, helped by his athletic and KGB past. This image was attractive to voters. After a decade of inflation and declining living standards in the 2000s, Russia began a period of economic growth, falling unemployment and rising living standards. The strong economy growth was due to the rising price of oil and gas (*increasing value of Russia's exports*) and strong macroeconomic management.

Early in his leadership, he reached an agreement with the new Russian "oligarchs", the powerful businessmen who had gained control of former state-owned industries. Putin made an agreement in which they agreed to start paying taxes and avoiding politics. In return, they were free to pursue their business interests. This contributed to increased revenue for the government and reduced oligarchic political influence.

In 2008, without being able to be elected for a third term as president, Dmitry Medvedev was elected President. During Medvedev's presidency, Vladimir Putin was Russia's prime minister. But it was Vladimir Putin who remained the most powerful person.

In 2012, Putin was re-elected for a third term as president, but for the first time, this led to widespread protests against the country's lack of democracy. Vladimir Putin's regime has been increasingly criticized for being dictatorial and avoiding real democracy.

For example, the former Russian President Mikhail Gorbachev, who was originally a supporter of Vladimir Putin, was disappointed by the growing disrespect for democracy and authoritarian tendencies.

In 2007, Mikhail Gorbachev said that Vladimir Putin had "taken Russia out of chaos".

In 2011, he criticized Vladimir Putin for seeking a third term as president.

Mikhail Gorbachev was very critical of the 2011 election. "The result doesn't reflect the will of the people," Mikhail Gorbachev said at the time. "Therefore, I believe that Russia's leaders can only make one decision - annul the election result and hold new ones." (*Mikhail Gorbachev calls upon Vladimir Putin to resign*). This would have been a completely wrong decision.

As for *Mikhail Gorbachev's criticism of Vladimir Putin, then it is unjustified. At the time of Mikhail Gorbachev's departure, Russia was in bankruptcy, poverty and disintegration.*

*Nothing worked in Russia at that time.*

In May 2007, Patriarch Alexius II of the Russian Orthodox Church praised Vladimir Putin for healing the 80-year-old schism between the leadership and the Russian Orthodox Church.

In March 2014, following the unrest in Ukraine, Vladimir Putin approved the use of Russian troops to enter the Crimean region. Shortly afterwards, a referendum was held in which a majority of the people voted to leave Ukraine and re-enter Russia. There was criticism of the legitimacy of the referendum, but Crimea has effectively left Ukraine for Russia. The Ukraine issue has led to increased tensions between Russia and the West.

During the 2016 US election, the CIA in the US and MI 6 in the UK claimed that Russian agents were trying to influence the presidential election by publishing social media news that helped Donald Trump and prevented Hillary Clinton from becoming president.

Knowing Hillary Clinton's immoral background, which has been kept secret from the whole world by the Illuminati, she would be prevented by any means from being elected the new president of the United States.

There are ethical and moral rules that a head of state should follow if about to shoulder the responsibility for an entire nation or the whole world.

Hillary Clinton did not meet that criterion.

Similar allegations were made against Vladimir Putin over Britain's vote on Brexit.

President Putin is the only President in Europe who cares about the prosperity and preservation of his own people, but also to create peace on earth. The United States, through NATO, has over 800 military bases around the world, while Russia has only four, and China two. So who is the enemy and who is striving for peace - and then out of the blue, Russia is portrayed as the number one enemy.

Vladimir Putin is accused of having influenced both the US presidential election and the British election when it comes to Brexit.

Vladimir Putin is the only leader in the world who has the possibility to prevent the US, Illuminati, CABAL (*deep state*) - led agenda of the planned "New World Order" from coming into being.

Vladimir Putin is the only one who can prevent the extinction and enslavement of humanity on earth.

This is thanks to the cooperation that has been going on between the Pleiadian Federation and the KGB (now GRU) since 1963. Here, Russia has gained access to more sophisticated defense technology to be able to guarantee peace for the Russian people and for the countries, nations that want Russia's protection. This protection must be contrasted with NATO's agenda, with its extraterrestrial perverted species from the Orion constellation, Betelgeuse, who the Hitler regime previously cooperated with.

*Russian military technology is far superior to both the American and Chinese.*

The Russian people have undergone an extensive hardening process, in the same way as coal before it became a diamond.

# Helena Petrovna Blavatsky

The well-known Russian mystic and founder of the Theosophical Society, Helena Petrovna Blavatsky, foretold as early as the 19th century the rise of the Russian people out of suffering and poverty and its coming heyday in the 21st century.

She predicted the return of Vladimir Putin (*alias Peter the Great*) to lead the Russian people into the New Age.

Who was H.P. Blavatsky?

Figure 3. Helena Petrovna Blavatsky, 1831-1891, founder of the World Wide Theosophical Society.

**Helena Petrovna von Hahn** was born into a Russian noble family in 1831 in Ukraine. Already in her childhood, Helena demonstrated her extraordinary talents, as well as her clairvoyance and other cross-border inner abilities. She was a stubborn child, with a will that could not be controlled by anything but reasonable arguments. She received her education from governesses, an education that she immersed herself in through own studies in her grandfather's large library.

At 16 years of age, she was divorced from the 69-year-old General **Nikofor Blavatsky**. After three months of marriage, she left him. She had other plans. She set out on her own on a long journey that lasted about 25 years. She had no problem with finances because her family was rich. She had an innate ability for occultism (mysticism), which made her want to go on adventures to find the answer to the mystery of life that she wanted to seek in different cultures.

In 1848, when she was 17 years old, she came to Constantinople in Turkey.

In 1850 she was in Cairo, studying ancient Egyptian and Coptic mysticism. She continued her journey to the United States, New Mexico, Colorado, etc., where she studied "The Way of Life" according to the Inca culture and the Hopi peoples. She traveled to Peru, Bolivia and Ecuador to study the ancient Native American cultures and the lost wisdom of the gods.

Then she went to Asia. She traveled to India, Burma, Siam and China. She wanted to find various masters and holy men and women who practiced various kinds of ritual magic, yoga and more.

In India, she was fascinated by the miraculous abilities of yogis and fakirs, and it struck her that it was not just about advanced magic, but that their achievements were the results of many years of training and development. It wasn't something you learned in a few weeks of courses, or a short stay with a yoga master or guru, or with some Western people who have opened different kinds of schools in the West where they practice a lower quality mind-related skill - these kinds of skills that usually lead to dead ends.

In the end, her trip went to Tibet. She had heard that the spiritual Masters were there, those who belonged to the secret White Brotherhood.

She tried several times to enter Tibet but was denied entry by the English authorities who believed she was a Russian spy. She claimed that she finally managed to enter the most closed of all countries and reached the Masters' Oasis, where she stayed for seven years, hence the film: "*Seven Years in Tibet*" which was played with Brad Pitt in the lead role.

The film largely was about the current **14th Dalai Lama** and his upbringing in Lhasa, Tibet. The current Dalai Lama is Tibet's religious and political leader. This office has nothing to do with the title of "Panchen" or "Tashi" Lama. During H P Blavatsky's visit to Tibet, the Panchen Lama was the Supreme Spiritual Head of the Tibetan people and the monks of the Tashilunpo Monastery (*main monastery*) in Shigatse.

Figure 4. Tashilhunpo Monastery in Shagatse.

Some who have studied her life doubt her claim. There are no other sources than her own information and they are sometimes strongly contradictory. Some things are not told to anyone, because it does not concern anyone else, only oneself.

What if the intelligence services CIA, NSA, FSB, GRU, MI 6, MOSAD or the Swedish SÄPO were to reveal everything they know or have knowledge of?

How would it work for people who don't understand more than just the most necessary in life - those who doubt or reject what they don't understand? They have to seek the truth on their own. This applies to all kinds of experiences.

But whether one believes or mistrusts H.P. Blavatsky, if she was in Tibet or not, she was very engaged in finding the Masters of the Orient and gaining access to their wisdom.

H.P. Blavatsky claimed that she had been able to see the Masters in <u>visions</u> since her childhood and that on at least one occasion she had met her own Master, Kuthumi Lal Singh.

There has been a lot of speculation about H.P. Blavatsky's life, travels, what places she visited or who she met, things that cannot be documented. This has created speculation, conspiracy theories and questioning among those who have nothing to do with it. It is her knowledge and teachings that is of interest and not who she met and why?

I have been subjected to similar criticisms where journalists, uninitiated question the truthfulness of what is being said, without having any knowledge or experience of what they are questioning. This instead of using the information and knowledge you convey.

The existence of H.P. Blavatsky's Master, his authenticity, I can attest through one of the attached documents I have in my possession, which is both written and signed by Master Kuthumi Lal Sing, dated to my own Master Teacher "Johnny Lovewisdom" in Ecuador, South America, in May 1947.

The name "Kuthumi Lal Singh" is an official title of a Master Teacher who reincarnates and uses the same title in the same way as "Dalai Lama" is an official title.

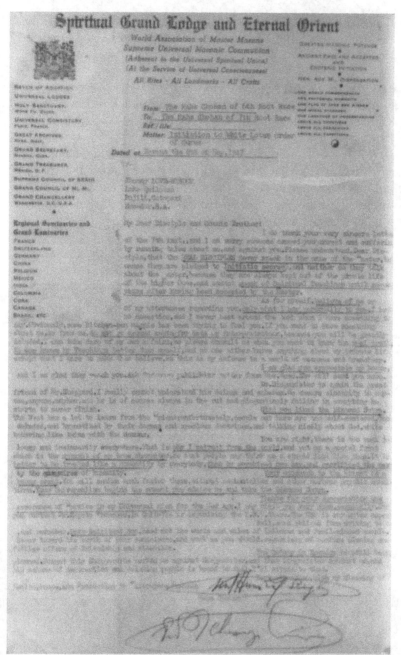

Figure 5. Letter from Master Kuthumi Lal Singh, dated May 1947 to Johnny Lovewisdom in Ecuador, South America.

One day when H.P. Blavatsky took a walk in Hyde Park, as she stood by Lake Serpentine, immersed in thought, the Master suddenly was standing in front of her, smiling. He declared that he belonged to the Great White Brotherhood (*the Cosmic Federation on Earth*), which at that time was headquartered in Tashilunpo, Shigatse, Tibet. The Brotherhood needed her help to promote a powerful spiritual impulse for the good of mankind. She would be at the forefront of an extensive spiritual movement, and for this important task she would have to prepare for many years.

Helena Petrovna Blavatsky decided to answer yes to the Masters' wish. She had just turned 20 years old.

*The notion of the Masters and the Great White Brotherhood has played a major role in theosophy and also in several other occult directions. The official theosophical designation is Mahatma (great soul) but in English the word Master is often used. According to Theosophy, a Master is consecrated, initiated to the highest degree, an elevated being, in possession of a wisdom and power corresponding to the status he has attained in spiritual evolvement.*

*According to theosophy, spiritual evolvement presupposes reincarnation.*

*Man undergoes evolution through millions of years and thousands of earthly incarnations. During each incarnation, man gains experiences that take him a step further on the infinitely long path to the goal, which is to make aware the Higher Self, which means that the human being achieves a divine status.*

*The theosophists believed that the Masters lived in an inaccessible area of Tibet and that they controlled the cosmic forces to such an extent that they could appear either in their physical body or in their spiritual form, according to their own will. They were not bound by distance but could move from Tibet to London in an instant. The theosophists also thought that all the Masters together constituted the Great White Brotherhood, leading world development by inspiring people to reach higher consciousness.*

That which made Madame Blavatsky embark on the endless journeys was the conviction that earlier high cultures had access to a mystery wisdom that was later lost. She thought that if there were still fragments of this occult wisdom left in different parts of the world, it was necessary to collect these pieces and reconstruct a coherent spiritual world explanation.

At the same time, she was looking for ways that could develop and open her spiritual senses and make her see into the spiritual world.

In the early 1860s, she spent a long time in the Caucasus. There she went into a meditative existence. She needed peace and quiet to digest the impressions of many years of travel, and in addition, she sought solitude in order to practice certain magical techniques she had learned. Suddenly she became ill with a violent and long-lasting fever. Sometimes she was in a coma, sometimes in an awake, apathetic state. During the illness, she experienced that her inner self was split in two personalities. In this meditative state, there was a significant change in her *psychic* abilities.

When her meditative state was over, she discovered that she had gained full control over her medial abilities. She resumed her travels. But in the early 1870s, she felt a strong need to do more than pursue secret wisdom for her own part. She felt that the time had come for an organized attack on materialism and selfishness.

In 1871 she started in Cairo the **Societé Spirité**, which consisted of a group of people who would undertake a *scientific* study in spiritualism. But the group soon disbanded, and again she began to wander in Europe until in 1873, at the age of 42, she received a clear *order* from Master *Kuthumi Lal Singh* urging her to go to the United States.

In 1875 she founded in New York together with Colonel H.S. Olcott the *Theosophical Society*.

In 1877 she published the book *Isis Unveiled*.

According to her diary entries, it was always Master *Kuthumi Lal Singh* who inspired her.

She had developed the ability to put herself in a state of total relaxation, at the Theta stage of consciousness. At this stage of consciousness, she was able to telepathically establish communication with her Master Teacher.

Isis Unveiled is a huge work of 1300 pages, which deals with the most subjects in occultism, magic and ancient mystery wisdom. She refers to over a hundred sources, most of which were forgotten and legendary manuscripts that in her time did not exist in any Western library. The book is an attempt to establish an occult world declaration.

One part of the content describes the fourth dimension (4D): the parallel *astral and etheric world* and the five-dimensional (5D) *Akasha chronicle*, which contains information about the entire universe and the evolution of the human species.

The astral world (4D) is explained as part of the reality that exists between the earthly physical three-dimensional world (3D) and the five-dimensional (5D) spiritual world. This 4D world is also called the parallel world. It permeates the physical world and is an extension of this and the place where the dead reside and where everything has a much stronger intensity than in the physical world.

The human being also has an *astral body* where the psychic processes take place. The human astral body connects her with the macrocosmic astral world, and it is possible through meditative efforts to develop astral sensory organs and become seeing in that part of reality. The astral substance is non-physical, but subtle, and has still a certain extent in space and time and above all, the astral world is governed by completely different laws than those that govern the physical world. Madam Blavatsky claimed, among other things that the Masters could detach their astral body (etheric body) from the physical body and move with the speed of thought to any place on earth.

The Akasha Chronicle is the 5D matrix (*unity field*) where everything that happens within creation is imprinted. The initiates can look into the Akasha chronicle and thus get to know everything that has happened in history.

The theosophist *Scott Elliot*, who published a book about Atlantis in 1896, claimed that the book's content was the result of a clairvoyant study of the astral world. In addition to the astral world and the astral body, the theosophists believe that there is a supersensible etheric world and an etheric body that are located between the astral world and the physical world.

In the book The Secret Doctrine, in which Madame Blavatsky tried to give the Theosophical thoughts a final written form, it was again the Masters who spoke through her.

She was told by her Master *Kuthumi Lal Singh* that Russia will once again become a great power and lead the development on earth during the New Age with the influence of the Supreme Pleiadian Federation. The Russian leadership is a consequence of the fact that the Russian people belong to the people who has suffered the most on earth under the oppression of various rulers and thus has the most experience in life.

# Xi Jinping

Figure 6. Xi Jinping, President of the
People's Republic of China.

Xi Jinping was born on June 15, 1953 in Beijing.

Xi Jinping comes from the Shaanxi Province. He is the youngest son of Xi Zhongxun, one of the founders of the former communist guerrilla movement in the province. His father later became vice Prime Minister of the People's Republic of China. Xi Jinping is therefore usually considered the "crown prince" among today's Chinese leaders.

Xi Jinping belongs to the generation of the Chinese leaders who engaged in physical labor during the Cultural Revolution and who got educated at the beginning of the Reformation period. During the Cultural Revolution, Xi Jinping's father lost all his political positions and was exiled to the Henan Province. He was not rehabilitated until 1980. Xi Jinping himself, however, managed to escape direct persecution, but was deported to Liangjiahe Village in Yanchuan between 1969 and 1975. Xi Jinping himself has said that this experience was a turning point in his life. In 1975, Xi Jinping had to leave the village when he was admitted to Tsinghua University on the recommendation of party comrades in the village.

Local politician (1982–1993)

In 1982, Xi Jinping received his first position as deputy party secretary in the Zhengding district in Hebei, and was promoted a year later to full party secretary of the same district in 1983. He remained there until 1985, when he became deputy mayor of the important city of Xiamen in Fujian. Still in Fujian, he became party secretary for Ningde since 1988 and then party secretary for the provincial capital of Fuzhou in 1990.

Provincial politician (1993–2007)

Xi rose to the provincial level as he was elected to the board of Fujian's party department in 1993, and in 1995 became deputy party secretary of the province, a position he held for a year 1995-1996 in parallel with his duties as party secretary for Fuzhou.

At the party congress in 1997, Xi became a deputy in the Central Committee. He became acting governor of Fujian in 1999 and then permanent governor in 2000. Note that a governor in China has less power than the provincial party secretary, as illustrated by the fact that Xi was still only deputy party secretary despite the governorship.

In 2002, Xi became a permanent member of the Central Committee and finally got his own province, as he became party secretary of Zhejiang. He stayed there until 2007 before being allowed to step in as party secretary for prestigious Shanghai for a year after a corruption scandal in the city's party apparatus, which hit Jiang Zemin's "Shanghai clique" hard.

During his time as party secretary, Xi wrote a number of theoretical works, including two essays on Karl Marx's "Theses on Feuerbach" and a collection of essays published at the Zhejiang People's Publishing House in 2007.

National politicians (2007–2012)

Xi Jinping was elected to the Politburo's standing committee at the party congress in 2007, and he was also elected chairman of the secretariat and principal of the Central Party School. The following year, he was elected Vice President of the People's Republic of China. His position was further strengthened when in 2010 he became vice chairman of both the party's and the state's central military commissions. It was then clear that the party leader, president and chairman of the Central Military Commissions Hu Jintao had appointed Xi Jinping as his successor.

Since Xi was elected to the Politburo's standing committee, he has, among other things, had overall responsibility for the 2008 Summer Olympics. He also visited the Gansu and Shaanxi provinces in connection with the 2008 Sichuan earthquake.

Supreme Leader (2012–)

At the 18th Congress of the Communist Party in 2012, Xi was elected Secretary General of the Communist Party of China and Chairman of the Central Military Commission of the Communist Party of China. A few months later, he was elected by the 12th National People's Congress (2013) President and Chairman of the Central Military Commission of the People's Republic of China. Together, these four titles make him what is informally called "China's supreme leader". As a way to strengthen his position of power within the party, Xi has created his own clique with trusted party leaders, all of whom are connected to the Xi family's home province of Shaanxi. This "Shaanxi clique" includes Wang Qishan and Yu Zhengsheng, who both sit on the party's standing committee. One of the strongest bastions of the Shaanxi clique is the People's Liberation Army, where Xi has close contacts with several top-level officers.

The presidency was originally limited to two five-year terms, which would force Xi to resign by 2023. However, the 13th National People's Congress (2018), after very brief preparation, passed a constitutional amendment that removed the term of office, so that Xi can now theoretically be re-elected to any number of five-year periods. The constitution also included the concept of "Xi Jinping's thinking on socialism with Chinese nature for a new age" as part of the state's official values.

As supreme leader, Xi Jinping has launched an extensive anti-corruption campaign that promises to strike at "both flies and tigers". Efforts against corruption under previous leaders had been criticized for largely prosecuting politicians at the district level ("flies") but turning a blind eye to villains at the municipal, provincial and national levels ("tigers").

Xi Jinping's slogan as a leader is "the Chinese dream", a parallel to "the American dream".

Unlike the American counterpart, the Chinese dream is less about individual self-realization but more about collective self-realization, a society that strives for unity. This is achieved through joint efforts, and not as in Sweden or in the so-called material countries where you more or less only think of yourself and ignore your fellow human beings.

One month after Xi Jinping was elected president in 2012, he signed his vision for the next two decades: *to abolish inequality "socialist modernization"* by 2012, and, by 2049, to transform China into *"a great modern socialist country, prosperous, wellbeing, strong, democratic, culturally advanced, harmonious and beautiful"*.

To allow Xi Jinping to realize China's new vision, his colleagues granted him a special leadership status in 2017 and amended the constitution in 2018, so that he and a prime minister can remain in office for a second term so that the new phase will have a good start.

Since Xi Jinping will remain in office until at least 2027, it may be a good idea to get to know him, before the mainstream media (MSM) intensifies their attacks on him. Here is a short biography.

*People who have little experience of power - because they have had none - tend to view politics as mysterious and exciting. But for my part, I prefer to look beyond the surface, the power, the flowers, the honor, and the applause. I see the detention facilities, the deficient human relationships. I see politics on a deeper level.*

- Xi Jinping, President of China

Since President Xi Jinping is a reincarnation of the YELLOW EMPEROR (QIN HUANGDI), his ambitions should not be underestimated.

He has plans to become a world leader.

But to become a world leader, he must first and foremost address the escalating environmental problems and increasing population.

He must move about 800,000,000 of his people in a peaceful way, outside China.

And time is short!

To which countries - it remains to be seen?

Today's big challenge for the western world is that China has managed all too well, with methods that are increasingly being questioned. It is not enough that e.g. all the world's car manufacturers are there in "joint ventures" with Chinese state-owned companies in a market that consumes 25 million cars a year. Major investments are being made in the fourth-generation technology.

This and the ongoing global shift in power is what the trade war between the United States and China is ultimately about.

In 2015, the Chinese government launched *Made in China 2025*, a strategy to place China at the forefront when it comes to *robots, autonomous cars, biotechnology* and, not least, the *new information technology*.

Figure 7. China Telecom tested 5G in Chengdu in March 2019.

At the center of this drama is the issue of 5G, the foundation of the entire world's future Internet architecture, and the vision of a connected world.

Chinese Huawei, the main symbol of China's dramatic development, is a central part of this new architecture.

The company is today the world's biggest telecom company with a turnover of 100 billion dollars, where half of it is outside China, and with a research budget that is three times as large as Ericsson's, and with almost as many patents as Ericsson.

The United States has no equivalent.

Now Huawei plays a key role in the development of the global standard that will apply to 5G, a wireless communication that is expected to increase internet speed 100 times compared to 4G and form the basis for the "smart cities" of the future, driverless cars, healthcare, and AI (Artificial Intelligence).

*This is a scary scenario for most of the world's populations from a health and survival point of view!*

Given the pandemic Covid-19/20, the world health situation will worsen significantly due to 5G.

The biggest problem is that the entire earthly civilization suffers from malnutrition due to nutrient-poor foods (*junk food*), unhealthy drinks and increased air pollution, especially in big cities. To all this are added different kinds of chemicals, heavy metals, bacteria and viruses. These lower the immune system and pave the way for epidemics, diseases of various kinds and escalated mortality.

We are experiencing a deepening polarization with far-reaching consequences for the global economy and international cooperation. This is a fact. It is also a fact that the rising China is a technological superpower, and that the emerging entailing risks must be managed. It is also a fact that China is deeply integrated into the global economy and its value chains as well as the world's technological development.

China is making the same mistakes that the United States made, when mainly thinking of power, control, economics and materialism, instead of minimalism. Increased materialism contributes to selfishness and division instead of unity.

This mistake will sooner or later lead to the downfall of the empire.

The Pleiadian alternative that the President of the Russian Federation Vladimir Putin chose, is first and foremost about human development and a gradual adaptation to increased technology, and not the other way around, as the United States and now China are working for.

If technology goes too far as is happening in China, then there will be a robot society where the robots take over and decide over humans. Man isn't able to and will not have the time to develop at the same pace as technology.

This is exactly the thought structure that the Western Illuminati, CABAL, (*the shadow government*) is applying in its pursuit of Globalization and the New World Order.

*The society of the New Age that we from the AIC are working for is mainly about human evolvement in the first place, and technological development in the second place. This must be done in parallel.*

The Earth is an integration and development planet whose task is to cooperate with nature and the cosmic laws and follow the directives that the Council of the Intergalactic Federation has decided for us to follow. We must not invent our own paths that lead to destructiveness and destruction of all life.

An individual or nation that is at the primary school level of its consciousness, cannot understand what is being taught at the secondary school level. Therefore, it is important that we first and foremost develop a higher qualitative consciousness in order to be able to master the technology in a constructive and sensible way. Relying solely on the 3D mind, the intellect without pursuing a 5D unity consciousness will result in none of the goals that Xi Jinping or anyone else have set as their goals.

President Xi Jinping should listen to his inner intuition and follow the DAO like he did when he was incarnated in the form of the Yellow Emperor. Then he will make sure that the people will follow the DAO "the cosmic path". Otherwise, he will fail with the plan that he wants to realize. To leave the animal-human stage of consciousness and enter the human stage of consciousness requires knowledge, self-knowledge and experience of life as a whole, and not as hitherto only parts of it.

That is why the Council of the Intergalactic Federation has chosen President Vladimir Putin to lead the earthly civilization into the New Age, the Golden Age. The ones who are mature of the earthly people will be able to enter the New Age.

Russia has, through long experience of suffering, gained patience, perseverance in the same way as China. Russia's technological progress is based on mutual cooperation with highly evolved extraterrestrial beings from the Pleiades. This collaboration has led to development and scientific know-how in all sectors over a period of about 50 years.

In China, it has been a matter of quickly copying Western knowledge and technology and starting to sell this cheaper than has been possible in the Western world due to completely different costs.

*Being able to copy a product is not the same as developing it.*

We ourselves have been involved in helping a Chinese company to develop laser technology that would meet the requirements for a corresponding Western technical product. It has taken us almost four years with several adjustments where communication, lack of language skills had to be bridged in order to be able to implement the instructions and adjustments that our wishes demanded. This is to be able to complete the product which then meets the requirements set according to European or Western standard. One can improve technology and change design, which makes it ethically and morally defensible to circumvent patent. If you can also keep a lower manufacturing cost, it is favorable for the consumer. But copying a product with the belief that a lower cost will make you sell more of it, while the new product does not meet the same standard as the Western product - is not morally defensible. Furthermore with inadequate manual with poor language translation due to ignorance does not make it serious. In this way, China cannot yet compare itself with the experience of the Western world. Even today, some Chinese companies find it difficult to understand that their products cannot be marketed in the Western world before they meet the requirements of the product according to European and Western standards. The Western world has a different mindset about quality compared to China for the time being. These problems make most consumers skeptical of Chinese-made products.

E.g. when a Chinese Company that manufactures medical-technological products copied from an EU country, changes design and price at certain intervals, to speed up the marketing of the product - is not serious.

Mass-producing goods or services that don't meet the quality requirements promised and demanded is the wrong way to go just to accelerate economic and technological growth without following given ethical and moral rules.

China cannot compare itself with the Western world in terms of technological know-how. China lacks knowledge and experience.

Russia is a leader in military and civilian technology that concerns e.g. the future medicine. These technologies are based on Quantum Physics, Metaphysics, where the causal connection behind a conceivable symptom is the most important to find, in comparison with the outdated biochemical approach which is based exclusively on biochemistry and its side effects. It is more important to focus from the beginning on preventing a disease instead of ascertaining an already existing symptom, a disease that has arisen. The Russians' medical technology has been used on their spaceships and space stations for decades to prevent their astronauts from getting sick.

China must learn to accelerate slowly and to develop its technological know-how at the same pace. It takes a Taoist spirit to be able to handle technology in an ethical and humanitarian way. Otherwise, technology takes control of man, and this is not allowed by the Intergalactic Federation, which is responsible for the continued development of the Earth and the new civilization during the New Age. The nowadays "earthy" laws set by the Illuminati, CABAL (*the deep state*) are no longer valid, the ones that were enacted to be enforced. These laws will no longer be allowed by the Intergalactic Federation, which governs all evolution in our galaxy, our solar system and Earth during the New Age.

In the new society, no form of imperialism will be allowed in the same way as so far on earth. The United States is the last of its kind.

Every nation, every people must defend its sovereignty, the right to self-determination in the same way as our organism, our organs in our body function. We must all together strive for a 5D unity consciousness that includes and benefits everything and everyone in the universe, hyperspace.

An Interplanetary Council Assembly consisting of the most evolutionarily conscious of the Earth's people in leadership together with the President of the Russian Federation Vladimir Putin, will lead the Earthly civilization into the New Age, the Golden Age, in which we already entered in 2012, when many believed that the earth would go under.

The entire earthly civilization is facing major changes, restructurings that are occurring for the first time in the earth's many thousands of years of history. Nothing will be as before. It's impossible to build a new society on an outdated thought structure that we have been used to so far.

It requires a "New Consciousness in a New Time" which is also the title of one of our books.

Many of you are wondering and will react to the fact that we have proposed President Vladimir Putin as the "World Leader" for the new society that is slowly beginning to take shape.

It is not we who have chosen him, but the Council of the Intergalactic Federation.

After the end of World War II, this Council offered the United States technological assistance at the same rate as the earthly man progresses in his consciousness development, in parallel with increased ethical and moral awareness and rules. This is the basic foundation for a constructive societal development. The former US President David "Ike" Eisenhower, the CIA and the DIA were not interested in the Intergalactic Council's offer, and the US was already involved with extraterrestrial destructive creatures from Orion, who were behind the technological development in the former Nazi Hitler Germany.

In 1945, at the end of World War II, about a thousand researchers and scientists with Werner von Braun in the lead from Nazi Germany were recruited to continue their work for the US military and administration. This development included the development of extraterrestrial technology, nuclear technology, laser technology, sound technology, robot technology, aviation technology and more. The Nazis didn't have time to complete all since the war ended. All of these Nazi-loyal scientists were immediately granted U.S. citizenships and began their work for NASA.

The United States took over in principle the same role and pursuit as Hitler had, i.e. to reach World Dominion, A New Roman Empire.

The next scenario arose in connection with the Cuban Missile Crisis when the whole world held its breath, when a nuclear war became almost imminent and almost inevitable between the United States and the former USSR (The Soviet Regime). Neither party wanted to give up. The United States were more advanced technologically, so they refused to negotiate with the former President of the Soviet Union, Nikita Khrushchev, who was equally determined. The Interplanetary Federation Council sent a Pleiadian envoy to the President Kennedy administration to negotiate peace. But the US military and the CIA refused to comply with the envoy's request. Then the Pleiadian envoy turned to President Nikita Khrushchev and explained the situation, what would happen if they chose to start a nuclear war. At the same time, the Pleiadian envoy offered President Nikita Khrushchev technological cooperation between the Intergalactic Federation and the former Soviet government.

Nikita Khrushchev suspended his nuclear threat and withdrew his planned military cooperation with the Cuban President Fidel Castro.

Nikita Khrushchev presented the proposal he had received from the Pleiadian envoy to the Duma (Soviet Parliament), but they were not directly interested. The Soviet intelligence service KGB contacted President Nikita Khrushchev and expressed interest in cooperating with the Intergalactic Federation. This happened the following year, in 1963. Since then, the KGB, now the GRU has cooperated with the Intergalactic Federation and their Pleiadian representatives. This has contributed to the fact that the Russian Federation today has military and civilian medical technology that far exceeds the technology available to NATO or China. The military technology that NATO has at its disposal is limited due to the technical knowledge and level of consciousness of their alien allies. In the event that the United States or any of its allies dare to trigger a confrontation with Russia, they themselves would suffer. US and Allied communications systems related to Satellite, Air, Navy or Land-based defense systems would be shut down immediately. The Intergalactic Defense Force's spacecrafts (UFOs) are superior and invulnerable compared to the spaceships and technologies of the Orion and Reptile Creatures.

No world leader can compete with Vladimir Putin. You are born a World Leader and aren't appointed by any earthly committee. To be able to shoulder the mantle required to lead the development of a civilization, a higher qualitative quantum consciousness is needed, compared to what the rest of the population is equipped with.

It is not about choosing a shepherd who will make sure the sheep have food, somewhere to sleep and protection. No significant knowledge or experience is required for this latter task. In our world in various contexts so far, there were and are some sheep that have greater knowledge and insight than the shepherd himself. That is the reason why our civilization is on the brink of a major catastrophe, which continues to escalate if nothing is done or happens.

It is time for all countries in the world, including Sweden, to start a more comprehensive collaboration with President Vladimir Putin and his Council to save the world, the world economy through BRICS currency cooperation and stop the Illuminati's, CABAL's (*deep state's*) planned world order, whose purpose is to exterminate most of the earth's current civilization and enslave the rest.

Adolf Hitler's so-called "final solution" is nothing compared to the Illuminati's current plan to exterminate nearly 7 billion of the earthly population through various kinds of diabolical measures.

# Illuminati, CABAL (The Deep State), Agenda

The information below is about humanity's present and future situation on earth according to the destructive mind-influenced Illuminati, CABAL (*the deep state*), their agenda.

This is happening in the world and the society without human knowledge.

The negative world government (*the deep state*), which is a "*miniature state*", controls since World War II all citizens on earth, regardless of their national, political or religious affiliation.

This control has increased more during the last decade due to the revelation of the involvement and participation of the Illuminati, CABAL (*the deep state*) in the decision-making and in the violation of the independence of countries and peoples.

No state, no government or individual has the right to impose its power and control on any other country or people through threats, economic pressure or otherwise.

That which is happening in the US and in the EU is also happening in Sweden and other countries, except in Russia and China, which refuse to submit to the influence of these destructive forces. The US, EU and others constantly violate the sovereignty and participation of different countries, while constantly talking about democracy and democratic rights.

What we are experiencing in society today, in the world, is a mentally driven and seemingly totally emotionally cold declaration from the destructive extraterrestrial Orion-influenced groups and their earthly allies, the *Bilderberg Group*, the *Trilateral Commission* and the *Council on Foreign Relations*, which are part of the invisible shadow government Illuminati, CABAL (*the deep state*).

How is the Illuminati structured? Who governs the Illuminati?

The Illuminati Order is a secret society.

The word Illuminati means "*people who have been enlightened*" or Illuminated "*by receiving knowledge from a higher source*". This is not the case with the "Illuminati" we are referring to here in the book. The Illuminati mentioned here are about the secret societies known as the "*Bilderberg Group*, the *Trilateral Commission* and the *Council of Foreign Relations*". Their members constitute the leadership and business elite of the world, the so-called CABAL, (*the deep state*).

CABAL in this context refers to a small group of knowledgeable people who work together in silence to achieve their political goals. The word "Cabal" is originally derived from the Jewish tradition associated with the term cabala / kabbala, which by outsiders has been associated with precisely secrecy, which non-initiates have no insight into.

The deep (hidden) state, is a State within the state (French: *L'État dans l'État*) and is a political concept. It refers to an organization that acts as if it was a state authority, and that operates within another state apparatus.

## The Bilderberg Group

From places behind closed doors and armed guards comes the true history of the world power elite and their secret plans for the future.

The group name, the "*Bilderberg Group*" comes from the "Hotel de Bilderberg" in Oosterbeek in the Netherlands, where the group had its first meeting on May 29, 1954, hosted by Prince Bernhard of the Netherlands.

Famous participants have been Henry Kissinger, Romano Prodi, David Rockefeller, Carl Bildt and Bill Clinton.

The Bilderberg Group was created by David Rockefeller.

The Bilderberg Group holds two annual meetings, one in the spring and one in the autumn, where 120-150 invited participants that represent the global power elite in business and industry, media and political activities from different countries, meet to receive information on continued political and economic governance in the world.

The meeting has been held every year since 1954.

The meetings are organized by 34 people in the steering committee.

Since then, all Presidents and Government Representatives have attended these secret meetings with the Bilderberg Group and the Trilateral Commission.

The first Swedish representative to participate in the Bilderberg meeting in 1955 was Herbert Tingsten. He was followed by Tage Erlander, Arne Geijer, Marcus Wallenberg, Olof Palme in the 1960s. The next Swedish representatives were Marcus Wallenberg, Christer Wikman, Gunnar Sträng and Thorbjörn Fälldin in the 1970s. Pehr G Gyllenhammar joined in the 1980s. King Carl XVI Gustav and Carl Bildt joined in the 1990s. Fredrik Reinfeldt, Jan Björklund, Maud Olofsson, Carin Jämtin, Percy Barnevik, Leif Pagrotsky joined in the 2000s. Jacob Wallenberg, Stefan Löfvén, Annie Lööf, Anders Borg, Magdalena Andersson, Leif Johansson and Jonas Bonnier and others were added in the 2010s.

Sweden, which is a small country with only 10.6 million inhabitants, has for several decades been overrepresented in the Bilderberg Club's annual meetings.

At the Bilderberg meeting in 2017, which took place at Westfields Marriott in Chantilly, Virginia, USA, the Bilderberg group's steering committee proposed that the Center Party leader Annie Lööf would be the leader of the new alliance (Minister of State) in Sweden after the 2022 election. How can you do that if you don't manipulate the election via Social Media and MSM?

Russia and Vladimir Putin were accused of having influenced the US election when Donald Tramp was elected president, instead of Hillary Clinton who "had several skeletons" in the closet. This latter had afterwards been sensitive to reveal to the public and the world.

## The Trilateral Commission

The "*Trilateral Commission*" is a global private elite organization second only to the Bilderberg Group.

The idea is that the members should meet in an informal environment without transparency from the media. The purpose is to influence from behind the scenes and thus control the decisions that governments make far from values that characterize, for example, social liberals.

What merits does Annie Lööf have that the Bilderberg Group and the Trilateral Commission see in her, which others don't see, and proposes her as future Minister of State for Sweden and the Swedish people?

The organization, the "*Trilateral Commission*" was formed 45 years ago by among others David Rockefeller, Henry Kissinger and Zbigniew Brzezinski. They wanted to gather the "best brains" in Western Europe, North America and Japan so that they could act as advisors to the world's formal decision-makers. The main brains turned out to be mainly among the representatives of monetary interests such as transnational companies, financiers, banks and their supporters in the media world.

The purpose is not to safeguard either democracy or democratic institutions. On the contrary, it is instead a matter of being an active party leader and allow oneself to become elected a member of this organization. This indicates extremely bad judgment on her part. Annie Lööf has Margaret Thatcher as role model of neoliberalism, but lacks all the knowledge and experience that Margaret Thatcher had when she was appointed Prime Minister of the United Kingdom by the Bilderbergs and the Trilateral Commission.

Sitting in a government is a position of trust by the Swedish people who live in Sweden. The purpose is primarily to safeguard the interests of the Swedish people, and not the interests of the globalizing recent capitalism, which both the Bilderberg Group and the Trilateral Commission represent and advocate.

Sweden does not need a Minister of State - or even one cabinet minister - who is a member of a private global organization with the purpose behind closed doors to lead the world.

Her immigration policy is about importing about 250 million immigrants, (mainly) Muslims to Europe, of which about 30 million of these to Sweden. She has previously spoken out about polygamy, which is a Muslim tradition. It would have been easier for her to emigrate to one of the Muslim countries and take part of their traditions and views of women instead of promoting their ideology here at home in Sweden. She has been given this task by the spokesman for the Illuminati, the Bilderberg Group and the Trilateral Commission, the Hungarian George Soros, who, among other things, through his Open-Society-Foundation contributed to the increased immigration to Europe, and also financed left-wing extremist movements in

Sweden and in some countries in Europe so that nationalists who protect their people and their country's independence will not be able to come to power. Annie Lööf knows the financier George Soros very well and runs his policy in Sweden.

If she aims at the position as Minister of State in Sweden in 2022, which she will not be able to reach due to her attitude, view of Russia and China, which she constantly criticizes, and also due to the new development that the whole world is facing, including Sweden.

Annie Lööf as well as her political associates in various parties are unaware of how the Illuminati, CABAL (*the deep state*), which includes the Bilderberg Group and the Trilateral Commission, are driving the world towards total collapse.

This process involves 5 stages of collapse.

1) Economic Collapse, 2) Commercial Collapse, 3) Political Collapse, 4) Social Collapse and 5) Cultural Collapse.

The first stage of "economic collapse" has already begun with the made-up pandemic Covid-19. This is staged by the Illuminati, CABAL (*the deep state*) in which she herself is a member. From that scenario she cannot escape unless she changes guidelines in her policy and starts thinking of Sweden and the Swedish people and starts collaborating with the Sweden Democrats for a new society. Instead, she sees them as enemies. If she doesn't do this, she will perish together with her clients the Bilderberg Group and the Trilateral Commission, whose time is numbered.

It is Vladimir Putin who has the ability and possibility to save the world, the earthly civilization and also the Swedish society from total collapse. China also supports this rescue operation. The time of the United States, the European Union and the Illuminati is over. A New Consciousness in a New Time is at the door.

In the first instance, Annie Lööf must ensure that Sweden joins the currency co-operation BRICS to secure the Swedish economy instead of continuing with the Fiat currency which only has its paper value. It is important not to accept the World Order that the Illuminati, CABAL (*the deep state*) chooses to implement, which will result in the five stages of collapse that we have mentioned above.

She must change her attitude when it comes to immigration policy to Europe and to Sweden. In the New Age in which we have already entered, all countries will become independent and will protect their countries and their populations. This will take place in the same way as our organs in the body carry out their own tasks and interact with each other to create symbiosis, balance between each other.

Christ said: *Man, get to know yourself, and you will understand how the universe works*. This rule also applies to our society in which we are individual cells seen from a cosmic perspective.

The earthly man must wake up from his Sleeping Beauty sleep and become aware of what is going on around him, instead of believing in the tales and stories served to him by a leadership elite that consciously or unconsciously manipulates, deceives their own citizens.

The destructive extraterrestrial entities (*beings*) from Orion that the United States has associated with after the end of World War II, as well as their earthly allies, the Western Illuminati, Cabal (*the deep state*), have chosen the "COVID-19" pandemic as the reason for the launch and implementation of their plan with the aim their New World Order, and this has been their plan for a long time. Milestones of the plan Madonna showed on stage at the Eurovision song contest in Tel Aviv, Israel, in 2019, when she performed the song "Future".

Not many in the audience or in the world understood her performance about the Illuminati, CABAL, their future for humanity on earth, "*That those who did not listen, who were not sensitive to what is happening, will have to leave the earth for good*".

*The Bilderberg Group, the Trilateral Commission* and *the Council on Foreign Relations* have always been a cover for the Western Illuminati, Cabal (*the deep state*), which has hitherto been able to operate in the dark, without the humanity knowing. They have controlled all the revolutions (*including the Russian*), all the world wars and the depression of the 1930s, the rise and fall of Adolf Hitler, all the unemployment, the economic development in different countries, all the banks and their credits, the whole pharmaceutical industry, medical education, science, education, EU, UN, Vatican City (*the Pope*), everything you can imagine.

In 2019, I was contacted for the first time by Illuminati representatives and was offered $ 2.0 million in advance, plus Royalty, as well as a guarantee that this newly authored book would be published in various languages worldwide, i.e. if the book's content was in line with the agenda of the Illuminati, CABAL (*Deep State*).

I was also offered the office as Secretary General of the Illuminati for Northern Europe and an unlimited amount of money for our International Academy for Total Human Culture (AIC) and its approximately 6,000-page text material and health concept etc. that would serve the purpose of the Illuminati.

I declined their offer, as I know their intention with their New World Order. It goes against the law and order of the cosmos (*universe*).

I would rather be *Poor* and *Rich* than *Rich* and *Poor*.

Bible Quote: *It is easier for a camel to pass through the eye of a needle than for a materially rich man to enter the kingdom of heaven.*

Now is the time to reveal the events that are slowly but surely creeping into our society, your workplace, your home, without you knowing it.

It may be good for you to know what is going on in your country, in the world and how your elected political representatives are deceiving you, manipulating you through beautiful promises and through the help of mainstream media (MSM) to make you believe in everything they say and claim.

Your political representatives and authorities are the only thing they are interested in more than their own egos, power and economy. They choose different ways to manipulate you to get your vote to stay in power. We saw how it went in the last election in 2019 in Sweden. How the incumbent Minister of State refused to resign and relinquish power, even though his party did not have a majority of the Swedish people. We saw how they opposed the "Sweden Democrats", both before and after the election, even though they had 18% of the Swedish people's votes, how some of the Sweden Democrats' ballot papers had suddenly disappeared in various places. We also saw how the Bilderberg representative, the billionaire George Soros via the Center Party leader, who constantly advocated for increased immigration to Europe and Sweden, split the bourgeois alliance and supported the Minister of State in power, along with the Liberals and the Green Party's spokesmen.

The United States and the European Union have also accused Vladimir Putin of personally having influenced the US election, as well as the Brexit election in Britain.

The former US President George W Bush mentioned during his term "*those who are not with us are against us*". He was referring to the "*New World Order*", which is created by the lower quality, destructively influenced extraterrestrial beings from Orion/Sirius B and their earthly allies, the Illuminati, CABAL (*the deep state*) to exterminate about 95% of the earth's population and enslave and make the rest into obedient tools, robots.

As a robot in their plans, you are not included.

Only about 500 million people are needed to complete the important tasks that cannot be replaced by robots.

How would these unethical, immoral people lead a country towards a higher qualitative development when they themselves are at the primary school level from the point of view of development and consciousness? They hardly notice themselves what is going on around them - that their empire is collapsing like a house of cards.

*It is important that you understand the content behind their intention in order to better contribute to your own liberation. Otherwise you stagnate in your human development.*

*We want to offer you a new opportunity.*

*We within our Association and Order are aware of exactly what is happening on Earth and why?*

*It is not our intention or task to interfere with the actions of the destructive forces or to fight against their followers, i.e. leaders, politicians, government officials, decision makers at various levels. They have to settle the battle between them themselves.*

*Our task is to inform, illuminate what is going on without your knowledge.*

These negative, destructive forces have hitherto been as necessary for the cosmic development of the earthly human being as the positive forces. Without this opposite (*negative*) polarity, man cannot develop his inner ability to understand creation in its entirety.

Therefore, some of us have chosen to incarnate (*be born*) here on earth from higher evolved civilizations to learn what is not possible to learn anywhere else in the universe, and also to help those who seek the meaning of life, which requires the right knowledge and experience.

Our task within the AIC is to "help those who want to help themselves" to be able to more easily free themselves from the dungeon and bondage of the lower quality mind.

It is not our job to *criticize, smear, condemn* and *fight* the forces that have been necessary for the development of the earth, civilization and the individual from the point of view of consciousness. Thanks to these forces, the earthly man has had the opportunity to learn to count, write and become more aware than before.

But now development has reached the level where man must choose a new path, the path of the soul (*self*) over the mind (*intellect*) in order to move forward in his human development.

But to be able to do that it requires willpower, perseverance and commitment. Nothing happens by itself.

Our task is to bring to life, clarify the game of chess, spectacle that is constantly going on within the lower levels of creation.

The people who are dissatisfied with life and believe that through political debates, discussions, subversive activities, criticism, etc., they can change society, the world for the better; they don't understand how creation works in its entirety. We have all been assigned different roles in the Theater of the Mind. Some of us are unaware of what the role play itself is all about. We all have to take the consequences of the role play we have undertaken to play in the world, in society, in family life.

Think of all the revolutions, all the wars that have been fought between individuals, countries, nations throughout history.

Has life become better? - In that case, for whom?

Perhaps for some seen from a material point of view, but not for civilization as a whole.

*Democracy, democratic rights, freedom of speech, equality, brotherhood are beautiful words for those who are both blind and deaf to the truth. The more often the lie is repeated, the more one believes in it.*

*There is a saying: while the lie has reached to Baghdad, the truth is still looking for its sandals.*

What some people perceive as injustices does not have to be injustices if you look at the whole, or at the law of karma - the law of fate (*action and reaction*).

*What you sow, you must also reap,* said Christ - for better or for worse.

Without darkness, light does not exist. Without cold we cannot experience heat. Without sorrow there is no joy. Without hatred, there is no unconditional love.

But there is a big difference between the negative mind power and the destructive part of it. The latter wants to destroy, divide, destroy cultures, societies, people, etc.

As long as creation exists, as long will these polarities also exist in the lower qualitative 3D worlds to which our planet Earth still belong.

We want you to know the truth about the planned agenda of the Western-dominated Illuminati, Cabal (*the deep state*) for the New World Order - the one they have planned to execute, realize.


**What is the purpose of the Illuminati?**

Their aim is to get rid of about 95% of the earth's total population as soon as possible, which they no longer consider necessary.

They have learned from their destructive employers from Orion that you can replace them all with robots that can work around the clock (24/7) without coffee breaks, time off and without pay or pension.

They don't dare to start a nuclear war because then they themselves will be exterminated or stopped by the defense forces of the Intergalactic Federation and Vladimir Putin's high-tech defense system.

*The pandemic covid-19 is the beginning of this scenario.*

But what these destructive forces haven't thought of is the extensive extraterrestrial activity initiated by the Intergalactic Federation and their cooperation with President Vladimir Putin and his organization. All the politicians, bankers, businessmen who are members and cooperate with the Bilderberg Group, the Trilateral Commission and the Council on Foreign Relations in all countries where the CABAL (*the deep state*) has its influence, will be revealed to the people and prevented in various ways from succeeding in their plans. They have consciously or unconsciously betrayed their own people who have chosen them and believed in them. Instead they have followed their own power and selfish interests.

They didn't take into account the role of Russia - Vladimir Putin and China - Xi Jinping.

They have not taken into account the role of the Intergalactic Federation and the Pleiadian Federation in the evolution of the earth.

They haven't known that since 1963 the KGB military intelligence service has been indirectly cooperating with the Pleiadian Federation, which monitors all developments on earth regarding military and civilian technology and their use.

The United States has on three different occasions declined the Pleiadian offer, which was about the development of primarily the ethical, moral attitudes and rules of the earthly man before contributing to high technological knowledge and development. The US administration together with the DIA and the CIA has thus chosen the opposite.

Instead of choosing the slower technological development and develop the consciousness of the people, the United States chose to cooperate with the former Nazi scientists from former Hitler Germany, who collaborated with destructive extraterrestrial entities (beings) from Orion, the so-called Gray. These promised rapid technological development. The United States sought world domination, a kind of new Roman Empire, rather than raising the level of consciousness in its own people and the rest of the world.

The United States basically sold out the entire population of the earth to these destructive extraterrestrial beings from Orion/Draco in order to reach the position of power they hold today through NATO. These are the same alien destructive creatures from Orion/Draco that are behind the Illuminati, CABAL (*the deep state*), the Bilderberg Group, the Trilateral Commission, the

Council on Foreign Relations and their members from most governments, including Sweden. They manipulate, control through the economy, the banking system the policies of all countries.

The Rothschild family privately owns about 165 of all Central Banks in the world, including the Swedish one. The power within the Illuminati, CABAL (*the deep state*) is handled by the 13 richest families in the world.

Of these, the Rothschild family is No. 1.

Everything you think and do is devised by the Illuminati.

From the moment you were born here on earth until you have left your biological 3D form through the so-called death, you have been under the influence and surveillance of the Illuminati and the destructive extraterrestrial beings without your knowledge.

You have been indoctrinated by your parents, who in turn were indoctrinated by their parents. You have been misled by your surroundings, schools, neighbors, friends, workplaces, mainstream media (MSM), politics, religions and world events. The Illuminati has been behind all this. Have you ever thought about who you are? Are you thinking your thoughts or do they belong to someone else? Have you thought about whether your thoughts are right or wrong from an ethical, moral point of view?

Have you thought about when you indebt yourself through bank loans to buy a car, boat, summer cottage or villa, who owns these?

Is it you or the Rothschild Family who owns the Riksbank (Swedish Central Bank), which in turn lends useless Fiat currency (*alleged currency*) to your private bank Nordea, SEB etc., for which you have to pay interest?

Here is an example: You go to your bank to buy a summer place. 15 % is the down payment you need to have yourself. If the summer place costs SEK 1 million, you must have SEK 150,000 for the down payment and the rest of the money SEK 850,000 you can borrow from the bank, which the bank does not really has but is printed when the loan is given. The house becomes the security for the loan, that it has even been printed. With a fictitious currency, the bank has written over the house to itself. The bank transfers SEK 850,000 in digital digits to your account. On the 850,000 SEK (non-existent currency) you have to pay interest, which is also made up, and which has never even been printed. On your loan, which is only fictitious figures, you have to pay interest plus amortization. If you cannot pay, the bank will take the summer place or the house away from you.

In reality, you have "bought" the bank a house for worthless currency that you don't own until you have paid your debt to the Bank. If you do not pay, the debt goes to the Senior Enforcement Officer for attachment and sale. You will be privately indebted and declared bankrupt and won't be allowed to borrow money, rent an apartment or own a car, boat, house or anything else. You have paid your debt to the Crown's bailiff at the same time as you have lost the house that was not your house but the bank's. When the debt bubble around the world bursts, the countries linked to the Rothschild Central Banks become liable for repayment, along with all citizens, which means that all property and private assets are transferred to the deep state. This makes all people serfs - "owned by the deep state".

All this has taken place in accordance with the Swedish Financial Supervisory Authority's law and arbitrariness. Here we can hardly talk about democracy and democratic rights that have become a slogan in Sweden.

Mainstream media "TV, Radio, Newspapers, Google, Facebook, YouTube etc." are still controlled by the Illuminati, Cabal (*the deep state*), but their empire is coming to an end thanks to the strong leader of the Russian Federation, Vladimir Putin, but also to China's leader Xi Jinping.

## The Agenda of the Illuminati Order

*Listen to the Illuminati Order's Agenda and you will understand what we mean.*

## My World Citizens!

"We cannot stress enough what difficulties you will have to go through if you oppose us. We have our ways when it comes to dealing with opponents. We say that now, because it is far too late to return.

That day is long gone when you could have stopped us. We have full control over Mother Earth and its finances as well as the main media propaganda. There is simply no way any nation or power can defeat us.

We have eyes on every level in all the governments of the world and know what is planned, because our eyes and ears are always present. State secrets are fully known to us. China accused the US media of lying about Kosovo. Oh, you gullible people, of course we're lying. That way we can keep people in ignorance and they always have to face controversies, which is very helpful for us.

Have you never seen the talk shows?

Some of you think we are liberals and the good people are the conservatives.

In reality, both promote our purposes. Each camp simply offers what we have approved, but they are not allowed to present the real conditions. By creating controversies at all levels, no one knows what to do. They are powerless. So, in all this confusion, we go ahead and do what we want without obstacles.

Just look at the President of the United States. Even though he regularly violates every known obstacle in his power - who can stop him? He goes ahead and does what we want anyway. Congress has no power to stop him. He does what we want, whenever we want, because he knows that if he does not, because of his rather dark nature, we can remove him in an instant. Isn't that a pretty brilliant strategy from our part?

You cannot bring us to justice because you cannot see us and you do not know who we are. The courts are also our servants. We control everything and yet you don't know who to attack. I must say that this invisible plan is wonderfully well thought out and without any comparable historical event on this scale.

*We control the world and the world cannot even figure out who controls it!*

This is truly a wonderful thing. In the media world, we present to you exactly what we want you to know. Then, like lightning, our little servants obey. We can send American or European troops under the auspices of the UN wherever we want, whenever we want and for whatever reason we want and you dutifully carry out our orders.

How many more proofs do you need? We can make you long to go to war and leave home and family on our command. We just need to present some kind of nonsense to you from our president's or mayor's podium or through the evening news and we can get you to stand up for anything we want. You can do nothing but what we present to you!

## *Your vain resistance*

When any of you try to oppose us, we have ways to make you seem ridiculous, just as we did with your Home Guard movements. We have gladly used these movements to show the world how powerless every resistance is. They look so stupid as they walk around with their rifles in the woods as if they were a match for our military.

We have generously taxed you and used the money to make the most sophisticated weapons you can find without any competition. Your own money has served to forge the chain we bind you with, because we have control over all the money.

Some of you think that you can escape by acquiring land in the countryside and start planting a garden. Let me remind you that you are still paying us land rent. Oh, you might call it property tax, but it's still going to us.

As you can see, you need money for whatever you do. If you cannot pay property tax to us, we will take your property and sell it to someone who can pay the rent. Don't you think we can do this? And with your property tax, we pay for the indoctrination of your children in the municipal schools we have started. We want them to grow up indoctrinated in the system with our way of thinking. Your children learn what we want them to learn, when we want them to learn it and you pay for it via the municipal tax or property tax if you so wish.

These assets are also used for other projects that we have in mind and our builders get paid well for their work. You may doubt that we own your children, or have such control, but you will understand that it is so. We can report that you hit your children when you spank them and then take them away from you. If they do not show up for the indoctrination lessons, we can accuse you of negligence and thereby leave them to us.

Your children are not yours - they are ours! You have to vaccinate them, you have to take them to our hospitals if we decide, otherwise we will take them away from you. You know this, and we know it. And now when we have made you believe that covid-19 is something other than respiratory disease and force you to wear a mask that is totally useless if you are not living in a similar environment as in Wuhang in China, where the city stinks of air pollution. The Covid epidemic does not only exist in the imagination that we have created for you. You can ask a knowledgeable doctor if you doubt what we are saying. By wearing a mask all day, you can get sick by inhaling your own toxins, bacteria that thrive in the moist mask, and the lack of oxygen gives brain damages. We can fine you or put you in jail if you refuse to obey our orders.

We will force you to be vaccinated in the belief that it protects you against the Corona virus. In reality, we vaccinate you and your children to bring in mercury and aluminum that are life-threatening toxins and result in respiratory diseases and nerve diseases that can kill you.

We will also introduce nanochips via vaccination to be able to control you, monitor you and know what you are doing on a daily basis. You will not even be able to go to the toilet without our knowledge. We can monitor you if required 24/7.

Through our electronic monitoring system, we have the opportunity to see where you are, what you buy and how much you have to buy for. From where do you think we got our monthly financial statistics? Through the Internet and other sources, we can also know how you think and what you say. It does not matter to us what you believe in, as long as you do as we say. What you think is nonsense anyway.

But if we see that you have a follower, and we assume that you are in some way dangerous to our agenda, then we have ways to deal with you. We have a Pandora's box of mischief that we can use to trap you. We can easily drain your assets for one or another sweeping reason. We have an inexhaustible fund from which we can take money to our lawyers to ensnare you.

These lawyers are paid by you through your taxes.

You don't have these vast stores of wealth. We know how to divide and conquer. Haven't we overthrown rulers in different countries through our inventions? So you think your little self would be a match for us? You are just one sheep among all other sheep.

### Your meaningless organizations

Let us consider your religions and the "moral majority". The "*moral majority*" has neither morality nor is in the majority. We look forward to using this opportunity to ridicule the Christian faith. The fools who run that organization always end up with rotten eggs thrown in their faces. We have always placed them in a defensive position as we have done with such success when it comes to the NRA (*National Rifle Association*).

Haven't we taken the American Republican movement by the ear?

If it serves our purposes, we can use Democrats to take Republicans by the ear. It makes no difference to us, but it serves to make you believe that there are two sides fighting for their position. This helps to make it look like honesty and freedom because everyone has a voice. In fact, there is only one side with all kinds of masks on, but you cannot see through our intentions. You understand that we can do whatever we want and you can do nothing about it. Doesn't it sound wise and reasonable that you simply obey and serve us?

Otherwise, you will be devoured by the resistance that you thought would set you free.

You cannot be set free. Imagine how you can do that. We supply you with petrol for your cars. We can turn off the flow whenever we want by claiming that it is some kind of shortage or deficit. What happens if your car breaks down? You cannot get parts for it without us. We provide you with all the money you spend. With every whim or sudden whim from our part, we can stop the flow of money or cause a complete crash in the economy. It is all about electronic numbers. We can then order the president to declare all money worthless and that we must have new money.

All your cash goes up in smoke in an instant!

Don't you need food? If necessary, we can cause a transport strike that would stop deliveries of food to your local store. We can starve you whenever we want. You only have food because we have provided you with it from our table. During the Great Depression, we controlled the food. We piled mountains of food behind fences and let it rot. The hungry were then allowed to work in our labor camps, even though there was plenty and more than enough to eat for them.

Do you really think you can defeat us?

You say you want to collect gold secretly so that you still have money at the time of the crash. We can easily enact a law that makes it illegal to own gold - just as we have done before. If we suspect or find gold in your possession, we would simply confiscate it and put you in jail for breaking the law. When you are in prison, you will be asked to work in one of our prison industries. We have created an image of the labor camps in our prisons these days that no one seems to mind. We tell people that killers have to pay for their own living. No one seems to think that we have the power to let tomato growers be there as well.

We can pass laws banning gardens and then come up with some scientific explanation for why you should only buy foods from our sources. If anyone sees you growing tomatoes, they will report it to us and then you will have to work in our fields for us. Oh, you stupid nationalists, there's no way to escape, for long before you were born we planned your capture.

Your teachers and pastors have been formulating your thoughts for us for generations. You cannot hurt us, find us or even imagine what we are doing. I throw to you these few crumbs just so that you may, if you have any sense at all, obey and follow our orders. We have different ways available to control the population of the earth. And we have already decided how many of you will remain here on earth.

### Your controlled consciousness

We control Hollywood. Movies like Terminator and Armageddon, along with loads of others, were created simply to make you think in accordance with our directives. We have made you fond of violence so that when we send you to kill any bad person in our opinion who appears in front of you, you react without hesitating. We have placed violent games in your computers and in your gaming halls. We have developed these games to be used via the computer to prepare the minds of your young people with the art of fighting and killing without thinking.

We have arranged for you to see armies and police as the good force and you accept things that were unthinkable a few decades ago. Our cunning programs are all designed to help you accept and also help with the realization of the new world order.

Star Trek and other similar creations have taught you to simply obey orders from the new rulers.

Oh, unconscious people, you thought you were entertained while in reality you were taught!

Can I use the term brainwashed or brain-controlled?

From one to the other, have you seen the new Star Wars?

What a masterpiece of mental manipulation. People confer with indescribable beasts of all shapes and sizes and they confer in English!

I wonder where these space monsters learned English. Oh, the simplicity of the citizen's mind! Earthly man never thinks that he has been brought into a virtual world. It's something we want you to learn from these movies. Or maybe you can say that it's something we don't want you to learn. In any case, we get what we want and when we want it.

Do you remember that most of the American presidents were against violence? This did not solve the problem but only made people believe that they were working for peace.

Barack Obama received the Nobel Peace Prize before he was even elected president.

We have accused Russia and China of threatening world peace.

In how many countries does Russia or China have military bases?

How many countries have Russia or China attacked, used to replenish their oil reserves?

We have made the Swedish government believe that Russia is their real enemy, just to make them believe that NATO is their protector.

NATO, for its part, ignores Sweden.

Sex and violence are the absolute best force to use to help us increase our superiority. People strongly dislike giving up sex and violence, so we put everything they want in front of them on the TV screen, in newspapers, in movies and in literature.

In that way, we keep them so busy that they have neither the integrity nor the brainpower to deal with the really important events in their lives, which are thus entirely in our hands.

President Clinton has been of great help to us. We know what figure he was before we installed him as president. Revealing him was very helpful in adjusting the moral habits of the young generation in society. This is to our advantage. Even more pleasing to us were the vain attempts of those who thought they could remove President Clinton against our will. He has been useful to us and he has not been able to be removed from power by anyone until we were willing to remove him. This is what we have done with all presidents or important people.

It's the same with Hillary Clinton. We did not want her as president because of her perverted sexual behavior. She would have hurt us if she had been elected president and revealed by the Russian intelligence service, which has all information about her.

We would rather choose Donald Trump, even if we were not so fond of his different ways of expressing himself or acting. We had no one else to choose from.

Excuse me if I seem to be pushing your beliefs, but they are pretty old-fashioned.

Don't you have eyes to see that your meaningless freedoms and your righteous conduct are not for us?

You can only do what we say you can do. We remove presidents, heads of state when we are ready for it and the leader we have appointed will stay there until it serves us to have another.

At that time, we place our proposed leader in front of you and you vote for the one we want. Look at the French President Emmanuel Macron. We made him president in a few months and before he was completely unknown to the majority in France.

We removed the nationalist Marine Le Pen in a simple way who would otherwise have won the election if we had not intervened. We are not nationalists. In this way, we give you an exercise in the meaningless voting in the belief that you have something to do with the placement of your leader.

This applies to most countries in the world, including Sweden.

We have already decided who will be the new Minister of State of Sweden in 2022 and no one can stop us. We are the ones who decide the outcome of the election. The people naively believe that they have something to say about who will lead Sweden. We are the ones who decide. We often use the word democracy because most people believe in it. But we are not democrats. How would we have reached our goal if we had let the people decide? But we use different means to make them believe that they are the ones who decide. We only need to increase the child benefit a little to get families with children who are in the majority to vote for our pre-appointed candidate. Or to use pensioners by promising to improve their pension, which we obviously do in the run-up to the election. But afterwards we remove it again by blaming that the money is needed for a more important project.

## *Our unexplored mysteries*

The war in Serbia as well as in Iraq had many intentions, but we are not talking openly about these things. We let the talk show hosts chatter all sorts of nonsense, but none of them touches the core. First of all, there was a wealth of natural resources in Kosovo that we had to have complete control over. Kosovo had large supplies of uranium in the ground and uranium is very valuable to our regime. It also suits us to keep all such minerals from the hands of potential enemies.

Then the Serbian President Milosevic was not very helpful in giving us these resources, so we simply made things difficult for him until he did as we wanted. We reduced this proud nation to the level of humility that we expect from all peoples. After the war, when Milosevic was not humble enough, we took him to the war crimes tribunal in The Hague and accused him of war crimes.

We did the same thing with Saddam Hussein in Iraq.

We were not interested in fighting in Iraq with religious fanatics, fundamentalists.

We were interested in the Oil and taking care of our interests.

We made that designation, pretty ingenious, don't you think?

How can there be such a term as "war crime"?

The whole nature of war is that all rules are gone.

It is so entertaining to see the nations try to fight wars in accordance with the laws we have placed before them. The only war crime that really exists involves the crime of being against us. Everyone who is against us is jeopardizing our team.

We have named them terrorists.

As you have seen, when someone is for us, we do not care what he does.

Wasn't Nelson Mandela a terrorist who carried bombs and killed many of his enemies?

We made him a hero when he sided with us.

We do not follow any laws when it comes to war. We do what we want, when we want and where we want. We can starve nations to death. We can ruin civilians and any other threatening danger, and take our enemy to court.

Look at our example.

We bombed Serbia senselessly; we bombed Kosovo out of their homes; poisoned their rivers and streams, turned off their electricity and created a great crisis in that country and then masterfully made it appear that everything was Milosevic's fault and he had to go to court for it.

In the same way we did when we made the inferno in Waco look like it was Koresh's fault.

Then there was our master villain Saddam Hussein, who we accused of having access to weapons of mass destruction, which of course was false.

There are many dozens of bad people and we can conjure up one at any time that suits us.

This is really quite fun when you think about it. I'm not the one who usually jokes, but I found myself laughing sometimes at the absolute absurdity of the ideas and ideas we put in front of you and which you easily accept.

Do you wonder why the leaders in the world tremble through our presence?

They know that they have no power other than the power we give them.

We are not afraid of Russia or China because we already have full control over their systems.

China knows that we can freeze as many of their companies in the United States as we want and we can erase all their capital with a single stroke of the pen. We use the nations for what we want to use them for. Everyone knows they have to submit or die. Fortunately, we have had opponents such as Saddam and Milosevic who have been very helpful in showing world leaders what we will do with them if they don't accept what we want.

There is only glory by following our intentions and doing as we say. If someone doesn't do that, it will be such a sad and tragic result.

I really want you to be spared such an end.

But then, again, if you are not spared this, it will have no consequences for us. We will use you to alleviate some of the problem of overpopulation.

### You stupid rebel against our domination

Some of you have thought that you can stop us by placing a bomb in a government building. Dumb-asses! How can it hurt us? All it does is give us a reason how we can use it to perhaps put more control and heavy burdens on the population.

We love when you rebel and detonate bombs. We love when you demonstrate, burn our flag and shout slogans. You give us reasons to enact more laws against all these boredoms that limit your freedom even more. If someone didn't blow up something for some reason then we had no justification to put up more fences around you.

Can you not realize how impossible it is for you to resist us? The more you are tricked, the more we tighten the rope around your neck. In the end, you cannot breathe.

Our kingdom is the kingdom of money. Excuse me, but I must admit that we are the rulers of the kingdom of non-existent money! You have to see the humor in this statement. We have given you a piece of paper or some electronic numbers on a computer screen that we have called money. They are backed up by nothing and proven by nothing but what we say it is. We create it from nothing, we print it, we lend it, we give it its value and we remove its value.

Everything that has to do with money is in our hands.

Think about it, what can you do against us without money? If you try to resist, we can erase your credit or freeze your assets. Your cash can be easily confiscated. We have made so many regulations in the kingdom of life that you cannot live without money.

If you camp on government land then you must move within two weeks. You cannot get anything to germinate in a garden in two weeks. Many of our wilderness trailers can only enter with permission. We have entry permits that don't allow you to live in a trailer for a certain period without moving to another location. We want you to be in our system. When you buy a house, we not only get tax revenues to use for our purposes, but we get large sums from the interest on the loans. You may pay for your house two or three times just by the interest cost. The interest cost is also taxed, which is again used by us for the sectors of influence that we choose.

We do not want you to get away and be free and that is why we have done everything as we have done.

You are our property. We have made you a slave. We do not allow you to buy or sell without accepting our provision. If you go to court to put us there, we will passivate, tire you out and eventually you will lose. If you use force, you end up in one of our camps, more specifically called prison industries. You need our money, our entertainment, our petrol and our community service to be able to function and if you do not have this, you will feel deprived of everything.

Through our actions, your neck is bent and you give in to our will.

You do not even know how to think anymore because we have carefully unmasked your religions and your faith in God.

Now you only have yourself and we have made you run after your own tail in a pretty good way nowadays.

I hope this little story is enough to inform you what the new century will be about. We have named it the New World Order.

The twenty-first century is our century. You may get into it if you do as you are told. We have no intention whatsoever of engaging in your so-called "human rights" or the so-called constitution. They were only intended for our purposes for a certain period of time.

Your constitution is a joke to us and we can do with it as we wish.

Has it never occurred to you that 50 years ago the US Constitution was used to refuse abortions! When we decided to legalize abortions, we used the same constitution to justify it.

Your so-called human rights are what we say they are and your constitution is what we say it is.

We have only used the word "*human rights*" to keep you calm. The more worries or troubles in society, the more reason we have to enslave you, to keep you in captivity.

The pandemic Covid-19 that we have invented and made you follow is just the beginning to show you that it is we who decide. We use mainstream media to scare you 24/7. You will be fed around the clock with what we want you to hear. We have sent our so-called experts to tell you how dangerous this virus is, because we want you to believe in it. We will isolate you; make you unemployed and financially destitute. Many of you become mentally ill, depressed. Healthcare cannot take care of you. Not because there is a lack of doctors, personnel, but because they too can stay at home like you. They also become isolated. Where this scenario will end, I do not want to reveal.

This information may bother you, as I speak plainly - but none of it affects us.

It sucks, right?"

*Illuminati Order*

# The Orion Influence

Since 1945, when World War II ended, the United States has waged war in 37 countries and 20-30 million people have been killed in these wars. During World War II, some 50 million people, both civilian and military, died. These don't include those who were injured, disabled and had post-traumatic stress disorder of various kinds.

Some of these countries in which the United States has been waging war since 1945 are Angola, Afghanistan, Cambodia, Colombia, Congo, Guatemala, Iraq, North and South Korea, Pakistan, Sudan, Vietnam and Yugoslavia.

In Vietnam 3-7 million people died, in Iraq at least 1 million people, in Cambodia over 2 million people, in Congo 3 million, in Guatemala about 200,000 and the list just goes on.

20-30 million dead in 70 years, that's pretty much exactly 1,000 people a day who die or have died in wars where the United States has participated. The official number of deaths per year by "terrorists" is about 5,000. This means that more people die in a week of war in which the United States is involved than the terrorists kill in a whole year.

From the American side, it has always been claimed that they defend American lives. How can they do it 2000-3000 km outside the US territorial borders? First you invade a country to access its natural resources. Then, when the country in question defends itself against the intruder, it is claimed that the US defends their own lives and territories against those who were attacked. How does this math sum up? It has always been claimed that Russia, China, North Korea, etc. are the real enemies. Have these countries shown any kind of hostility against the United States or European countries, without being provoked?

The answer is No.

Has the United States as a superpower since the Second World War acted hostilely against these mentioned countries or peoples?

The answer is Yes.

The United States has more than 800 military bases outside its own territorial borders, spread across the world, according to the recently published book "Base Nation" by David Vine.

David Vine visited more than 50 of these bases during the six years he wrote the book.

In Germany there are 174 of the US military bases, in England 27, in Italy 50, in Japan 113, in South Korea 83, in Romania 5, in Bulgaria 4, in Turkey 17, in Iraq 6, just to mention a few.

Russia is basically surrounded by all these American bases.

How would the United States react if Russia had 150 military bases in Canada and 100 in Mexico?

This is a highly relevant question to ask.

Russia has only four military bases outside the Russian border.

According to Stockholm International Peace Research Institute's (SIPRI) figures from 2016, the United States spends 36 percent of the world's total military expenditures on its military apparatus.

Russia accounts for only four percent, China 13 percent, Saudi Arabia 5.2 percent and the United Kingdom 3.3 percent.

The US military industry, where the main manufacturers are Boeing, Raytheon and Lockheed Martin, earn astronomical sums from these wars. This is also the reason why the illusion of a threatening Russia must be maintained. Without this "threat", the US military industry would not be able to justify to the public the enormous sums of money spent on weapons. Instead of investing this enormous energy of money in peace activities and mutual cooperation between countries, nations, these resources are being spent on new wars and the extermination of humanity.

The United States has started and continues to wage war completely without the UN support and in direct violation of international law. The former US presence in Syria was against international law, while Russia's presence is completely legal, something that official media never say. In Sweden, Russia and China are considered its biggest enemies and close their eyes to the real enemy, which is the wolf dressed in sheep's clothing.

A number of reliable sources have also reported that the CIA is arming and financing the rebels and terrorists against whom we officially claim to be waging war on. This tells e.g. Tulsi Gabbard, a Member of the United States House of Representatives.

However, she is just one of hundreds of whistleblowers.

On July 19, 2017, it was reported in the official media, the Washington Post, and the New York Times that Barack Obama has been arming rebels in Syria since 2013 with the intention of overthrowing the Syrian President al-Assad.

We must not forget that Barack Obama previously received the Nobel Peace Prize for his pursuit of peace.

I mentioned in my biography that my experience in the Hungarian Great Plain, which took place after my graduation in 1953, when an alien being contacted me and urged me to leave Hungary and go to Sweden, that I was given the task to lay the foundation for a center in Cultural Ecology (life sciences) in Europe. I also saw the historical people who previously acted in various historical events and contexts.

I saw how these actors would gather at the end of the 20th century due to their karmic roles and work together for a complete collapse of the economy and societal structure of the earthly civilization.

The United States is the last empire on earth that, along with its allies, is contributing to this collapse. It marks the end of a long cosmic cycle and the beginning of a new Era, which will bring the earthly civilization to higher heights on the spiral of evolution. This will lead to lasting peace between people and countries and to a Golden Age.

# Conflict areas

### The Arctic is a risk area of conflict

What are the geo- and security policy consequences when China now seriously challenges US dominance in the world - especially economically, technically and commercially?

China's economy is soon larger than the United States' and the realization that the balance of power is shifting from the West to Asia/Africa is slowly beginning to be understood in the average citizen.

Figure 8. A Canadian combat unit moving during the exercise Trident Juncture in the autumn of 2018 in Gåsbakken, Norway. The exercise prepares for war in northern Europe and the Arctic.

The discussion about the ongoing development is conducted intensively within so-called think tanks around the world; can and does the United States want to adapt or will there be more asymmetric conflicts and thereafter also proxy wars between the United States and China and between the United States and Russia?

To challenge Russia is probably not the smartest move.

Russia is technologically superior when it comes to long-range robots and to knock out radio and data communications, thanks to Pleiadian space technology.

The United States has long been a militarily superior superpower in the world, but is no longer as obvious in all areas.

Russia and China are on the offensive, as are some other nuclear-armed countries - India, Pakistan, Iran and the North Korea.

## The American superpower is on the verge of collapse

The US military has long been completely superior in the world.

The US military is very experienced, well-trained and well-equipped. The management and logistics also work well, which makes it possible to conduct operations all over the world, including with the help of aircraft carriers. But in recent years, the Armed Forces have become "worn out". Many of the soldiers who have been to Afghanistan, Iraq and other countries have been killed or injured. The suicide rate among military personnel in the United States has also increased. Many veterans suffer from post-traumatic stress disorder.

The technological superiority that the United States had is now also threatened, as all technological development that used to take place within the country, but now takes place in different parts of the world, far from American control.

*Conflict areas today* are the South and East China Sea. The United States, with its allies, has domination there today, but China is now claiming influence. China's military goal is to be able to make peace with the United States in the immediate area and has modernized its military over the past 20 years.

*Conflict areas tomorrow are* the Arctic. The Northeast Passage along the Russian coast opens up a new faster transport route to Asia and China. Russia's military goal has already been reached, which is to control the Northeast Passage, which runs within the Russian economic zone.

The United States seems to have made up its mind. Those who, under President Donald Trump, advocated global cooperation and multilateralism, lost. The Nationalists won and Donald Trump began his trade war against China and the goal is to undermine China's ambitions to become a global leading nation. He will never succeed in this.

The ongoing trade war is a part of that power struggle. The US strategy seems to be "containment" or "decoupling" - that they disconnect China from the economic system, isolate the country that was successfully done to the former Soviet Union.

That they succeeded with that back then is partly due to the fact that the Soviet Union was in a weak economic situation compared to China, and the dollar had a different value from what it has today. The dollar today is very weak and has hardly the paper value compared to the Chinese currency Yuan-Renminbi or the Russian Ruble. Behind these later currencies are large gold reserves, which are non-existent for the dollar. Both China and Russia have considered a joint currency system to avoid an economic crash, which will affect all the countries that are dependent on the dollar.

China's situation today is different from what it was a few decades ago. China today is incorporated into international regulations. China's ambitions consist of a web in which economic policy is part of foreign, security and defense policy.

China is investing in its "soft power" through huge investments in infrastructure in the developing countries Asia and Africa through the Belt and Road Initiative (BRI). China is primarily planning for the long term.

The EU and Sweden have begun to wake up from their Sleeping Beauty sleep and seems not to know what position to hold on to.

Sweden has lack of knowledge about modern China, i.e. what has happened in the country since the 1980s and what is going on, what is expected, and how the Chinese think.

When the former Minister of Infrastructure Anna Johansson, for example, attended the very first Silk Road Conference (Belt & Road) in Beijing in 2017, she showed, according to China experts who participated, an astonishing indifference and inability to understand what BRI (Belt & Road initiative) implies.

Since 2017, Sweden has also deliberately boycotted the subsequent major BRI conferences and not even responded to the invitations to conferences in Sweden. This has been seen as indifference and disrespect.

<u>The Swedish upbringing is the worst in the world.</u>

The Ministry for Foreign Affairs (UD) in Sweden is currently devising a China strategy and how to build up its own "thought structure" for increased knowledge about China. It is likely that it will follow the line that the EU has recently set out: *indecisive, critical and wait-and-see but co-operative inwards* - for economic reasons.

The economic and societal collapse that is on the doorstep should wake the Swedes from their Sleeping Beauty sleep and make them realize the fact that the value of the dollar is no more than the paper value. It is not about whether it happens, but when the economic crash happens. Then Sweden stands alone without help.

The interesting question is what type of collapse can affect us in Sweden and how we can survive it. It will be very difficult without the support of the BRICS countries that have laid the foundations for monetary cooperation.

The Swedish Riksbank should act before the collapse really takes place.

It is time to look to the East and consider BRICS currency cooperation with Brazil, Russia, India, China and South Africa, to ensure a currency system - instead of being dependent on the US currency system, which is on the verge of collapse.

The Russian author Dmitry Orlov mentions in his book "The Five Stages of Collapse" that a collapse always happens step by step in the same way as a disease. The steps towards collapse are:

1. Economic collapse
2. Commercial collapse
3. Political collapse
4. Social collapse
5. Cultural collapse

In "The Five Stages of Collapse", Dmitry Orlov describes what characterizes each individual stage. What measures can be taken to cope with the adaptation to the new social circumstances and prevent the collapse from proceeding to a higher, more devastating stage.

Sweden, like other EU member states, is in the danger zone due to their indifference and inability to think and act beforehand. Countries like Sweden that have built their welfare on borrowed money from outside, on high taxes and benefit systems will not be able to maintain their welfare.

Sweden will have a hard time when stage 1: The economic collapse occurs.

It is soon followed by stage 2: the commercial collapse, which is followed by stage 3: the political collapse, stage 4: the social collapse and stage 5: the cultural collapse.

Thereafter, the whole societal system falls apart like a house of cards where only anarchy, the disintegration of society remains. This happens unless something drastic happens, i.e. if Sweden would start cooperating with the new BRICS currency system and abandon the dollar, which no longer has any value.

Otherwise, Sweden will become a prototype for a crumbling society because it has done nothing but criticize other countries' policies and infrastructure, instead of learning both from their mistakes as well as their success like both China and Russia have experienced.

There is a saying that goes: *to criticize requires knowledge, to judge requires total knowledge. How many politicians, decision makers of various kinds possess total knowledge?*

A total knowledge is based on a 5D consciousness (*multi-dimensional consciousness*).

It is not limited to a 3D consciousness (*three-dimensional*) intellectual knowledge.

## The mythology of the Dragon

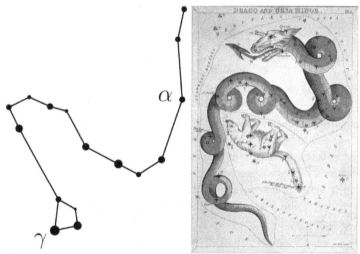

Figure 9. We communicate on several levels to convey this message in a way that is easier to understand.

1. Since the beginning, there have been dragons on earth. They come from a Draco/Reptilian species, probably from the constellation Dragon between Ursa major and Ursa minor in the northern starry sky.

2. Dragons impregnated earthly women and thereby created bloodlines with earthly people, who in turn constituted the Imperial and Royal families who have governed the development of man and the earthly civilization on earth until now. According to legend, the Emperor of the Han dynasty came from here.

3. The first of many biblical references is in the * Genesis, about Eve and the serpent (the dragon) and Adam and their eldest son Cain.

4. The Draconian bloodline is still on earth and most of the royal families belong to their bloodlines.

5. Most of the truth about the Draconian family has been hidden and covered by the so-called myths and legends.

6. The Draconian family can decipher the cosmic hieroglyphs. This is why dragons and reptiles in every culture tell about history and predict what will happen on earth in the future. Keep in mind that myths and legends are often hidden in symbols or in fairy tales and myths. There are Dragons who don't want us to know the truth about history.

* The serpent was the most cunning of all the wild animals that the Lord God had created. The serpent asked the woman, "Has God really told you not to eat from any tree in the garden?" The woman replied, "We may eat fruit from the trees, but about the fruit from the tree in the middle of the garden, God has said: Do not eat it or touch it! If you do, you will die." The serpent said, "Surely you will not die. But God knows that on the day you eat of the fruit your eyes will be opened, and you will become like gods with knowledge of good and evil." The woman saw that the tree was good as food: it was a delight to the eye and a glorious tree, because it gave wisdom. And she took the fruit and ate. She also gave to her husband, who was with her, and he ate. Then their eyes were opened, and they saw that they were naked. And they attached fig leaves and tied them around the hips.

They heard the Lord God walking in the garden in the cool evening breeze. Then the man and the woman hid themselves among the trees before the

Lord God. But the Lord God cried out to the man, "Where are you?" He replied, "I heard you coming in the garden and I was afraid, because I am naked, and so I hid." The Lord God said, "Who told you that you were naked? Have you eaten from the tree that I forbade you to eat of?" The man answered, "The woman whom you have set beside me, she gave me of the tree, and I ate." And the Lord God said unto the woman: What is this that thou hast done? She replied, "The serpent deceived me, and I ate."

## The five Dragon types

Since the beginning, there have been five Dragon Species on Earth. These have colonized the earth and controlled man and evolution. Each of these species was endowed with varying degrees (levels) of consciousness. They created with the earthly species different bloodlines and communication, especially within select leadership elite.

*Different kinds of Imperial and Royal houses were under their influence.*

These five Dragon species are:

1. The Golden Dragon (Society)
2. The White Dragon (Society)
3. The Red Dragon (Society)
4. The Green Dragon (Society)
5. The Black Dragon (Society)

Each of these groups belongs to the Asian and Western Illuminati "the Enlightened".

Could it be that when the dragons colonized the earth, that they decided who would rule certain regions? - where some of them chose to be peaceful, protective, while others chose to be more aggressive, power-hungry. Will any of them have any influence in the development during the New Age? Could it be that there has been a cosmic sibling rivalry that has been ongoing on earth for thousands of years?

Has the earthly human being been used as a slave for economic and power purposes, in wars (*nation against nation, religion against religion, race against race*) at the expense of satisfying the enormous ego of the negative, destructive dragons, reptiles?

Is there an end in sight for the game where the human being functions as a ping-pong ball?

Yes!

For the first time in the 26,000-year history of the earthly man, war and violence are coming to an end, so that the new earthly man can develop his inner higher qualitative ability and allow himself be guided by the soul quality (*reasoning, ethics and morality*) over the lower mind, the destructive qualities, and live and work in peace with each other.

If you listen to the messengers of DAOISM (Tao) and GNOSTICS (Sun Theology) and follow the law of the universe - the law of Morality: "*As you want to be treated, so you must also treat your fellow human beings*", then peace and harmony will prevail on earth.

## The dragon in Chinese mythology

The Chinese White Dragon is not like the Western Dragons (*with whom they are probably not related at all*), which are often seen as fire-breathing monsters. The Chinese White Dragon is usually associated with water and stands for *power, wisdom, peace and harmony*.

The Yellow Emperor was a devoted DAOIST (Taoist) and achieved immortality at the foot of Mount Qiao.

There, an alien spacecraft (UFO) in the shape of a golden dragon hovered down and took the YELLOW EMPEROR (*Qin Huang-Di*) and 70 of the royal officials up to the sky (*space*).

Dragons are central in Chinese mythology and there are often dragon motifs on textiles and ceramics.

The Chinese dragon differs from the Western image of a winged fire-breathing monster.

The Chinese dragon does not breathe fire but fog (*water vapor*) and is associated with water. The dragon is often depicted as snake-like with power over rivers, lakes and streams. The dragon is a recurring symbol of the emperor, but also of wisdom. The dragons were generally not considered evil and could sometimes appear in human form, even though they were mostly in the world of the immortals (*the parallel world*).

There is and has always been a plan to get rid of the evil dragons who have ruled the world in injustice. They have created most of humanity (*homo ercetus, homo habilis and homo sapiens*) and have also created the human reptile brain to be able to control it through emotions and fears.

They have created most of the earthly civilization through genetic modification (*see Darwin's philosophy*) to use them as slaves for their own purposes.

In the beginning of their evolution, the earthly man regarded them as their gods. Dragons are very wise, conscious, and intelligent and have the ability to manipulate those who have not reached a similar consciousness themselves.

The below text in Revelation 12: 7,8,9, is very relevant for 2012 when many people believed that the earth would go under.

7 And there arose a battle in heaven: Michael and his angels fought against the dragon; and the dragon and his angels fought against them,
8 but they could do nothing against them, and there was no place for them in heaven.
9 And the great dragon, that old serpent, was cast out, he who is called Devil and Satan, who deceived the whole world: he was cast down to the earth, and his angels were cast down beside him.

In reality, this is about the entry into the New Age, the Age of Aquarius (*The Golden Age*) - an age when peace will reign on earth. The evil dragons that create wars, anarchy and the disintegration of society no longer have a place among the earthly people. They cannot keep up with the 5D level of consciousness that the sons of the sun "The Yellow Emperor in East Asia and the Unifier in the Nordic countries" convey.

We cannot get into the many hidden messages in this writing.

Prophecies are written and given to be interpreted multi-dimensionally.

There are clear astrological references, historical and many other symbols.

What many don't realize is that there is a literal futuristic event that can be seen in the sky.

Figure 10. The President of the People's Republic of China Xi Jinping points at the signs of the Future.

He should know because he is a reincarnation of the Yellow Emperor, Qin Shi Huangdi.

## The Golden Dragon

Figure 11. The President of the People's Republic of China Xi Jinping is a Reincarnation of the Yellow Emperor Qin Shi Huangdi, reign 246 BC – 210 BC.

Qin Shi Huangdi was called the Yellow Emperor. Huang means "yellow" in Chinese and is a color associated with the Sun and with Royalty. He is the last of China's prehistoric rulers.

He is also considered the ancestor of the Han Chinese and has remained an important nationalist symbol.

When it comes to Chinese mythology, it is sometimes questionable to talk about gods. The Yellow Emperor is such a case where it is mainly a mysterious figure who is also considered by some to have been a historical person.

Like Shennong (the founder of TCM), the Yellow Emperor was helpful to the people and he is praised for having created stability in society. All prehistoric emperors are praised as inventors of various sciences and other things that benefit humans. Therefore, they also have the function of serving as role models for later emperors to relate to.

*The Golden Dragon* in Chinese philosophy and rules of life symbolizes the inner (hidden), neutral force (neutrinos) of the SUN, which according to ancient Chinese philosophy was called "DAO" (TAO), the Way.

To live according to DAO (Tao) is to avoid the extreme and thus balance yin and yang. It is also an understanding that all life is dependent on each other and to identify with everything else in creation. This holistic view of life makes violence unthinkable, because you realize that if you hurt someone, you hurt yourself. The Taoist also knows that there is a perpetual interaction in nature. Life is dynamic and constantly changing, so it is also pointless to seek security outside oneself.

DAO in Western philosophy corresponds to the SOUL, SOUL CONSCIOUSNESS in all manifestation. From here comes the saying that (GOD) is omnipresent. God sees everything and knows everything.

Tao is a mystery to most because it goes beyond the logic that belongs to the domain of the Mind. It is not about faith, but about education, experience, consciousness and knowledge, primarily about oneself and nature. The Eastern approach - to let <u>intuition</u> take precedence over logic or <u>instinct</u> - permeates Taoism.

The hidden, mysterious cosmic neutrino force (*zero point or neutral energy*) is not seen, heard or felt. It manifests itself in our intuitive consciousness and can only be perceived through its effect on ourselves and our surroundings, on our ideas, events and human development. The underlying principle in the doctrine is the complementary, the polar. Each action gives rise to a sequel. Each pole gives rise to an opposite pole.

Electricity is created by both + (plus) and - (minus).

The day would not be a day if night had not existed.

There must be "a couple" behind every form of relationship and creation. William Shakespeare's "Be or not to be " arises from each other. Difficult and easy explain each other. Long and short are in opposition to each other. Before and after follow each other.

To set up a theater or film requires two opposite poles - a "script writer" and a "director". The script writer is equated with the *Creator* and the Director with the *Executor*. Without the collaboration of these two poles, there would be no theater or film.

So it is within the Cosmic Spectacle as well.

The (*inner*) hidden, implicit force of the SUN is *neutral or zero point energy*, which corresponds to the "SOUL ENERGY, SELF, I" according to Metaphysics, Quantum Physics.

The (*external*) manifesting force of the SUN is *electromagnetic energy* which corresponds to the "MIND POWER, MIND" according to Metaphysics, Quantum Physics.

In ancient Chinese philosophy, "I CHING" is referred to as restructuring, transformation, change - which relates to the Mind Power.

Within creation, the manifestation, there is no GOD other than the SUN. The SUN is the Creator, Sustainer and Dissolver or Transformer of all life, form, manifestation within the all-encompassing hyperspace.

*The Self-consciousness slumbers in the mineral kingdom, awakens in the plant kingdom, moves in the animal kingdom and thinks in the human kingdom.*

Man is the crown of creation and has self-consciousness. The three other natural kingdoms have a collective unconscious consciousness and lack self-identity.

The next stage in the human development is the 5th in order, which occurs during the present age, the Age of Aquarius. It is also called the Golden Age. During this age, man on earth will develop a collective universal consciousness. Man will understand that nothing is separate. Everything exists and works at the same time at all levels - from high school to primary school.

In primary school, you don't see the forest for all the trees.

In intermediate school you don't see the lake beyond the forest.

In high school you see the tree, the forest and the lake.

It is not easy to understand what we don't have knowledge or experience of, but you can learn everything!

## The Golden Dragon and the White Dragon

DAO (TAO) is the "*The Golden Dragon*", the Essence (*the inner power*), "The Soul Power" and I CHING is the "*The White Dragon*", the Substance, Creation (*the outer power*), "The Mind Power" or Executer.

The Golden Dragon Society is the inner operation of the Asian Illuminati in China, while the White Dragon Society is the outer, manifested part of China.

Therefore, the external activity in China consists of the "White Dragon Society", which belongs to certain Asian countries.

These two forces must coexist and interact with each other; otherwise an imbalance arises where either the spiritual or the mind-related, intellectual force predominates.

Without the interaction of these two forces, neither life nor form exists.

Therefore, the SUN is the HIGHEST SOURCE and the only true GODHEAD that HUANG-DI (*The Yellow Emperor*) and PHARAOH AKHENATON saw as the Creator of the Universe (GOD). Everything else is just Illusion.

All other beings that the unconscious earthly man calls his gods are nothing but virtual forms created by the mind.

Figure 12. The White Dragon is the guardian and protector of all human life on earth, as dragons did in ancient times.

This ancient society is today led by a group of elders (sages) from the Golden Dragon Society who live in the "*forbidden zone*" in China.

*They are considered immortal due to their extremely long lifespan.*

# Consciousness and Reality

Consciousness is a relative concept and depends on what we compare with.

Consciousness is a term that refers to the relationship between the mind and the world of the mind, the environment with which it interacts.

Consciousness has been defined as: subjectivity, the ability to experience or feel, alertness, having a sense of the self and the executive control system the mind. Despite the difficulty of defining consciousness, many philosophers believe that there is an all-encompassing underlying intuition about what consciousness is.

We all know what consciousness is.

We are conscious when we are awake, when we think and when we think about the universe. But can anyone explain what consciousness is in its proper context?

Or even what distinguishes a conscious thought from an unconscious thought?

The debate about consciousness has been handed over to philosophers, religious scholars and brain scientists, but none of these have understood the true nature of consciousness.

There is a cosmic (*holistic*) truth about consciousness:

* Consciousness slumbers in the mineral kingdom
* Awakens in the plant kingdom
* Moves in the animal kingdom
* Thinks in the human kingdom
* Understand creation in the divine kingdom

The earthly man uses his brain capacity (*brain computer*) more and more consciously, and her ability to understand more and more of the whole increases.

But as our understanding of the brain is constantly increasing, researchers are more and more able to address this difficult subject.

Imagine the difference between the image of an apple that we visualize in our brain and the image taken by a digital camera.

The raw image of the apple is the same whether it is taken with a camera or if we imagine it in our head. The camera processes each "pixel" independently. However, our brain will combine parts of the image to identify an object, i.e. that it is an apple and that it is food. Here the camera can be seen as "unconscious state" and the brain as "conscious state".

A pixel is the smallest part of the grid graphics that is used to e.g. show images on a monitor.

Figure 13. Image of an apple: The camera is seen as "unconscious state" and the brain in subjective interpretation as "conscious state."

Grid graphics are images made up of rows of pixels. Each pixel is given a color.

The word pixel comes from the English *Picture Element*, where "pix" is an abbreviation for Pictures. The abbreviation "px" is often used when talking about pixels as units.

A pixel can be considered a point with a certain color and location. The resolution of a computer screen can be specified as, for example, 1024x768, which means 1024 pixels horizontally and 768 pixels vertically.

Here, the camera image, or pixel by pixel division, can be seen as "unreal with the absence of consciousness" and in our brain as "real and with the presence of consciousness, a kind of reality".

Man is both a Soul (self) conscious and a Mind Conscious being.

*"Everything we are aware of at any given time is part of our consciousness. Having conscious experience is the most familiar and most mysterious aspect of our lives."*

Our individual and collective "reality" is the sum of our consciousness, which in turn is the sum of our experience.

*Achieving a multidimensional consciousness is an expression that has become popular in some circles and many people use this expression without understanding its true meaning.*

To have a multidimensional - multistructural 5D consciousness means to be aware of the spiritual, virtual, implicit (*folded*), hidden, by the mind imperceptible unmanifested part and the mind-related 3D explicit (*unfolded*) perceptible, manifested (appearing) part of reality .

5D consciousness means that we have an absolute consciousness, of both to the mind hidden part and the manifested part of reality. We have full insight into our original identity. Not on an intellectual level, but on an intuitive level, of insight.

It is easy to use expressions just to impress your surroundings. But it is not as easy to understand its true meaning.

I see in my students whom I have taught for decades, how difficult it is for them to distinguish the intellectual, learned part of reality from their intuitive, inner perceptible part of reality. The majority believe that what they have learned intellectually is the same as they have experienced during their course of development, life.

## Who is the Human Being?

Man is an AI "Artificial Intelligence" that has been created and assigned different roles to play in different dimensional worlds. The earthly man belongs to the lowest, most sluggish species that belong to the human kingdom in creation, manifestation.

Man is an "actor", a chess piece on earth who has been assigned different kinds of roles by the so-called Director (*Creator*) - the Casting Director within creation (in the theater of the mind) in the lowest, slowest 3D part of the creation, manifestation.

Figure 14. Man is an actor on the universal stage.

We have all so far worn masks to hide our true identity to not to be recognized by our surroundings.

But at 12 o'clock (at midnight) when the darkness slowly fades and the light increases, we must remove the mask we have worn through life and show our true identity.

*We must show who we really are - the one we have hidden behind the mask.*

Some of us don't want to take off the mask. We don't want to be recognized by our loved ones, i.e. parents, siblings, friends or by our surroundings. It's easier to keep the mask and continue to play our different roles, than to get rid of our role-playing games. We are afraid of getting rid of the role play we have undertaken to portray in life, which is not the real role we carry within us, but a role we have constantly taken on for convenience, which can be leaders, politicians, decision makers, etc.

Figure 15. We make our choice in life now.

It is clear that some don't want to be recognized and refuse to the end to unmask.

Here we have the Illuminati, CABAL (*the deep or hidden state*), destructive alien intelligences from Betelgeuse from the Orion's planetary system whose allies, government representatives, government officials, leaders of various kinds until now have influenced and controlled all life and development on earth. These destructive subspecies regard earth as their planet and a large part of humanity as their slaves.

They have controlled *politics, philosophy, religion, science and teachings*. They have controlled everything that man can imagine in his wildest fantasy.

It goes without saying that they don't want to unmask and reveal their identities. This also applies to their earthly representatives who act through different roles in the theater of the mind.

A 5D cosmic conscious being cannot be fooled. He sees what or who is hiding behind the mask. He sees but does not judge anyone.

He knows the reason why we all wear masks here on earth.

*But now that we have entered a new phase of development to become more conscious during the New Age, we must remove the mask we have worn through incarnations, life after life.*

*Otherwise we will be recognized and revealed into public view.*

That is what is happening to the Illuminati, CABAL (*the deep state*) who to the very last want to hide their true identity from humanity.

This process has already begun.

Countries, States and their representatives, politicians, decision makers, mainstream media "MSM" which engage in *misleading information, untruth, corruption, fraud, exercise of power, defamation, slander* - have begun to be revealed.

And this is just the beginning.

Everything that has been swept under the carpet will come to the surface.

We can ask ourselves the following question:

What is the difference between consciousness and thought, intellect?

"Cogito, ergo sum" - "I think, therefore I am" is a philosophical statement formulated by the French philosopher René Descartes. This also applies to the last species of our humanity, Homo Sapiens "*the thinking human being*", which is our current species.

According to Descartes, the only knowledge one could be sure of was that of consciousness, that if one thinks, one exists. One who does not think does not exist according to Descartes.

This is obviously not correct.

The ego is the recognition of our identity with our thoughts, opinions, mental perceptions, attitudes, etc.

The ego is a kind of separated, fragmented identity of our existence.

It corresponds to the drop of the ocean - a holographic part of the whole.

Figure 16. The ego is like a drop of the ocean.

We imagine that in order to be conscious we must think, but thought and consciousness are two different phenomena.

Thinking is a normal phenomenon on our 3D level, to which our planet earth belongs. Here, the Ego is in a lower qualitative state.

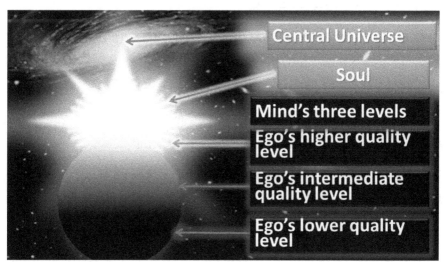

Figure 17. There are three main mind qualities. On earth at present, the population is mainly aware of the lower and intermediate qualitative levels of the ego.

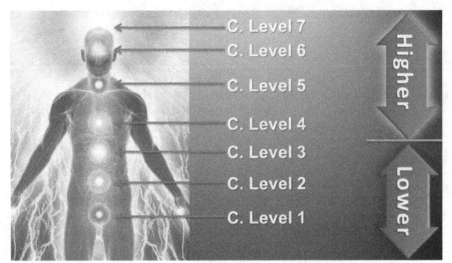

Figure 18. The human levels of consciousness. Humanity today is at consciousness level 1-3, with few exceptions.

Extraterrestrial intelligences that are at a higher dimensional level as well as a few individuals on earth with a higher qualitative consciousness, <u>don't think</u>.

They have an <u>intuitive knowledge</u>!

They are aware of what is going to happen and why it is happening?

Their "Ego" is in a higher qualitative state, i.e. in indirect connection with the Original Source, the Ocean, the Absolute 5D Field of Consciousness.

These types of beings have access to the universal matrix, where the past, present and future exist simultaneously.

We can put ourselves in a neutral state (zero), where we are aware on a delta level and yet we are awake. Today's earthly normal individual is unconscious in this state.

The animals don't think. Plants don't think. Still, they can scan, sense their surroundings, feel dangers or approaching changes in their surroundings in advance - weather changes, approaching thunderstorms, cold, rain, etc.

Consciousness can mean: *thoughts, feelings, perceptions, moods, dreams and self-awareness.*

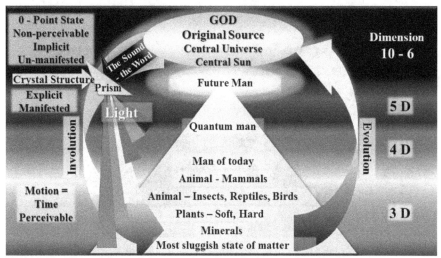

Figure 19. Illustration of the creation. Involution and evolution.

Consciousness can be seen as a state of mind - a way of perceiving what is happening - a relationship between oneself and the outside world.

Consciousness has been described as "The Self, the Ego", the existence of "being someone and something".

Many philosophers see consciousness as the most important thing in the universe.

On the other hand, many researchers believe that the word "*consciousness*" is too diffuse to be useful.

Consciousness is the subject of much research within *philosophy, psychology, neuroscience, cognitive science* and *artificial intelligence*.

There is disagreement about whether consciousness can be assessed in seriously ill people or people who are in a coma (*in an unconscious state*).

**Conscious**                    **Unconscious**

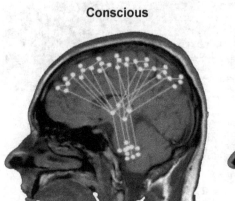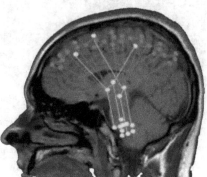

Figure 20. The more conscious you are, the more dendritic connections there are in the brain, brain cell branches and connections to other nerve cells.

If the absent human consciousness exists - how can it then be measured *at what point in the fetal development the consciousness begins*? In my experience, it happens about 3 months before birth, when the unity consciousness (soul) has entered the fetus.

Can a human-like robot achieve a conscious state?

The answer is Yes.

Consciousness also stands for the "*unconscious*", the "*subconscious*" and the "*waking-conscious*" consciousness. These include *unconscious state, dream state* and *waking state*. The waking state is the mind's and the senses' reaction to the surroundings. This is in contrast to when we sleep and are in a *dream state* or an *unconscious state*.

We are in a matrix, hologram or virtual programmed reality that we think is real because our brain perceives and expresses it.

**Who are we and who created us?**

Most people on earth claim that there is someone we call God who has created the human being. Who is God and where is he?

If you have read the Bible (book of books) in the Gospel of John 10:34, Christ answers: "*Is it not written in your law; I said that you are gods?*"

Have you thought of that we have created everything that exists in our 3D world and reality, i.e. everything without the natural kingdoms? We are co-creators in creation.

Have you ever heard that the Pleadians have created our 3D world and reality from the 5D matrix, the hologram (Akasha) that makes up the Central Sun Alcyone and its software program, the information structure of our galaxy? To have extracted from this information matrix all the energy and information required to create worlds, civilizations, dimensional materials of different quality and density. They have created the mineral kingdom, the plant kingdom, the animal kingdom and the human kingdom with the power of thought.

Does that sound unlikely? No not at all.

For about 1 year in the early 1990s, I worked with a former Soviet KGB colonel at my Biophysiological Institute in Stockholm. He wasn't a spy. He was employed at the intelligence service's department of psychology during the 1980s Presidency of Mikhail Gorbachev. The KGB colonel talked about how their researchers have been able to influence molecular structures in different substances to improve their quality.

He also told me that he was trained onboard a Pleiadian spaceship, and that he could leave his biological body and move into parallel worlds. He was able to monitor President Mikhail Gorbachev when he was on business trips abroad to cut off any threats to which he might be exposed to from the parallel world.

This is not a fantasy. The CIA has been practicing this since the 1970s and Russia as early as the 1960s. The public isn't informed about this, because they would not understand it and it would create confusion in individuals. Everything that doesn't belong to man's so-called normal behavior and habitual thought structures are called *fabrications, fantasies, untruths or conspiracy theories*.

Today's James Bond agents work outside the body. They can access secret information without having to break into any building. They can also conduct so-called industrial espionage by teleporting, moving their bodies, their consciousness and using remote viewing.

They can access information without having to be physically present.

How many of you understand or believe this?

But this is true.

Extraterrestrial beings can hack into the internet at any time and access information. They are constantly updated about what happens on earth and in our society. I experienced this already in the 1960s when a Pleiadian woman who called herself Borealis interrupted the news program I was watching and appeared on the TV screen and communicated with me telepathically. She wore a dark blue tight-fitting uniform with a silver-like belt around her waist and matching boots. She showed herself on two occasions when I was alone. On the next occasion, she was accompanied by a dark-haired extraterrestrial man dressed in a different kind of uniform. She mentioned that he came from another planetary system. They worked together on the spaceship and were studying plants here on earth.

I have made some demonstrations to my life science students in various contexts when I told them what they had thought or done in secret or what questions they had written down that they would ask me the last day on the seminar. But by then they had already had their questions answered. This type of reading, scanning often creates fear in the majority, instead of curiosity. They think I can read all their thoughts and see what they are doing at home or at work.

Then you can imagine that both the CIA and the GRU already know for real that which you deny or don't believe in, that it exists in reality.

Anyone who has the will, interest and patience can develop their communicative ability through telepathy and intuition. I mention this so you understand why President Vladimir Putin is more suitable as a world leader than Xi Jinping or any other leader or head of state in the world. Vladimir Putin is endowed with a different kind of consciousness than the other leaders, the heads of state in the world. On the one hand, he has inborn knowledge and experience as Peter the Great from one of his previous incarnations, and on the other hand through his contemporary knowledge and experience from the political game and from the intelligence service.

Vladimir Putin knows what others think or suspect.

One day not so far away you will learn and master what the intelligence services CIA, KGB (GRU) since long have been busy with. It will be completely normal for you what until now you have regarded as mystery, fantasy and unreality. In school your children will learn: *telepathy, thought transfer, remote vision, traveling outside the body and traveling in different types of spacecrafts.* This will become completely normal in the New Age society.

Man on earth will learn in schools a whole new scientific way of thinking, which includes quantum physics, metaphysics (higher physics) compared to what the present modern human being is endowed with, aware of.

## The Future Medicine is Individually Based Harmonization

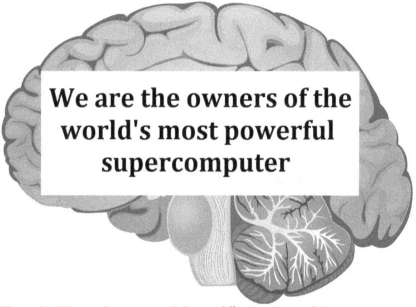

Figure 21. We are the owners of the world's most powerful supercomputer.

**The future medicine is already here**

Everything in creation is Energy and Information consisting of Frequencies.

*Everything exists at the same time both as energy and information.*

Energy is the carrier for information. Neither energy nor information can exist separately. Only together they can create, maintain and dissolve (restructure) matter (form) in its entirety. Without matter - form, neither the primary original program (soul program, unity program), nor the secondary separated mind program, mind can come to expression.

All matter consists of atoms that oscillate at different speeds (frequencies) and these frequencies form electromagnetic fields.

All living matter thus has a certain frequency and intensity, which means that it vibrates with a certain wavelength.

These frequencies can be used to stimulate or inhibit specific components in the body, or to neutralize invasive parasitic life forms or pathogenic energies.

This energy effect is called energy medicine, frequency medicine because they are effective at different frequencies.

Energy medicine is based on the principle of metaphysics - quantum physics: *all matter from its highest subtle state to its lowest condensed state is Energy and Information*.

For example, light is available in two forms, quantum which is the physical part and wavelength which is the energy part/form. By wavelength is meant the distance that a wave e.g. sound travels during one oscillation. Sound with the frequency 1 Hz performs one oscillation per second, and since the speed in air is 340 m/s, the wavelength becomes 340 meters; the higher the sound frequency, the shorter the wavelength.

Different biochemical and electrical processes generate low frequencies of 1–100 Hz (Hertz, or oscillations per second).

These vibrations from various biochemical reactions are constantly present in our body parts, tissues and organs. You can see it as a background noise, a constant, often inaudibly low humming. At a strong physical effort, you can hear your body more.

The frequency - or tone - is different for different cells in different parts of the body.

For example, different ions (electric charges) have different frequencies: potassium has 7 Hz; manganese has 21 Hz and calcium 28 Hz.

A healthy cell has one frequency and a cancer cell has another.

The treatment effect lies in the fact that we modulate the frequency, either by:

- Resonance (*amplification*) or
- Interference (*disturbance or extinction of the wavelength*).

In the same way as light, man consists of both matter and undulations. So, if we influence the energy body, we influence the physical part, the body.

This is done for example through the help of subtle energies or via electromagnetic energy in the form of sound waves and light waves.

These energy treatments can therefore be called <u>Energy Medicine</u>, <u>Frequency Medicine</u> - or <u>Bioresonance</u> - because they work with different frequencies.

Each organ has its own vibration frequency (*oscillations per second*). You can see the body as an orchestra, and it is important that the various instruments interact to maintain high function and efficiency.

As long as the energy flows in the body unimpeded and different parts interact (*are in symbiosis*), in harmony, you feel healthy and full of energy.

Each organ or part of the body thus has an optimal oscillation rate.

Even our thoughts and feelings fluctuate with different frequencies, and their frequencies affect the body and organs.

## Thoughts are energy

Thoughts are also energy. Thoughts like "*I feel worthless*" or "*no one wants me*" can lower the whole system energy, while thoughts like "*life is wonderful*" and "*I love myself and others*" higher the energy.

If you compare with tones, the words *love, joy, peace* and *harmony* vibrate with the highest, clearest and purest frequencies.

At the bottom of the "*tone scale*" we find the heavier vibrations such as *shame* and *guilt*.

In the same way, love, light, joy, peace, harmony and balance are words with high energy that lift us up. It is important what kind of energy we surround ourselves with, what we take in and what we cultivate, what we allow within us.

## Blocked energy flow

We humans are designed for flow of energy and information between the cells and the organism to work without interruption. But if we are exposed to inner and external stress or pressure for a long time, parts of our energy flow can be slowed down, blocked or "shut down completely". This slows down communication, cleansing and renewal of the physical body. Even a blockage in an area of the body can affect the rest of the energy system; where e.g. an inflammation in a tooth root can increase the risk of inflammation throughout the body. This causes the energy system to become unbalanced, at first in one part but over time the entire system is affected, which can give rise to physical or mental symptoms.

The body itself, of course, works all the time in silence to balance and distribute the energy and repair minor damages. But we may need extra help, and energy treatments offer this.

By using different specific frequencies in the treatment of our energy body, which is the mold, the prototype (*bioplasma, etheric body, plasma body*) for our biological (*physical*) body and organism, the physical body is affected to a higher function and wholeness.

Harmonization means that the body's inherent harmony is restored. It is a sophisticated science that operates at the energy level. It is done with the so-called "Quantum Generator".

If you want to find the secrets of the universe, think in terms of energy, frequency and vibration.

Figure 22. According to Albert Einstein, Nikola Tesla was one of the most important contributors to the birth of electricity.

Quantum medical analysis and treatment technology is a result of research and development in Space Medicine. Quantum medicine works through information in electromagnetic oscillation rates, and the method is based on the fact that the human interior is like a constantly waving sea of energy waves (*oscillations*) that in good health are in harmony.

In connection with the analysis via headphone-based sensors or via telemetry[2], the human 100 billion neurons (nerve cells) in the brain transmit information as energy waves and "listen" to the resonance from her biological body, organism.

In case of imbalance, the Quantum Analyzer reads deviating frequencies in organs, muscles, bones and also that which concerns the mental and emotional state. These imbalances can be restored (normalized) by "harmonizing" the energy field of the body, the organism.

---

[2] Telemetry (from the Greek "tele" and "metros") actually means remote measurement. Telemetry is the wireless transmission of measurement data from a measurement object. The transmission of measurement data can take place via radio waves, scalar waves or optically by means of, for example, infrared light or laser.

This is perhaps easier to understand if you compare it to playing an instrument. The resonant structure of the musical instrument amplifies the tone by starting to vibrate at the same frequency as the sound source. In the same way, you only receive a radio channel if the frequency of the radio receiver corresponds to that of the radio station. The same applies to our TV channels.

So the treatment of the body, the organism responds to frequencies that are in resonance, where susceptibility exists for precisely these frequencies.

The frequencies are transmitted to the body through the energy body, the etheric body or the bioplasma. It is an extremely fast system.

It's ingenious and simple!

## Stimulating frequencies

Russian scientists, who are at the forefront of research in the field of plasma fields, have for about 60 years studied the effects of energy medicine on the body, organism, thoughts and feelings in both humans and animals.

Bio-efficient frequencies have been found that resonate with various organs and systems in the body.

These frequencies are used to improve or restore the function of the body, the organism, the cell structure, molecules - all the way down to the RNA and DNA level, to the molecular level.

Through the CelesteMethod®, we can detect and remedy possible disease-causing bacteria, viruses, fungi, etc. at an early stage, which otherwise contribute to symptom-related malfunctions, diseases, from chromosome and DNA level to organ level. Only then can traditional healthcare detect a possible illness, and then it is already too late.

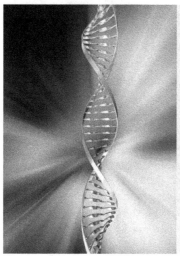

**DNA works as a permanent transmitter and receiver of information.**

**Cells communicate with each other.**

DR F. A. POPP
DR B. RUTH

Figure 23. The DNA acts as a constant transmitter and receiver of information. Cells communicate with each other.

Here are some examples: 20 Hz is the lowest audible sound in air for humans and the wavelength is 17 meters. Sound with a longer wavelength is called infrasound.

- The parasympathetic nervous system is stimulated by 1–10 Hz.
- The sympathetic nervous system is stimulated by 25–100 Hz.
- 0.5–30 Hz affects the rhythm of the brain and can be used to induce alpha, beta, theta and delta waves, for example to relieve stress.
- The muscles are activated by 20–30 Hz etc.

At our research institute in Sweden, we use two specific instruments, which are based on space technology. These two are "significant analyzer" and "quantum generator". These are the latest in AI "*Artificial Intelligence*", which have been developed by Russian and Czech researchers. We can use these equipments both at our research institute, but also via telemetry at a distance.

For analysis and measures, we use only scalar waves, which are about 1.5 times faster than the speed of light, or faster.

**Biophilia** means: "**love of life and all living things**". Biophilia is a theory that tries to explain man's inner will to be close to nature and live in symbiosis with nature and with his natural traits.

The original Health Analyzer the "Russian Oberon and Metatron GR 4025" is the most revolutionary in "Energy Medicine" in this century. It is a result of space research in Russia and was developed in Omsk, Russia by the physicists Dr. Vladimir Igorevich Nesterov, Dr. Vera Nestarova, Dr. Natalina Ogluzdina and Dr. Miroslav Nosec at the Institute of Practical Psychophysics (IPP), which Dr. Vladimir Nesterov founded in 1990.

Professor Vladimir Nesterov, Dr. Vera Nestarova and Dr. Miroslav Nosec are members of the "*Russian Academy of Medical Sciences*" (Moscow).

The latest automated model of the Quantum Analyzer and the Quantum Generator for "Multidimensional Virtual Scanning and Harmonization" has been developed by Dr. Miroslav Nosec, Ph.D., MD, the Czech Physicist Alex Waldemar Laufersweller and Civil Engineer Thomas Mariancic, who is a software specialist.

## The function of the Quantum Analyzer - Quantum Generator

There is a very weak low-frequency magnetic field around biological systems. The scientific discoveries on which Oberon is based are based on oriental medicine and the energetic conception of acupuncture as a means of biological system control.

The distinct oscillations of each organ and cell are recorded in the Quantum Analyzer's software as a spectral analysis of vortex magnetic fields. Electronic oscillators in the Quantum Analyzer resonate at electromagnetic wavelengths and energy levels that are sufficient to break weak bonds and read the activity of body tissues while selectively amplifying signals against the background noise.

After registering the frequency characteristics of the organ, the Quantum Analyzer compares them with reference processes (healthy tissue, disease-affected tissue, infectious agents) and reveals the most likely pathological process or tendency to pathological expression. The Quantum Analyzer's software contains a large number of pathological processes with a certain degree of manifestation, age, sex and other differences taken into account. In this way, the Quantum Analyzer identifies stresses that can lead to diseases, and therefore indicates problems sometimes before they occur.

In an unpublished study of 100 clients, "The Dove Clinic", UK, reported an 80% correlation between known pathology and what the Quantum Analyzer revealed.

Pathological areas in the human body are identified by the Quantum Analyzer in terms of entropy values (degree of quantum organization) - the lower the entropy, the greater the level of structural organization and function; the higher the entropy, the lower the level of structural organization and function. The entropy values of specific structures are displayed in colors on a computer screen. Areas with low entropy (fully functioning) are shown in light yellow. As entropy increases, the color displayed on the Oberon becomes darker, ranging from orange to red, purple and almost black.

The Quantum Analyzer also provides a unique possibility to record frequency fluctuations in drug preparations. According to spectral properties, the Oberon can make an immediate comparison with all the preparations stored in the computer memory (which can be several thousand in number) and the properties of the pathological process and reveal what remedies can be the most effective.

## Treatment with the Quantum Generator

The information therapy provided by the Oberon affects the individual's body with a combination of different modulated electromagnetic oscillations. The Oberon therapy aims to correct the disturbed inner balance in the organism and corresponding electromagnetic radiation through information preparations (metazodes).

The metazodes in the Quantum Analyzer are specific combinations of frequencies found in the current state of ill health (the pathological waveforms are inverted 180°). They can be received by the individual via the Quantum Analyzer at a clinic, or transmitted to the individual via remote telemetry. The same procedure applies to animals of different kinds (horses, dogs, cats, etc.)

Delivery of therapy via the "Quantum Generator" is achieved through Scalar waves to affect the energy fields of the pathologically damaged organs.

With the "Quantum Analyzer and the Quantum Generator" we can both analyze and harmonize the human brain's subconscious data fields and map the primary cause behind every conceivable symptom, regardless of whether they are mentally related, emotionally related or biologically related (physical) problems.

Through a special method called *telemetry*, we can both analyze and transmit harmonization to the body (organism) at a distance through scalar waves, without the individual having to be present. This type of health program is of particular interest now when humans in connection with "pandemics, 4G and 5G impacts" no longer have access to the health care and medical care required for a healthy life.

Both analysis and action take place via DNA.

NOTE. No known university in the world has access to this knowledge.

Our AI (*Artificial Intelligence*) is connected to virtual servers located in the Northern and Southern Hemisphere. Should any of them stop communicating, the other server automatically takes over the communication.

The quantum generator has access to 40 different categories of measure programs.

Our AI "*Artificial Intelligence*" can handle hundreds or thousands of people at the same time via telemetry, regardless of whether they are on Earth; regardless of whether their problems are mental, emotional or biological (physical).

This technology is based on knowledge in Metaphysics and Quantum Physics by highly conscious Russian and Czech scientists in collaboration with extraterrestrial intelligences from the Pleiades.

We can detect physiological changes in the body, the organism long before they have had time to result in a noticeable biological symptom (*disease*), e.g. breast cancer, prostate cancer, bowel cancer, lung cancer, etc., which affect hundreds of thousands of people worldwide every year.

The entire current healthcare and biochemical pharmaceutical industry will collapse within the next few decades.

This has already begun in connection with the "Covid-19 pandemic".

The future medicine is about "*Harmonization of Man's Etheric Plasma Housing*" through AI "*Artificial Intelligence*".

People who want to survive on earth and be part of the new civilization must take personal responsibility for their own health - mental, emotional and biological well-being. These people must also think about a nutritious diet and the right kind of environment to live in.

*A New Consciousness in A New Time is a necessity for the survival of the earthly civilization.*

For this purpose, we have developed the CelesteMethod®.

# The CelesteMethod®

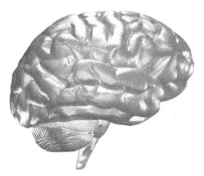

Bild 24. The Golden Brain

**Man's Inner Resource Development and Future Health are based on the CelesteMethod®**

The CelesteMethod® was developed by the UNIFIER, Sandor Alexander Markus, Ph.D., MD (MA) (*alias Saint Germain*) together with (*the protector of the World Doctrine*) Ann-Sofie Hammarbäck, STD, in order for the human being in the New Age to reach a Soul-related, Higher Qualitative, Quantum Consciousness - become a Master in Life.

This millennial knowledge, taught through online teachings, seminars, and literatures, has never before been offered to man in its entirety.

Until now, parts of this knowledge have only been available to chosen elite.

Now the wholeness about creation is taught and added information from the implicit (*hidden*) virtual part of the universe, i.e. from the 8th, 7th and 6th dimensional levels to our 5D (*matrix*) reality. This in order to show the wholeness within the form-manifested universe, i.e. within the 4th subtle and the 3rd condensed dimensional manifestation.

We offer the keys to the riddle of life, the ancient universal knowledge that exists within all of us to turn our lower qualitative (*intellectual*) development toward a higher qualitative (*unity-related cosmic*) development.

The knowledge is now available to you so that you can change and adapt your life to the New Age (*Age of Aquarius*) in which we entered on December 21-23, 2012, when our solar system and our sun crossed the equatorial line in our galaxy and entered a photon belt around the galaxy sun Alcyone in the Pleiadian constellation.

The CelesteMethod® is a three-step program that through self-realization leads man to increased consciousness (*quantum*) or increased consciousness of the unmanifested, hidden (*implicit*) and manifested (*explicit*) universe.

The CelesteMethod® restores the unity consciousness (*Soul Control*) in a Mind-Controlled human being, which means that one can find the originality, one's true identity, instead of a mind-constructed, mind-controlled (*illusory*) reality.

## 1. Information:

Every individual who wants to realize the CelesteMethod® in his life, in his thinking and action, can take part of the education and development program via membership of the "AIC Association" (www.worlddoctrine.org).

## 2. Analysis:

Individual analyzes and harmonization of our inner quality through high-tech-AI "Artificial Intelligence", gives each member a tailored individualized program.

## 3. Measure Program:

Individual application of our high-tech analysis and measure program (development program) gradually leads to increased consciousness about ourselves and to better health and increased well-being. This is a necessity for all of us who want to adapt to the demands of the New Age (*Golden Age*).

The earthly civilization is on the brink of a global catastrophe. This occurs for the first time in the earth's approximately 26,000-year history. Major epidemics, natural disasters, radiation from 4-5 G base-station-masts, mobile phones, destructiveness of various kinds: *materialism, selfishness, lust for power, war, hatred, etc.*, are growing to uncontrollable proportions, especially in the Western-controlled world.

Ethics - morality, consideration for one's neighbor, nature, animals, etc. are, in today's thinking a utopia.

*Many talk about ethics and morality, but only a few practice it in their daily lives.*

Ethics - morality is the basic foundation according to the law of the cosmos.

Ethics is "how we think" and Morality is "how we act".

If man continues to destroy the foundation of his existence, survival, on which the destiny of man rests, then the present civilization as well as previous civilizations will be only memories. Man believes in his ignorance, unconsciousness (*naivety*) that everything changes, without having to do anything himself. People count on that there is always someone else who takes care of everything.

She has a hard time freeing herself from her sheep mentality.

If so, who would solve her problems that she has created for herself due to ignorance, unconsciousness?

*A paradigmatic shift, an altered consciousness is a necessity for the survival of the earthly civilization.*

To protect the total human culture, which includes creation, the hyperspace in its entirety, both the terrestrial and the extraterrestrial, we have created the CelesteMethod®.

The CelesteMethod® is the most comprehensive and profound cosmic science ever presented in modern times.

Parts of this science have previously been intended for only certain select students. Today, this cosmic knowledge is available to anyone searching for the truth.

All serious seekers, interested can take part of this knowledge.

The CelesteMethod® is a cosmic, universal science (*knowing*) which is the basic foundation in all *philosophies, religions, sciences and all life.*

The CelesteMethod® leads us into the deepest mysteries of the universe, hyperspace and gives us knowledge - wisdom about what concerns both the unmanifested, the so-called virtual (*spiritual*), the implicit order, the folded universe, and the manifested, explicit order (*mind-influenced*), the unfolded part of creation. These together constitute the universe, the hyperspace in its entirety.

*Throw all obsolete ideas and traditions in a dustbin and start a new life. Only then can we survive as individuals and civilization on earth.*

The waking-conscious (*intellectual*) part of our brain in today's most developed humans is responsible for only about 17% of our brain computer's (*quantum computer's*) total capacity, strength and ability according to the latest neuroscience. Unfortunately, most people continue to use only this part of the brain consciously. In reality, humans have access to a quantum computer with infinite capacity.

The CelesteMethod® gives you the opportunity to change your life, your current life situation for the better through increased consciousness of what concerns your inner potential.

Most people are afraid to ransack themselves, take responsibility for their actions or even care about what happens after physical death. They believe everything ends after the earthly life. They stress through life to catch up with as much as possible in this very life.

These people become deeply disappointed after the removal of the physical body when they discover that life continues as usual at another level of existence, another dimensional level, and that their problems are still unsolved.

<u>No one can escape their own shadow. Many have tried but none have succeeded so far.</u>

We recommend these so-called non-believers to get more information from the mainstream media (msm) about ghosts, communication with the unknown, UFO-phenomena etc., and read information on the subject available on the Internet, in literatures. It's not so easy to explain away these things.

One day, they may have a similar experience.

The CelesteMethod® makes you see clearly in the infinite, boundless worlds.

This is the first time the opportunity is offered on a larger scale to become aware of the unconscious!

Many adolescents think life is meaningless and see no brightening in life.

Why is that?

What can we do to reverse this trend?

First we must get to know ourselves, who we really are, and get to know our true self, true identity?

Who are we?

What is the meaning of our life? We must find the right tools to achieve the goal that we want, desire or have intended.

All of humanity is in a chaotic state which we have never experienced before here on earth.

A minority on earth equals about 0.1% of about 7.8 billion people have decided to exterminate the majority of humanity through various kinds of measures. They believe that these people no longer fill the function that the modern society demands.

An altered consciousness (*paradigmatic shift*) is a necessity in all areas for the survival of the human being and the civilization.

*Our International Association for Total Human Culture "AIC", in Sweden, is the only educational institution currently in the world that teaches the Life Sciences - Cultural Ecology according to the CelesteMethod®.*

The word "*Celeste*" is derived from the French language meaning "*Heavenly*". It corresponds to 5D (*the fifth dimension*), the unity field, the matrix, the source of all knowledge, both the hidden (*implicit*) and the manifested (*explicit*) part of creation.

The CelesteMethod® is a method that has to do with the entire cosmic development. It is not limited to just a three-dimensional level of physical consciousness.

It encompasses the whole of creation, the hyperspace in its entirety.

The CelesteMethod® has been a registered and protected trademark for several decades.

The CelesteMethod® is a method for reaching an altered consciousness, here and now.

If you follow our instructions, you will reach MASTERSHIP IN LIFE.

*Prof. Dr. Sandor A. Markus, PhD., MD (MA)., STD.*
*Founder of the AIC and the CelesteMethod®*
*Secretary General of the AIC*


# Cultural Ecology

The word "CULTURE" as it has been interpreted so far has been completely misunderstood.

CULTURAL ECOLOGY in its original context is about the science of the human being as a whole. The human being is a dynamic system with a mutual effect and isn't incomprehensible either collectively or individually.

CULTURAL ECOLOGY includes WORLD CULTURE, NATIONAL CULTURE as well as INDIVIDUAL CULTURE.

CULTURAL ECOLOGY can be defined as feedback to the original individual's soul quality (original quality) and to the original social culture from which man has deviated through the influence of the lower qualitative mind.

World culture, social culture and individual culture are based on the original consciousness of man, the operating system of the soul atom, the "soul" and have nothing to do with the lower qualitative mind consciousness, the 3D material consciousness to do.

The individual part is the inherent, original source program or the original primary consciousness, the absolute consciousness, the unity consciousness, which contributes to a mutual interaction between the soul matrix (the operative program) and the mind matrix (control program), between intuition and intellect, between the eternal, virtual, implicit (folded), unmanifested order, 10th - 6th dimension and the mind-related, explicit (unfolded), manifested, time-bound order, 5th 4th and 3rd dimensions.

## A Cultural Rebirth

A cultural rebirth means a paradigmatic shift (an altered thought structure, consciousness), which gradually leads to an increased consensus and to peace among individuals, species and nations.

In order to create peace on earth, we must create peace within ourselves and thereby with our surroundings.

This is not something that is achieved simply by belonging to any peace organization or simply by propagating for peace.

To achieve peace within us, we must first begin to remove the computer viruses, data bugs that have been stored in our subconscious database and our DNA structure for millennia.

Here we have the opportunity to use our AI "Artificial Intelligence", Quantum Generator, Quantum Harmonizer to help those who want to reach a higher qualitative consciousness by removing the bugs, virus programs that are stored in their subconscious database that prevent them from becoming free from their cause-related problems. These can be Mental, Emotional and Physical problems of various kinds.

For this reason, we have created the CelesteMethod®.

The data viruses that affect our way of thinking, feeling and acting in real time (now) must be removed from our subconscious database in order to be able to change our individual, society-related and world-related problems of various kinds. When the individual is affected, the entire social community is affected.

If we want to adapt to the demands and challenges of the future, then we must change our thinking and acting.

This can only happen if we add new knowledge to what we already have at our disposal and get rid of the computer viruses, data bugs that constantly prevent us from reaching our goal in life, what we deep down want, dream about or are entitled to according to the law of the cosmos. We are not talking about material goals but goals related to happiness, harmony and community in life.

The New Age, "The Golden Age", which stands on the threshold, means a total restructuring of our thoughts and feelings, which in turn contributes to a completely new social structure that we haven't experienced on earth so far.

We are faced with the choice - either we choose to adapt to the demands and challenges of tomorrow both individually and collectively, or we choose to remain in our outdated paradigm (thought structure) and then we must take the consequences thereof, what it means.

Many will choose to remain in their individual dungeons because of convenience, so-called economic and social security that they have been used to so far or for some other reason. These people will have a hard time in tomorrow's society as external security will gradually change.

There is no security outside of ourselves that most people believe or imagine. All this is just false security, illusion, wishful thinking, perception that the lower qualitative part of our ego, the mind through the senses has created for us. Material security is only a means and not a goal in our pursuit of peace, harmony and happiness in life. The only security that exists is our innermost being, the security of the Soul, the Higher Self which is in resonance with the Source, the 1st Source, the Central Universe - that which we call the essence of God.

It all began about 1200 years ago, during the 800s, when an alien race visited Earth and created an underground museum with a time capsule in the Chaco Canyon in the New Mexico desert that was then inhabited by the Chacobsa tribe from the Anasazi Indian culture. This extraterrestrial race also laid the foundation of another six time capsules, deployed on the six other continents. These time capsules will gradually be activated.

The Anasazi culture originated in the southwestern United States, long before the whites came and left a lot of archaeological evidences. These can be seen now in the four states of Arizona, New Mexico, Utah and Colorado.

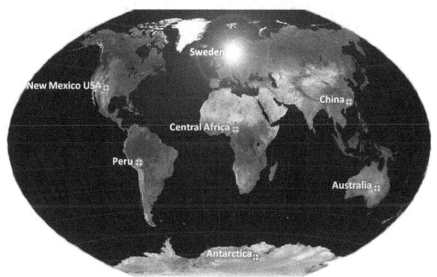

Figure 25. The seven time capsules are located on the earth's seven continents.

The Lake Siljan in Sweden, which was formed after a meteorite impact, is the site on the European continent, where the 7th time capsule is located as a scalar field, energy vortex. The 7th energy vortex in Northern Europe (in Sweden) is the birthplace of the UNIFIER's appearance in the Nordic region. This is the starting point for a "New Consciousness in a New Time".

Figure 26. The Siljan ring is the seat of the 7th time capsule.

# Action plan for Fair Societal Development

The AIC has developed an "*Action Plan for Fair Societal Development*". This "Action Plan" is a higher sanctioned approach that society needs for the transition to a more humane societal development than so far. More attention must be paid to the individual and what is good for the Swedish people, above the ill-considered globalization plan that some politicians and decision-makers run because of self-interests, ignorance and unconsciousness; a globalization plan that contributes to the individual's limited freedom of speech, freedom of movement, the right to decide over his or her own life and destiny, and which hinders the individual and the nation in their cosmic - spiritual (soul) development. The plan of globalization is oedipal and nihilistic in nature and contributes to the downfall of the individual and civilization. Everything that deviates from the AIC's eight-point program is against the law of the universe, the cosmos.

The Action Plan for Fair Societal Development:
https://www.unifier.se/action-plan-for-fair-societal-development

# AIC World - "Bright Future" - Action Plan for Fair Societal Development

**International Alliance for Cultural Ecology - Key words: A New Consciousness in a New Time!**

This is the only action program that will work in the time we have entered. All the old "structures" will fall into pieces.

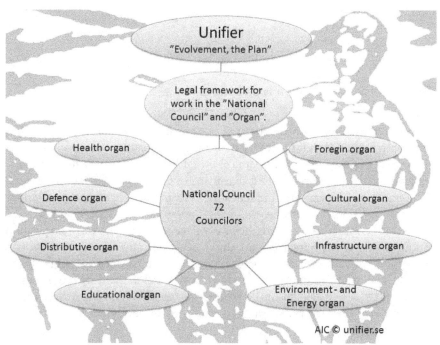

Figure 27. The New Age Government that will be established on earth when a higher Ethics - Morality has become the Guiding Star.

## Background

The background to this initiative on ethical and moral rule of Sweden can be read in the book "The Matrix Reality" written by Dr. Sandor A. Markus and Lars Helge Swahn.

Action Plan for Fair Societal Development works for:

- One World Commonwealth
- One Fraternal Humanity
- A Flag of Love – Wisdom
- One Moral Standard
- One Language of Understanding
- Above All Frontiers
- Above All Prejudices
- Above All Traditions

## The aim of the action plan is as follows

We want to work to ensure that all people in society have an individual possibility for the development of their inherent qualities, which contributes to increased consciousness and ethical-moral living. Man must live a healthy life where ideas are implemented that is in harmony with the laws of nature. Cooperation, understanding and harmony between people are the guiding star where competition is passed on to its origin, the animal kingdom. We collaborate consciously towards heights of technical facilitations, acquisition of knowledge about ourselves and about how the universe works. Sweden's population, as well as all the peoples of the earth, must once again be aligned with the task we have in the cosmos - to work hand in hand with the laws of nature and the universe instead of opposing them. We work with a multi-thousand year plan for prosperity and long lives in development towards the future.

## Background:

## The earthly man's present situation

The human civilization on earth is facing an ecological crisis that has become more critical in recent decades. Man destroys both his inner and outer environment through artificial influence and the consequences of this will be incalculable in the form of natural disasters, epidemics of various kinds. No one can be personally accused for this. It is based on ignorance of the earthly human species as a whole. Nor can any government, political party or religious organization be blamed for the situation in which the earth is at present, but is entirely a consequence of natural development, in which the negative mind power has hitherto had a predominant influence, in comparison with the positive, so-called spiritual.

In this case, as with all simple problems, the solution becomes self-evident, as man understands what the matter is. In order to get a proper grasp of the problem, we must try to present it as simply as possible, even if it involves some difficulties due to the different degree of human consciousness.

An individual at the primary school level has a harder time understanding the equation than one who attends high school. It is perfectly normal for man to understand differently much of life and of events that take place around him.

There are three branches of science in the universe, the <u>cosmic</u>, the <u>social</u>, and the <u>material</u>, which are necessary for the survival, development, and advancement of the earthly civilization. The <u>Cosmic</u> and <u>Social</u> science must come first. There can be no material progress if there is no basis of cosmic and social knowledge to build on. The material progress that has taken place on earth over the past half century has, from a spiritual perspective, created stress, insecurity and stagnation.

When we speak of the "spiritual", we do not mean the "religious".

<u>Spirituality is a cosmic, universal concept and has nothing to do with institutional religion, idolatry or sectarianism.</u>

117

Religion is based exclusively on faith, emotional thinking and emotional will, while the cosmic, spiritual is based on knowledge, knowing, science of man and of hyperspace as a whole.

What man cannot perceive with his five sensory senses (sight, hearing, feeling, taste and smell), he calls non-existent, unreal, subjective, supernatural, transcendental or spiritual. This without really understanding what is meant by the term "spiritual" or "supernatural". Everything that exists in hyperspace is natural. What the earthly man can perceive with his five sensory senses she calls real, objective, and scientific.

We must keep in mind that it is only our limited three-dimensional intellectual consciousness and our five senses that scan the environment around us, that exclude us from the true reality, the creation, the hyperspace in its entirety. We perceive only a small part, a limited part of creation in our current state of consciousness. And from this experience of reality, we try to explain how the whole creation was created.

We can imagine a vibration scale, an electromagnetic scale from zero to infinity. The objective visible world that the earthly man with his five sensory functions perceives as reality, amounts to only about 400-700 nm on this infinite scale. (1 nanometer is one billionth of a meter). Everything else is outside the normal individual's ability to understand, but still exists as reality. The word reality is a relative term. What is real to one individual is unreal to another. We ourselves can be convinced of this correctness, when we think of the difference between the ability of animals and man to perceive reality. The reality of a beetle is completely different from that of the elephant.

Animals have no cosmic or social consciousness but react instinctively unconsciously and consequently have not been able to get anywhere in material science.

In some insects, e.g. the ant and the bee, there is an approach to social community, to the extent that they can live together in large numbers, work for their common welfare and have a kind of discipline that applies to them all.

As a result, they have also developed very limited material group consciousness. They build anthills and collect food for future needs. However, every trace of cosmic knowledge is missing, which has proved to be absolutely necessary for further development. Therefore, in thousands of years, they have not advanced one single step.

Mankind, on the other hand, has from the very beginning of its development had an intuitive sense of a higher power or cosmic intelligence, which arranges and supervises the whole of nature. The human attitude to this power has varied between fear and reluctance to reverence and love, but one has always wanted to know more about its nature.

Cosmic science has its roots right down to the first awakening of human intelligence. And when people began to realize that only through cooperation one could improve their living conditions, the first tribes were formed and thus the foundation for social science was laid.

From these two sciences and the influence of extraterrestrial civilizations, material knowledge has since emerged and this is where the problem starts.
The development in the material field is continuously stimulated by the body through its ever-increasing desires and needs. We can very easily be convinced of this, by comparing the inventions and material development of the last fifty years with the corresponding progress over the last hundred years before that, and this in turn with what happened during a thousand years before.

It is evident that scientific development in the material field is taking place at an ever faster pace. While the cosmic and social sciences only progress in direct proportion to time and sometimes not even that fast. This has caused the chaos that humanity on earth currently is in.

Consider the following problem:

A large massive building is being erected. The walls rise in height at an ever faster pace and the foundation, which supports the entire structure, is also completed at the same time but at a much slower pace. Unless one finds a way to stimulate the work pace on the foundation, it is inevitable that the time will come when the building will collapse on its foundation and both will be completely destroyed.

This has happened before on earth, and the development has come to the stage where the probability is high that the same type of event will be repeated once more.

The danger of the earthly civilization being decimated again is imminent through its increased destructiveness and the means of destruction it has brought forth.

How then can a civilization be threatened by its own work?

The reason is simply that man has not made sufficient progress in the cosmic (spiritual) field to be able to determine how society can best be developed and how material production should best be adapted to the laws of nature.

Those in our civilization who really think clearly understand the danger that lies in the use of unconventional weapons (nuclear weapons). This is especially true in those countries that want to stay out of international control and ignore the regulations governing the use of these weapons. These are the countries where emotions still control common sense.

In addition, there is another problem in this regard, which the earthly man has not hitherto realized. Unless unity between nations can be achieved, the fact that such weapons exist, even if never used, will lead to the total collapse of the present civilization. The truth of this can be understood by anyone who wants to strain the brain capacity a bit. We must not forget that war is constantly going on somewhere on earth as long as man for religious-ideological reasons and abuse of power wants to take control of others.

The earth belongs to the primary school in hyperspace from the point of view of consciousness where hatred, war, selfishness, lust for power, abuse of power are still dominant. Although intelligences from higher-developed extraterrestrial civilizations have for a long time informed man on earth what selfishness, acquisitiveness, lust for power, and abuse of power can lead to, the earthly race has so far ignored these warnings. She continues on the same path to destroy her future opportunities to survive as a civilization on earth. How can such a race call itself intelligent?

Civilization is built and maintained by thinking, conscious and perceptive people, who work with the aim on the future, and not by the ignorant, unconscious mass.

But who wants to devote their lives to improving the conditions of the newborn or unborn generations, if the foreseeable future does not even extend over the next twenty-four hours?

The entire current civilization is threatened by the ever-increasing environmental degradation, which will result in unforeseen natural disasters and epidemics unless man takes constructive actions. Even if these measures are taken at the expense of material welfare, it is necessary. The time is five minutes to twelve. We only have five minutes at our disposal to complete our course to avoid major disasters of various kinds.

But in order to realize the seriousness behind these threats, we must develop our consciousness from its current three-dimensional embryonic stage to a five-dimensional cosmic level of consciousness.

A phenomenon that is discussed daily in the mass media around the world is the strong increase in juvenile delinquency and crime. Some people blame the parents or the schools, others the church or the state. At the same time, no institution has any direct responsibility for the emergence of the current situation, which has arisen mainly from the fact that young people are more sensitive to the general state of insecurity.

Young people feel insecure and insecure about the future. Many commit suicide or use psychotropic drugs to bear the burden to live. The accuracy of this can be attested by any psychologist. Never in the history of the earthly civilization has the future seemed more uncertain than at present. The rising generation sees no future and the institutional church does nothing either. Everyone sits with their arms crossed and blames each other.

The institutional church that claims to have a monopoly on the cosmic (spiritual) truth cannot give the new generations anything but references to the Bible (the book of books) or to the so-called holy scriptures, which have been created through stories, myths and traditions.

Man has not understood what extraterrestrial intelligences like Akhenaten, Jesus ben Pandira, John the Baptist, Buddha, Muhammad, Guru Nanak, and others have proclaimed to them at the time when they were illiterates. Man's daily life consisted mainly of hard work to provide food for their families. Only a few could write or read. What these highly evolved extraterrestrial beings conveyed to the earthly man was not recorded until long after their deaths. Not even their closest disciples understood what these teachers actually said or meant. In the same way today the earthly man understands nothing but what he is indoctrinated into believing from his surroundings.

The political and military tensions in the world continue at the same pace, even if it looks calm on the surface. The superpowers monitor and don't dare to trust each other even if they talk about peace. The change that has taken place in the 1990s in Eastern Europe is only the beginning of a global process of change.

Various religious faiths claim that their religion is the only right one and are prepared to go to war for it in the name of God. This means that new generations would be born and raised under constant threat of an imminent annihilation. Hyperspace has not yet produced the civilization on the three-dimensional level to which the earth belongs, which could develop under such conditions.

While the intelligentsia is discussing and debating whether to intervene to stop this impending catastrophe, environmental degradation and destructiveness are advancing at an ever-increasing rate. No one with responsibility wants to realize what this means for the entire civilization of the earth. The result can be only one - increased crime, destructiveness, natural disasters in the form of earthquakes, storms, floods, climate change, epidemics of diseases, which in turn will result in material damage and to an economic collapse.

There are different views on how to fix the problem.

Some argue that the scientific development in the material field should be halted by ceasing work on all kinds of advanced plans and banning or restricting the study and research in nuclear physics.

Others go even further, saying that one should completely destroy the fruits of material science and return to nature and to the conditions of the animals.

Then there are people who believe that only through increased religiosity, the introduction of religious education in schools, etc., can one improve life and create peace on earth. But history testifies to how religion has so far failed to improve human conditions, except possibly for the institutional church.

If you were building a large building and suddenly discovered that the foundation would not be strong enough to support it through a miscalculation, would you immediately start tearing it all down? No - if you have a bit of human intelligence, you would instead start researching how you could best strengthen the foundation and not have to tear down the building and then rebuild it.

The development of material science cannot be halted. Either development will continue without hindrance, or it will stagnate. If it stagnates, it will collapse. It is not the case that material science has grown out of erroneous basic assumptions, but it will advance and achieve hitherto unimaginable results, if the people on earth develop a high quality cosmic consciousness, quantum consciousness and thereby ensure that they thereby obtain a viable basis.

And if they don't, what happens then?

Then civilization, like previous civilizations, will perish. It will collapse in a disaster with only a limited number of survivors. These few will have neither the ability nor the will to resume scientific research.

Within a few generations, the descendants have returned to almost the animal stage. Then the development curve starts to go up again. In fifteen to twenty thousand years, a new civilization will arise, thanks to higher developed extraterrestrial intelligences, civilizations. The civilization will face the same problems as the current one and will be faced with the same possible solutions. Should they also fail, they will in turn perish. It is one of the relentless laws of the cosmos, even if it leaves the human race free to choose.

Neither race nor culture is made to be wiped out. If we change our way of thinking and restructure our egocentric characteristics, we will be able to follow the upward curve of civilization and leave the risk of disaster behind. The choice is in the human hands and it is urgent.

*We have only two options to choose from, either to succumb because of our ignorance and foolhardiness, or to develop our consciousness to be able to continue our existence on this planet.*

As the earthly man develops his current three-dimensional consciousness to a five-dimensional cosmic level of consciousness, he can come into possession of hitherto unknown forces and knowledge, which will result in cosmic dynamic creation.

Regarding science, we can state the following: Admittedly, we have come a long way in nuclear physics, but physics is still at the embryonic stage. It is a fact that man has individual consciousness and possesses the ability to coordinate his senses in meaningful images and logical thought systems. This indicates that there must be a cosmic universal mind of which our individual mind is an "image, copy".

Due to the limitation of the sensory organs and the inherited animal instincts in man, his conception of the universal mind becomes one-sided and distorted. Despite her imperfections, however, it remains an "image" of "something" that she can guess, but not fully understand or scientifically describe at present.

Beyond the world that our sensory functions give us knowledge of, we are beginning to discern more and more clearly an omnipotence, which is the original source of primary energy (soul energy) and secondary energy (mind energy). From this source known as the "CENTRAL SUN" emanates our individual ability to think and create. Our ethical beliefs also stem from this source, whose admonitions we hear through what we call the "voice of conscience." A familiar name of this source of omnipotence is GOD, which is GOOD and HARMONIC.

Everything in the world of the mind, in the form-bound hyperspace, is bound to time and space and is perishable, i.e. undergoes constant change, transformation, restructuring.

The 2nd cosmic region, the 5th mental-causal dimension can be described with the terms "non-physical space" and "non-physical time".

Non-physical space cannot be measured by length, nor can non-physical time be measured by clock. Distances in time and space can therefore not be considered as long or short. They are qualitative and mental concepts, which should be well distinguished from the quantitative and physical concepts with the same names.

Physical time or clock time is, as we clearly realize, a measurable quantity. It determines not only duration but also progress. That time moves in a certain direction must have a deep meaning, but it should be remembered that progress and change are not the same thing. Progress we think of as meaningful and with an intention, which can be clear or hidden.

Changes without goals usually lead to chaotic states, while purposeful changes lead to order and often to the introduction of specific functions. Since time has a definite direction, we can talk with Eddington about the "arrow of time". This arrow can be likened to a signpost. It shows us the way to the future and away from the past. Sometimes the view has been expressed that the direction of the time arrow in a certain direction depends on an immediate reaction in our consciousness, which has its cause in a partial disorganization of the brain substance.

Intuitively, however, we feel that time has a more fundamental significance than just being a measure of the size of degenerative tendencies in our body and that it has something to do with development and progress.

Actually, eternity should not be considered a timeless world. We can compare the chronology of our memory with the content of a historical story. As we read it, we can skip certain chapters and read the history of the present, before we read the past. But within a limited part of the book we must read the words in their natural sequence, otherwise they would completely lose their meaning. Usually the arrow of physical time points in the same direction as the non-physical time, but as often happens in dreams memories from very different periods of our lives can be mixed up.

Facts of this kind could possibly serve as a starting point for explanations of future predictions. They also show that the dimension of eternity is not a static world where nothing happens.

Our conscious memory functions are seldom counted among the psychic phenomena, which, however, should definitely be the case. They are important manifestations of the human psyche, but we are so used to our memories that we easily forget that the ability to remember needs an explanation. If man had been able to solve the mystery of memory, then he would have received an explanation for many other psychic phenomena.

It has been claimed that potential memories create "tracks" in the physical brain. But the brain is, scientifically speaking, a liquid body and therefore subject to the heat effect of the movement of its molecules. As little as we are able to make complex and lasting impressions in the brain, just as little can we write the history of our lives in water or flying sand and have it preserved.

Furthermore, the metabolism in a biochemical brain is associated with the uptake of new matter and elimination, removal of spent material, so that within a few years only a few molecules of the old brain remain. But apart from this, it is impossible for most people to understand how the mechanical structure of the brain can produce mental memories in our consciousness. The procedure is the same as when programming a data disk or hard disk.

The physical brain, which we can see with our physical eyes and examine with physical aids, can be considered a space-time aspect of something else, which is not currently described in physical terms. We can imagine that it consists of a non-physical or "cosmic" (electromagnetic) equivalent to the physical brain.

The non-physical, virtual brain is responsible for the structure and functions of the biochemical brain.

Both the physical and the non-physical brain are a product of ideas in the human consciousness, which have arisen through logical conclusions on the basis of observations within very different fields of research. Of course, we must assume some kind of equivalent between the physical and the non-physical brain, the former belonging to the material, the latter to the immaterial, subtle world.

A potential memory image transfer to a current and efficient image can be described as follows. Every person has his own cosmic memory complex in the eternal world of the universe, which exists beyond space and time. When certain nerve ganglia (nerve centers) in our brain are stimulated by electrical, electromagnetic, chemical or mechanical means, a resonance can be achieved between a particular brain center and its cosmic equivalent.

Immediately, a certain memory image arises in our consciousness, often followed by a series of other memories, in one way or another connected with the first. All have their origin in the cosmic memory bank (universal database), the collective unconscious according to Dr. Jung's theory, for memories and thoughts, which are often intimately interconnected.

Since the cosmic memory complex has nothing to do with the physical space, it cannot be located in a particular place and since it is also beyond physical time, it is indestructible.

It is now a well-known fact that an individual during <u>relaxation and relaxation of thought activity</u> can recall in <u>detail what happens during a particular period in his or her life</u>. This is probably not due to any particularly strong stimulation of the brain, but rather to a suppression of sensations and memories, which could lead to a disturbance in the connection with the cosmic memory complex.

The well-known so-called prenatal memories (memories from before birth), which are evoked in a hypnotic way, do not necessarily have to be interpreted as evidence of past lives or previous incarnations.

Since reincarnation (rebirth) really exists, the evidence must be based on more certain facts than man can establish only through hypnosis, regression, or similar experiences.

This is because the memory is located in the five-dimensional matrix space.

But since man in his present state is the product of his past lives and experiences, it does not matter much what he has been in his previous lives, incarnations. She has only taken on different roles in the scene of life. What good is it if you have been a wealthy person in your past life but live in poverty in your current one? What good is it if you were a king or queen in your past life and is a common worker in your current life?

If we accept the theory that the memory content is indestructible, we must also conclude that every event, which has been registered in our consciousness, is also registered in the universal memory bank, the database, the matrix. In this way we return to the old idea of an indestructible "matrix / akasha chronicle" well known from Eastern philosophy, but here expressed in a scientific form. The fifth dimension in the human development is based on many thousands of years of experience.

It looks like we were able to pick out our own experiences from the huge collection of cosmic memories. But sometimes we seem to pick out memories that belong to a completely different person. This in itself is not more difficult to understand than the known facts of telepathy (thought transfer). But strange as it may seem, the memory complex we contact under special circumstances may very well belong to a person who has just died, or someone who has been dead for a long time.

There are facts that support this view. It has been found that communication during hypnosis, regression or through trance psychics can sometimes contain unknown facts for the persons concerned, but which have later been verified through investigations. Although such so-called "astral messages" are rare, it should not be difficult to verify them. If it can be proven that such messages occur, it directly indicates the existence of a world of preserved memories from deceased people. This idea of a common human memory reminds of the well-known psychologist Dr. Jung's conception of a "collective" subconscious, or group consciousness, which is referred to as the matrix.

An extremely important thing about our memory complex is its unity or indivisibility. We have a definite feeling of no matter how much our personality may change during a long life, there is something in our cosmic structure that remains unchanged and that cannot be divided into smaller parts. Individuals of all races have instinctively felt the presence of a unified spiritual essence and have given it a name, i.e. the soul.

The well-known fact that one thought leads to another thought and that the recollection of an event usually leads to another recollection of an event shows that there are links between the elements of our thoughts and memory. This connective system belongs to the immaterial, non-physical world, i.e. the virtual equivalent of the physical brain, the super-memory, which exists in a world beyond space and time and that can be likened to a kind of "cement", which binds together all our mental experiences in an indivisible unit, a so-called soul seed, soul atom, seed atom.

The existence of personality split shows that soul atoms, seed atoms (original consciousnesses) with different memory complexes can exist in the same physical body. Here the idea of a temporary behavior, mental connection with other soul atoms comes to our aid. The examination of the subconscious soul life in an individual with a personality split can be greatly facilitated by putting the individual in a transcendental state, a hypnotic state of sleep.

It has then been shown that behind the foreign intruders there is a unified personality, i.e. an indivisible soul atom. We can now more easily understand the connection between the past and the future. The axis of eternity has two extensions, <u>one extending towards the past</u> and <u>one towards the future</u>.

The past cannot be changed; it is fixed in immutable form in the realm of eternity. In the direction towards the future the links (causal chains) which before have been considered completely unchangeable and determine all events in the future, have recently proved to be changeable to some extent. This new discovery in physics is expressed in the "principle of uncertainty" and is applicable on scientific theories and is a manifestation of the cosmic will, commonly called "God's will".

The corpus pinealis plexus, the epiphysis (Tisra Til) located behind the forehead bone is limited in its functionality in the three-dimensional conscious human being. By activating this center of consciousness, one can raise one's current level of consciousness to a higher qualitative quantum level.

The CelesteMethod® aims to activate a higher degree of consciousness in humans and thereby raise the current three-dimensional consciousness to a multidimensional level of consciousness.

Only through a change of consciousness, which leads to increased understanding, consideration, tolerance, can we overcome disagreements and misunderstandings between individuals, races and nations and thereby achieve lasting peace on earth.

The earthly man is in need of a cosmic consciousness, quantum consciousness in order to become a better citizen and decision-maker, or to be able to function better in family life, society life and in working life.

Man's decisions in different situations are the synthesis of his current thoughts and feelings. If she does not develop from the point of view of consciousness, then she can also not function as a leader or decision-maker in society. Then her different kinds of decisions will only be temporary, short-term.

The current Parliamentary Democracy must be replaced by a Cosmocracy.

If we look at the current political system, we can see the following: the current parliamentary democracy cannot solve the current or future situation of man effectively, because the parliamentary democracy is in an oedipal, nihilistic state. This condition only creates chaos through its temporary, short-term solutions. A long-term solution can only be found in cosmic democracy, i.e. a dynamic cosmic program.

Our current democratic system is based on a de-cosmization process. It has a nihilistic dynamic, which in the long run is destructive, degenerate for man and for society, and sooner or later leads to chaos, anarchy. Democracy must be guided into a cosmic dynamic creativity.

The great goal of the future development of man on earth is to transform the current parliamentary de-cosmization democracy into a cosmocratic democracy (cosmic democracy).

Cosmocracy is a dynamic cosmic democratic process. Only a cosmic dynamic process can guarantee the development and survival of civilization.

How can we change the current democracy from oedipal to cosmic dynamic democracy?

By becoming more aware of ourselves and our own role and relationship with the universe - that we strengthen the qualitative, ethical, moral qualities that are characteristics of our innermost core. This can only happen through increased cosmic consciousness.

If we integrate the intellectual part of our brain activity that currently makes up about 17 percent of our waking consciousness with the subconscious "non-waking consciousness", the intuitive part, which makes up 83 percent of our consciousness, we reach a high quality level of consciousness compared to which most people access today.

## The form of Government is changed

*We need a new way to govern Sweden - the old party system locks itself in bloc politics and changes for the better fail. In reality, Sweden's policy has in recent decades gradually dismantled Swedish society.*

## *The party system of today is abolished.*

A governing "National Council" is established with 72 individuals. This council shall consist of the most developed, evolved and insightful individuals in society. They must have competence in different areas and there must be requirements for experience and high knowledge. They must be responsible with a view set on a multi-thousand year perspective.

Key words for their characteristics are: harmony, universalism, holistic view and development.

All Ministries (organs) in society shall be governed and supervised by these Council members.

To push through solutions as today because they are economically advantageous in the short term or for other pernicious purposes is made history. Today's economic system is rooted in the lower qualities of selfishness, greed, anger, vanity, lust, and all versions of all these five qualities. Today's economic thinking leads to disharmony within man and thus within nature. Today's economic system works against the universal laws we all obey regardless of whether the government dictates other laws.

Today's economic system is abolished. But a new economic system is established during a transitional period. It will look different from the current one.

The reason for abolishing the economic system is simply because the debt saturation has reached the level where the printing of new money doesn't even cover the interest costs that exist. Today's economic system will thus collapse on itself.

From the ashes "when everything crashes" arises a new type of thinking "A New Consciousness in a New Time".

The universal task of the world teacher "UNIFIER" is established officially - to supervise the National Council and provide universal insights to drive the work of evolutionary development further. This is the task of the World Teacher on all planets - but the earth differs from this procedure in that it belongs to the least developed from cosmic comparison. When intellectualism develops and is seen from a three-dimensional perspective as the only thing of value, then the level of development has reached its lowest level.

## The individual

The individual must be evolutionarily given the opportunity for studies in peace and quiet, contemplation, research, good health at all levels, evolution.

The reality that man has within himself in the form of emotions, stress, quality of consciousness and other qualities is the reality that the individual projects into his exterior. A human being can never create a different reality in the exterior than what he has in his interior. Once man has solved his inner problems then family situation, social situation, country situation and the world situation will become harmonious and based on universal understanding.

Today's society is the result of people feeling bad physically, mentally and emotionally, which gives disharmony with competition and stress within man and society with environmental degradation that gives a degenerative further downward spiral on all levels.

## Society – World

Healthy individuals make society healthy and the country healthy on all levels. In a broader perspective, when the thought structure becomes international, the planet earth will also be healthy and harmonious on all levels.

## General working method in all procedures

The general working method that is established in all areas: individual, family, societal, national and international - is the CelesteMethod®. This method is the very foundation of everything.

The CelesteMethod® includes three parts which are information, analysis and measure. The CelesteMethod® was originally developed for individual development toward better health and higher consciousness, which is a matter of course as the mind consciousness must give way to soul consciousness. This is the only viable path in the time we are in now - all other approaches will be dead ends. With the CelesteMethod® the individual becomes healthier and develops a higher consciousness where the inner healthier environment is projected into the exterior. Individual, family, societal, national and international problems are thus solved automatically. By working with our health and inner resource development we achieve a unity consciousness and become aware of the cosmic law to which everyone is subject. In this way, the future becomes bright - "Bright Future" - we will make the right decisions. The slogan will be "A New Consciousness in a New Time". When people feel good about themselves, harmony arises.

The CelesteMethod® is applied in all areas. The result of this will help the individual and society to achieve the goal of the action plan - i.e. higher consciousness and a healthy society where there is a good and bright feeling about the future in all areas.

Working for "A New Consciousness in a New Time" gives a "Bright Future".

# AIC World - "Bright Future"

Action Plan for Fair Societal Development. International Alliance for Cultural Ecology.

# Program

## Citizen task

The goal benefits the individual, society and the world.

The key words are harmony, evolution, knowledge acquisition and understanding of the laws of the universe.

We abolish today's competitive society and instead of people working against each other individually, in groups or against other countries to gain competitive advantages, we focus instead on cooperation.

Different companies in Sweden that work with the same things are given the opportunity to collaborate on a much broader level than before. Patent rights are removed and all inventions are released. Patents so far have only existed to benefit the old competitive mindset.

The release allows people, groups in peace and quiet to construct natural harmonious solutions to facilitate in all areas of society.

Automation and robot solutions are used as far as possible and heavy work is made history.

Life expectancy and quality of life are increased and instead studies and research can be used to develop new solutions.

## Working environment

The working environment must be as temperate, harmonious, contemplative and evolutionarily developing as possible.

Heavy lifting and health-damaging environments are abolished. Man must work as best he can in health-promoting environments. Tasks are automated with robots as far as possible.

## Accomodations

Housings are acquired as needed.

People still live in the homes and houses they currently have, and have their belongings at their disposal. In cases where houses are lacking, then new houses must be built with housing modules. Everything evens out in the long run as the level of consciousness increases.

Some types of housing modules can be ordered that can be moved when you need to move yourself. More ornamental buildings or other buildings may be available for special needs and purposes.

You don't have to own the home but are allowed to live there for as long as you need.

## Democracy – Cosmocracy

Today's Parliamentary so-called "Democracy" shall be replaced by a Cosmic Democracy (Cosmocracy).

What is meant by Cosmic Democracy - Cosmocracy?

Cosmocracy means a changed state of consciousness that leads to increased universalism and internationalism and reduced material attachment. Materialism (material attachment) leads man to increased selfishness, abuse of power and sooner or later to stagnation and disintegration of society. Reduced materialism does not mean that man should live in misery without material conveniences and technical aids. What we mean is that the material should be a means and not a goal as in today's human pursuit.

## Animal protection

The animal kingdom is prior to the human kingdom. It therefore gives us the responsibility to care for the animals. We must always respect the animals and learn more about them so we understand their role in nature and in their stages of development.

Human food should not, as now, include the animal kingdom. In a transitional phase, we can use certain animal products such as eggs and milk and what these products can generate in the form of foods. When we do this, we must ensure that these animals are as well off as possible but still have possibilities to evolve.

Animals should age as naturally as possible and be treated respectfully even late in their lives.

## From economy to citizen tasks

### *This is how it looks like today*

We are for the abolition of the monetary system as such - and it will anyway implode on itself. Today's monetary system exists for some people to rudely plunder assets and for other people to suffer the consequences of not even having enough food for the day. The system is created to fatten the mind's five negative properties and this is most evident today in the banks where money is created when lending money. People thus become indebted and must slave and work for money that has never existed and a fictitious interest rate that has been created. The bottom line is that the bank gets back the money they lent when they created it, as well as an interest rate that grows into an unmanageable mountain of debt. The bottom line is that the mountain of debt is growing and can never be repaid. The banks have thus created indebted individuals in a "legal" way. These people owe money to the banks - a debt of money to the banks that the banks never had at their disposal. This currently legal system aims to create a slave society where all citizens in one way or another owe money to banks and the state. The result is shamelessly wealthy bankers and an increasingly poor and indebted population. The country Sweden also has a mountain of debt and the banks "own" virtually everything that the state claims to have at its disposal. In the same way, the banks own virtually everything that private individuals have indebted.

But in practice, no one can own anything. What we call our own can be taken away from us at any time through natural disasters, accidents, deaths, etc. We don't even own our own body. We also have this on loan and must return it to nature when our physical body has served its purpose. We then leave the third dimension and move on to the fourth dimension, the parallel world. Here we must ransack ourselves and see what we have created in the form of harmony and disharmony on Earth - no one can escape their shadow. We reap in the next life for better or worse what we have created in the previous life. Here we see the explanation for why it looks like as it does today in the world, individually, in family, in terms of relatives, society, in different countries. We can never escape the laws of the universe. They are there for the evolvement of our soul, which is the task of our life.

### *This is how we want it*

Measures in the present situation:

1. The Swedish state expropriates the Swedish Riksbank (Central Bank in Sweden). Today, all national banks worldwide, including in Sweden, are owned by the Rothschild family, as is the Federal Reserve. This family has a private fortune of about $ 500 trillion. This family has so far controlled the entire world economy. The Swedish Riksbank shall be owned by the Swedish people and all other profit-making power activities now may be seen as universally criminal as it is contrary to universal basic ethics and morality, i.e. against the laws of the universe.

2. The state must consider withdrawing the banking licenses issued to the banks in Sweden. The Riksbank must handle today's Swedish banks as distribution channels - i.e. no profit.

3. A "citizens' right (salary)" is introduced which is equal for all citizens. Women and men's basic needs are met. Families with children should of course have more support.

### Immigration, migration, integration

Sweden must work for peace and harmony at all levels and for the abolition of war.

People who have problems due to war should first and foremost take refuge in neighboring countries. Here, world cooperation must in the best way solve basic needs such as housing, food and care. Development opportunities must be given to those in need.

Immigration to our country can take place under certain conditions.

First and foremost: *Man must have reached the "Citizenship requirement"*.

Immigration can take place as extra labor in various areas, prominent researchers, experts and other people who fit in and are estimated to have met the "Citizenship requirement".

## Citizenship requirement:

Man must be free of lower qualitative qualities seen in the animal kingdom. A certain threshold must have been reached so that man can control himself and have got rid of the lower qualities of lust, anger, greed, vanity and selfishness and all the varieties of these five qualities.

People who try to immigrate to Sweden who speak untruths for their own gain, use violence, slander, seek happiness, work to introduce their own non-democratic order based on their own religion, etc., out of convenience, hunger, low material standards, care and the need for surgery shall not be able to immigrate to the country Sweden.

No energy and resources should be wasted on bringing people with different *intolerant views* into Sweden. These people develop best in their home countries with their own country's own problems. When the problem is solved, these individuals have risen developmentally.

It is the interior of man that is projected into society. When the people have solved their inner problems then the situation in the country has automatically been solved.

In other respects, the number of people can immigrate that the country is considered to be able to accommodate. At present, we cannot accept more immigrants. At present, we have a ticking "immigration problem" where undesirable qualities deviating from the "Citizenship requirement" are held by many.

## The solution to this recent "integration problem" is the following.

Persons who have not reached the "citizenship requirement" in their development shall be taken care of in the following manner.

Integration centers are being built in the country. People who evidently not meet the citizenship requirement are taken care of in the integration center.

If this person can be returned to his home country when it comes to asylum immigration, this must be done as far as possible.

Integration centers shall offer citizenship training where consciousness training, basic education, and education for various types of employments that contribute to societal development shall take place. Basic emotional tests should be performed so that the person's emotional status can be monitored. The individual's level of consciousness must have reached a certain threshold before he/she can be incorporated into society among other citizens.

An unconscious - violent person cannot live in a society where he threatens, slanders and behaves aggressively towards his surroundings. This unconscious person then works in line with the mind's five opponents with disharmony and destructiveness as a result. In the human body and nature problems are encapsulated and not allowed to affect the healthy organism.

Planet Earth is a classroom where different things are taught in different countries. People are born into a family in a country where they have the most to learn in the form of consciousness training, and where they have to come to terms with certain things (animal characteristics or perverted animal characteristics, the mind's five opponents) before the next step can take place on the evolutionary spiral. One country can never be said to be better than another - the fundamental thing in human development is to be able to evolve in the best way from the individual's level of development.

Today's society's 55 (now more) no-go zones must be "taken back". Here there are higher concentrations of people who don't meet the citizenship requirement and lack the prerequisites for integration. Such people should be detained, or deported to their previous environments, where possible. In severe cases, the whole family will be deported.

**Fish protection**

Fish must be allowed to thrive in the oceans, seas and waters. We must pursue a policy that does not lead to depletion. The general thing is that we will eat more natural products to later completely switch to vegetarian food.

**Energy**

Free energy from the universe is used. This energy is free for all of us to use. Our human bodies are constantly using this energy, even though we have currently only studied the biochemical aspect, i.e. ATP and its use in the body. The cosmic energy is used to drive both photosynthesis and the body's energy recovery in the mitochondria.

This cosmic energy consists of scalar waves and is on a four- and five-dimensional level and is completely free to use. In historical times, Nikolai Tesla was the first to use this and today has e.g. the German professor Konstantin Meyl continued the research. Using scalar waves and down-transforming technology is the solution to energetically supply every city with energy. In this way every city is made self-sufficient.

All heating and everything that today is powered by electricity can use this energy source. A transition is to run today's electrical installations on this energy and in the long run phase out these installations so that alternating current is avoided as well as the entire wiring network. The universe uses scalar waves for energy and information exchange. The country Sweden will also use these waves.

Boats, cars, planes and other energy-intensive transports can use this technology. Tuned power plants are set up that wirelessly supply these transports with energy. Alternatively, smaller power plants are set up that can be installed in homes or carried where they are needed, e.g. in means of transport.

## Evolution

*This is a new officially instituted important part*

Evolution is about "Cultural ecology". Evolution must enter the culture.

### Culture - Cultural Ecology - Evolution

The concept of "culture" in its cosmic - multidimensional context means total control of the five-dimensional, matrix unit system, focused on the three-dimensional conscious human being.

Culture in its current form is nothing more but a cross-section of history.

The human-being's evolution is the sum total of man's previously acquired experiences and thus shows the level of his present consciousness. Man's present state is the result of his heritage, environment and way of life.

## Culture seen from a multidimensional cosmic perspective

The concept of "culture" in its cosmic context means total control of the five-dimensional, matrix unity system, focused on the three-dimensional conscious human being. Thus, cultural value in the cosmic context is the product of a higher qualitative process of consciousness, which when it starts its operating system on the three-dimensional physical-material plane, comes out of control of the multidimensional cosmic energy or the matrix unity system. The result is a "de-cosmization process", i.e. an increased mind influence that leads to increased attachment and decreased spirituality (limited consciousness and freedom).

By spirituality is not meant religiosity, but a higher qualitative multidimensional consciousness of unity.

Culture as man knows it today is education, anthropology and social science and is generally involved in politics and thus culture is of a secondary nature. Especially great misunderstanding and illusion prevails when talking about culture as an idea. Culture in its current form is nothing but a cross-section of history.

A three-dimensional consciousness based on a five-dimensional consciousness control is the only viable way to new thinking and thus to the survival of civilization.

Innovation is of a cosmic multidimensional nature and not limited within the three- and four-dimensional matter, form.

The central idea of a social community is not increased mind control, materialism or religiosity, but a transformation, integration with the original zero point energy, primary energy, solar energy, scalar energy.

It is a constant interaction between the primary power (original energy), the zero point energy consisting of sound and light, and the secondary power (mind energy), where the mind power stands for the creation of matter or form.

### Cultural Ecology

Cultural ecology is the science of the whole. Cultural ecology is a dynamic process with mutual effect which is thus not incomprehensible either collectively or individually and thus does not lead to incomprehensible systems such as religiosity, mysticism, occultism, intellectualism, etc.

Cultural ecology is a very important concept that involves knowledge of the development of the humanoid species under different conditions, their different levels of consciousness and societal development and how these different cultural levels can interact and coexist with each other.

Cultural ecology is the inner and outer environment that connects humans with each other and with all forms of creation in the vast hyperspace.

Cultural ecology is the source of social science.

Cultural ecology includes world culture, national culture as well as individual culture. Cultural ecology can be defined by feedback to the original cosmic consciousness, to the original social culture.

The real foundation of ecology is culture which changes us, develops us and restores our relationships with the universe. The kind of culture that people mean by culture is not evolving, developing viewed from a cosmic point of view. It materially changes our behavior.

Material revolution is a path that leads to increased consumption and thus to material attachment.

Matter is a means to our development and not the goal itself, but that does not mean we have to live in misery.

It has been stated through long experience that material revolution only leads to a higher material standard of living, which only contributes to increased materialism, egoism, acquisitiveness, jealousy, vanity, lust for power and more. In this way, man does not change significantly from the point of view of consciousness.

The three-dimensional and materially conscious human being is predominantly a materially producing being in a cultural context. The education is based on striving for consumption instead of on higher qualitative (cosmic) development, evolvement.

The result is well known: Inhuman relations, unfair distribution policy, exploitation, environmental degradation, wars, more and more serious illnesses, etc.

All this contributes to the degeneration and disintegration of society.

Materialism is degenerate in the long run and results in short-term happiness that later turns into suffering and misery. Materialism contributes to human degeneration further to the animal stage from the point of view of emotion and consciousness.

Only through a cosmic dynamic process and through a cosmic brain program can we contribute to a cultural rebirth, which is the only thing that can guarantee the survival of civilization. In the material renaissance, man has been a consuming being. The education and development have been based on the consumption of material products, while the spiritual (higher qualitative) "cosmic" development has given way to nihilistic egoism and materialism.

### Evolution

Man's evolution is the sum of his previously acquired experiences during his involution (entry into the third dimension) and thus shows the degree of his current consciousness.

Man's current state is the result of his inheritance (previously acquired experience) and the environment in which man currently resides. Applied to each individual, his current level of consciousness, his mental, emotional and biological well-being, are direct results of his hereditary ancestry and of the environment in which he lives and which affects him from birth to the present day.

A good mental, emotional and biological-physical well-being is the result of a good inheritance and of a favorable environment. The inheritance is constant and unchanging. The inheritance is inscribed (encoded) in man's individual soul atom and DNA's own possibilities and limitations. The environment in which man lives and acts can be changed, at the same time as it influences and interacts with him from birth to the end of life in the three-dimensional physical universe or matter.

Our past lives (hereditary factors), voluntary or forced lifestyles, our environment and their impacts on us are the cause of the health or illness we live with today.

The current well-being is often the result of several intertwined causes, heredity, environment, and way of life. But by changing our bad traits by removing negative thoughts from our subconscious data field and ensuring that our actions are in harmony with our original (cosmic, natural) environment, we can create the conditions for a change in the current state. This leads us to regain a state of well-being and an increased consciousness.

If the individual's own will and capacity is provided the right guidance by a competent teacher, you get the fastest and best result.

Mental, emotional and physical well-being is the basic foundation of the human development process toward higher dimensions. Therefore, a higher quality cosmic master teacher is necessary in order to teach us knowledge of the universe - the hyperspace in its entirety.

Only such a teacher (professor) in Cultural Ecology, who is endowed with a multidimensional cosmic consciousness, has access to all the knowledge concerning man's spiritual, implicit (folded) unmanifested spiritual nature and the mind-related explicit (manifested), mental, physical consciousness and development.

Only such a teacher can teach us how we can re-evoke the timeless truth in our innermost being and thereby free ourselves from all kinds of limitations.

NOTE: Since the "human-being" in its so-called spiritual, virtual original context is a "soul-bearing atom", it is referred to as "He" and not as "She" in our writings, literature and teachings. The soul atom is neutral and positively charged and dons both "masculine" and "feminine" forms (housings) during its development process. The soul as a neutral and positively charged atom has nothing to do with the masculine or feminine form in creation. The form belongs to the world of the mind, which constitutes the negative charge and is the contributing factor to the creation of the mind world, the form.

The Soul, the Spirit belongs to the unmanifested zero point energy, the First Source, the Central Universe, and the Mind to the 2nd Source, the manifested kinetic energy, the electromagnetism. These two forces together make up the creation in its entirety.


**Nation – Internation**


*Sweden, the Nordic region, EU-politics, world politics, foreign politics*

## Sweden

First, we must create an ideal society or work to create this on a smaller scale. We therefore start in Sweden and show the harmony and the popular commitment we create to solve one disharmony after another into harmony and harmony with the laws of nature in cooperation and with enthusiasm.

When we have shown the positive effects, we can integrate the other Nordic countries when they so wish.

## The Nordic Region

We want to have very good collaboration with our Nordic neighbors who think and function much like the people in Sweden. We enthuse our Nordic neighbors to work in a similar way for natural harmonious solutions where the evolutionary development of the individual human being is promoted.

## EU-politics

The EU does not function today. Greed, lust for power and one's own selfish desires come first. Decisions are made that benefit some individuals, agendas and countries more than others, some directly and others in the long run.

The Swedish people must leave the EU cooperation for the time being and work for their own ideal society in the first place. Cooperation with the EU can only take place when both Sweden and the EU comply with the 8 points we have presented. The same rules apply to UN cooperation. A Federation that does not follow the universal laws that prevail in the universe, the hyperspace, of which we are all citizens, cannot claim international leadership.

## World politics

Diplomatic cooperation between Sweden and other countries in the world is a necessity for the realization of the 8-point program.

## Foreign politics

We must work to neutralize discords at all levels. Sweden must regain its role as a neutral society and actively contribute to the creation of peace. This will be done by showing the way to an ideal society, which will be a requirement in the New Age that we have already entered.

Countries should be able to be offered help if we can offer this. The aid must be able to be applied practically in the countries that want our help. It is help to self-help. For example, we will not drill wells in other countries, but instead we can show how this can be done. It is then up to each country and society to use this technology or not. If they don't want to, then the country is left with the problems they have and have to come up with solutions themselves.

To help a country that does not want to be helped in the way we offer, i.e. with no demands on themselves, is wasting resources and energy from the part of Sweden. The country is then left to its fate.

## Functional organizations (former enterprises)

Companies or organizations for industry and manufacturing must once again be given good opportunities for development in Sweden.

Industries have so far more and more moved abroad and now it is important that these industries and companies can stay in the country without problems. As leaders of these companies, people with responsibility, environmental thinking and long-term planning are needed. Since the competition will disappear, during the transition, punitive customs will apply to goods that can instead be manufactured in Sweden. Manufacturing is then gradually transferred to Sweden. All industries and skills needed for all functions for entrepreneurship and industry in the country must be in Sweden - in our immediate area - as far as possible.

The feeling to contribute with what you do best and where you instill your ideals is the driving force in the company management. The lure should then not have to be money (parachute) or higher salary. To be able to work with what you think is the most fun is instead the driving force - and to instill the responsibility for the business that is in accordance with high morals and ethics. This shall be the case in all organizations where everything is interconnected by the "National Council".

## New solutions – Innovation

Under calm contemplative conditions, new ideas are "hatched". It is important to know where new ideas come from. Ideas already exist and it is only a matter of being able to tune in on them and realize them. Patents are no longer needed but can be used freely where they are needed.

When we see that a new product or function would be needed, the functional organization works out a new concept. The functional group then works to create this innovative new function or product - which of course must be in line with its area of activity.

Of course, it can be sold abroad as well - but to manage in the country, this should not be needed for Sweden's survival.

Here, a certain exchange with the rest of the world will be made possible. We can exchange goods and services but these must be in line with the 8 points we presented above.

Innovation cooperation must exist with the rest of the world - which of course must benefit both parties.

It is also important to create automation and robot systems in most areas.

## Family

Families should have more resources so that their children can develop and also have a good life. With a good distribution, everyone should be able to manage well.

## Wellness

We will be able to significantly increase life expectancy with the help of preventive healthcare (Health & Resource Development) and the other reforms we are now implementing. The CelesteMethod® is applied with:

Information: Information to every person about what health really is, or is not.
Analysis: Healthcare aims to map energetic imbalances in the human body at an early stage, the organism that at a later stage can otherwise cause a disease state.
Measure: Appropriate measures are taken to neutralize the energy deviations. The CelesteMethod® today has unique measure (action) systems that work

multi-dimensionally to solve the human multi-dimensional and multi-structural problems.

## Defense

Right now, the western world is working on strategies to weaken Europe, the Nordic countries and Sweden. We want to change this trend. Car fires are commonplace in Sweden and occur every day in the larger cities. Murder using weapons has become more common. This trend must be stopped. *The tactics of the authorities to create as many conflicts at home as possible and to proclaim Russia as some kind of enemy must cease.* The media are deliberately careful not to report on the great uncertainty that is building up in Sweden. When it is obvious that it is no longer possible to gag the media, it is believed that the Swedish people will raise their voices for a Swedish NATO membership. They want to introduce more control and a police state in Sweden. In this way, they have gone from a veiled dictatorship to an open dictatorship. This must not happen. Forces exist to unite the Western world in an aggression against Russia. This will not be easy as humans are much more aware than that, and people are becoming increasingly aware now as the solar influence (energy, information) is increasing on the planet and in our solar system. Major changes are taking place and will take place on earth, in society and in the human being in the coming decades. The extent of this man cannot imagine even in his wildest fantasy.

When we are sure that foreign governing influences are away from Sweden, we want to create our own defense that will be used to protect Sweden against external as well as internal aggression. Thereafter, we want to create Nordic defense co-operation. We work for the 8 points we have presented above.

The degree of self-sufficiency must be 100%. We must re-establish agriculture in Sweden so that we can become self-sufficient in basic food in the event of natural disasters or wars. In major national crises, there must be resources, e.g. in case of forest fires, floods and storms. Receiving help from abroad or helping other countries in crises is also important.

*We need free information. A country that is afraid to let its citizens judge the truth and the lie is a country that is afraid of its citizens.* (President John F. Kennedy, February 1962)

## The information society

Initially, the fiber network will be expanded to facilitate the dissemination of information. Wireless information is added to a favorable "frequency" for humans. By extension, the information society should be based on scalar energy and information.

Paper newspapers are abolished. Today's "newspaper support" or "media support" is abolished as it is today given to newspapers that are considered to print or send the correct (pc) information, which is angled for a special purpose. The media with appointed representatives who stand for truth from a higher comic perspective can be considered entitled to inform the population regarding societal information from an evolving and developmental perspective.

Current information to Sweden's residents must be independent and inform about what is really happening in society and how the development society is progressing, both in terms of technology and evolution. <u>The information shall not be kept secret or manipulated</u>.

## Infrastructure – Traffic

Research must be done making cities use natural harmonic materials so that health can improve even more for individuals. It is important to build energetically so that the structures provide energy instead of reducing the energy for humans.

The same applies to common areas in cities where the structures are made harmonious and provide energy and inspiration to reach higher heights in all areas that we undertake. We know that pyramids and globe-shaped structures produce these effects.

All communication (train, plane, boat, car, motorcycle) must be operated on free energy described under energy politics. Interventions to a minor extent can be done in nature to make this system work. The vehicles can be common and different solutions for transport will be instituted.

The key words are energy, inspiration, harmony, development and evolvement of consciousness.

## Citizen task (the jobs)

All people in Sweden must work according to their own prerequisites. Since the inhabitants of Sweden will benefit greatly in terms of food, clothing, housing, healthcare, wellness, evolution, etc.... it is important that everyone comes forwards and works with input to the system.

After having completed education, and during the study time, input must be given to the system. The input is in the form of labor for one of the functional organizations or public activities that one is interested in or for some "service system - robot system."

## Robotization and automation

As far as possible, monotonous heavy work must be automated with robot technology. It is not the intention of man in a modern technological society to wear out their bodies with hard physical work under unhealthy conditions. Robots take care of all this work.

## Service systems – robot systems

A service system is a term for the function of servicing the robots and the automation used in various areas. During the transition to this system, many people will become unemployed according to today's way of seeing it. The process has already started towards robotization and automation. People who become unemployed will receive temporary support during a transitional period at the same time as training for future new tasks.

## Supportive tasks

This is to help with all practical things during a transition period. These tasks can be within entrepreneurship (functional organizations) or other public activities. Public activities are the basic support organizations that exist today and in some new areas. So far we have schools, healthcare, defense, and the police. New public activities will be *wellness* and *evolution*. One part of agriculture will become public.

## Agriculture

Sweden must be self-sufficient in food. However, we can exchange certain foods with other countries.

Sweden's agriculture and food production will be re-established and the degree of self-sufficiency will amount to 100%.

## Criminal elements

### *People who don't meet the citizen requirement*

People who don't meet the citizenship requirement are sent to one of Sweden's integration centers.

### *People who don't meet the citizen requirement and are heavily criminal*

Changing the behavioral pattern is a pervasive process that requires a lot of work from the persons concerned. Various karmic (fated) structures must be worked off and in many cases this is a process that takes a lot of time and effort if there is even an interest in this in the individual in question.

If a person doesn't want to receive the help offered to work with the self, the person is sent to some area on planet earth where he or she may be confronted with like-minded people. We work together internationally to establish such a place on the planet for these people to reside on. The place can be remote and quite impossible to get away from without modern technology. The person in question meets other people on the same level with similar fated qualities - equal solves equal - it is up to these people themselves to want to develop into more cosmically aligned people, probably in a more distant future. What is happening now is that these types of individuals will not be reborn on the earth. These souls will be moved to other three-dimensional worlds that take over the role of developing these individuals. The lowest astral plane belonging to the earth is phased out now as the earth is entering the new age.

To begin with, we set up special detention centers for these types of serious criminal recidivists who cannot change their behavior.

## Spare time, Enjoyment, Culture

In the spare time, it must be offered to do completely different things compared to the task you have in the social apparatus. It can be completely different activities that can be seen as interesting, developing for the person in question. It can be travels to different areas for recreation or to train certain sports or join certain organizations.

## Travels

Traveling and broadening one's horizons is a good way to get new input for more ideas or as a relaxation from citizen activities.

## Sports

Common to the sports is that they belong to entertainment and are not included as social support activities. Sport may take place in parallel with studies and the task of sustaining society. The sport should be enjoyable and uplifting. Sport should not be based on profit. All the funds that sports clubs receive from the state or from private donors, will be used to promote the club's continued existence and as inspiration for the stimulation of a new generation.

## Organizations

Participating in some organization or club for a specific purpose can also be enriching.

## Countryside

The countryside must have a harmonious environment for all the people who live there; people and animals must be able to live in a fantastic nature. The oceans must be cared for as well as land and air.

## Environment

Whatever we do in the country, it must be done in a natural harmonious way.

Emissions must be reduced and harmful chemicals that harm nature and groundwater must be banned. According to the transition policy, the cars will be operated with free energy without exhaust gases described under the heading energy politics. It is common for all combustion gases to be purified as best as possible, especially in the case of industries and waste incineration plants.

Water, air and soil must be purified where needed. Areas that are poisoned must be detoxified with new technology that does not involve a new environmental impact. Environmental toxins are neutralized with scalar energy technology.

## Cooperation (we abolish competition)

We propose the abolition of a competitive society and propose the introduction of cooperation in all areas. Competition contributes to increased selfishness and discord between individuals and nations. We choose cooperation over competition.

## Wellness (preventive healthcare) – Healthcare

Healthcare gets a new ally, namely "wellness". Healthcare aims to provide urgent solutions to people's problems and wellness (preventive healthcare) aims to inform, inspect and give people back their quality of life by preventing any imbalances in the body, the organism's functionality, which otherwise result in disease states.

Wellness is neglected today and we often wait until we are acutely ill before we think we need to do something about it. Maintaining good health and preventing problems should be a matter of course for every human being promoting long life and well-being. The CelesteMethod® is applied.

When we work with wellness, health care as today will not be needed in the long run.

## Schools, education, research

Various tests and analyzes are done early so we can see what inherent talents and skills the child has. The child must be stimulated within his field of talent so that the child can develop and strengthen his self-confidence.

Since different children have different talents, we need a school system that meets this. Different types of schools are needed. The students are grouped according to their level so that all students can develop from the right level and at the right pace that is suitable for the individual. The student's skills and talents are mapped, utilized and developed in the best way.

Teachers should be offered increased knowledge in philosophy of life and ethical moral living. This must then be implemented and included in the teaching in both primary and secondary school.

Consciousness development is a subject that is common to all schools.

Religion should be included as an optional subject in school education and not a must. This is because religion is largely about history and is not a universal philosophy of life. Religion is to be replaced by Gnostics - Solar Theology, which has been excluded by the Church out of power interests. Gnosticism is the original - esoteric doctrine of creation in its entirety.

Depending on consciousness and talent, the school is offered that is needed to stimulate that particular student's need to become an important cog in society. The main tasks in society will be to run the public activities and functional organizations. The functional organizations will develop new innovations, new technology and service the existing technology. Other information will in principle not be available.

Student loans are abolished. Existing student loans are declared invalid. No student loans are needed as all individuals have a civil right to "citizen's income".

When the student has completed his or her education that he or she receives free of charge from society, it is important to support society with what the studies have generated. The graduate student is therefore required to repay in work at least a ten-year period to Sweden. Later, when more countries adopt the "AIC World", the effort can be made in some of these countries as well.

## Forests

Today, there are only primeval forests on a few per mille of the forest land. We want to see more of the forest untouched and that more trees can grow and align with the natural energy that exists in the area. The energetic field then becomes stronger and the experience of being there becomes even more energy-charging.

Running forestry as today with major interventions in nature creates energy problems in these areas. We want to build a strong energetic structure in Sweden that people benefit from. As today, Sweden does not need to contribute 10% of the world's raw materials for wood, pulp and paper.

## Elder people

As you grow older, it should be possible to reduce the work effort. No one will retire. We work together in the societal body for everything to work and the tasks will be stimulating. We interact and collaborate in harmony with life and nature.

As an older person, you have gathered a lot of experience and this will benefit the up-growing generations. Being a support in different working groups is then a matter of course. As an older person, you can choose the action level that fits you.

Elderly care where it is needed must be properly cared for. Any energetic imbalances must be neutralized as far as possible. If we help our elderly in the best way, their next lives will be better with better development opportunities. Elderly care must also, like other health care or medical care, be multi-dimensional and multi-structural.

# The Constitutional Laws, New Constitutional Laws

New Constitutional laws are established. These are the previous ones: http://www.riksdagen.se/sv/sa-funkar-riksdagen/demokrati/grundlagarna/

## * Form of government

The form of government:
https://www.riksdagen.se/sv/dokument-lagar/dokument/svensk-forfattningssamling/kungorelse-1974152-om-beslutad-ny-regeringsform_sfs-1974-152

The form of government must be changed.

## * The Succession Act

Monarchy needs to be restructured and adapted to the society of tomorrow.

## * Freedom of Press Act

The press ethics rules that apply today have been designed by the various press organizations themselves. These own established rules must be reviewed as information is often angled to create sensation and blacken individuals or countries. This is contrary to the current Freedom of Press Act. In other respects, the Freedom of Press Act can apply as hitherto.

## * The Freedom of Expression Act

The Freedom of Expression Act may apply as hitherto. You must be allowed to express your position wherever it applies. Today there are some other laws that limit this right - these laws must be reviewed. One must distinguish between criticism and statement. If you aren't allowed to state errors, shortcomings in an individual or social system, then we cannot develop or evolve. If a swear word is directed at an individual, he should be able to receive this without overreacting emotionally as today. It is important for everyone to neutralize their five inherent negative mind properties (often perverted). New views may be seen as a springboard for development.

Debate should cease and be replaced by factual dialogues. Debates belong to the sandbox level of consciousness. One should learn to listen and not unnecessarily interrupt a dialogue just to get more points than the other. All this belongs to the kindergarten stage of consciousness.

**\* The Riksdag Act (almost a constitutional law)**

https://www.riksdagen.se/sv/dokument-lagar/dokument/svensk-forfattningssamling/riksdagsordning-2014801_sfs-2014-801

The Riksdag (Swedish Parliament) procedure is very detailed and shows in detail how everything works in the Riksdag. The Riksdag agenda may be changed.

**World Teacher (1 in number)**

The task of the world teacher will be supervising, monitoring and overall communication with the National Council and the Ministries (organs). The World Teacher - UNIFIER appoints the successor, as the UNIFIER represents the Galactic Federation on Earth.

**National Council (72 councilors)**

The Ministries (organs) will be 8 in numbers. The Ministry of Labor and Ministry of Justice are removed. The Ministry of Social Affairs is renamed the Ministry of Health.

The council members lead the various ministries and have priority in communication with the World Teacher - UNIFIER when advising on various issues.

It is always difficult to appoint councilors at first. Once the system is established, it becomes easier because the level of consciousness has been raised and the choice of members can be made with long forward planning. When the council is appointed, the most suitable individuals shall be nominated for the respective council function. We have eight ministries with a preliminary nine council members each. Council members must be tailored to their task - i.e. the right person is chosen for the right task. A universal nomination committee does this in consultation with the World Teacher.

Ministries (organs, 8 in number)

- Foreign Ministry
- Defence Ministry
- Health Ministry
- Distributive Ministry
- Education Ministry
- Environment and Energy Ministry
- Infrastructure Ministry
- Cultural Ministry

## Foreign Ministry

Sweden's relations with other countries, foreign exchange, trade with other countries, universal exchange and agreements, positions. This applies between Sweden and other countries as well as Sweden and Extraterrestrial Intelligences.

## Defense Ministry

The Defense Ministry handles national security, defense of borders, sea, land, security.

The Defense Ministry runs the judiciary, the police (terrorism, prison care, crisis preparedness, migration, and asylum). The Defense Ministry includes the total defense, military, civil defense, duty service, volunteer services, security policy, the Home Guard, the rescue service, the Coast Guard.

## Health Ministry

The Health Ministry handles Care and Health, Health Care, Wellness.

## Distributive Ministry

This Ministry handles national coordination in terms of resource allocation, coordination and support. The Distribution Ministry has great communication with all the country's municipalities that handle distribution at the local level - which takes place in both directions, i.e. within the municipality and between municipalities in the country.

### Education Ministry

The Education Ministry handles education and research in various areas.

### Environment and Energy Ministry

This Ministry handles various energy solutions for the country and works overall for environmental issues when it comes to improving the environment.

### Infrastructure Ministry

The Infrastructure Ministry handles housing, administration, state development, rural areas, communication, transport, urban development, rural areas, IT, transport and infrastructure issues as well as functional organizations, leisure and tourism issues.

### Culture Ministry

The Culture Ministry handles questions regarding Cultural Ecology, Evolution, Cosmocracy, Culture, Ethics - Morality.

### Working Groups

Various working groups are appointed to work on certain issues on behalf of the ministries.

### Municipalities

The municipalities in the country can be the same as before. They work with local distribution of resources and with other assignments that come from the local level or ministry levels (organ levels).

### County Council

The county councils can be the same as before. They work with local distribution of resources and with other assignments that come from the local level or ministry levels (organ levels).

// *This is what the action plan for a fair societal development looks like right now. It will be supplemented on an ongoing basis (2020-10-17).*

*// More background information can be found in the books, courses and teachings materials that the AIC provides. The information here becomes more and more obvious as the readers work with their own health and inner resource development according to the CelesteMethod® at the AIC Association.*

https://www.unifier.se/action-plan-for-fair-societal-development/

# Part 2

# The Filter

Besides seeing through yourself and working off all your energy blockages, impurities and reaching the higher quality multi-dimensional quantum consciousness - this is the filter that you and every person must live trough and survive until the filter is no longer existent, and has been dissolved along with its wielders, protectors and allies.

**The eye of the needle that everyone must pass, the connections to the negative, destructive force**

The new society, which in the long run will become a reality after all the changes, will not be for all people. In fact, only a few of today's people will be part of it. Many of these are not even born yet, and many of these will come from different civilizations in the cosmos, i.e. extraterrestrial intelligences. Most people living on earth now will after they have passed away be transferred to other planets that correspond to their inner qualities - other three-dimensional planets. Their connections to the earth disappear as the earth is restructured and their development continues on another planet in the cosmos, and this is how evolution takes place. No human being is forgotten - everyone develops and evolves from their current qualitative level.

The filter that has now been constructed aims to separate the individuals who can continue their development on the earth in terms of quality - and those who will be removed from here.

The filter is constructed by negative intelligences working behind the scenes with the development of the earthly population. This can be considered negative and malignant, but is of utmost importance for human development. The five animal mind qualities that we have developed in the animal kingdom and that we have later perverted in the human kingdom, must be seen through by us individually, and we must voluntarily work off these and work toward a neutral state, i.e. when we have had enough of the three-dimensional degrading classroom climate - i.e. the three-dimensional earthly reality that we live in physically here on the planet earth.

Some people work consciously to achieve a more neutral and positive state, and some are still immersed in a gloomier negative state, to where they are drawn emotionally between different versions of the five mind opponents, i.e. lust, anger, greed, vanity, selfishness. These people, who are completely immersed or don't even want to emancipate, will have to leave the planet earth after their physical death. Right now, more and more extraterrestrial highly evolved neutral beings are being born to earth, and will be part of the new civilization, and will ascend the most important supporting societal positions and ensure that evolution follows the plan for the planet earth.

## The basis of the Filter

Since we all humans are more or less connected to the three-dimensional reality and many also deeply immersed and engrossed, there are players who automatically help in establishing the filter and maintain it - defend it - with the help of the five mind opponents - i.e. which benefits themselves, and only a little, and only short-term.

The beings who work to allow man to pervert their mind abilities are behind the scenes on a four-dimensional level. These are not visible to the earth-born man but influence them without them being aware of it. Everyone is more or less affected and this is the purpose. The more man follows these influences, the more immersed he becomes. Some people have completely surrendered to the control of these beings and here we have the root cause of the social development that has accelerated over the last two centuries.

The people who are unconscious and fully controlled by this negative power run the errands of the negative power, in everything. They do it completely naturally and socialize with peers. This ruling elite can without being questioned by people at the same level calmly and methodically build up the filter that is now ready for the people of the earth to walk through. The filter has been constructed over a long time and is defended completely automatically with the schooling we all received through primary school, high schools, university educations to give us an OK stamp to enable us to work certified with any of the jobs available in society today - to support the filter and keep the filter going. To a very large extent this affects our emotions, health and consciousness, i.e. affect us in most cases completely.

The people who have a higher consciousness and better health and see through what is happening now will be able to pass through the filter.

The people who have too much unsolved karma accumulated and cannot see through the established filter, will have their situations worsened and their characteristics will get more energy from the sun, and expand and worsen. These people will experience emotional disturbances to an even greater extent, which will affect their essence more, which will lead to death through disease or other sudden death.

This process will go pretty fast and the filter will help with this. An already poor health must be activated to the extent that death occurs. These people have for themselves created their own mind programming unconsciously, which now meets the filter, and every single human being will now reap the consequences of this.

The filter has been established and institutionalized in society as more or less a matter of course. It all starts with the early school education, which teaches everything except how we develop as individuals toward higher consciousness with higher ethics and morality. We learn instead technically evolving information, distorted history and social sciences; we stretch our intellects to the utmost to learn everything possible in terms of mathematics, science, etc. The intellectualism that we develop here is a tool that when disconnected from higher consciousness instead with the help of the five opponents of the mind will become an enemy to ourselves, we degenerate further - and believe in all kinds of intellectual information, especially if repeated many times - e.g. as with the carbon dioxide as a global warming agent of the earth's climate - when reality is the opposite. Generations of growing children are indoctrinated and inclined in a degenerate direction with an accompanying societal climate. The indoctrination continues until death occurs. Teachers follow the curriculum and receive a small salary, which they must, as they want to continue living in the society. People do anything for a salary. Generations are deceived.

The restructuring of the police has made serious and organized crime increase to the extent that society is heading for a complete ravage. To keep the clearance rate of crimes high, they use automatic cameras to catch speeding offenders in traffic. Governing people at different levels in society raise wages and see no strange in these structural changes - that these lead to a more insecure and immoral society. Immorality and violence are spreading and mushrooming.

Healthcare, which should instead keep people healthy, aims to make efforts when people have already become seriously ill. The conditions are solved with unnatural emergency medicines in the forms of pills, vaccinations and surgery. The healthcare staff sees that certain efforts in the long run actually help to kill people, but since they are required to perform the work they are trained for, very little is questioned. As a healthcare employee, you get a salary - and you want to keep it. You therefore become a good henchman of death, but at the same time you are indoctrinated and demoralized to the extent that you don't see through this but happily with great conviction carry out the work.

The people living in society today have been drilled in countless lives to get the intellectual training necessary to maintain the society that now exists, and some of these citizens to the extent that they unconsciously firmly instruct their subjects in how everything should proceed. These people get paid more for their efforts.

The negative power would express it as "*if you worship me, I'll give you the whole world.*" These people are richly rewarded for their efforts by the negative power - but create a wasp's nest of karma for themselves.

This karmic load is clearly visible on the four- and five-dimensional level, in the human being's astral cause-related field, which governs the individual in everything he is drilled to perform.

You only question this procedure when you are able to begin to see through your five mind opponents, and work these obstructions off from your being. Very few individuals do this. Most often people defend their actions and perceptions so that the degenerating social system is maintained as well as the individual's own distorted mind programming. Blaming others is standard - it's always someone else's fault.

*We are all therefore guilty in the maintaining of the filter - it is completely in line with the development period we are in now.*

## The creation of the Filter

Now people are more or less poisoned through bad, poisoned and nutrition poor foods, wrong thoughts, immoral living, where the influence of the sun now increasingly activates the over thousands of years of woven karmic webs, now having the opportunity to have them worked off and dissolved. Each individual will be confronted with oneself where many will die as they face their unsolved karmic situations. As icing on the cake, the situation is now even more at its peak as the negative force with the United States at the forefront, the Western world through the Globalists have done everything to poison people for a long time (read *The Matrix Reality*), but now also through 3G, 4G, 5G in combination with the Corona strategy and associated vaccinations. This radiation in combination with our karmic situation, poisoned organisms at different levels will kill very many people and dismantle society to the ground. This is done to pave the way for Putin's new world of development. No one can be blamed for this death policy, "cult" - but all people are more or less involved in enforcing this sentence. If you want to change it, you have to work with yourself to become a better world citizen. Then you can pass the filter yourself. It is therefore important to strive to develop the higher-quality multidimensional quantum consciousness - free from all attachments. Few people will succeed in this - but it is important to start the process.

# Part 3

# The Filter - the measures

### Sweden is over-represented in the Bilderberg group

Sweden's highest politicians have for a long time and in total secret gone to the annual Bilderberg meeting which takes place twice a year. This is to get instructions from the power elite in the Bilderberg group.

Carl Bildt (M) has participated since 1996 at the Bilderberg's annual meetings. He is an active member, as is Jacob Wallenberg. Carl Bildt has worked for Sweden's membership of NATO. Fredrik Reinfeldt (M) was called 3 months before the 2006 Swedish election to Bilderberg's meeting for instructions. Similarly, Stefan Löfven (S) was invited in the spring of 2013 before he was elected Prime Minister. Other former participants are Göran Person, Mona Sahlin (S) and Anders Borg (M) and others.

So far, not the Swedish people but the Bilderberg Group has decided who will lead the politics in Sweden.

The power of the mass media and deceptive information to the people, various political pickpocketing, etc., are excellent ways to gain power and lull people into an illusion of a welfare based on debt, on digital figures and worthless paper money.

I grew up under Stalinist dictatorship in Hungary and what I experience in Sweden today does not differ much from the Stalin era. The difference is that, so far, mental torture is used in Sweden over physical, which was a standard method under Stalinism in Hungary and other eastern states.

It would be better if these authoritarian personalities would devote their time and energy to help their own country and people to develop and prosper, rather than running matters for negative, despotic, authoritarian governments that want to create a totalitarian dictatorship on earth and enslave and eradicate humanity. This is to sell one's soul to the devil.

Almost all journalists and politicians in Sweden have been totally deceived by this company.

David Rockefeller - another very high positioned Bilderberg who together with Jacob Rothschild think they own the whole world, wrote this in his memoirs:

*"Some even believe that we are part of a secret society that work against the interests of the United States, and characterize me and my family as 'internationalists' and that we are conspiring with others around the world to build a more integrated global political and economic structure, a unified world so to speak. If this is the accusation, then I am guilty, and I am proud of it."*

He also said the following in a 1994 speech to the UN:

*"We are on the verge of a global restructuring. All we need is the right major crisis and the nations will accept the new world order."*

How many people know something about the Federal Emergency Management Agency (FEMA), which has built so-called concentration camps in various states of the United States?

Thus, they have built over 800 concentration camps in the United States. These are closely guarded full-time, but currently empty.

*They have planned in advance that all people who do not want to align themselves with the "New World Order", its agenda, should be expelled to these concentration camps, similar to the Guantanamo Prison in Cuba.*

These camps are also run by FEMA. If there are major natural disasters, demonstrations, riots in a larger scale, or illegal immigrants are crossing a border, which happened in Europe, or if Republicans and Democrats after an election clash start a civil war, then the laws of war will come into force in the United States. This can be done with just a simple order from the president. All camps have rail links as well as roads and highways that lead straight into them. Almost all camps have an airport close by. Most of FEMA's camps can accommodate about 20,000 individuals, plus staff. The largest of all these camps is in Alaska and can hold up to 2 million people. This is as many as half the number of Los Angeles residents in California.

Remember that the Nazi death camps (concentration camps) in Germany during World War II really existed. Their existence was a conspiracy theory only until after the war, when the existence of the camps was really verified. Remains of these camps are still there for the public to see today. Concentration camps were also used during the 1900s by the Russians against Russians (e.g. Siberian concentration camps), by Yugoslavs against Yugoslavs (Tito's death camps) and also during the Yugoslavian civil war in 1991-2001, etc.

Important persons who have disclosed information about these FEMA camps have been liquidated.

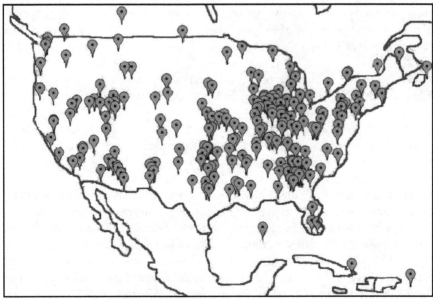

Figure 28. FEMA camps are spread all across the US.

Figure 29. Every concentration camp can accommodate up to 20,000 people.

The Illuminati Order and their sub-organizations (Freemasons, Bilderberg Group, Skull & Bones and others) believe that there is only room for about 500 million people on earth. The remaining approximately 7 billion people could be gradually removed from the earth through various kinds of measures. Several of these planned actions are described in this book.

In order to reduce the number of people on earth, it requires triggering extensive natural disasters, storms, floods, earthquakes via Chemtrails and HAARP in the atmosphere. Furthermore, they want to significantly reduce the quality of life in humans by letting them eat GMO crops (*genetically modified foods*). They want to release bacteria and viruses into the air and freshwater. They want to spray plants and arable land, increase electro smog, increase consumption of alcoholic beverages. They want to let narcotic, psychedelic (hallucinogenic) drugs free. They want to introduce mass vaccination and mentally affect humans through Chip implants, synthetic drugs, chemical additives in food and drink, etc., wines with a high proportion of pesticides (often found in wines grown in hot, humid climates) and wines with high sulfite content (more than 100 mg/liter). White wines have higher sulfite content than reds.

Wines produced without pesticides and fertilizers are called organic. Producers of so-called natural wines have taken a step further and are making wines completely without additives. Only minor amounts of sulfite is sometimes used in the bottling itself to increase shelf life. In principle, all wines before the 1950s were natural wines, i.e. "real deal".

## The New World Order

The New World Order is about universal membership in a totalitarian state governed by an autocratic government, whose purpose and objectives are dictatorship.

The UN constitution refers to Article 21 (3) "Universal Declaration of Human Rights". This means that every citizen has the right to life, freedom and personal security according to the UN Declaration on Human Rights.

The word "Human Rights" is a utopia that exists only in human imagination, as is the word "democracy". There is no nation in the world that applies human rights or lives by democratic principles, except in exceptional cases.

The "New World Order's General Secretariat" has its seat in Washington D.C., USA.

In order to get a 7-language international passport, you must sign a document assuring that you follow all the points of the new world order. If for some reason you want to drop out or break the content of the charter, you will get punished either through life imprisonment or by being killed.

Ordinary people can change "nationality" overnight and are then guaranteed world citizenship. They then join the "New World Order".

In Sweden, human rights are constantly being talked about, at the same time as new legislations come in order to limit people's rights to their own views concerning the state and their way of handling human rights in accordance with democratic principles.

The state does not want transparency and involvement in its business that can shed light on what they are doing behind the scenes, or what they are planning behind the backs of their citizens.

Figure 30. World Passport for World Citizens in seven languages.

We must not forget that the UN Charter on Human Rights does not concern all citizens in the world.

Some citizens or groups of people benefit more at the expense of others.

The UN is entirely governed by Washington and the intelligence services NSA, CIA, DIA and FBI.

As soon as you vote for any proposition that is in conflict with the national or international interests of the United States, the United States will veto it. Except when it comes to war declaration against some member state, then the United States is first to vote for it.

I have never understood what the UN means by human rights.

Rather, they are about humanity's obligations to a totalitarian state, authority or organization, which is inviolable and wants to limit people's opinions and freedom of speech. Human rights under the New World Order mean that one must, without question, follow what the World Government dictates for its citizens.

Exactly the same agenda the EU government wants to impose on all its Member States and its citizens in Europe. Isn't this the same agenda as the Hitler regime or the Stalin regime worked for?

## What does it mean to be a World Citizen in a Totalitarian State?

"All registered world citizens will receive the World Citizen Card, laminated and in 7 languages: English, French, Spanish, Arabic, Russian, Chinese and Esperanto.

The possession of this card is evidence of a global political status allied with each and every other declared and registered World Citizen."

## Credo of a world citizen

"A World Citizen is a human being who lives intellectually, morally and physically in the present. A World Citizen accepts the dynamic fact that the planetary human community is interdependent and whole, that humankind is essentially one. A World Citizen is a peaceful and peacemaking individual, both in daily life and contacts with others.

As a global person, a World Citizen relates directly to humankind and to all fellow humans spontaneously, generously and openly.

Mutual trust is basic to his/her lifestyle.

Politically, a World Citizen accepts a sanctioning institution of representative government, expressing the general and individual sovereign will in order to establish and maintain a system of just and equitable world law with appropriate legislative, judiciary and enforcement bodies.

A World Citizen brings about better understanding and protection of different cultures, ethnic groups and language communities by promoting the use of a neutral international language, such as Esperanto (*meaning that English is no longer a world language*).

A World Citizen makes this world a better place to live in harmoniously by studying and respecting the viewpoints of fellow citizens from anywhere in the world."

## Affirmation

"I, the undersigned, do hereby, willingly and consciously, declare myself to be a Citizen of the World. As a World Citizen, I affirm my planetary civic commitment to WORLD GOVERNMENT, founded on three universal principles of One Absolute Value, One World, and One Humanity which constitute the basis of World Law.

As a World Citizen I acknowledge the WORLD GOVERNMENT as having the right and duty to represent me in all that concerns the General Good of humankind and the Good of All. As a Citizen of World Government, I affirm my awareness of my inherent responsibilities and rights as a legitimate member of the total world community of all men, women, and children, and will endeavor to fulfill and practice these whenever and wherever the opportunity presents itself.

As a Citizen of World Government, I recognize and reaffirm citizenship loyalties and responsibilities within the communal state, and/or national groupings consistent with the principles of unity above which constitute now my planetary civic commitment."

## The Illuminates' greatest fear is organized resistance

Everything that weakens a person's thought and emotional ability creates confusion. This can happen through false information via the media and

170

contributes to anxiety, stress, hopelessness, inability to act, and ultimately to suicide. These are things that are encouraged by the Illuminates. War, anarchy, disintegration of society makes man cry out for help and protection from the same negative beings who created all this.

The more chaos, the more control and surveillance.

The end product is slavery under more modern forms.

## Rockefeller's Dynasty

John D. Rockefeller, the founder of Standard Oil, was one of the world's first dollar billionaires. He built one of history's greatest family fortunes with the help of illegal, unethical and manipulative business ways that lacked all contact with sound and free market economics. Despite the intervention of the United States Supreme Court in 1911, the highly debatable business ways of the Rockefeller family were not stopped, and they continue today.

The Rockefeller family also played a prominent role in the creation of the UN. Their plan was to eventually be able to launch a new world order with a supranational government within the UN framework, where they had a decisive Western influence. 3 out of 5 permanent seats in the Security Council were assigned to the west. The initiative to the foundation of the NATO was also taken by the Rockefellers during the Cold War. Despite the end of the war, the NATO is now aggressively expanding, whose real role is to manipulate and prepare a market for the oligarchs' enormous expansive weapons industries.

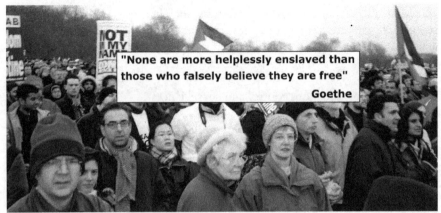

Figure 31. People showing their dissatisfaction with the unfair societal development.

**The Bilderberg Group was created by David Rockefeller**

To create a World Government the following is required:

1. An international identity
2. Centralized control of the people
3. A society with zero growth
4. A state of perpetual imbalance
5. Centralized control of all education
6. Centralized control of all foreign and domestic policies
7. A United Nations (UN) with self-determination, power
8. A western trade block
9. An expansion of NATO
10. A legal system
11. A social welfare state

➢ **An International Identity:** By authorizing international authorities to completely destroy all national identity through undermining from within, they intend to introduce a set of universal values. No others will be allowed to flourish in the future.

➢ **Centralized control of the people:** Through mind control (mental control) which also includes propaganda, disinformation, chip implants, etc., they want to control all of humanity to become obedient citizens. The blueprint of their plan is described in

Zbigniew Brezinski's book "Between Two Ages": America's Role in the Technotronic Era. With a Bachelor's degree from Harvard University in 1953, and as founder of the Rockefeller-controlled "Trilateral Commission," Zbigniew Brezinski has an impressive curriculum vitae. Not only because he was President Jimmy Carter's national security adviser, but also because he was a member of Ronald Reagan's "Foreign Intelligence Advisory Board" and shared the presidency of Georg H.W. Bush's "National Security Advisory Task Force" in 1988. He is also a colleague of Henry Kissinger and well-known for his presentations at several Bilderberg conferences. He wants to abolish the middle class and wants only one ruling class during the new world order.

➤ **A society with zero growth:** During a post-industrial period, zero growth will be necessary to destroy all public prosperity. When there is prosperity, there is progress. Prosperity and progress make it impossible to carry out repression, and you need repression if you want to divide society into owners and slaves. The end of prosperity will lead to the end of nuclear-generated electric power and all industrialization, except for the computer and service industries. The remaining Canadian and American industries will be exported to poor countries, where slave labor is cheap. One of the main objectives of NAFTA will then be realized.

➤ **A state of perpetual imbalance:** Artificial constructed crises will put people under constant threat. Mental, emotional and physical crises make it possible to keep people in a perpetual state of imbalance. People will be too tired and exhausted to decide their own destiny. They will be so confused and demonized that "apathy" on a massive scale will be the result when faced with too many choices.

➤ **Centralized control of all education:** One of the reasons why the European Union (EU), the American Union and the future Asian Union strive for bigger general control of education is that they want to allow the world's globalists (intellectually brainwashed) to sterilize the world's true past. Their efforts bear amazing fruit. Today's youth is almost completely unknowing of the lessons of history, individual liberty, rights and the importance of freedom. From the perspective of the globalists, this fact simplifies the curriculum.

➤ **Centralized control of all foreign and domestic policies:** What the United States is doing is affecting the entire world. The

173

Bilderbergs seem to exert some control over all US presidents and their policies. Although Canada appears to be able to maintain its own sovereignty, it is following point by point the demands of the United States. It is still unclear how this influence will affect, and is influenced by Donald Trump's new government. But none of these powerful high-handed know there will be major changes on earth in the coming decade.

➢ **A United Nations (UN) with self-determination, power:** By using what the UN already has in place, the plan is to transform it into a lawful and then an actual world government. They also plan to levy a direct UN tax on world citizens. Sweden who feels inferior to the United States is eager to meet its big brother, especially when having the President's Club in 2017.

➢ **A Western Trade Block:** By expanding the NAFTA across the Western Hemisphere into South America, an American Union will eventually be formed, similar to the European Union.

➢ **An expansion of NATO:** Since the UN intervenes in several trouble spots in the world, such as in Afghanistan, the NATO will become the United Nation's World Army. They don't expect to incorporate China and Russia into their association. It would be unfortunate if Sweden, for prestige reasons, wants to allow NATO on its ground. In principle, this would mean that Sweden's neutrality would cease and Sweden as a country would be counted among the other NATO members as a belligerent country. It would not be surprising if the parties that NATO sympathizes with in Sweden would have their wishes fulfilled. Although it will be short-lived.

➢ **One legal system:** The International Court of Justice in The Hague will be the only legal system in the world.

➢ **One social welfare state:** The Bilderbergs envision a socialist welfare state, where obedient slaves will be rewarded and dissidents become targets for extinction through various kinds of measures.

The Bilderbergs very high-positioned politician, Peter Sutherland, said in 2012 the following:

*"The EU must do its best to undermine the ethnic homogeneity in their member states."*

## The US is desperate and prepares for a third world war

When something happens in the world, you have to ask yourself what really is happening, what is the agenda and who is making money from it.

To date, the Illuminates, under the leadership of the Rothschild and Rockefeller families, have profited on all wars, both World War I, World War II, and the planned World War III, which is already ongoing to a lesser extent.

Initially, Iraq, Afghanistan and Libya have fallen victims of US terror and power interests. In Syria, they have so far failed.

Now it is about Russia, China and Iran.

Why does the United States want world domination under the slogan "A New World Order" and is prepared to start a war to achieve its purpose?

It is primarily about natural resources, oil, natural gas, raw materials, etc. This is difficult to understand given that all countries have access to "free energy", without any major cost. We can run our entire society on free energy, "scalar energy" (*zero point energy*) found in nature around us, without much cost. But it is difficult to make money on free energy.

The next US problem that needs to be solved in order to establish the "New World Order" is the problem with the world economy. The Illuminates want a single currency (*dollar*). This has been opposed by both Russia and China. Russia, China and India want their own currencies not to risk an economic collapse in their countries.

America's imminent dollar collapse is the root of the problem.

The US dollar has been special since it has been used as a world currency and means of oil payment at the same time. Ever since the end of World War II, the US dollar has been the world currency and was to be backed by real gold.

In the late 1960s, it became evident that the private Federal Reserve Bank (FRB) owned by the Rothschild family had printed up a lot of dollars without having the corresponding gold reserve.

According to the International Monetary Fund (IMF), foreign banks held $ 14 billion at the same time as FRB had only $ 3.2 billion in gold to cover the foreign part of the currency.

When other countries began to realize that the United States was stealing their purchased dollars, they wanted it back in gold from the United States.

The United States therefore removed the dollar from the gold standard in 1971 and continued to print more money, and this procedure has escalated since 2008 to later stabilize at an extremely high level in 2014.

Since the dollar is used as a world currency and to trade oil, other countries are forced to use dollars. As a result, the US steals purchasing power and welfare from these countries every time new dollars are printed.

This is a very lucrative game as long as the monopoly can be maintained.

This was the reason for the Iraq war since Saddam Hussein in 2000 instead of dollars wanted euro as payment for the oil. This was not liked by the United States, as Iraq was a big oil producing country.

Another event was that the Talibans in Afghanistan banned opium production in the summer of 2000 and a major source of income for the hidden powers in the West was threatened. In 2001, opium production in Afghanistan was non-existent and in October the same year the United States invaded the country. Opium production was quickly started, and today Afghanistan produces about 90% of the world's opium under US and NATO control. Most of the CIA's spending is financed by drug trafficking from Afghanistan.

In order to deceive their own people and the entire population of the world, they launched the terrorist attack on the "World Trade Center", where they pointed out Al Qaeda as responsible. 2974 people were killed. Then the CIA threatened to murder those who reveal the truth. All information leaked about this event that is true is written off as conspiracy theories. This is a way to hide the reality from the people.

Today, there should really be no doubt that the disaster that occurred in New York on September 11, 2001 was an insider job to get a reason to attack Afghanistan and Iraq. There is countless evidence of this. The motive for deliberately murdering so many people was to increase their power over the American people, meet the tremendous pressure of the weapons industry, increase political influence in the Middle East, and for a few to make huge sums of money on oil, e.g. for the Bush-Cheney family.

The reason why people in Sweden haven't been told the truth depends on the US power over the media and politicians. Sweden simply does not dare to question the US single-world empire.

The Swedish politicians are good examples of cowardly politicians who defend the lie and counteract the truth. They do not protect the people but themselves.

They complain about Russia and accuse President Vladimir Putin's regime of being the number one enemy. Russia is accused of violating human rights and threatening world peace. This is a lie. If you see how many NATO bases there are in the world compared to Russian, then it is easy to see that the United States is the number one enemy and not Russia. This is happening at the same time as the United States is murdering, raping and oppressing millions of people in the world for the purpose of seeking world domination with total dictatorship over the people with the help of NATO. This USA is considered a friend and ally.

How can you consider yourself a sensible and serious politician, representative of your own people when you close your eyes to the truth and use the lie, when you aren't interested in learning discernment to be able to distinguish the lie from the truth?

People call the truth a lie, and the lie a truth. People smear those who tell the truth.

There is a saying: *while the lie has reached to Baghdad, the truth is still searching for its sandals.*

We repeat President John F. Kennedy's words from February 1962:
*"We need free information. A nation that is afraid to let its people judge the truth and falsehood in an open market is a nation that is afraid of its people."*

In 2003, the war against Iraq started and the three alleged reasons were that Iraq had weapons of mass destruction, connections with Al-Qaeda and that Iraq had purchased nuclear material from Nigeria.

All this was lie.

At Hans Blixt's visit to Iraq, no evidence was found for these claims.

Hans Blixt is a lawyer and politician. He became known as Director General of the International Atomic Energy Agency from 1981 to 1997 as well as for his work within the UN.

Nor should it be forgotten that the wars put into debt the taxpayers and transfers huge sums of money from them to the power elite that owns the large industries such as the weapons industry, the chemical industry and the drug industry. Of course, they also make huge money on exporting weapons and are dependent on an uncertain world filled with conflicts.

The US and EU are facing strong competition from industrialized countries with cheap labor, while meeting a big oil and gas dependence from other countries. When we in the West import more than we export, the other countries will of course gain the financial power. This distorted trade the US is trying to balance by devaluing its own currency and forcing the rest of the world's countries to keep the dollar with the help of the oil-dollar monopoly.

The reason why, with the help of Sweden, they were bombing Libya was that President Muammar Abu Minyar al-Gaddafi, whom the United States and other countries called dictator, wanted gold in payment for the oil. At the same time, Gaddafi was trying to start an African central bank to break out of the Rothschild-owned central bank, forming a "United States of Africa". This was a direct threat to the dominance of the Illuminates and the US in the world and the cheap African natural resources.

The next state on the agenda today is Iran.

Iran is big in oil production and rich in uranium deposits.

If the countries of the world were serious, they would invest in free energy, scalar wave energy, which exists in nature and is free. But here it isn't possible to make money in the same way as it isn't possible to monopolize and make money on medicinal plants. The rulers don't think of the well-being of the people, but of their material abuses.

The Illuminati's plan to reduce the world's population and gain total control of the world was put into practice already at the first symposium in 1957, which concerned the future development of the world.

President Eisenhower, Rockefeller and Rothschild and others participated in this consultation. As previously mentioned, they would agree on one of three alternatives for the implementation of the New World Order. The astonishing conclusion of this symposium was that overpopulation and excessive exploitation of the environment would lead to self-destruction until the turn of the century in 2000, or shortly thereafter. Therefore, many predicted that the earth would go under on December 21, 2012. To those governments that play into the hands of the US and constantly portray Russia as the number one enemy, to them it is good to know how much money the US is spending on its military rearmament during one single year.

**President's Proposed Total Spending 2015**

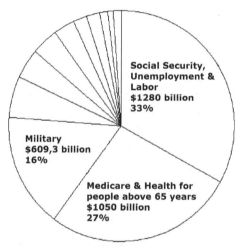

Figure 32. Source: National Priorities Project.

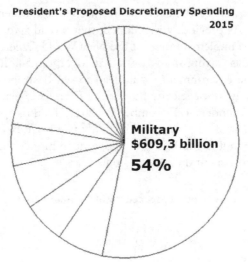

**President's Proposed Discretionary Spending 2015**

Military
$609,3 billion
**54%**

Figure 33. Source: National Priorities Project.

If we count out Social Security, Unemployment, Labour, Health Insurance for people over 65 and health, then we see the funds that remain and can be directed to various aims. Then we can see that the US has spent most of the poor tax payers' money on military debauchery, which is then recalculated to about 54%. If we add the cost that is paid to their war veterans annually, it will be an additional 6% to this total budget. Then we have a military budget of about 60% per year for war and devastation of infrastructure in nations, and eradication of human life.

Then, not included is the money that NATO countries pay for protection and to fight pretended enemies that in reality don't exist to the extent claimed by the mass media.

Listed below are the costs that the taxpayers pay per hour in the United States:

$ 615,482 per hour to fight ISIS.
$ 3.42 million per hour to the Pentagon Defense Headquarters.
$ 4.0 million per hour for the war in Afghanistan.
$ 117,035 per hour for the Iraq War.
$ 8.36 million per hour in total cost for Wars since 2001.
$ 57.52 million per hour to the Department of Defense, 2016.
$ 936,703 per hour for F-35 Joint Strike Fighter, 2016.
$ 2.19 million per hour for Nuclear Weapons, 2016.
$ 116,063 per hour for Drones, 2016.

$ 1.42 million per hour for US foreign military assistance, 2016.
$ 6.74 million per hour for "Homeland Security" after 11/9.
$ 11.64 million per hour in Education Cost, 2016.
$ 2.95 million per hour for Environmental Investment, 2016.
$ 2.93 million per hour for Economic Aid, 2016.
$ 4.87 million per hour in Building of Quarters, 2016
$ 40.68 million per hour in Medical Venture, 2016
$ 12.68 million per hour in Food Assistance, 2016

Source: National Priorities Project.

## One World Government according to the CABAL (the deep state)

The illuminati Order is infiltrated in all social institutions, both political and private, and is secretly preparing for the introduction of "Total Dictatorship" and military takeover via NATO.

The Illuminati has infiltrated governments at local, state and national levels, school systems and financial institutions, religions and the media.

With Europe as the base, the Illuminati is planning the "New World Order" which will be trial number 3 after World War I and World War II. Nazism and communism will appear as lame attempts in comparison with their new agenda.

The Illuminati people are soulless, unhappy and lonely beings. They have no others to spend time with than their peers.

They have nothing but money and material abundance.

Christ said: *those who are the poorest among the poor are those who have nothing but money.*

Each region in the United States has its own "nerve center" or centers of power for regional activities. The US has been divided into seven major geographical regions. Each region has locations that house military camps and bases hidden in remote areas or on large private properties. These bases are regularly used to train new generations in military technology, combat man against man, non-visible control, weapons use and all aspects of military weapons use.

One may ask the question, Why?

The answer is that the Illuminates are completely convinced that all governments in the world will collapse.

Themselves they have planned these collapses and these will take place as follows:

First, they will arrange an economic collapse that triggers a major depression that the world has never seen before. This is done by maneuvering the major banks and financial institutions in the world through stock manipulation and interesting changes in interest rates, since all the central banks in the world, except for a few exceptions, are subordinate the Federal Reserve, which is privately owned by the Rothschild family.

Most people will be indebted to the World Bank through their loans, credit card credits, etc.

The government in each country will withdraw all their credits immediately, and most people will be unable to pay and will go bankrupt.

This will cause a general financial panic, which will emerge simultaneously worldwide, which the Illuminates believe they can control through finances.

The good news is that a person who is without debts, who doesn't owe the state, who doesn't have credit debts to banks, who doesn't own anything that the banks can claim, who can live sufficiently independent, will be able to do better than others.

If I myself had been interested in speculating in business, then I would have invested in gold and not in shares. This is because the dollar lacks even the paper value without the support of precious metals. What people borrow from the bank is nothing but digital figures, with no value, on which they pay interest.

Man pays interest rate on what he does not own. Man does not own the house, car, boat or company as long as he borrows money from the bank.

I remember what happened after World War II in Hungary. We had worthless paper money printed by the communist dictatorship (*regime*), and all less valuable coins were made of aluminum.

The state confiscated (stole) all properties from the people and the people had to work 10-12 hours a day on their lost properties, which the state had seized. In return, they got paid for their work with some useless paper money and aluminum coins to buy from the state the food and utensils they'd made themselves to survive as human beings.

*The dictatorship that is currently emerging in the world under the guise of "Globalization, World Order, Democracy" is the same dictatorship but in a much larger scale.*

We are heading in the same direction unless we are ready to change our current life situation, but instead we continue to believe and trust in all the pompous promises of democracy, welfare, human rights, decision-making, freedom of speech, etc., which has become an "eco" in society. These are just empty words and just as worthless as the Swedish currency, which is just electronic numbers of ones and zeros that lack even the paper value.

The whole world is facing economic collapse today. The exception is partly the BRICS countries, i.e. Brazil, Russia, India, China, South Africa, etc., that want their own currency instead of the dollar to avoid economic collapse with bankruptcy, mass unemployment, anarchy, disintegration of society. These countries will to some extent manage to escape the depression. Russia has broken with the Rothschild Bank and nationalized the Central Bank in Russia. This example should Sweden and the other countries follow if they want to avoid economic collapse.

All governments in the world, with a few exceptions, will allow economic collapse and afterwards intervene politically and militarily to regain control of panicking people. This will primarily be done through NATO troops, their intervention in countries that are associated with NATO.

The ultimate world government "EU" has already been created as a prototype of what is to come when the "New World Order" begins.

Members of this "New World Government" meet annually within the Bilderberg Group in Europe where, among other things, Sweden is involved. Here, financial directions, policies, etc. are discussed and solutions to problems that arise that don't benefit the agenda.

The Rothschild family has leading positions in the UK and France.

The descendants of the Habsburg dynasty have a generation-based post.

The descendants of leading families in the UK and France have a generation-based post.

The Rockefeller family in the United States has a lifelong place in the Order of the Illuminati.

This is why the Illuminates have remained "anonymous" all these years. The governing members are very, very, wealthy and powerful.

The Illuminati leadership means that they consider themselves the descendants of royal blood, just as they consider themselves to be occult descendants in a straight descending line from the ANUNAKI in Sumeria.

Two definitions of "royal" could be used.

The first is public royalty as one can see today, and the second is "hidden royalty" as a royal feature of extreme occult power.

Sometimes these two are one and the same, as in the case of the Prince of Wales.

Descendants of Hanover and Habsburg rule in Germany over Bruderheist. They are also known for their strong connections to the occult.

The British dynasty is subordinate the Habsburg Monarchy.

They definitely rule the British branch under Rothschild and within the occult, and also within the parliament they reign openly.

In France, Rothschild rules them all.

The United States is lower on the scale, no matter its national size and is younger than the European branches.

Germany, France and the UK rule the European cult.

Russia is considered important, and has the strongest military power in the world.

Russia has been given the fourth position in the Illuminati's "New World Order".

Previously, the United States had that role. In the past, the Illuminates felt that Russia had become more cooperative over the years regarding the future agenda. But that is not the case.

Descendants of former ruling families are also involved in the leadership along with the younger ones.

China is ranked after Russia and then comes the United States.

Some of the American leadership is in Europe where many have their homes. That is why the EU is important to the Illuminates.

The Illuminates want Russia to become a military power in Europe above NATO, as they regard the Russian military leadership as the most disciplined and the best in the World.

But President Vladimir Putin does the opposite of what the Illuminates want by leaving Rothschild's Federal Reserve and Rotschild's control over the Russian Central Bank. He will go for another joint currency with China, India, South Africa, Brazil and others backed by gold. This will overturn the Illuminates' and Bilderbergs' plans for a European globalization under the New World Order.

For this reason, the Illuminates elected Donald Trump as president instead of Hillary Clinton. She is too hostile to Russia in comparison with Donald Trump.

Through this play, the Illuminates hope to regain Russia and get Russia aligned with the New World Order.

But I trust Vladimir Putin. His agenda fits better into the New Age, where people should live in harmony and community rather than in constant worries, stress, insecurity and fear of war. He is much smarter than any Western or Eastern president who has ruled so far.

No president so far has been able to build up Russia in as short a time as he has.

It is easy to criticize him as in Sweden because of ignorance and unconsciousness. Sweden itself cannot even manage to take care of its own inhabitants who are only 10 million and make the society work well. But to criticize a head of government that is responsible for a country as big as the whole of Europe and has a population of about 146,8 million - that is to be presumptuous.

The Swedish government should realize that.

There is a proverb that says: *to criticize, knowledge is required, but to assess, total knowledge is required.*

How many of the Swedish politicians can judge what is right or wrong?

Illuminates love smart intelligent people. The rest of the people they consider sheep and themselves shepherds.

During the year 1972 I saw a vision in my meditation. I was in a wide open field. The horizon was dressed in a reddish dawn. The sun had not yet risen over the horizon. As I watched this beautiful dawn, I saw a figure slowly moving towards me in the open field. He was wearing armor. I recognized him. It was Satan, the Devil embodied in a Knights figure. I felt his strong negative vibrations. I focused on him with my energy. When he was halfway on the open field, he stopped. My power forced him not to come any closer.

We communicated with each other via telepathy.

He stated the following. Why do we fight each other when we work for the same thing? Then he dissolved and I returned to my waking consciousness. I have long thought about what he meant. One day I suddenly realized the following.

We both work for the development of humanity. It is his job to put obstacles in the way of people so that they gain experience and will be able to develop. That's why all people on this planet are here. The Earth is an integration planet where different humanoid species are to meet and learn from each other through resistance. That some of us experience this resistance as evil is because we are equipped with a reptile brain, a limbic system that translates the negative energies that surround us into emotions, which we then experience as negativity, evil of various kinds. How can we experience the light if we haven't been in darkness? How would we know what happiness is if we have never been unhappy? How would we know what love is if we have never experienced hatred? How would we know what heat is if we have never frozen? We can go on forever with these parables.

Do you understand how important this negative power or force has been in our lives - in all of our lives? Without it, we would stagnate in our human development. We would constantly be in a neutral state, without knowing anything about creation - about both sides of the coin.

But what then is the problem? Well, that we are stuck in the fine meshed net of this negative power and we cannot take ourselves out without help. That is why I am here as the UNIFIER - to unite you with your true origin - what you once were, before you descended into this part of creation, which is the lowest, most sluggish state of creation. You are hereby given the opportunity to leave this constructed reality in which you have existed for approximately 26,000 years of your development, evolution.

If you don't, then you will have problems. Satan, the Devil will not let you go so easily. You have already seen this power genius through the Illuminati which is his tool here on earth. The Illuminati aren't evil beings even though they control and have you under surveillance.

I received a written invitation from the Order of the Illuminati during the early 2000s. Here is the content which I wish to make public.

*Dear Sire,*

*When I saw the history of your name I instantly knew we had to contact you!*
*I can sense this first spark of Success and immortality in every new member. Yours in one of the best!*

*We know people around you may not see it, but we know that you, Sire, has experienced moments in which you feel spiritually gifted.*

*In those euphoric moments, you know you are special, you absolutely know it, and you feel you are here to do great thing with your life. Right? Well, we know it, too, Sire. And yes, you are meant to do great things, exactly as we are going to show you.*

*How do we know? Be honest: have you ever felt like God or some higher power may be communicating with you, giving you a sign?*

*If you answer yes, and we know you did, then you are indeed that special person we are looking for. And this is your calling. It's as simple as that.*

*Yours Sincerely*

*Mr. X*

*PS. Your Invitation form is enclosed. Simply mail or fax that entire page back to me, today.*

*PPS, Sire, you have one of the most exiting profiles we have yet encountered. Few people possess such a promising profile as yours!*

I had to refuse this invitation for the same reason that the Order of the Illuminati would refuse an invitation from "The Sovereign Imperial Order of Saint Germain", SIOSG that we officially represent on earth.

SIOSG is the opposite pole of the Illuminati.

These two poles are like oil and water, which are of different qualities. Without their interaction, no development takes place. However, when the balance between these two forces is disturbed so that the negative force becomes dominant as on earth, then there will be problems in all of creation.

My paranormal experience on the Hungarian Great Plains was primarily about my task of helping people into the New Age, i.e. to contribute to human flourishing and evolution, and not to human destruction and extinction. In all my life (incarnations), I have worked to unite man on a common platform, which is Love-Wisdom.

For this purpose, I have already established in 1989 an International Academy for Total Human Culture, "L'Académie Internationale de Culture Humaine Intégrale" (AIC), "The Northern Pontifical Academy" (NPA) and the "Sovereign Imperial Order of Saint Germain "(SIOSG).

These organizations work only for the humanity of the "New Age".

The real power will be concentrated in Europe and not in the United States.

China, on the other hand, has its roots in Oriental occultism. Depending on the country's large population, it will also be included by the Illuminates, but as it seems now that China has chosen Russia as its partner.

The Illuminati wants Russia included in its agenda of Globalization, World Order.

But President Vladimir Putin is a good chess player. Like Alexander the Great, he made Russia the great power of Europe when Charles XII lost the war against Russia in Poltava, in 1709.

Carl Bildt back then was incarnated in the shape of Charles XII. That's why the former Swedish Minister of State and Minister of Foreign Affairs Carl Bildt hates Vladimir Putin. Fate has brought these two historical figures together again to settle their karmic problems in this incarnation, which may be their last on earth.

I hope you understand why Vladimir Putin wants to make Russia a great power in Europe. He will succeed. Nothing can stop him. There is no reason to fear that Russia will invade neither Sweden nor other countries in Europe. Vladimir Putin wants peace and cooperation on equal terms with all countries.

The propaganda that is going on in the world, even in Sweden, describing Russia as the number one enemy, as a threat to Sweden and NATO, is nothing more than fabricated conspiracy theory - a false information that is deliberately spread through the media.

All the media in the western world is controlled by the CIA, which in turn is controlled by the shadow government - the Illuminati.

So when President Donald Trump in the United States accuses the media of spreading lies, he speaks the truth with some modification.

Swedish media is the same. It withholds the truth from the Swedish people and conveys what creates sensation or is absolutely unimportant to the Swedish people.

The truth spread through the free press is dismissed by the establishment as a conspiracy theory.

But since most politicians and people haven't developed discernment, they cannot separate the lie from the truth.

The UN was formed in 1945 to help overcome the major obstacles in the way of the New World Order. One of the obstacles was nationalism.

Therefore parties such as the "Sweden Democrats" (SD) and similar organizations are a direct obstacle to the realization of the "New World Order" under the guise of Globalization.

The Sweden Democrats are regarded as "racists", which is a completely wrong term for a political organization that protects the Swedish Society, the Swedish people's right to freedom, to decide their own welfare and destiny. We shouldn't have to depend on the Rothschild family's and Rockefeller's involvement in the Swedish economy via the Riksbank (Swedish Central Bank). Nor need Sweden, the Swedish politics and social development to be involved in the Bilderberg group.

There must be put an end to political pickpocketing, trade-offs, which is constantly going on among different political actors behind the backs of their citizens. Representatives of the people and society must primarily protect the well-being and development of the citizens, and not primarily their own interests as they do. Power means responsibility. If you don't take responsibility for the task you have undertaken, then you are inappropriate for the task.

The Estonian-Swedish publicist Jüri Lina advocates that we should introduce a psychopath test for all leading positions in society. If the test shows that the person in question is a psychopath, then the person is inappropriate for the task, and should not have it.

The task of the elected politicians is not to look on themselves as small popes and plot devilishness behind the backs of their voters. The task of politicians is to ensure that the people in society can live in security and harmony as they deserve. Politicians should not lure them into a pious globalization that works for the eradication and enslavement of people instead of their freedom and development, evolvement.

Sweden, like the other Nordic countries, should work for a "Nordic Cooperation" both when it comes to economy and trade. Sweden, together with like-minded countries, should oppose a centrally controlled EU policy and banking that exploits the people financially to earn billions on the inhabitants of the countries.

Man must have the right to control their lives instead of being slaves under the slave drivers.

Slavery has never been abolished - it has just changed form.

Globalization is not possible as long as man hasn't stopped his negative thoughts, feelings and actions, as long as he does not strive for ethical-moral living.

Living in harmony and communion with nature and with others is a prerequisite for Globalization.

The Globalization on Earth that the shadow government, the Illuminates have planned for centuries, cannot be achieved peacefully, but only through threats, violence, totalitarian control, destruction and the enslavement of humanity.

Who among the people are interested in a Globalization that cannot be implemented peacefully?

When different political and religious representatives in different countries cannot agree with each other in their own country, with their own people whom they claim to represent, without imposing their views through legislation, threats and control, how then could they make peace with other peoples, other cultures, other countries in the world?

As long as man cannot create peace within himself, with his family, his children, his friends, how then can he make peace in Europe or the World?

Globalization as well as democracy are a utopia, a dream, which can only be realized when differences between people no longer exist.

It's good to have an idea of a community with everyone in the world. But it must also work in practice which it doesn't do today.

How can you call yourself a Christian and claim to believe in God, serve God, while serving Satan, the Devil, the dark forces that want to destroy, destroy all life?

It isn't possible to serve two masters, two forces simultaneously.

You have to choose which one you want to serve and must take the consequences of your choice.

It is time for man to wake up from his Sleeping Beauty sleep and see reality as it is, and not as he imagines in his vivid phantasy.

I described this already in 1995 in my books: "*Satan Is the Man of Today*" (not published in English. Instead read the book *Saint Germain - The mysterious Count that never dies*) and "*From Barbarism the Super Consciousness*".

"*The story takes place at an inn in the Swiss Alps during the 20th century. At the inn, a number of people assemble that together represent the ruling forces in society. A mysterious stranger joins the party and claims that it's not God that is the ruling power in the world; God who people talk about and worship with ceremonies and rituals. It is not the altruistic love that Christ advocates that governs the world, but it is the power of the mind, the ego embodied in Satan's, the Devil's, the Beast's form. Thus, Satan controls human activities in politics, business, economics, media, religion and even family life*".

I wanted to make people aware of the power that governs and still controls the destiny of the world. If we want to change the world and our destiny, we must become more aware of ourselves and of the forces acting within us and in the universe, the cosmic spectacle. We must learn true love above the love which is nothing but passion. The choice lies in our hands. Who will rule the world, God or the Devil - that we have to decide for ourselves. But we cannot influence the cosmic plan, the destiny for the evolution of the earth. The plan is decided from elsewhere, from a higher level compared to what George Soros and his peers can understand with their limited intelligence, awareness. They consider themselves as smart, but those who see the plan are even smarter.

Sandor Alexander Markus

## The negative despotic extraterrestrial beings and their earthly allies

The negative extraterrestrial Reptilians, being, their extraterrestrial hybrids from Orion and Zeta and their terrestrial counterparts can be held responsible for all the negative events that have occurred in world history and that occur on earth.

The fear of being revealed, seen through, is the only reason why the Draconian Hierarchy and their terrestrial allies the Illuminates and their sub-organizations have not yet taken the final step towards the "New World Order". They are afraid of resistance.

In order to work for the establishment of a world government, the Illuminates have founded various kinds of organizations in the world which they control entirely.

Examples of these organizations are the UN, Unicef, EU, WHO, UNESCO, IMF, WBG (*World Bank*), Federal Reserve, CIA, NSA, NASA, Bilderberg, Thule, Skull & Bones, Freemasons and other organizations. The corresponding organizations to some of these we can also find in both China and Russia.

The negative forces control the entire banking system worldwide. They control the stock market, the media, the pharmaceutical industry, the food industry, the oil industry, governments, most in the legal systems, security services, armies and the weapons industry.

They influence and control all science, school literature, teachings, journalism, film industry, sports as well as the music industry and the gaming industry.

Inventors who invent something in e.g. free energy or something else that could be a threat to the establishment are bought out, threatened or murdered.

The negative forces are the owners of the largest precious metal mines in the world. They control all casinos, gaming, drugs and sex trade through the CIA, FBI and DEA, etc.

These organizations have been presented in the mass media to the people as those who want to create and maintain order in society, but in reality they do the opposite.

As long as citizens live a law-abiding life, pay their taxes on time and cooperate with their authorities, they are left alone.

But as soon as someone deviates from the paying path or starts asking difficult questions or doing something that hinders the plans of the powerful leaders, the individual's life can be turned upside down in an instant.

The Illuminates are not spiritually evolved beings, and therefore they do not believe in destiny (*karma*), its existence.

They believe that whatever suffering they cause others remains unpunished.

Unfortunately for these people, the laws of destiny work continuously and everywhere in the universe. No one can escape his destiny.

There will come a time, in this life or the next, when these people will be forced to bear the consequences of their actions. In fact, every earthly human being must evaluate his or her own life in heaven or hell after biological death.

**Population control, fear is the tool**

The Power has at all times used an uncompromising method for influencing opinions - namely fear. Like the villain in the film "Superman" Lex Luthor said: *The more fear you make, the more loot you take.* When you do a little research into the globalists' business, you see this strategy clearly. Already in 1968, they supported in the media Paul R. Ehrlich's book "*The Population Bomb*" and a campaign for global actions against a claimed coming famine disaster. Four years later came the Rome Club's first attempt to intimidate with the writing "*Limits to Growth*". Of course, everything was just false alarm and the development has gone in the complete opposite direction compared to the propaganda.

The hyped environmental conference organized by the UN in Rio in 1992 was led by the Globalists who succeeded in bringing in the Rockefeller family's very close associate Maurice Strong as chairman. Preparations were made for the launch of the UN Agenda 21 through yet another alarmist writing from the Club of Rome. The grand title was "*The First Global Revolution*". There, the idea was introduced in using the "alarming" low anthropogenic climate impact from emissions of life-giving carbon dioxide to scare the world into a global world order - Agenda 21. Later, the UN has added the Agenda 2030.

In order to speed up the people's fears, which did not really want to take hold, the globalists' own torpedo George Soros entered in 2006 with a lot of millions and financed the doomsday prophet Al Gore's film "*An Inconvenient Truth*". This was an extremely cynical title, as there is almost no truth in the film. Through their control over the MSM (*Main Stream Media*), it was possible to launch the film worldwide and create the fear that was sought. Since the Globalists had a firm grip on the political establishment in the west, they also made sure to put the turbo on the scare campaign with a Nobel Prize (peace prize) to the charlatan Al Gore. Of course, just like all the Globalists' earlier doomsday prophecies, reality has become the exact opposite this time as well.

The globalists left nothing to chance. In 2008, with money channeled through Soros, the presidential campaign was funded for their lay-figure Barak Obama. Here they made sure to place the doomsday prophet and close co-worker to Paul Ehrlich - John Holdren as Obama's right hand in scientific matters. He orchestrated Obama's actions and he instigated falsifications of past temperature data within the leading state research organization NOAA (the US equivalent to the Swedish SMHI). By interfering in historical temperature data and changing temperatures, the false picture of a global warming has been created that has not occurred. The one best known in history for this type of rewriting before Obama was Stalin. However, he did not change temperatures but only erased things in old photographs.

The Globalists wanted to blame Carbon dioxide as a greenhouse gas for the warming. Carbon Dioxide is a strong component in plant growth as it is a major component in their photosynthesis.

On the other hand, not so much noticed are the rising levels of industrial chemicals in the atmosphere such as e.g. sulfur hexafluoride, which has a much wider absorption spectrum than carbon dioxide and thus a greenhouse effect that is 24,000 times higher. In addition, the retention times of these stable compounds in the atmosphere are much longer than for methane and carbon dioxide. But the Globalists don't want us to notice this.

The resources available to society for environmental measures are needed to stop the deforestations of our rainforests, over-fishing and poisoning of the seas, and measures to break the rampant metabolic morbidity caused by the life-threatening industrial foods of the globalists' Big Food and the deadly pills of their Big Pharma. The pursuit of the life-giving carbon dioxide is only about global power and is a diversion to motivate the new global world order and take people's attention away from the real threats to our environment.

Rockefeller is also responsible for the formation of the very influential Bilderberg group whose first chairman was the old Nazi Prince Bernhardt, who also co-founded the neo-colonial environmental organization, the World Wildlife Fund WWF.

David Rockefeller along with Alexander King and Aurelio Peccei are also behind the formation of the lobby organization Club of Rome, where the former Secretary General of the Swedish Red Cross Anders Wijkman since 2012 is a chairman. He advocates Climate Threats and requires legislation for those parts that are non-existent threats. Together with Stefan Löfvén, he wants the Swedish people and other EU members to pay environmental taxes for these. Anders Wijkman was previously also Vice Chairman of the Tällberg Foundation, which is owned by Bo Ekman.

Carbon dioxide emissions have been linked to the most important driving force behind the exaggerated climate threat which the Green Party in Sweden has driven as its cause. So far, this has cost the western world thousands of billions in meaningless costs. For the Swedish taxpayers, the climate threat costs about SEK 4.3 billion annually.

To blame for the climate change is increased solar activity. The activity of the sun is now gradually increasing after the entry of our solar system and the earth into a gigantic plasma field around the local Central Universe, the Central Sun Alcyone in the Pleiadian constellation. The entry took place on December 21-23, in 2012, when our solar system and our planet passed the equatorial plane of our galaxy.

Furthermore, HAARP installations in various parts of the world constitute a major environmental threat. These are also found on Tromsö in Norway and in Kiruna in Sweden, but are not mentioned by any politician.

Next in order are Chemtrails, i.e. toxic emissions into the atmosphere that cause weather changes.

Of course, carbon dioxide emissions affect to a certain extent climate, but to a lesser extent and in the opposite direction than various organizations and politicians have hitherto stated.

Environmental alarms have been the tools of these lobbyists who try to apply a brake to global economic growth, which is the biggest threat to the oligarchs' power. This activity has largely been a failure, which has mostly reflected the economic development in the western world. However, the oligarchs' bankers have been able to enjoy an increasing indebtedness in countries that have been forced to pay these wasted climate billions.

Instead of finding out the facts, some individuals and organizations come up with different tasks to benefit themselves, or to mislead the public.

We want to recommend reading the White House report, a 44-page document from October 22, 2015. The report under the title "National Space Weather Action Plan" clearly shows what the increase in solar activity means for the US, Europe and the world.

Already during the first half of 2016, natural disasters have cost the world approximately $ 70 billion, which is equivalent to about SEK 600 billion.

Then we have not counted the loss of people's lives and suffering.

The entire earth's communication system is largely based on electricity and computer technology today.

Increased solar activity causes disruptions to power grids, computers, satellites, radio and television broadcasts, internet communication etc.

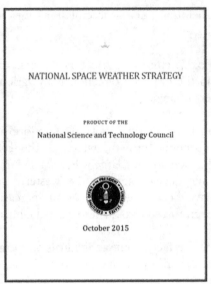

Figure 34. The White House report on increased solar storms (solar activity) and their effects on humans and infrastructure.

Solar storms not only affect the climate itself, but create natural disasters (*earthquakes, volcanic eruptions, storms, floods and droughts*) that destroy the infrastructure and human life of communities.

Increased solar activity means vibratory increase on our planet, affecting all life, including man.

Figure 35. Increased solar activity affects the electromagnetic field of nature and man.

Now that our solar system's sun has entered the giant plasma field around the Central Sun, Alcyone, solar activity will increase significantly. This will affect the climate and infrastructure throughout the world.

Increased solar activity affects nature and man's electromagnetic fields, plasma fields and contributes to an increased awakening of all the negative, constructed, destructive properties that man has created for himself through generations. These will affect man's daily life and future destiny. These qualities are stored in the human subconscious.

Taxpayers cannot be charged for the climate impact that occurs because of increased solar activity and destructive technology such as electric smog, HAARP and Chemtrails created by unscrupulous people who want to destroy life on earth.

### The majority of the political power elite are confabulators, psychopaths and sociopaths

As a confabulator, you come up with different stories, lies, which you later change to something else when you meet resistance. They turn the sails by the wind. We find many among the politicians, government officials and leaders of various organizations.

To be considered a psychopath or sociopath, a person should have three or more of the following characteristics that are said to describe an "antisocial personality disorder".

1. Frequently breaks or tampers with the law.
2. Constantly lies and deceives others.
3. Is impulsive and rarely or never plans in advance.
4. Cares very little about the safety or well-being of others.
5. Tends to be often aggressive, conflict-seeking and using physical violence.
6. Irresponsible, e.g. takes no responsibility for finances or public order.
7. Doesn't feel regret or guilt.
8. Doesn't listen to others who have different opinions.
9. Always blames own failures on others.

The list applies to both sociopaths and psychopaths.

The psychopath suffers from psychopathy, which is a collective term for mental disorders, i.e. such people who are selfish, high-handed, feel superior to others, want constant attention, suffer from delusions of grandeur, have a need for assertion because of inferiority and inner uncertainty.

In general, psychopaths are considered cold, calculating and lack empathy. This allows them to camouflage their disorders and, for example, manage to keep a job or appear completely normal on the surface.

Psychopathy is often a combination of hereditary, inborn, destructive traits and social factors such as childhood trauma.

Psychopaths are to 99% men.

Psychopaths usually search leadership positions in society, where they can control and decide over others.

The sociopath according to the American way of thinking is a product of his surroundings. Poor upbringing, childhood experiences or other difficult experiences can be a contributing cause of a person's altered state of mind.

The psychopath is more calculating and conscious in his behavior, while the sociopath is more unpredictable and chaotic.

In Sweden, the terminology sociopath is questioned and is generally not used in any official context.

If you study the Illuminates' way of acting throughout history, you can see that they are negative, despotic beings who are behind everything that contributes to violence, wars, destructiveness, disintegration between individuals, groups or nations.

# The tools of the Illuminates

Here are some of the tools used by the Illuminates to keep people unaware, with a negative destructive mood, ill and in need of care as much as possible. The idea is that the person with a weak function as slave should live until retirement and then die on his 65th birthday.

Much of what is mentioned below is intended to be used as tools to allow man to live longer with good health. But unfortunately, when it comes to the human intellect, and when used by a mind that lacks soul contact, the intellect becomes a tool for a soulless mind to use for the most destructive purposes only. The result is the same as if the "Devil would interpret the Bible," or the writings of other religions.

Viruses - epidemics of diseases:
They expose groups or nations to epidemics of various diseases (*Swine Flu, Ebola, AIDS and more*).

Vaccinations:
They expose people to harmful vaccines that cause autoimmune diseases and cancer.

Medication:
They manufacture and distribute artificial medicines with severe side effects as results. Many of the side effects require further medication with more side effects and disabilities as a result. According to the pharmaceutical industry, one wants to be able to diagnose all people, and this "disease state" should be medicated. When the medication is started, you can control the course of the disease according to the template, i.e. "nurture" the disease state so that the "disease" persists but the symptoms to some extent cease and where the disease can be further medicated.

The pharmaceutical industry opposes natural harmonious methods:
Authorities are gradually banning herbal medicines that would otherwise benefit human health and well-being. They want to completely ban homeopathic preparations.

Liquidation of Alternative Medicine:
Alternative medicine has been counteracted since the early 1900s. The aim is to keep humans ill but free of symptoms, which benefits the pharmaceutical industry.

Emissions of vaccines:
Emissions of vaccines from aircrafts.

Geoengineering - Chemtrails:
Emissions of thousands (millions) of metric tonnes of harmful nanoparticles of aluminum, strontium, barium etc.

HAARP:
An exotic weapon system designed to damage natural ecosystems, e.g. ionosphere, atmosphere, climate, weather or tectonic systems with the aim of causing damage or destruction to a target population or region on earth or in space.

Smart electricity meters:
Many of these work on microwaves.

Cellphones (4G, 5G):
Mental control, brain control, radiation, brain tumors.

Chipping - mind control:
Artificial impact on the brain with chip implants, 4G and 5G technology, artificial impact on the brain (TMS) and other human monitoring.

Obsession and "New World Order":
Holders of power and people in key positions receive the inspiration they need to launch the "New World Order".

Form of government:
Block politics - the power behind.

## NATO, EU, etc:

As a step on the way to "Global Dictatorship", they want to create large associations that can be more easily centrally controlled, with force if needed, or when needed.

## Immigration:

There is a plan with the increasing immigration. They want to lead the society into a police state and dictatorship.

## Adult education:

Sometimes referendums may be needed, which are best avoided.

## Prohibit demonstrations:

On the way to dictatorship comes a stage where demonstrations will be banned.

## Law enforcement:

If today's conscientious police officers cannot cope with the trend towards dictatorship, then a new type of police must be appointed.

## Acceptance of certain types of crimes:

Fear and duality must be instilled in the population.

## Fluorine:

Fluorine reduces the ability for humans to evolve by adversely affecting the pineal gland (corpus pinealis plexus).

## Harmful foods:

They develop and distribute harmful foods (junk food) and beverages.

## GMOs:

They work to get all agricultural land converted and used for GMO crops where the crops must have genetically built protection against certain pesticides and aluminum. The crops endanger human and animal health and reproductive health.

## Acidification:

The accelerated acidification leaches toxic metal ions to the groundwater. These metal ions end up in our drinking water and are absorbed by the plants and arable crops we eat.

Climate lies - the climate issue:
One wants to create a climate policy framework based on carbon dioxide taxation.

Agenda 21 and Agenda 2030:
The Globalists have formulated these two standards. The contents sound good but the underlying agenda is total control of man.

Ending:
The conclusion briefly mentions some sentences about low frequency music (junk music), fracking (hydraulic cracking), oil extraction, mining industry, toxic heavy metals and chemicals, toxins, religions, economics, media, negative affirmations, schooling, research, libraries, drugs, alcohol , tobacco and drugs, and that nature is medicated through the release of harmful pharmaceuticals through urine, wars and conflicts.

**Viruses - epidemics of diseases**

*"Swine flu"... H1N1 etc...*

Influenza viruses can develop, evolve and change structure. This happens continuously. Influenza viruses can also mutate in larger steps and this occurs in animals. The change can then be so abrupt that people have less resistance to the virus. Some of these types are more contagious and can be spread to humans. Some viruses have also been claimed to skip evolutionary steps, and the change would then be too big to be probable. In these cases, the viruses would be created in laboratory environments. There are also viruses that are patented.

"Swine flu" is a term that refers to different types of swine flu viruses, which can give rise to influenza. It is also experimented with "swine flu virus" where they try to make them more infectious, i.e. more easily transferable to humans. This is done under the guise of researching for better vaccines.

No progress has been done with the old technology of producing flu vaccines since the 1980s. The protective effect is low, side effects occur and the price must be considered unreasonably high.

## Ebola

The last known Ebola epidemic mentioned in the media is the one in West Africa (Guinea, Liberia and Sierra Leone) in 2014. The epidemic is said to have started in a hollow bat-filled tree in Guinea. In order for an infection to spread among people, a bodily fluid e.g. blood from an infected person, must be transferred and come in contact with another person's wound or open skin. The bats then "must" have attacked and perhaps bit people to cause the epidemic to "break out".

Defectors from pharmaceutical companies have said that vaccines against Ebola were tested in the region before the outbreak in 2014. During the year 2014, the "Ebola epidemic" started in West Africa. It was probably a highly questionable vaccine that was used. The WHO stated that the Ebola epidemic had ended also in Sierra Leone in 2015 and doctors without borders as late as 2016 for the whole of West Africa. The vaccine used should now be 100% effective and safe to use.

The United States had no soldiers stationed before the epidemic but during the epidemic about 3000 "aid workers" were stationed in West Africa. The US military is still in Liberia as West Africa is very rich when it comes to exporting diamonds.

## HIV and AIDS

The official idea is that AIDS (Acquired Immune Deficiency Syndrome) started with a monkey in Africa, and that the infection then spread to Africans. A leading personality in the pharmaceutical industry, Robert Gallo, has acknowledged on video that he imported "green monkeys" from Africa to the United States. Gallo wanted to develop a polio vaccine with the help of the monkeys. What he didn't know was that the monkeys brought with them 40 viruses alien to humans, i.e. SV40. These were included in the polio vaccine. Robert Gallo believes that this was a contributing cause of the AIDS, i.e. that it began to cause autoimmune diseases in humans.

AIDS is used to limit childbirth in Africans. It was to be a race-selective disease that would affect Africans.

HIV is not the same as AIDS. HIV (human immunodeficiency virus) does not exist in the way as described in the media. HIV is genes in our immune system that are variable and RNA and proteins are created that respond positively to HIV testing. No HIV virus exists, and therefore also no HIV test works. The tests are not standardized. This means that one can test positive in one country and at the same time negative in another country. No infection comes from outside. Those who were diagnosed HIV positive initially suffered harmful treatments and many people died. Now the treatments are lighter. The doctor should only diagnose and treat, nothing more.

HIV tests respond to certain genetic factors. Africans have a different genetic spectrum and are therefore more often diagnosed HIV positive. This stems from their heritage and background. The "treatment" they then receive is harmful, and turns into a genocide. Therefore, HIV is a race-selective diagnosis.

Pregnant women produce more antibodies as 50% of the fetal genes come from the father. The antibodies are there to protect the fetus. Pregnant women can therefore be tested HIV positive.

Similarly, people infected with malaria, tuberculosis or leprosy can be tested positive. Dirty drinking water and malnutrition can also cause a physical reaction that can give a positive HIV test. Gay people have a larger proportion of certain proteins and this can also result in a positive HIV test. Even an influenza vaccine can provide a positive HIV test, i.e. an in-vaccinated immune system impairment. This immune system impairment may also be drug-related.

The antibodies looked for can thus arise from various reasons, i.e. from something that has lowered the immune system in the person being tested.

HIV is thus a diagnosis and there are no scientific studies that HIV can develop into AIDS. AIDS is a collective name for a variety of symptoms which can be dry cough, high fever, diarrhea for several weeks, 10% weight loss, etc. classic symptoms of malnutrition, tuberculosis and poverty. So AIDS does not exist but is a series of symptoms.

If you want to help Africans, you must help them get out of poverty, malnutrition and make sure they drink clean water. It is also better to cure tuberculosis, leprosy and malaria than to diagnose the condition as HIV-like diseases, i.e. AIDS. As soon as HIV vaccines and AIDS medications begin to be used, the "patient" has surrendered to the pharmaceutical industry, which then controls the patient's health with a lot of medication for a long time that ultimately results in the patient's death. Fear is induced in the population and people are intimidated into various galas for raising money for further research to solve the problem, which never happens.

That AIDS would be sexually transmitted is also a lie - it has never been proven. AIDS medications are basically chemotherapy that lower the immune system, affect the liver, etc., and then the health curve goes down. HIV medication kills people and causes AIDS symptoms.

## Vaccinations

When you get vaccinated, an antigen is injected. It is a body-alien substance that triggers a response in the immune system as it enters the organism. The antigen may be a living but weakened pathogen or an inactivated or killed pathogen. The reaction leads to the formation of antibodies and the recruitment of white blood cells that attack the antigen. The immune system is updated which then gains a defense against the disease-causing factor, e.g. bacteria, viruses or parasites.

But is this completely true?

In addition to the antigen itself that is to build up resistance to a disease, there are toxic adjuvants (reinforcing agents), and preservatives as well as other questionable ingredients.

Adjuvants added to the vaccine are often aluminum salts, e.g. aluminum phosphate, aluminum hydroxide or potassium aluminum sulfate. Aluminum is a well-known poison for the nervous system. Aluminum is stored in the human brain and its concentration increases with age. At the age of 70, a pathological concentration of aluminum may have been reached. Experimental research clearly shows that aluminum adjuvants have the potential to induce severe immunological malfunctions in humans, i.e. the immune system attacks its own tissues. Aluminum has been associated with three types of dementia which are Alzheimer's disease, Parkinson's dementia and dialysis dementia. Aluminum releases free radicals and reduces fats in the brain. Aluminum can also affect the parathyroid glands and lead to abnormal bone loss. Excessive concentration of aluminum can lead to impaired memory, concentration difficulties, gastrointestinal disorders, skin rashes and nausea.

Thus, with the first polio vaccine, SV40 followed. This is a virus that can cause cancer, as many other viruses do. SV40 was used in polio vaccines until 1963. Even today, SV40 can be found in brain, bone and lung tumors. Our vaccines are contaminated with viruses.

Robert Gallo's research group also experimented with other cancer-causing viruses similar to the SV40 and brought forth mutant ones that caused AIDS (white blood cell dysfunction), leukemia, lymphoma, sarcoma that caused the final death of cats, mice, chickens and humans. These were given in the presence of other slightly mutated retrovirus contaminants. An epidemic of cancer began to emerge. In 1960 they wanted to vaccinate against cancer. It only got worse.

Various viruses were radiated and they hoped that something better would be the result. Instead, they developed the ultimate cancer-causing vaccine that could kill a human in 28 days. Until 1971, deadly viruses were created that caused, among other things, Adenovirus, Leukemia, Lymphatic Leukemia, Sarcoma, Herpes Simplex, Hodgin's Disease, Herpes Virus, Influenza, Kuru, Lymphoma, Meningitis, Malignant Lymphoma. Thus, SV40 and similar viruses that are injected together with prolonged radiation e.g. X-rays cause cancer and death.

Alien to human viruses together with radiation causes cancer.

If we inject an influenza vaccine, then a dormant virus that we have in our body could bloom and activate. Viruses can be transmitted through body fluids such as blood, urine, saliva, breast milk, tears, semen and vaginal fluids and not through simple body contact.

Here comes a list of what a modern vaccine can contain of body foreign substances.

Rubella:
- various human cells from aborted fetuses

Diphtheria, tetanus, whooping cough:
- washed red blood cells from sheep

Smallpox:
- vesicle fluids from calfskin

Influenza vaccine:
- embryonic fluids from chicken

Chicken-pox:
- embryonic cells from guinea pigs, bovine serum, human blood albumin, various aborted fetal cells.

Hepatitus A:
- different cells from aborted fetuses

Measles, mumps, rubella, chicken pox (combined):
- human albumin, human various cells from aborted fetal tissues, bovine serum, chicken fetuses.

Japanese encephalite:
- serum, proteins from mice.

Rubella for adults and Hepatitis B vaccine:
- produces chronic arthritis that lasts for at least one year. Causes autoimmune diseases.

Hepatitis B and Influenza Vaccine:
- Guillain-Barré syndrome.

Gardasil has given rise to some Guillain-Barré syndromes.

Of course, with these vaccines, body foreign viruses come along. The American doctor Tent says that we now have an expanding autoimmune epidemic.

Immunization has been erroneously mistaken for vaccine.

Immunization is caused by natural exposure to various proteins that challenge our immune system.

Vaccines cause hypersensitive reactions including allergies, autoimmune diseases, asthma and cancer can be triggered.

Viruses, wild or combined for vaccines can silently trigger autoimmune diseases in the central nervous system. Aborted fetuses have been used to induce rubella, measles, mumps, rabies, polio, smallpox, hepatitis A, chickenpox, vaccines against herpes zoster. Every time someone uses a vaccine with original human cells, you get DNA and protein structures from human aborted fetuses. This leads to having foreign DNA in the bloodstream. The body will attack this. This is called autoimmune disease. Dr.

Tent claims that Sweden has sent aborted fetuses to the US for the vaccine industry.

Our immune system is weakened by e.g. antibiotics, given blood transfusion, vaccination, certain medications, surgery, poisoned food, water and air, stress, chemicals, fear, certain working environments etc. We must have a good immune system or a virus can be activated.

Brain tumors and cancers can appear long after a vaccine has been given. With this flora of various foreign viruses, parts of virus, mutated variants that man carries, more and more people will get autoimmune diseases, i.e. the body's defense attacks its own body. Cancer will also increase.

Also in Sweden there is a strong lobby that wants compulsory vaccinations in the population to release this problem at a larger scale. It is also no wonder that it has been "decided" at the parliamentary level that mobile radiation is not dangerous. Proper radiation in combination with the above should be a fully adequate cocktail to create an avalanche of bad immune systems with autoimmune diseases and topped with an avalanche of cancer.

Furthermore, there is a preservative in several vaccines called thiomersal, i.e. methyl mercury. Methyl mercury can induce damage to the central nervous system, lower the immune system, cause stomach problems and worsen liver detoxification. Furthermore, the mobility of mercury in the body is increased by mobile phone radiation and Wifi. In vaccines for children there is instead the preservative phenoxyethanol. It is a well-known allergen and a probable neurotoxin.

In a study of child vaccine was found lead, iron, titanium, aluminum, tungsten, chromium, nickel, copper and tin. The researchers have discussed the consequences of this and found "that mineral particles are foreign to the organism and for this reason they will induce an inflammatory reaction. These substances can enter the cell nucleus and interact with its DNA".

In a previous study by Dr. Tore Persson at KI (Karolinska Institutet) in collaboration with KTH (Royal Institute of Technology) was found in Pandemrix both arsenic and tin.

The contents in vaccines (including tissue proteins) can cause encephalitis in infants. This may occur immediately or after vaccination of infants. They have not fully developed their myelination of their nervous system, which has taken place fully in their 20s. Encephalitis can manifest itself with various horrible symptoms when the child's nervous system is attacked. There are voices that say that sudden infant death has to do with vaccination. The US court has now stated that multi vaccination of infants can lead to sudden infant death. One study also shows that repeated vaccination against influenza in women can cause miscarriage, but researchers believe that more research is needed before this can be determined with greater certainty.

Some believe that the childhood diseases that the health care vaccinates against were reduced by about 95% before the 1950s before the vaccination programs started. The reason was that the standard of living was raised in the West with better sanitary conditions, nutritional intake and no starvation. Furthermore, the housing conditions were better and the houses less draughty.

We end this section with a few words by the internationally recognized epidemiologist Lars Olof Kallings: "Everyone seems to have lost judgment". He makes the statement in the Swedish paper "Svenska Dagbladet" and this regards the Swedish mass vaccination against "swine flu".

Today, the vaccines are approved centrally in the EU and the Swedish Medicines Agency's judgment of this is based on the documentation available if there is any benefit with the vaccine. Thus, the Swedish Medicines Agency does not make its own tests - but relies "blindly" on what is written, only it is done correctly.


## Medication

If we feel ill or have a temporary illness, the body is phenomenal in restoring the balance of the body. If we have an internal imbalance due to the law of karma (fate) which makes us continue on a theme in our lives that eventually culminates in a physical state of symptoms or illness, then it is an inner deep-rooted imbalance that we must rebalance. Since diseases have a big underlying basis, we may need help to restore balance. In this state, we have often been in a state of powerlessness and we need someone who "gnostics" us and prescribes what we should do to restore balance. An individual who is familiar with the body's multi-dimensional structure and clearly can see the reason behind our condition can help us restore balance. This knowledge is lacking in today's school medical care. Therefore, it is dedicated to diagnosis instead. Diagnosis means "not knowing", i.e. two people who don't know; the doctor and the patient.

The school medicine used is chemical laboratory-derived preparations which in most cases lack a natural hologram created by nature. When a human unbalanced mind develops a medicine on an intellectual way, the medication gets an artificial imprint that is both alienating and hostile. The body then does everything to defend itself against the attack. These school medicines are thus suitable as emergency medicines, and the real cause should be adjusted with the help of energy medicine by a competent health care provider.

The body protects itself against a school medical attack as follows:
When a medical school medication is taken by a patient, side effects occur. In the book "FASS" which is the Swedish doctors' Bible, the side effects are described. It is not uncommon for a drug to have about 80 side effects. School medicine is poison, and doctors should be very restrictive with prescribing medications.

The placebo effect, i.e. the belief that a remedy helps should not be detract from either. It can be up to 50% of a drug's effect. The placebo effect along with the body's own healing ability may be sufficient for the body to regain balance. After all, it is still only the body that can heal itself, or rather the body's various dimensional radiation fields.

The National Board of Health estimates that "almost 6.5 million people took at least one prescribed medicine in 2016. This corresponds to about 66 percent of the population. Most users are found in the older age groups. Paracetamol, Omeprazole and Penicillin V are the most used prescription drugs that are used by most patients. Between 2006 and 2016, the proportion of patients taking at least one prescription for Penicillin has decreased while the corresponding figure for ADHD drugs has increased."

Paracetamol is a pain relieving substance found in Citodon, Alvedon and Panodil. It breaks down in the liver like all prescription drugs. High doses cause liver cells to break down and continuous use does the same. Chronic abuse in combination with alcohol makes it all worse - you can die from it.

Common side effects are many and more or less noticeable and the synergy of different drugs should make the list even more severe, even if you try to avoid it.

One side effect can be that you use more drugs to fight side effects, then even more side effects appear, etc. The result is a degenerative health state with an impaired immune system, which leaves the body open for awakening of body-alien latent viruses. We get autoimmune diseases or cancer.

Pharmaceutical companies are strongly lobbying for prescription drugs as they make money from this. Doctors and government are targeted. In a review by the magazine Aftonbladet, 1200 doctors received in average SEK 20,000 from the pharmaceutical industry in 2015. In 2015, 34,176 doctors worked in Sweden and abroad. How much these doctors received is not included in the Aftonbladet's study. Of course, this dependency ratio increases prescriptions.

The prescription of antidepressants is increasing in Sweden. This is a sign of that the Swedish population is generally feeling worse. Today, over 10% of Sweden's population takes antidepressant drugs, and the increase is constantly increasing. The increase is highest in young girls and the intake is highest in women.

If you look at countries like the United States, the sales of antidepressants has reached an even higher percentage.

Psychoactive drugs are chemical substances that affect the brain function and cause changes in behavior, mood, perception and consciousness. Examples of these are sedative hypnotic drugs and anxiolytics, antipsychotics, antidepressants, mood stabilizers, narcotic analgesics, psychomotor stimulants, psychedelics and hallucinogens.

Seen from a development point of view, it is completely reprehensible to medicate with psychoactive drugs. It should only be done in urgent cases and everything must be done to get the underlying karmic situation sorted out - to be balanced. That man is feeling bad is an acute sign of imbalance that needs to be addressed. Basically, psychiatry has never cured a single patient.

A world organization behind large pharmaceutical companies lobbies to make it possible to make a diagnosis for all normal people, a diagnosis that can be medicated. The goal is to be able to reprogram man into a "World Citizen", i.e. a person adapted to the "New World Order". In the 1950s, the first psychiatric drugs came and it was now possible to take to the work on a larger scale.

Now, school students were also targeted. Thus, there is a tendency to medicate problems that aren't medical. By creating more named diseases, a market for more drugs is created. The phenomenon is called disease mongering. ADHD (attention deficit hyperactivity disorder) is one example of this. By medicating small doses of amphetamine, it should be easier for these individuals to concentrate. Amphetamine is a central stimulant and a narcotic drug. The use of this drug hinders expanded consciousness development, and stops short or long-term development of expanded consciousness development (see the heading below "Psychoactive drugs and narcotics from a consciousness perspective ").

As long as man uses a distorted and perverted intellect to design school medicines that are not produced by nature, but in a disharmonious laboratory, the school medicines will of course also have a mind distorting effect - where the problem to the individual in a wider perspective becomes increasingly severe.

According to the "Citizens Commission on Human Rights" (CCHR), 15,000 people internationally lobby politicians at all levels. Anti-depressants in 2015 cost internationally SEK 131 billion and 539,000 die prematurely of psychiatric drugs. CCHR believes that 80% instead would have gained better health with placebo.

In the clinical trials of psychotropics, the documentation can be given a more positive inclination in several stages. The clinical trials are done by psychiatrists and these are linked to the pharmaceutical companies. Many believe that this has not much to do with science - but more with marketing. One can ask where the biochemical trials are in the documentation; where is the research; where is the evidence? Some psychiatrists believe that these evidences don't exist. The scientific testing does not exist but clinical tests have been carried out with the drugs instead. The drugs should be tested for toxicity, efficiency and comparison with placebo. This approach is subjective and full of opportunities for manipulation. In many ways the documentation can be angled. The study can also be influenced in a certain direction. It is possible to manipulate data. The people who are tested can deviate from going through all tests and these people can simply be excluded from the documentation. If e.g. 100 people are tested and 40 don't follow through, then 30 can show a positive response and the remaining 30 none at all. The test could then claim that 50% showed a positive response. If people after taking part in the trial of e.g. antidepressant get suicidal thoughts, or commit suicide, this can be removed from the trial by excluding this check option in the documentation. A clinical trial of psychoactive drugs may take between 4 and 8 weeks. It can therefore be short-term studies. In the long run, you know nothing. In this way, a psychoactive drug can be approved which in the short term may only relieve the psychotic symptoms one or two percent better than sugar pills, i.e. placebo.

After a subjective assessment, the drug may be out on the market. The subjective assessment can be further enhanced by the fact that doctors at the FDA or the Swedish Equivalent are also linked to the pharmaceutical industry in one way or another. If 6 out of 10 are positive to an approval, the drug can be approved.

Thus, the effects of the drug aren't studied. These are tested on the population and show up directly or after a certain time, after maybe 1, 2 or 3 years. Here suicides can show up.

According to the National Board of Health, the prescription of ADHD medicine is increasing and more and more young people are taking antidepressants.

According to the Public Health Authority, suicide among young people in Sweden is increasing. Depression increases suicide risk 15-20 times. Affected professional groups are farmers, doctors, veterinarians, nurses and dentists. Sweden is above the average suicide rate in the world with 18.7 suicides in 100,000 inhabitants.

In the US, suicides are increasing among whites and American Indians.

One may wonder why people don't recover after taking prescribed synthetic drugs but need to eat them throughout life. Isn't the meaning to be healed by them? At the same time, the pharmaceutical industry is flourishing.

### Psychoactive drugs and narcotics from a consciousness perspective

We at the AIC want to inform everyone about the danger in using psychoactive drugs, both legal and illegal. We also want to warn against narcotic drugs and modified molecules that have not yet become illegal.

We see that especially young people are in the danger zone of using many of the drugs available on the market, where accessibility is great through several internet sites, especially now when unemployment is high and the belief in the future is weak.

It is said that many of these drugs give spiritual experiences and higher multidimensional consciousness. A higher multidimensional consciousness will definitely not be the result. Instead, drugs end all further human consciousness evolvement.

How can people believe that e.g. heroin, opium, cocaine, amphetamine, LSD, peyote, ayahuasca, hashish, cannabis, tablets etc. could raise the consciousness in the user to a higher qualitative multi-dimensional level?

Many people think that there are easy ways to raise their consciousness - or that they don't have to do anything at all.

This is where the forces of darkness come in and these lurk everywhere in society, without people knowing it.

A higher qualitative multidimensional quantum consciousness is achieved through constant training of consciousness through a special meditation program. This specific meditation training takes place over a long period of time and has the task of releasing and neutralize at a reasonable pace all the stored negative preconceived notions that the individual has accumulated over thousands of years of incarnations (births) on this planet. There is no other way to expand consciousness than this form of training, which requires focus, self-control and perseverance as well as the genuine desire to free oneself from all the illusions that people have created for themselves over many thousands of years.

To think that drugs can achieve the same thing is naive.

The psychedelic drug does the following to its victim, and in most cases it happens unconsciously. First, it can give a high, i.e. an experience, e.g. a feeling or a view into the lower qualitative part of the parallel world, the astral world.

The visions into the astral (parallel) world are completely connected to the user i.e. the victim. If you see angels or demons, the devil or Jesus, different colors, patterns, or whatever it may be, this is entirely linked to the victim's inner composition of preconceived opinions, attitudes, worldviews, self-knowledge, relationship to one's own family, one's country, the conflicts that take place in one's country, i.e. all that is connected to one's life, i.e. one's own inner essence, being. You will never get any other experience. Some believe during the high that they have a higher consciousness or that it persists afterwards. Of course, an experience can give a certain type of information, but it is completely colored by one's own being, one's own composition, etc., which is an illusion, i.e. completely individual. Some hear voices telling them that they are chosen to help humanity, while they cannot even help themselves.

What happens is that one weakens the brain's electromagnetic protection against astral sensations, energies, beings, while still retaining all individual composition, i.e. problems, which have not been eliminated through proper meditation. This weakening of one's electromagnetic protection is of course not good.

Outside in the parallel world, there are innumerable subtle (astral) beings, and the least developed beings are entirely connected to our 3D physical world, i.e. murderers, criminals, drug addicts, power-prone individuals - yes, all those beings who's most dominant traits are of a lower qualitative nature.

When our electromagnetic protection is weakened or gradually becomes so, then these lower qualitative astral entities go in and dig their claws into their victims. In most cases, this is done without the knowledge of the individual. If the person in question has been using drugs for many years, the negative impact can be very strong, without the individual knowing anything at all about it. In fact, the individual may believe that he has a higher consciousness, since he feels so and receives information, or in some cases also hear voices talking about what he should do, voices that are initially friendly but which after a while begin to threaten the individual which it uses as its instrument, tool for its purpose. This occurs when the astral being's influence is so established that the individual begins to fully trust the contact. This is called obsession. That this would exist is denied by most psychologists or psychiatrists, unfortunately. In psychiatry, obsession is called schizophrenia, which is believed to be possible to cure. The voice may disappear but the demon is left.

Lower qualitative astral beings can enter already during the victim's first high. When you haven't got rid of inner lower experiences and structures through the right meditation and guidance, these structures within will resonate with similar structures in the parallel world, in the astral field of the earth. This always happens, but if you take drugs then the impact becomes much stronger and open, and the victim usually denies this categorically, as a self-deceit, and believes in it.

Drugs put an end - completely - to all further consciousness evolvement. In order to correct this type of blunder, many incarnations (rebirths) may be required just to figure out this little simple blunder that unfortunately was made. If you have entered the drug misery, you may need hundreds of incarnations if you at all are allowed to incarnate more here on earth; because if you have degenerated enough consciously, there are no parents on this planet who can commit to give birth to such a being. If things have gone too far, the child will already at an early age behave non-socially, i.e. can bite, tear down wallpapers, and be pretty much an unrestrained wreck. These worst children are rarely born, because no parents can handle them.

Think for yourself! We have lived here for many thousands of years during countless incarnations and some have lived here for more than 10,000 years. Over that time, an individual accumulates experiences that are also part of the meaning of our lives - experiences that ultimately bring consciousness. These experiences provide programming, skills to our energy structure. In the average individual there is so much mind matter programming stored that everything in our world becomes illusion, i.e. an individual reality. We all have different realities, because we reason emotionally different in different situations. We have created our own reality, i.e., the situation in which we have incarnated and which is now the sum of everything we have gone through. To this we can add all the indoctrination that we are exposed to in our new lives from our parents, siblings, relatives and others in the community which includes schools, authorities, the media and others. How would we know who we are? How can we free ourselves from all confinement, bondage unless a higher-evolved (quantum-conscious) teacher shows us the way out of our confusion?

There is a reason for why we have our electromagnetic protection in the brain. It is because we shouldn't become tools and end up in the claws of lower qualitative astral beings. The 4D lower qualitative astral beings who are closest to our three-dimensional (3D) world want to satisfy their own shortcomings through their victims, since the victims have a physical body which the possessing astral being has not.

A drug thus opens the door to a distorted astral world that one has created for himself. The advice is to keep the door closed and work off all own programming. Don't go down in the swamp of drugs. Drug use leads to passivity, addiction, degeneration, crimes, desperation and ultimately to death. All the promises that old and some new drugs would give a higher consciousness are completely wrong. We hope that we have made this clear here now when we have mentioned that all people must work off their own illusory mind programming (karma) before we can attain a higher qualitative consciousness, quantum consciousness.

Instead, train your consciousness, work off all your programming that keeps you in this world, and then open your consciousness to a higher level. Then you have become a Master in life and can decide for yourself if you want to be born back to earth, or live on a slightly higher dimensional level - but you choose yourself and take command of your life - as all great Teachers who have lived on earth have done and advocated. They have just as we, strongly discouraged from all drug use, and have argued that these put an end to all further human development.

Many have experienced near-death experiences. Such an experience is a direct indication of what world the individual ends up in after his earthly life. How do you want your life to be after your earthly life - and later in coming incarnations?

Make the decision in your life and start training for a genuine consciousness and an ethical-moral life. Stay totally away from all drugs! There are no shortcuts!

The choice is yours!

If you know that you have been taking drugs for a while and want to change your life, then you should. But at the same time, you must be aware of that influences from the lower regions of the astral plane can be a direct obstacle to your development. In these cases, of course, you must do your best to evolve, and additional protection programs and information may be needed to reduce the influences from the negative forces.

## The pharmaceutical industry counteracts natural harmonious methods

They want to exclude the possibility for man to recover in a natural way, i.e. with natural harmonic herbs.

Medicinal plants have been used by man throughout history. The Egyptian papyrus scroll "Papyrus Ebers" (1550 BC) describes how to "cure" about 800 ailments. In addition, there are 700 domestic and foreign herbal drugs included. Medicinal plants should have been used in most cultures that exist on earth.

Now the use of medicinal plants has been made more difficult and also to obtain for today's man. The use of natural remedies and natural products has gradually being banned.

Here is a decision that reduces the freedom of choice for man, but which financially benefits the pharmaceutical industry.

Traditional herbal medicine products sold today in the EU must be licensed. The directive was established in 2004 and became effective on 30 April 2011. Thereafter all the herbs must be approved by the Swedish Medicines Agency. The directive is called "The Traditional Herbal Medicinal Products Directive (THMPD)".

After that date a lot of herbal medicine products disappeared from the market.

To get herbal medicine approved is a costly procedure. First, the herbs must undergo testing. They are to be tested clinically to see if they are safe and effective. The herbs must then be approved by the Swedish Medical Products Agency, and here mainly doctors and pharmacists work. These have a schooling that is colored by the same theme, i.e. intellectually school medical. When consciousness is raised in the country, many will wish that also physicists and biochemists could work there as well. Man is multidimensional and not a chemical laboratory.

To the small company that wants to still sell their herbal medicines, it is costly first when it comes to the clinical testing and secondly when it comes to the fee to the Swedish Medicines Agency. An analysis can cost almost half a million Swedish Crowns. Thereafter, an annual fee of SEK 15,000 per product must be paid to the Swedish Medicines Agency.

People have to grow their own herbs at home instead.

Furthermore, in the media much derogatory information is written about herbs, but school medicine and psycho-drugs on the other hand are often criticized in a positive way. To the normal individual, what is written in the established media often appears as "carved in stone", i.e. 100% true.

The authorities take the liberty of deciding for us what is good for us when we feel bad. This is a violation against human rights. Not being able to use the herbs of nature as a private person is to limit the human freedom and also declare false the cultural heritage that we have gained from thousands of years of development.

It is man himself who recovers from an illness, never a medicine. A medicine can eliminate a symptom, but can never improve the causal karmic situation that man has created for himself. To claim this is to deceive man.

Even the enormous positive power of the placebo effect in the use of herbal medicines is denied to man.

Homeopathic preparations are completely prohibited. It is believed that it is absurd to call something so diluted a medicine compared to evidence-based medicine. It is claimed it has no effect. However, since the clinical trials are short and don't span several years, it is difficult to see any positive effects. The contemporary man now carries so much environmental toxins that the effects of homeopathic preparations become even more difficult to see, especially in the short term.

The annual report from the "U.S. National Poison Data System" shows that there are no deaths linked to food supplements in the United States. This shows that the supplements are safe to use. This applies to multivitamin preparations, vitamin B, vitamins A, C, D and E and all other vitamins.

Furthermore, there were no deaths due to amino acids or herbal products. This means no deaths because of Echinacea, ginkgo biloba, ginseng, kava, St. John's wort, valerian, Asian medicine, Ayurvedic medicine or others from the plant kingdom. There were no deaths from creatine, blue-green algae, glucosamine, chondroitin, melatonin or other homeopathic medications.

There were also no deaths in 2008 from mineral supplements. There were no deaths because of calcium, magnesium, chromium, zinc, colloidal silver, selenium, iron or multimineral supplements. Two children were reported to have died as a result of the medical use of sodium bicarbonate.

On the other hand, it is estimated that approximately 100,000 Americans die each year from prescribed prescriptions, but probably many-fold. The deaths have been based on the side effects of the medication, i.e. no mistakes, overdoses or other uses.

The doings of healthcare not many dare to question, but the alternative methods that can extend and save healthcare from crashing are being persecuted by our authorities.

If dietary supplements or alternative treatments would give rise to a single death, our authorities would have immediately moved out, tightened legislation and it had been dealt with quickly and in the media we had read about it the day after on the first page with big headlines. The fact that real food, supplements and alternative medicine make thousands of healthy and drug-free they don't speak of.

In 2016, half of all Americans ate supplements. If all some 160 million Americans who take supplements every day take one tablet a day, there will be 60 billion doses annually. If they take 3-4 pills, which most people do, the number becomes astronomical. No deaths.

*One can expect that the reporting of side effects to the FDA from school medicine is only 1 percent of the actual number.*

But the relationship between alternative medicine and school medicine is really interesting and then you can also understand how and why the media is manipulated.

One may also wonder why Chinese medicine and Ayurvedic medicine should be banned (zero deaths) in the EU, as well as virtually all herbal preparations and homeopathic remedies.

At the same time, unhealthy medicines and vaccines are sold in huge quantities. In particular, psychiatric antipsychotic drugs reap huge amounts of deaths each year. At the same time as the "disease state" is being oppressed, the patients are getting obesity, diabetes and premature death. Several pharmaceutical companies have been sued for billions.

## Abolishment of Alternative Medicine

Under the headings above, we can pretty much see where society stand today in terms of the preservation of human diseases, but at the same time, as far as possible, the removal of the symptoms. From where does this agenda stem?

At the end of the 1800s and in the early 1900s, there were homeopaths, osteopaths, chiropractors, naturopaths, acupuncturists, healers, electro-medicists and allopaths. The allopaths are today's traditionally school-medically trained physicians. These treat a body symptom with the opposite. Constipation is counteracted by laxatives etc. They mainly used bloodletting, toxic minerals and surgery. The allopaths did this instead of stimulating the body to self-healing, i.e. correct the imbalance in the body.

All of the above disciplines existed simultaneously. The pharmaceutical companies then hired a certain Abraham Flexner to travel across the country, i.e. USA, to do an inventory of schools that taught medicine where there were people who used and prescribed allopathic drugs. Flexner then left the list to

Carnegie and Rockefeller. After that, the allopathic medical schools were given free access to money. The laws were changed and only those who prescribed medical medicines were allowed to practice medicine.

From 1910 to 1935, half of the health care schools disappeared. Research money has ever since flowed to the allopathic medical school discipline and has been ongoing for more than 100 years. The reason has been economic and political, and the development has reached here with the help of legislation and drug money. All competing disciplines except for allopathy were called quackery.

They wanted to "carve in stone" that everything in the human body is the result of material interactions, including human consciousness, soul and mind. This can make money and control people.

The guidelines were written down in what came to be called "The Flexner Report". It was spread throughout the world and is now the world's school medical starting point. Pharmaceutical school medicine could now flourish without hindrance and the result we can see today. Man's symptoms are treated, but man's inherent imbalances that create these have increased, i.e. we are sicker today than ever. We take our imbalances into future incarnations. Today's doctors know very little about nutrients, natural treatments and nothing about man's controlling energy system.

The Flexner Report was published in 1910. Alternative medicine has since been fought worldwide.

Examples of counteracted alternative medicine include Dr. Royal Raymond Rife's research, which is counteracted even today. He was most active in his field of research in the 1920s and onwards (1888-1971). He studied bacteria with his own designed extremely magnifying microscope. He exposed bacteria to different electric frequencies until he found the frequency that killed the microorganism (MOR, mortality oscillatory rate). He could see the progress in real time. He could kill bacteria without damaging the body tissues. He found MOR for bacteria and even viruses. He found the frequencies that harmonize with the body's healthy tissues and organs. He cured 16 incurable cancer patients.

Dr. Raymond Rife's research is still today classified as quackery but is allowed to be used on animals. Dr. Raymond Rife was discouraged throughout his life by the school medical pharmaceutical establishment. His activities were stopped by the authorities and his coworkers were murdered. Himself he became an alcoholic. You can clearly see who rules the world - is it GOD or the DEVIL?

In 2005, Karolinska Institutet received a private donation of SEK 43 million to study acupuncture, herbal medicine, chiropractic and meditation and how these could be integrated into health care. The work was not carried out. The money was diverted. The researchers completely lacked alternative medicine knowledge.

On January 1, 2015, a law was passes that would increase patients' influence and choice in care. Since nothing happened they wanted to go a step further. In April 2017, the Swedish Ministry of Social Affairs initiated an investigation to help increase contacts and understanding between the established care and the care that is outside the established care. The purpose is to increase patient safety and the patients' right to choose the care and treatment they want. It may be a care that is alternative, complementary and integrative medicine, even if such care is not funded by the general public. Evidence-based information is sought about the effects of the methods. A patient shall be given information by the caregiver and be able to choose between care providers.

This is one of several attempts, and this is now taking place in Swedish health care. With the knowledge and orientation held by today's caregivers, it is all doomed to fail. "A good idea" it may seem, but the intention is another.

When the so-called investigation is finished, the conclusion will be as today's investigators lack knowledge in the field that no alternative medicine treatments work. If any form of treatment proves to be good, it will only be allowed to be performed by a legitimate doctor who has no insight into how the method or the whole work. As a patient, you will not be able to get "an informed choice of caregivers", as only medical knowledge will be offered. The result will be that the alternative medicine is depreciated again. An opening to a change has been set, but the result is already decided.

They want to collaborate with the Karolinska Institutet's Osher center, which ruined its previous chance due to ignorance and unwillingness. Sweden's Patient Safety Act already has limitations, and they want to again investigate whether or not mental illness should also be included there - i.e. not be allowed to be treated by a non-healthcare professional.

*The mental illnesses that are now expanding have not been treated at all by medical science. With today's medication, the growing avalanche of mental illnesses is pushed to the future.*

*The problems stem to a 100% from man's inherent karmic computer program - something today's healthcare doesn't know anything about at all.*

<u>Every service user (patient) must do all they can to enforce their choice of care within the framework of reasonableness - that is the service user's right!</u>

## Air releases of vaccines

During the 1990s, animals began to be vaccinated against rabies on a large scale. Up to now, in Texas, millions of vaccination baits have been released for animals to eat. This has also taken place from the air. The program continues today in 2017. The vaccines are embedded in fish oil and draped with crumbs of fishmeal. People are urged not to touch these baits.

In 2012, live rabies vaccine was released from the air. Rabies cases increased in number and accelerated and in 2015 it was reported that a new type of rabies had been found. At the same time it is officially stated that the number of rabies cases is decreasing. In any case, by tricking animals into eating and consuming rabies-like weakened virus versions, their immune system will decline. These animals will have a bigger tendency to develop various viral diseases, some certainly similar to rabies. The result of this type of vaccination we will certainly get in the coming years.

From 2014 to 2016, an increase in animals tested positive to rabies was reported to have increased from 4.8% to 12.8% in Canada.

## Geoengineering - Chemtrails

Figure 36. Are these condensation trails from aircrafts or chemtrails?

Chemtrails are the emissions of thousands (millions) of tonnes of harmful nanoparticles of alumina, strontium, barium, arsenic, lead, mycoplasma etc. The main ingredients are aluminum and barium. Chemtrailing, i.e. the spraying of these chemicals began in the 1980s and continues more intensively today.

These chemtrails are dangerous emissions of chemicals into the atmosphere. This is done via aircrafts and the emissions poison people, animals and nature and assist the US military in their warfare called weather modification. This approach means that one can control weather with more rainfall in some areas on the globe, while drought occurs elsewhere in the world.

Chemtrails are not ordinary condensation trails, but rather the deliberate spread of chemicals for primarily military purposes. *"This is devilish and will lead to a public health disaster."*

In Sweden, Chemtrails are dismissed as conspiracy theories.

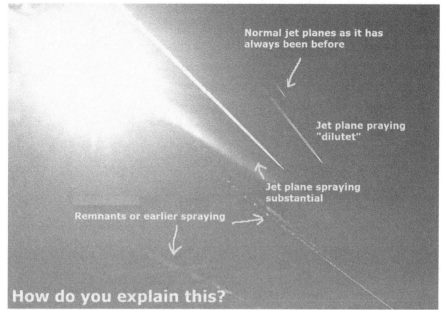

Figure 37: "[3] In Europe and Sweden, there are partly NATO planes that release these harmful substances over us. The rest is handled by some commercial civilian airlines or private weather manipulation companies. The Swedish government obviously allows this over its own territory".

Figure 38. This is what the inside may look like in a test aircraft. Similar tanks can also be filled with chemtrail gas.

---

[3] http://chemtrails-sverige.blogspot.se/

227

How can we allow NATO planes in Swedish airspace when we accuse Russia of war threats as soon as a Russian fighter plane appears near Sweden?

As far as we know, the Swedish people have not yet voted for NATO membership.

Figure 39. Chemtrails at the Onsala Church in Kungsbacka community, Sweden, 30th of June in 2015 at. 11.30. At 15.00 the trails were expanded by the wind.

Areas in Sweden that are mainly sprayed are Skåne, the West Coast and Sweden's most densely populated areas. Spraying is ongoing. These pollutants increase the incidence of respiratory diseases, and other serious diseases.

When you put together all the pieces of the puzzle it becomes very clear that what you see in the sky is something extremely devilish that is done to humanity.

This scenario is ongoing not only in the US and Europe, but elsewhere in the world as well. People really need to know what they are exposed to. Elected politicians must take responsibility for the health and well-being of their people and not hide their heads in the sand, whether they are aware or not of what is happening.

Figure 40. It is easier to hide the head in the sand than take responsibility.

"Chemtrails" is not a scientific name of these poisonous emissions, but the term was used in one of the United States Air Force manuals in the early 1990s for aviation students.

The various toxic substances that are spread are used for a variety of purposes: *defensive or offensive weapons, improved communications, but also impaired communications "disruptions", as well as experiments with humans.*

Chemtrails block sunlight from coming down to earth, but at the same time, the heat below the chemtrails is kept. You can create different weather scenarios. Initially, the purpose of chemtrails was to create drought or to stop a storm in an area. By chemtrailing with aluminum and barium and then allowing this fog to heat, a storm can develop faster and become more violent. Now weather in a large scale can be controlled and also of an entire continent.

When the relative humidity is about 25-40% and the fog trails after the aircraft remain, they are definitely chemtrails. If they were condensation trails, the trails would dissolve within a minute. After chemtrailing it starts to get foggy. The chemtrails add moisture from the air and can develop into clouds. The weather can get overcast. If there is a lot of humidity in the air, it can start raining.

With the help of HAARP (see the next heading below) you can radiate heat into the chemtrails. You can load heat into or extract heat from the atmosphere, i.e. control weather. You can sell different types of weather to customers, i.e. countries. You can use different weathers in warfare or expose different countries to inconveniences. You can let it rain in one area and create drought in another.

These chemicals rain down on the ground or in the sea and there are large amounts of it. Because the size of the particles is so small, they can pass straight through the skin and into the body. Furthermore, we get these through the drinking water and inhalation. The effects of the chemicals are starting to take effect now. They are found in our drinking water and adversely affect agriculture and forestry.

In plants, aluminum reduces root development, root respiration, decreases water uptake, reduces the function in the root plasma membrane, affects the transport and metabolism of essential nutrients. The absorption decreases in phosphorus, calcium, magnesium and iron, and especially calcium in wheat. Photosynthesis decreases. Water uptake is often affected but not always. Aluminum is stored to varying degrees in plants and trees. Secondary problems are trees that are more susceptible to fungus and insect infestation, and that the trees become less resistant to storm attacks, more susceptible to frost and drought. Today, groundwater contains the double amount of aluminum than 10 years ago.

Along with a low soil pH, the toxicity of aluminum is increased. There are voices saying that some forests on earth are slowly dying because of this extra aluminum impact from chemtrails.

To humans and animals, the impairments are neurological changes, weakening of the immune defense system, Alzheimer's, dementia, Parkinson's disease, anemia and impairments on the gastrointestinal tract, negative effects on reproduction, etc.

Respiratory tract infections caused by chemtrails are just the beginning of the problem. Now in recent years, Alzheimer's and Parkinson's disease as well as neurodegenerative disorders are said to have almost quadrupled among the population.

The most common ailment in people in heavily sprayed areas is caused by "mycoplasma", which is a bacterium. Some of these are genetically engineered pathogens, which then act as biological warfare agents. It can cause acute upper respiratory damage, intestinal problems, nasal bleeding, joint pain and dry coughing which can last for four or five weeks and then recur. Entailing autoimmune diseases, chronic fatigue, multiple sclerosis, lupus, transverse myelitis and meningitis may be triggered. There is also a mental-emotional component that can make people mentally confused with the inability to concentrate. Short-term memory loss can also occur.

The released particles or aerosols are used in combination with so-called "heaters" i.e. large radar systems such as HAARP (Kiruna, Sweden) and EISCAT (Tromsö, Norway). The result can be seen as rolling clouds in the sky, "frequency clouds". These clouds are the result of weather manipulation and are entirely artificial. They are now starting to appear everywhere and almost every day.

Why are there no more pilots and meteorologists, i.e. whistleblowers who go out and tell you that this is ongoing? The online newspaper NewsVoice asked the question to an American pilot who has been involved in the release of chemtrails.

The pilot said the following: *The pilots, meteorologists, military and politicians don't do it because of fear. They are afraid of losing their jobs.*

It is also very dangerous for a chemtrail pilot to reveal what they do. Pilots and their families have been threatened or murdered because of this by the CIA and NSA.

At the same time, politicians are blaming the warming on increased emissions of methane gas and carbon dioxide to burden businesses and citizens with additional taxes.

Greenpeace admits that they are silenced. The Swedish Environmental Party (the Green) has stated that politicians don't know what chemtrails are. Politicians believe they are condensation trails, and these people say they protect the environment. Talk about double standards.

With today's technology, the damage is already irreparable and the establishment has already contaminated the world's web - this is a fact.

Day by day it becomes more difficult to hide this elephant in the living room.

The official opinion is still that chemtrails don't exist.

## HAARP

Figure 41. HAARP is used to control the weather and as a warfare agent.

Figure 42. Some approximate locations of HAARP facilities. There are also HAARP-installations on Antarctica.

HAARP (*High Frequency Active Auroral Research Program*) is the next devilish weapon system used by the United States for Electronic Warfare and Climate Impact.

HAARP is used for:

1. Weather Changes.
2. To cause earthquakes and tsunamis.
3. To destroy global communication systems.
4. For electromagnetic warfare.

HAARP is an electromagnetic weapon that can send off an invisible swarm of directed energy pulses, hundreds of times more powerful than the electrical current found in lightning.

HAARP can shot down an enemy robot from the sky, or be used to blind soldiers in the battlefield, or control a riotous crowd by heating their skins.

If an electromagnetic pulse detonates over a large city, the weapon can destroy all electronics in the city in seconds.

HAARP uses directed energy to create a powerful electromagnetic pulse.

HAARP is such a powerful technique that it can be used to heat the atmosphere's ionosphere. At the right frequency, energy can be discharged from the ionosphere and directed towards the earth. The discharge can be 100 times stronger than a lightning flash.

With HAARP you can start famine on earth and kill huge numbers of people. Imagine using a river to flood an entire city or triggering a hurricane or tornado to decimate an enemy army in the desert.

The military has spent a lot of time to study weather changes as a concept to see how it can affect a war situation. If an electromagnetic pulse detonates over an entire city, then virtually every electrical object in the homes would cease to function and be destroyed.

HAARP has been extended throughout the globe and today there are many HAARP plants on every continent. All parts of HAARP are synchronized.

Norway, Finland and Sweden have acted as prostitutes to the US and are happy to contribute to big brother US HAARP activities and thus contribute to problems in the world instead of peace.

Norway's HAARP antenna system is located in Tromsö and is called EISCAT.

Sweden's HAARP is located in Kiruna, with the same name.

According to H.R.2977 "Space Preservation Act of 2001" HAARP would be prohibited if it was located more than 60 km up in the air, as well as chemtrails mentioned in the document. However, since HAARP and chemtrails are located closer to or on Earth, the document does not limit operations. The document mentions, among other things, that there must be no "exotic weapon systems designed to damage space or natural ecosystems, such as the ionosphere, atmosphere, climate, weather or tectonic systems with the aim of causing harm or destruction to a target population or region on earth or in space."

Sweden has recently built the antenna system LOIS located in southern Sweden from Gothenburg to Gotland, from Linköping to Lund. The LOIS is part of HAARP. The system consists of 10,000 antennas connected with fast fiber communications, and from here comes the fast expansion of the broadband fiber network in Sweden. Together, these antennas (cellmasts, 3G, 4G, TV masts, military antennas, radar systems, terra, etc.) make up a uniform large telescope, but the official announcement is to find the universe's first hydrogen atom and solve the riddle of the universe. The system's antennas use Microwaves and all connected mobile phones are a good extra source of radiation. You take control of the weather and have the opportunity to spy on the east.

On September 26, 2011, LOFAR was inaugurated on Råö on the Onsala Peninsula south of Gothenburg. Now you have a telescope that is said to be used to study the early history of the universe, how galaxies are formed, find new celestial bodies and investigate black holes. LOFAR consists of 192 antennas and operates together with Europe's other 5000 antennas of the same type. LOFAR, LOIS, EISCAT are all parts of HAARP and everything is centralized.

Microwave radiation has doubled many times in recent years. Microwave radiation makes mercury more mobile in our body. Experiments with rats have shown that microwaves make our blood-brain barrier more permeable. Microwaves thus open the way for mercury, aluminum and other toxins into our central nervous system (CNS). Both mercury and aluminum are very harmful to our nervous system. Further research on this should be very difficult to raise money for. Microwaves have, according to a court in Rome, been said to cause cancer and there is research that prove it, but Swedish authorities don't want to recognize such an announcement. For many years, the Swedish state has decided that the microwave radiation of mobile phones is not dangerous. Thus, HAARP is according to them not dangerous. We can only wait for the coming disease and cancer epidemic.

The list can be made much larger by various kinds of technologies and devilish ways of wanting to destroy the earth, countries, societies, civilizations, and make the earth habitable for only a certain select elite, negative prominent psychopaths and programmed robot creatures.

Today there are at least 175 weather modification patents.

## "Smart electricity meter" at home

The analogue electricity meters that were stationed in our homes have now been replaced with "smart electricity meters". Several of these work on microwaves, e.g. through Wi-Fi and send signals to the electricity suppliers about how much power we use in our homes. So here we also get an addition of microwave radiation often between 900 MHz and 2.4 GHz which is transmitted at least 9600 times a day.

Some of these network customers who have these smart electricity meters installed have shown symptoms such as fatigue, headache, palpitations and dizziness. Some have got electromagnetic hypersensitivity reactions after the installation.

## Mobil Phones (4G, 5G)

We have already said that microwaves, also used by mobile phones, induce cancer, brain tumors, increase the mobility of e.g. mercury in the body and increase the permeability of the blood-brain barrier, which makes toxic substances in the body e.g. aluminum and mercury even more easily harm the nervous system. The great thing about mobile phones is that they are designed to be held against the ear where of course some of the radiation is absorbed by the brain. The brain is thus highly exposed to this microwave radiation.

Figure 43. Smartphone with Wi-Fi, hotspot, bluetooth, mobile data transfer and mobile calls, are all based on microwave technology.

The next generation of mobile phones will be based on 5G.

5G will increase microwave radiation even more. 5G is the next standard for mobile broadband communication, which is expected to be in use from around 2020. 5G means greatly expanded data capacity and opens for applications such as, "Internet of Things".

"Internet of things" means that various technical devices will be connected to the internet. This applies to e.g. automatic control of cars and their ability to receive information from the immediate area. Furthermore, kitchen machines can be connected to the Internet, etc. Already today there are "smart homes" where very much is connected to the Internet and can be monitored via e.g. applications in mobile phones (smartphones).

5G is already being tested but with no political debate, investigations into the consequences for public health and the environment have not been conducted. All of Sweden becomes an experimental environment and people are uninformed and incorrectly informed about known health risks, which is unacceptable according to current international conventions and Swedish legislation.

Over 180 researchers from 36 countries have now (2017-09-13) sent a letter to the European Commission. They require a moratorium on the rollout of

5G. The researchers warn that the health consequences will be tragic and irreversible.

Cancer will increase further, as well as headaches, sleep difficulties, fatigue, impaired memory, learning problems, chest pressure, concentration problems, depression / mental illness, disturbed thyroid function, irritation, behavioral disorders and sweating.

Some type of mental illness has come to be called the "microwave syndrome" by some.

### *Mental control*

Mobile phones can be used to control people mentally. The mobile phone (smartphone) is a smart tool for brain control.

The question is whether the scientists understand the difference in "believing in God" compared to experiencing something that is extremely big, mysterious and impossible for the intellect to handle, but yet has a deep meaning and for the individual? A direct experience of something big and positive is different from having an idea of something that has not yet been experienced, but which can nevertheless be an element within the framework of a religious-political belief.

From a healthy paranoia perspective, a smartphone should be a perfect tool for regularly inhibiting the "*posterior medial frontal cortex*", provided that a Smartphone can generate such a magnetic field, which also proves to be the case.

Subliminal information has been incorporated into television programs and was already used in the 1960s. Subliminal information goes straight into our subconscious field and we can program and increase the inclination for certain things there. A TV can display 24 frames per second, and one of the frames may deviate from the series of images that build up the TV program. You can enter e.g. a message for something that e.g. increases anxiety and murder statistics. The person in front of the TV doesn't notice this and can automatically be programmed for certain things e.g. buying behavior, political views or the like.

Even a smartphone can be programmed for this. It can be programmed to send out e.g. subliminal sound. There are programs that can be used to hack a person's smartphone for eavesdropping or programming. There is not much a private person can do to protect himself. The mobile phone can be used by third parties even if it is switched off.

### Brain control worked already with old Nokia phones

An article entitled "Mind Control by Cell Phone" in the magazine "Scientific American" from 2008 describes how researchers at the Brain Science Institute in Australia and Loughborough University's Sleep Research Center in England with two models of Nokia (6110 and 6310) could affect the brain's EEG-activities with TMS technology. This technique uses powerful electromagnetic radiation pulses that are radiated into a person's brain to damage or excite special "circuits" in the brain.

Figure 44. Nokia mobile phone.

The researchers noticed against their own presumption that the mobile phone cannot only change the brain's EEG pattern. Also sleep can be greatly disturbed by the cell phone's "field" and the effect continues long after the phone is turned off.

Despite this discovery, the researchers sought to mitigate the significance of the discovery by speculatively comparing the results with the stressful effect of drinking coffee or being affected by a negative sleeping environment. This was done without scientific evidence.

Researcher James Horne at Loughborough University's Sleep Research Center in England nevertheless admits that telephone users can clearly be affected at certain frequencies and that the modern-day surroundings is filled with electromagnetic devices that emit impacting fields and radiation:

The experiments are now several years old. The old Nokia phones no longer exist and the market has been flooded with significantly more potent 4G smart phones that transmit even more powerful magnetic fields. It will get even worse with the introduction of the 5G technology.

### Brain tumors increase

The Swedish Radiation Safety Authority dismisses this claim.

The number of people suffering from brain tumor in Denmark has more than doubled since 1990 and the biggest increase has been in the last 10 years.

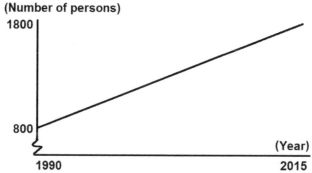

Figure 45. The number of new patients with tumors in the brain / central nervous system in Denmark 1990-2015. This is the trend.

Among young people aged 0-39, this is the sort of tumor that is increasing the most. This means that the Swedish Radiation Safety Authority's and some experts' main arguments for the harmlessness of mobile phones are incorrect, i.e. that brain tumors do not increase. According to the latest statistics from the Danish Cancer Registry that the "Strålskyddsstiftelsen" (Radiation Protection Foundation) has produced, the number of people affected by tumor in the brain or the spinal cord membranes, or in the central nervous system (including cranial nerves) in Denmark has increased recently; from 827 cases in 1990 to 1807 cases in 2015. This is a doubling, and then taken into account is also Denmark's population increase during the same period. The increase has speeded up over the last ten years. During the same period, the use of mobile phones has increased greatly.

The "Strålskyddsstiftelsen"[4] (Radiation Protection Foundation) wrote that "9 out of 10 mobile phones can exceed the limit value and 4 out of 10 double the limit value when held directly on the body. This is shown by the French authority ANFR. Apple 5 can expose users to 5.3 W/kg, well above the limit value 2 W/kg. Already at values of 0.04 W/kg has shown to promote tumors according to research. The reason why mobiles actually radiate far more than the limit value and more than stated by the manufacturers themselves is that the mobile radiation is not measured when the mobile phone is held directly on the body, but instead when used from a distance of usually between 5 and 15 mm, which leads to significantly lower measured radiation".

There are now experts in mobile radiation who say that there is scientific evidence of that radiation from wireless technology should be classified as a human carcinogen. This can no longer be ignored. The usage of cell phones increases the risk of brain tumors. Right now, children and young people are exposed to this radiation, especially in preschools and schools. People are also exposed to radiation at universities, in health care and in the care of old people. New research results were published in 2017 that show this. The radiation also inflicts mental illness and impaired learning. There is also strong evidence that the radiation gives rise to Alzheimer's and infertility in men.

On the other hand, Radiation Protection Authorities worldwide deny all the risks of wireless communication. The death march can continue - most of us join, and we are currently marching straight into the 5G society.

**Chipping - mind control**

Next in order in the Bilderberg agenda are:

1. Overshadowing
2. Monitoring via Chipp implants, camera and mobile phones
3. Reproductive cloning (hybrid program)
4. Shutdown of the brain's communicative ability through Transcranial Magnetic Stimulation (TMS)

Overshadowing and monitoring of an individual's behavior is usually done through MK Ultra (Mind Control). This is the easiest way for negative, despotic beings, authorities to influence people they want to exploit for their

---

[4] http://www.stralskyddsstiftelsen.se/2017/06/vanliga-mobiltelefoner-kan-strala-langt-over-gransvardet/

own perverse agendas, purposes. The mind control begins when the person gets a brain implant, i.e. a chip implanted in the brain.

We know that MK Ultra started in Sweden already during the 1940s. They began experimenting on unknowing patients through small inoperative electrodes, chips etc. This technology was then used and is used still today at the Karolinska Institutet in Stockholm and usually goes under the slightly more anonymous concept of "Biometric Telemetry", "Synthetic Telepathy" or other incomprehensible names to mask its true purpose. The one who opened the door to this cynical activity was no less than the Bilderberger and Freemason Olof Palme in Sweden.

Now it seems that the Karolinska Institutet's brain researchers have free hands to experiment in state-of-the-art laboratories in brand new buildings and use a very advanced supercomputer they have acquired, to invest in the development of artificial intelligence (AI), rather than refine their own intelligence with natural methods.

For a long time, Sweden was one of the leading countries in the world in mind control. As far as I know it was only the former Soviet Union and the US that were ahead. Surprising is that the corrupt researchers don't use this technology on their own children and relatives. They choose others to experiment on. So far in Sweden, about 500 people have volunteered to become chipped in good faith, in the belief that it will facilitate from the point of view of health examination, bank identity, travelling etc. This is scam and just the beginning of the misery. If they had been aware of what was planned by the negative, despotic rulers, then they would never allow this kind of artificial influence.

We must remember that the human body can be hacked in the same way as any computer program. This makes some believe that they can influence their own DNA in a positive direction, e.g. improve their health situation, become more cheerful, happier, get more energy, etc. This is just a dream that does not come true as long as you don't get rid of your suppressed thoughts and feelings, mental blockings and don't tune in on the scalar waves that form the innermost core of everything.

Those who voluntarily allow to become chipped are not aware of what they are getting into. They only see the advantages but not the disadvantages. These people are easily indoctrinated by the rulers to believe in some miracle.

Due to naivety, ignorance, these people don't see the problems that arise in connection with their chip implants.

This negative artificial technology has been used for many years in Sweden on completely unknowing people. One of the victims is Robert Näslund, whose story can be studied on YouTube.

The MK Ultra project was secret and an illegal CIA program that researched behavioral modification. The program began in the early 1950s and was officially ongoing until 1973. The program used unknowing American and Canadian citizens as experimental subjects. MK Ultra involved the use of several methods to manipulate people's individual mental states and brain functions, which included by stealth giving people drugs (*especially LSD*), hypnosis, sensory deprivation, isolation, verbal and sexual abuse as well as various types of torture.

The book "Trance Formation of America" is a documented autobiography of a victim of the CIA's thought control project MK Ultra. The book can be ordered from Amazon in the US.

Cathy O'Brien is the only survivor among dozens of experimental subjects who were kidnapped and forced to participate against their own will in the CIA's MK Ultra Project. Thanks to her programmer, who later became her deprogrammer and real husband, Mark Philip, she survived and now lectures in various states in the United States about the degradation she has suffered since childhood. She has been deliberately exploited by high-ranking politicians, both male and female.

Here we have an example of a criminal act where the perpetrator doesn't remember anything of the situation or incident he/she was involved in. He/she denies that he/she would have committed any crime. Here, man and the authorities don't know or understand the root cause of such crimes. The perpetrator can be sentenced to death, imprisonment or psychiatric care, but no one ever knows who or why this crime was committed. The cause of the crime remains unknown to the uninitiated.

Some civil and military intelligence services use psychological influence to put people into a kind of deep hypnosis, where the victims do what they have been programmed to do.

I myself have been trained in Clinical Hypnotherapy in Honolulu, Hawaii and have used it earlier at my Biophysical Institute to help people who feared flying and within regression. Regression is a return to past events (*past lives*) or to the fetal stage where one can be aware of what happened with the mother and her surroundings.

Chipping began to be introduced by negative alien beings from Orion and Zeta, in agreement with the US administration in the 1950s. This was primarily intended to control and direct the experimental subjects who would be brought aboard spaceships for medical examination or research purposes. Later, this technology was copied by CIA-supported research centers for chip implants in politicians, intelligence personnel and others.

This has been done for spreading false information, influencing citizens in society through mental and artificial control, legislation and for misleading people through mass medial propaganda.

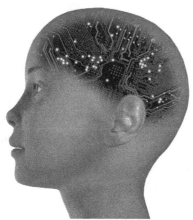

Figure 46. Man is on his way to become a soulless mind controlled cyborg.

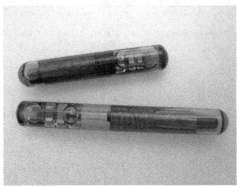

Figure 47. Chip implants in the brain. Today, the chip can be made incredibly small. With a single syringe, thousands of nano-chips can be injected.

It has also been done to monitor some people, due to medical experiments or for other reasons.

Nowadays, this technology is used in psychiatry and in the security services. This form of surveillance has been going on for half a century, both in Europe and in the rest of the world, without the public knowing about it.

I have already mentioned in my book under the title "Quantum Humanism" (not yet translated to English), which was published in Sweden in 1995, that chip implants were inserted and used at certain Psychiatric clinics in Sweden. This was approved by the Director General of the National Health Authorities in 1989 - 1995. The Karolinska Institutet in Sweden is leading in EU when it comes to MK Ultra chip implants.

In Sweden, until 2025, it is planned to insert chip implants in all people under the guise to protect their identity. This is a false statement. In reality, it is about ID checks linked to bank accounts and various types of government control, monitoring. A further check can be done via the person's SMS, applications, E-mails and Internet communications. They want complete control over the individual's thoughts, feelings and actions. They will try to chip people, if not voluntarily, then through legislation. People who allow to become chipped voluntarily don't know what they are doing. Also under the guise of virus threats or other threats people will be vaccinated and also added swarms of chips, without these people knowing it. It has already been planned by the Illuminates.

All kinds of mental (*mind*) control, negative influence of the mind, to oppress, enslave, exploit people for self-purposes without their consent, is contrary to the law of the cosmos and to human integrity (the right of self-determination over one's life and thinking).

Such a control is not tenable. What contradicts human development only leads to stagnation.

Those who are behind this agenda and control technological development on earth want complete destruction of everything that has to do with common sense. These beings are negative, destructive extraterrestrial beings who want to turn the earthly people into their slaves, obedient robots under the so-called "New World Order", and with Globalization as the cover, raise total control over the entire earthly civilization.

### What happens when 4G is replaced by 5G?

Tom Wheeler and Josh Del Sol warn against that 5G technology cannot only increase health risks, but also pave the way for a totalitarian surveillance community.

- 5G provides ultra-high frequencies of 24-100 GHz.
- The 5G expansion will be very infrastructure intensive, which means a massive installation of masts.
- 5G will generate billions of dollars for the financial players.
- American companies are to be first on the market.
- 5G is a national priority for the United States. "*Stay out of the way of technological development,*" says Tom Wheeler.
- No studies on 5G are needed. The future will invent itself. The market should be free and preferably unregulated.
- The first tests will take place in 2017 and full market introduction will take place in 2020.
- The applications of 5G are both commercial and military.
- Ground-based networks and satellite networks will merge.
- Everything will be able to be connected on the 5G network, everything from pillboxes to irrigation systems.

5G takes us straight into total monitoring with unimagined health risks.

Josh Del Sol warns against that not only will 5G increase health risks, but also pave the way for a totalitarian surveillance community.

Josh Del Sol works for the civic initiative "*Take Back Your Power*". In a longer video, Del Sol interviews some scholarly people who comment on the technical developments and how the media and authorities handle the topic 5G.

The application of 5G from the year 2020 means - if companies decide - that the industry will have much latitude to test, develop and use extremely high-frequency wireless technology, with no responsibility for either human personal integrity or health.

100's of billions of microchips will be integrated into the 5G network, which also includes humans. We get total monitoring of everything and everyone and each chip gets a unique IP number.

Each bottle of milk or human life cycle can be tracked and handled.

We are back in the same totalitarian surveillance that took place at the Betelgeuse in Orion; what the Hitler regime worked for if it would have won the war.

It is exactly this surveillance and dictatorial system that the Great Power USA, with its allies, wants to apply under the guise: "*The New World Order*".

Under the "New World Order", man is completely brainwashed into believing in nothing but the five rules governing their earthly, material existence. These five rules are to:

1. Work (*slave*) for their alien and terrestrial parasites.

2. Stress, chase money and status.

3. Engage in different kinds of entertainments, hobbies in their limited free time.

4. Sleeping.

5. Wait for death and die, leaving the family to fight for their entire material possessions.

These five rules dominate most of the human species on earth today.

So-called "burnout" that most people suffer from in society is due to people's fear, anxiety, stress both at work time and also at spare time.

Man has become indoctrinated to believe that the more you stress and devote yourself to various kinds of activities, the more capable and successful you are as an individual, even in your spare time.

On the contrary! - we are simply excluded from being able to communicate with our higher qualitative self, our soul consciousness and knowing ourselves, listening to ourselves through our intuition. What do I want for myself? What is good for me - and not what others think? What do I think myself?

Instead, we follow what others think - what we become indoctrinated to believe in. Thus we don't have time to devote any time to our own development before it is time to leave the body and die. What became of our life? What have we done? Is this the meaning and purpose of life?

### Artificial influence on the brain

Through artificial magnetic influence on the brain's plasmatic (*etheric*) field, we shut off the ability for self-communication and contact with our higher qualitative self with multidimensional worlds and reality. The same thing happens by influencing the brain with cell phone radiation fields if you don't use headphones. Young people who constantly use their mobile phones are at risk. This has been stated through researching on low-frequency electromagnetic effects on the brain. The bought so-called experts who speak positively about this kind of technology are either bought by companies, government agencies and lack the knowledge, experience or are indoctrinated to believe in the harmlessness of this technology.

A study conducted in collaboration with British researchers at the "University of York" and researchers at the "University of California" in the United States, allege that if the problem-solving part of the brain is weakened, both belief in God and other kinds of paranormal possibilities decrease.

The technique is called "Transcranial Magnetic Stimulation" (*TMS*) and is already used to reduce depression in psychiatric patients.

When the researchers used TMS on "*posterior medial frontal cortex*", the part of the brain that is active in identification and problem solving, it was discovered that 32,8% of the examination subjects experienced less faith in God or in paranormal phenomena. They were also less anxious to be comforted, even though they had been reminded of death.

The purpose of the study was to determine whether an area of the brain was affected in connection with problem solving, where the area could be related to ideology. This was done considering many individuals turn to religious or political ideologies when faced with certain dilemmas or threats.

During a TMS session, an electromagnetic coil is placed against the scalp near the experimental subject's forehead. The electromagnet provides a painless magnetic pulse that stimulates nerve cells in the region for mood control and depression. The idea is to be able to activate areas of the brain that have reduced activity in people with depression.

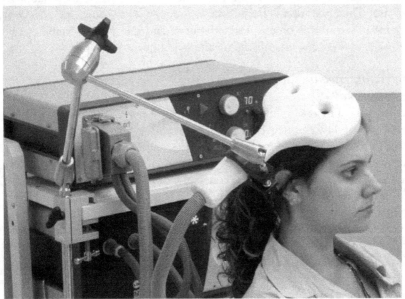

Figure 48. Transcranial Magnetic Stimulation (TMS).

Although biology is not entirely clear why TMS works, the stimulation appears to affect the function of this part of the brain. This in turn relieves the symptoms of depression and improves mood.

Treatment for depression involves delivering repetitive magnetic pulses.

The researchers suggest that a shutdown of the "*posterior medial frontal cortex*" makes man less prejudiced, less religious, less religious extremist and less superstitious.

The problem then becomes that man loses his full ability to genuinely experience spiritual experiences as well as identifying and solving problems, i.e. being able to think clearly. People are turned into living biological robots.

The part of humanity that benefits on stupid citizens who lack inspiration with a deeper meaning in life is, in fact, dictatorships, which then more easily can control a troubled and lost civilization.

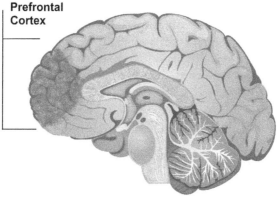

Figure 49. TMS stimulates the "frontal cortex". Man then becomes more robotic and not in the same way interested in the meaning of life.

Through mental influence, mental manipulation, man becomes completely cut off from his true identity and reality, his spiritual nature. In the same way as Reptilians from Alfa Draco enslaved the first human species i.e. Homo Erectus, Homo Habilis and Homo Sapiens, the thought is to enslave the earlier light-skinned Aryan species.

### Further monitoring of the human being

Controlling people is very simple. It can be done collectively or individually.

Chip can be inserted that get their power from the body's own scalar field or from powerful transmitter antennas that resonate with the chip. The energy to the chip allows the chip to send out exactly the electromagnetic signature needed for the individual to be put in the chosen state. Of course, the input information can be changed and the behavioral outcome or the ability to concentrate can be changed as needed. The chip sends out information about the person that a national or international central unit receives and reads and stores in a database. The chip is individually customized.

Of course, a mobile phone is excellent to use. It can be hacked from the outside and a base code is included in the phone's operating system. It can be updated as needed. The mobile phone reads the human health condition, mental state and physical condition as needed. It can monitor everything in real time. Similarly, the mobile phone can send the exact signature data to the person who needs it to become a pattern-friendly world citizen all according to the Globalists' desired New World Order. A chip in the individual can further locally strengthen the information where it needs to be the strongest.

Of course, a monitoring and control program for behavior and "health" can be included from the central taskmaster right from the beginning in e.g. the android operating system. Hidden in the machine code, the program can be difficult to detect and, as needed, the operating system can be updated.

## Obsession and the "New World Order"

Alien degenerate Reptilians as well as beings from Orion also chip people who have voluntarily chosen to cooperate with them for a variety of reasons. The agreement may have been made at an earlier stage in life or in a previous incarnation. An earthly political person or key person can be properly entrenched in the Reptilian agenda, i.e. the Globalists' Agenda with the "New World Order", so that the flow of information appears most natural. In this way, these earthly "representatives" hold together and cooperate very well. They don't know where the agenda is heading, but it feels very comfortable and frictionless for them. These chips are biological and work completely on scalar technology. They dissolve if the person dies or if the chip is removed from the body. These chips make the control of the individual quite accurate and everything can be monitored. Many politicians and leading people at very high positions also have a governing entity governing and controlling them, who in detail controls the individual's thoughts and provides energy and information to the person. The politician feels better than others and with increased energy gets the inspiration he or she needs to execute his or her part in launching the "New World Order".

It should be added that without this fourth-dimensional controlling entity, these leading individuals would have very low energy. The day the grip is released by the negative control being, the controlled individual will feel like a torn cloth. He or she will have very little energy left. The individual in question will not really understand what really happened. Furthermore, these individuals have a large karmic package where the underlying programmed pattern of actions makes these individuals very suitable to occupy and control in this way. Obsession is today denied by psychologists and psychiatrists - totally in line with being able to launch the "New World Order".

## Government

The political arenas are adapted in such a way that one can get elected candidates to be elected as presidents and heads of state. Putting one group against another is the tactic. If the voters are allowed to choose between two handpicked prospective candidates then the right policy is implemented - which benefits the "New World Order", i.e. the World Order of the Globalists. Gradually the snare is tightened and freedom is limited in steps to finally end up in an open dictatorial regime.

In Sweden, block policy is used as the basis. We have a left block and a right block. The block compositions are configured in such a way that the politically correct agenda is pursued. In reality, there are no different political parties, but a large party shaped like a cake, though with different "colored" pieces of the cake. Various statements are made to direct the policy in the politically correct direction.

E.g. before the 2014 election, the Swedish party the Moderates got too much support in the opinion polls before the election and the moderates' party leader stated in the election campaign that we should all "open our hearts" to the reception of asylum seekers. The party leader himself left Sweden for a top job in the US within the banking system. He did not have to open his heart to the asylum seekers himself. All voters did not like his statement and shortly thereafter the Social Democrats had received more support in the opinion polls. Moreover, many opinion polls are ordered to show support for certain things. Most recently, the new moderate leader in 2017 wanted to approach the nationalist party the Sweden Democrats. Subsequently, the moderates' opinion figures again declined and the Social Democrats again gained more support.

With strong lobbying from large market forces with central management from the Bilderberg group, politics can be steered in the chosen direction, i.e. in the direction of the "Globalists".

People must all the time choose between two actors, in Sweden between the right and the left block, in the United States between the Democratic and the Republican presidential candidates and now in France, the battle was fought between the extreme right Marine Le Pen and the Liberal Emmanuel Macron. Of course, all leader aspirants must be approved by the controlling invisible hand that controls the pieces on the chessboard.

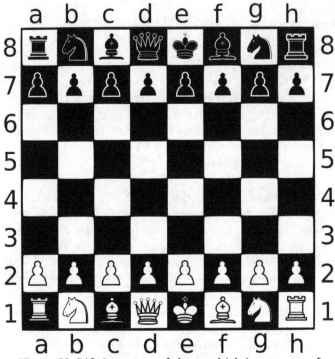

Figure 50. Life is a game of chess, which is your move?

Voters generally consider nothing more than giving their sympathy to one of the pieces of the cake that appear on the scene, which promise jam - but which don't at all have to hold any election promises afterwards. Once in a position of power you can do anything, i.e. no one knows how the cake tastes, and it can have a rather different taste, the taste of the dictatorship of the Globalists.

The Globalists' "integration" is about threatening and equal people and embedding them in dictatorship without any development or evolutionary opportunities whatsoever.

In fact, if you vote for any of the established party candidates that the media supports, then you vote for the Dictatorship of the Globalists.

## NATO, EU, etc.

As a step along the way to "Global Dictatorship", they want to create large associations that they can more easily control centrally, with force if needed, or when needed. As people become more inclined and control is increased, even larger associations will be formed. Finally, just as it was on Orion, "One Single Empire Will Rule Everything". It does not matter if it is the Left Wind or the Right Wind that pushes people towards the fold - only people end up there. This is integration under coercion.

In Sweden, the Globalists' spokesmen are doing everything to lobby NATO as a kind of contemporary Gestapo to control countries and their citizens. If domestic police officers had too high a morale, emergency forces like 2nd World War II German SS (Schutzstaffel, i.e. protective troops) are needed. These new police units can be chipped and centrally controlled like robots. In advance all types of conscience have been disabled with the help of TMS or the like. The security forces' efforts run smoothly without question.

The forces are led and operated in line with the establishment of the "New World Order".

The Swedish Parliament has agreed to Sweden's host country agreement with NATO. This is another step towards a full NATO membership for Sweden.

The people of Sweden are not asked for this allowance, but the decision has been taken above their heads. It would have been better if Sweden had stayed neutral and been able to contribute to serious social and world development instead of being a lackey to the Globalists.

## The Immigration

The plan with the increasing immigration is to facilitate the "New World Order".

Sweden is involved and equally guilty in this process, i.e. the "Arab Spring" that is happening now. This was declared openly when Sweden, with the support of all Sweden's parliamentary parties except the Left Party and the Sweden Democrats, sent the Swedish fighter JAS-Gripen to Libya to overthrow Gadaffi, i.e. Libya's "dictator". Many lies circulated in the media regarding Libya to justify this procedure. Furthermore, Sweden has sent troops to Afghanistan and also helped create streams of refugees. Cause and effect - refugee flows are created.

Together with liberal immigration policy, it is estimated that approximately 1.5 million people have come to Sweden since the year 2000. These include asylum refugees, family immigration, labor immigration and students who have all been granted residence permits. The majority are asylum refugees and their relatives.

<u>Integration can only happen within each individual - when the process is complete, people can be integrated with each other - but not before as the majority seems to believe today.</u>

A hot topic right now is integration. With supportive agendas, they are trying to integrate people with different backgrounds, different religions, different customs, different cultures, different characteristics, different upbringing conditions and attitudes in different countries - also in Sweden. They try to do this with the pretext that love is the guiding star and together we will succeed. We in Sweden have seen that this integration did not go particularly well in a smaller scale - but believe instead that it will go better in a larger scale.

This is a utopia and will not work. The integration we are talking about today works only when the people who are to be integrated have reached a certain level of consciousness and have seriously entered the human kingdom. First and foremost, you have to behave as those around do. To be considered a human being, one must follow certain ethical and moral rules that characterize a higher qualitatively conscious human being. As long as you do not do this, you still belong to the animal-human state (stage) in your development. The human state is only reached when you have created harmony within yourself and with your surroundings; when you have worked off all kinds of selfishness, power cravings, hatred, anger, greed, vanity and pleasure. Once there, you have become a cosmic universal being.

The characteristics of these individuals are that they radiate harmony, universalism and care for all individuals in society. You set the entire society first with goals such as good health, good environment and a society that is there for human longevity and evolutionary development. These individuals are extremely few in today's society. Therefore, integration will not work on the premises that exist today - not in Sweden and not anywhere else on the planet earth at its present stage.

Man's inherent characteristics consist of an underlying karmic (fated) reservoir that is gigantic. This reservoir controls every individual in everything they do and there are both good and bad qualities - all learned through thousands of years of living on this planet, incarnation after incarnation (*rebirths*).

Real integration takes place individually within each individual. Integration means getting rid of one's karmic (fated) reservoir and raising one's consciousness to the forehead region "*posterior medial frontal cortex*", where our higher qualitative part, the Soul Consciousness and the higher qualitative Mind Consciousness are located. Today, the majority of people have their consciousness energetically focused in the solar plexus and in below located energy and consciousness centers. Here you find traits of lower quality, i.e. lust, anger, hatred, greed, vanity and selfishness and every perversion of them (*the lower qualities of the mind*). Humans have differently much of these traits and people are born in countries that best correspond to the traits they need to have confronted in life for further development - since evolvement is the meaning of our life in the universe, regardless of what today's governing society is trying to accomplish. Today, it is believed that the goal of life is to meet the financial budget, whatever the cost; it doesn't matter how many people are grinded down the mill, or how much you are poisoning the planet earth with all its life.

During our individual evolutionary consciousness development process, our consciousness is gradually increased and certain qualities of ourselves are illuminated and we are given the opportunity to getting rid of these old characteristics and thus our development process continues. The process takes place with the same method for all people who are finished with the development in the most sluggish part of the three-dimensional level of existence, to which the planet earth has belonged until now.

Now our solar system and planet have entered a new energy constellation with increased energetic influence from the central sun, which affects all life in our solar system. This is a springboard for further development if we are willing to develop and adjust our being in accordance with the new current situation. All of our karmic traits are now receiving increased energy and everything will "expand", and will allow us to choose to evolve or to get stuck even more in the qualities we have tried to camouflage to our surroundings, but which have always been in us as a shadow we cannot leave. We have all created this shadow for ourselves in our lives over thousands of years on this planet - during times of war, famine and other hardships. These events have shaped our lives into what we are today.

Bringing together people with different qualities, where some are more harmonious and some have more of the negative mind qualities mentioned above, should be an obvious unreasonableness. But this agenda is now trying to be pushed through by many across the world. This is done in ignorance about the cosmos and the laws of the universe.

When we individually remove our karmic reservoir and elevate our consciousness to a higher qualitative four- and five-dimensional level - and in addition become aware of these dimensions, we are gradually integrating. We get an overall understanding of each other's differences, but we have a joint ground of unity, where we feel community with everyone, and where at this level we all feel the same. Here we can integrate - because we follow all the laws of the universe, and not any laws dictated by three-dimensional intellectually conscious beings, whose intermediate goal is to enrich their own ego, with all the five mind qualities we mentioned above, consciously or unconsciously.

The goal is soul integration and to gain control of our mind with associated mind properties - the mind that is our opponent in creation. Without the mind there would be no development, because there would be nothing to develop. The differences we all have are also used to provoke ongoing development in us. Everything has its meaning and place in the cosmos. Nothing happens by chance. We begin our development unconsciously and our soul program is made conscious by incarnating the program throughout the mineral kingdom, the plant kingdom, the animal kingdom and is individualized in the human kingdom. As we begin our training toward a multi-dimensional higher qualitative quantum consciousness, we become aware of ourselves and of the entire universe. We become one with all of creation; we become fully integrated, i.e. consciously conscious beings.

The work of integration doesn't happen by itself, although the sun gives us excellent possibilities now. We must want to get rid of our inherently acquired qualities, a process that is particularly laborious, especially mentally, but all people are left with this choice - to be integrated or to continue to be non-integrated. For those who choose integration, everything will be more positive in life - one looks positively at existence in quest for the multidimensional quantum consciousness - free from all bondage and entanglements.

If you choose not to be integrated, i.e. live as you do today, then the following will happen. You will embrace more of the mind's lower qualitative, negative qualities and you will attract other people who don't want to be integrated either - you will get a taste of your own medicine, and fall.

The earth has already entered a new phase of development. The question is whether you (*we*) want to follow or not. If we choose not to follow, this will be your our last incarnation here on earth as the lower regions of the 4D parallel world (*astral world*) now is closing and being evacuated. The human beings who reside there after their physical death now make their departure to other planetary systems that correspond to their inner characteristics - no one can skip classes in their development - as little as a preschooler cannot skip all classes and start studying at the university. Our eternal life is an endless evolution toward more consciousness - and we are all on different evolutionary steps.

Lower evolved people can never be allowed to threaten people with higher levels of development and understanding. The cosmos regulates this on the planet earth with incarnations to different families, different countries, different continents, etc. We are still on planet earth, and we are not even allowed in our present state to visit other planets of higher development - we don't even know that they exist.

The "integration" of the Globalists is about threatening, drug-medicating and standardize people and back them in a dictatorship without any possibilities for development whatsoever.

Cosmic integration is about developing cosmically toward a higher qualitative multi-dimensional quantum consciousness, which means mutual understanding (*harmony*) and free of all bondage, entanglement. Automatically man wakes up to a higher dimensional reality and the consensus on existence becomes obvious.

The latter option will be the way that is implemented as the earth has reached its lowest level of development and is now beginning its return path together with its inhabitants. The people who oppose this will disappear in the chaos that now awaits when the Globalists in desperation do everything possible to create an Orion-like dictatorship with an Empire that rules everything and everyone, i.e. a ruling class and where the rest of the population is made into unconscious slaves. The lower qualitative part of the mind expands more and more and society degenerates.

Many of the people who have come to Sweden are good people with fantastic possibilities for development. These have come to Sweden to integrate spiritually and follow the earth's cosmic agenda. Their different types of gene materials along with existing gene materials will create the new human being, being part of the 5th civilization.

The people who have come to Sweden with karmic (fated) misery will of course attract similar people with the same type of characteristics. In this way, we have moved many of the troublemakers on the planet earth to Sweden and Europe. These people as well as people who have lived here for a long time with similar situations are therefore given the opportunity to sort out their karmic (fate-related) themes, which will increase the chaos that is approaching.

In the wake of the immigration that is happening, people will want to have order. Globalists will show happy faces when people want to have more police officers in the community as well as a stronger military power. A Swedish NATO-membership is getting closer as well as an open dictatorship.

## Popular adult education

Sometimes people may need to have some education in order to have the politically correct course, especially before referendums, which you prefer to avoid.

The popular adult education that many people remember in Sweden regards the vote for or against nuclear power in 1980. In order for the Swedish people to make the right choice, the people needed preparatory education.

Just before 1979, the US nuclear power plant Harrisburg had an accident. Those in charge wanted to give the Swedish people the opportunity to learn that nuclear power is good after all, even though a single nuclear power failure can make large areas uninhabitable. Most recently, in 2011, the Fukushima nuclear power plant failed in Japan as a result of a tsunami. An enormous amount of radioactive material was spread and today the whole of the Pacific Ocean is affected.

The expertise of advisers who were there to help politicians to get the correct attitude about nuclear power before the 1980 referendum was mainly positive to nuclear power. The people should have a positive attitude and many would get this positive attitude in study circles. Once the referendum was to take place, there were three options to vote for. Option 1 referred to gradual phase-out, option 2 also gradual phase-out and option 3 phase-out within 10 years. Option 2 won. Since the forces behind the economy are controlling, we still have nuclear power in Sweden today, only one reactor has been closed down.

Furthermore, there was popular education before the EU elections in 1994. They wanted Sweden to be "mature" to join.

Today it is important that we all have a negative attitude towards carbon dioxide. People should accept "carbon dioxide tax" and "emission allowances" fees. If this is not accepted, you can be called a "climate denier" and "fact resistant". The people should be conformed and accept higher taxes and feel the burden of debt. It is then easier to steer them wherever you want, i.e. to obedient world citizens.

## Banning demonstrations

Demonstrations will be prohibited along the way towards World Dictatorship. Likewise, it will be prohibited for groups of people to gather at the same place.

Today, this is a reality in the EU country of Spain. On July 1, 2015, the decision was made to approve the "Gag Laws" or "The Law for the Protection of Citizen Security" and thus Spain became a "Non-Law-Safe Police State".

The laws go against the freedom of opinion, the freedom of speech and the right of demonstration. It is now impossible for citizens of Spain to safely and officially criticize the incumbent government, to exercise several of their most fundamental freedoms and rights, to criticize the country of Spain, its government and government employees on social media or through demonstrations. It is now illegal to gather outside government buildings without a permit. It is illegal to film, photograph or make audio recordings of policemen on duty. A policeman can fine a citizen with a sum of SEK 5 million without court proceedings.

Which country will be the next in order to introduce similar laws? The Globalists' snare is gradually being tightened. The media is silent about this. They run the errands of the Globalists. Therefore, it is important that we also have a free media that stick to the truth and describe the reality as it is and not as some believe or imagine, in their naivety, in their ignorance.

## The Police Service

In 1965, the responsibility of the police was transferred from the municipalities to the state. Shortly thereafter, the 119 police authorities were merged into 24 county authorities, which then became 21 independent police authorities.

On January 1, 2015, Sweden got a unified Police Authority, unlike the previous division of 21 police authorities, the National Police Board and the National Forensic Laboratory. The reason for the centralization was that they wanted more effective governance and management, and then an increased number of police in the local police areas, national standardization and uniform assessments. Instead, the centralization led to lack of local anchorage where the police know and are known by the residents. The focus was moved from the immediate area. It has been said that it becomes more impersonal for every meter of increased distance between those who serve and those who are to be served. The police become distanced from the citizens.

The result is that the resolution of crimes committed dropped significantly. In 2016, 13% of the crimes were cleared compared to 18% six years earlier. Sweden has a low clearance rate compared to other EU countries. Some say in defense that too many changes have taken place at the same time.

The centralization reform takes place contrary to more successful police work in for example New York and the United Kingdom where local governance is important, but also local division of responsibility and pressure from the top that policemen do their jobs in steps below.

Of course, it can be difficult to understand why you want to centralize the work of the police when you know that the result is not so good. The reason is that you want to prepare for anonymous robot-like efforts without having a feeling for the local neighborhood. As we described earlier, if the police have a too high morality and conscience, a new police force must be added to the existing one. This should then be an unscrupulous robotic force similar to the German SS or Gestapo. In Sweden in the current stage, they want to be able to employ police officers without police training for special tasks, e.g. investigation of IT crimes etc.

In this atmosphere, some special units will also be trained. Now it is possible to tailor a mind program in recruits by means of chipping. The units will be able to "radio" control and their missions will be robotic and efficient without the need for conscience. Unless Sweden is able to create such a police system, people for these tasks will be recruited from for example the United States or other NATO-allied countries. Swedish police units can be controlled centrally from NATO - all to launch the Globalists' "New World Order".

America has terrorist laws that allow its military to capture people on American ground and detain them for an indefinite period without trial. People can then be sent to jail or "Guantánamo Bay." As soon as a person is accused of terrorism, all laws and all human rights for the individual cease.

Other countries as well as Sweden have also instituted terrorist laws. These laws have been introduced in Sweden because "other countries have introduced them". Terrorist laws have been instituted to circumvent the laws we currently have when a conscience still remains in a large part of the population. Today, terrorist laws in Europe have given police and security services powers that jeopardize legal security. The new "normal state" is the exception laws and several countries can now be classified as surveillance states. These changes now exist in almost all EU countries. Sweden has also introduced terrorist laws, but these are further tightened after the terrorist attacks that took place in Paris, Berlin, London and Stockholm. Slowly but surely this leads to the dismantling of human rights. Anti-terrorism measures undermine the rule of law, strengthen executive power, peel away judicial control mechanisms, limit freedom of speech and subject all residents to almost unimpeded surveillance by governments. Today, among other things, The United Kingdom, France, Germany, Poland, Hungary, Austria, Belgium and the Netherlands are classified as surveillance states. Human rights are now being restricted in order to provide security.

After the "terrorist attack" in Stockholm, the Swedish people have been urged to wanting to have more police - fully in line with the plan towards the "New World Order".

Of course, it was no coincidence that Sweden was assisting with troops in Afghanistan and so-called "kill decisions", where Swedes have been involved in deciding what and who to liquidate with drones. Sweden is complicit in creating the refugee streams that are circulating in Europe now. In the wake of this comes the restriction of human rights for all.


## Acceptance of certain types of crimes

To more easily oppress people, fear must be evoked in them. This is most easily done by reducing the clearance rate for certain types of crimes and offensive abuse. Today, Sweden has already a low clearance rate of most types of crimes with the exception traffic crimes when compared to other countries e.g. in Europe.

In wars, rape is used on the civilians to instill fear and hatred in a population. Then it is easier to keep the conflict going so that it can "develop" and more players can sell weapons and services to the conflict. It creates employment and indebted populations.

The clearance rate of rapes is low in Sweden. Only a few people are sentenced of the crime each year.

Compared to other countries, Sweden appears to be a country where there are a lot of rapes. In defense, it has been said that people in other countries don't report rape to the same extent as in Sweden, and don't classify all rapes as rape.

We can expect the clearance rate to remain low in Sweden when it comes to rapes, whether they are native or foreign-born perpetrators. Sweden has no public statistics that reveal the provenance of rape offenders.

Further efforts are being made to make violent crimes more acceptable. We have a situation today in Sweden with many nationalities of people and differences of opinion and thus of course violence comes in the wake as man's inner oppressed qualities surface. Man's karmic (fated) accumulations catch up. Violence, honor violence and cultural clashes are increasing in Sweden.

Some immigrant extreme Muslims in Sweden have a different view of women compared to Sweden's more advanced liberal view of women. Some of these Muslims want the Swedish women to also cover their heads and hide in the home and be an obedient companion to the man. Some of these Muslims are abusing Swedish women and the fear is increasing among women and many don't want to spend the same time outdoors in cities in the evening or at night. They feel scared. If a rape is reported, which can be a group rape, this rarely leads to conviction. It may be a group rape that has reached the tipping point with many previous offenses. In lack of evidence, i.e. "unclear and in some cases, contradictory" information about what really happened, no verdict can be enforced.

There are also local sharia courts in many of Sweden's now so-called no-go-zones like Rinkeby, where ordinary people cannot stay as there is an animal overemotional hate mood in many immigrants. These have taken over the areas and have their own legal systems. They are introducing sharia-like laws and not even journalists or government officials are safe. Swedish journalists and journalists from other countries have been attacked. Police interventions are made more difficult and emergency vehicles are exposed to threats and stone throwing. In principle, lawlessness prevails here and Swedish authorities have no control over these areas - new countries have been formed in Sweden where a completely different flora prevails - a flora that is closer to the animal stage. No-go-zones are also established in many places in other European countries.

Of course, in a more developed society, there is total harmony and complete equality between women and men. Only in a barbaric state of consciousness they embrace the view of women that many still have.

The woman according to the law of the cosmos is equal to the man consciously. From a developmental perspective, the woman is equal to the man and usually more sensible in her position than the man who usually uses his intellectuality over common sense. There are only a few psychopaths among women compared to men. If the woman had been allowed to decide, it would have been peace on earth. It is not women who send their sons out to war, to rape, to mutilate, and to kill their brothers and sisters they don't even know. Even the clergy in various religions claiming to be God's sent messengers abuse the law of the cosmos by oppressing women and blessing wars. The Soul that is the drop of the Supreme Creator's (God's) consciousness dons both a feminine and a masculine form (body) in order to express itself in the mind world. It is the lower qualitative part of the mind that creates differences between a woman's consciousness and a man's. The type of thinking that most men have about women belongs to the animal stage of consciousness and not to the human stage. During the new age, these views will belong to the past.

The spiral of violence is increasing in Sweden. The Crime Prevention Council's statistics shows that in 2016 that 106 murders were committed in

Sweden. A well-known journalist in Sweden did her own investigation and found that 162 murders had been committed during the same period. Some of the media debate against the journalist's own investigations and others think the situation is not so good. It is easy to see that the public media information we are fed with is not correct. More crimes are being committed now and more murders than before.

Car fires are increasing in Sweden and this is admitted after the trend has continued and harmed the country for many years, especially in the suburbs of Malmö, Gothenburg, Stockholm and Uppsala. The media has been almost completely silent about this in recent years. Today it can burn about 30 cars in a city like Malmö in just one weekend. The clearance rate is low and a perpetrator can be connected in only 10 % of the cases.

Furthermore, for some time stone throwing against evacuation vehicles has begun to increase, a completely absurd trend. Some areas in Sweden cannot be visited by emergency vehicles without extra reinforcement being called for. Rescue efforts are delayed or missing. More violent riots occur. Stone throwing and looting of e.g. stores are reported.

The statistics of car fires are covered up to a large extent by the fact that the number of efforts made doesn't mean the number of cars. If several cars burn at the same place and time, they are counted as one effort. Likewise, if more car fires are discovered near a previous alarm, even then, it is counted as one effort. The number of efforts for car fires in Sweden has increased from 380 in 1998 to 1428 in 2015 (MSB).

Crimes are increasing in Sweden and the clearance rate is kept low. This shows that the violence is to be normalized and this leads to more police, Special Forces and the control of people increase all along. We are therefore approaching a police state in Sweden where people support this development since they don't speak out or aren't allowed to, or get the opportunity. The media selects who should be allowed to express themselves in the media - and they must follow the agenda that the employer has.

From the year 2000 to 2010, the number of police officers in Sweden increased from 16,000 to 20,000. After the "terrorist attack" in Stockholm on April 7, in 2017, the Swedish Minister of State announced that he would appoint 10,000 extra police officers over 7 years.

Police and authorities claim that there are no no-go-zones, because Swedish law prevails there, and government officials work there as well. The problems that exist there also exist in areas in other countries - what is the difference they say?

## Fluorine

In Fritz Springmeier's book, "The Illuminati Bloodlines", you clearly get a picture about who are the highest-ranking families in the Illuminati network. These are Rothschild, Rockefeller, DuPont, Collins, Van Duyn, Russell, Kennedy, Freeman, Onassis, Li, Astor, Merovingian, Disney, Reynolds, and Krupp.

The story of how fluorine began to be added to drinking water is directly linked to at least five of the families listed above. In addition, other high-level Illuminati families are also deeply involved.

The idea of adding fluorine to water first came from the aluminum industry - *the Mellon Institute of Industrial Research*. This is a company founded by the brothers Andrew Mellon and Richard Mellon (*Mellon is a well-known top illuminati family*). The same institute was a strong advocate for the asbestos industry and produced research for decades saying that asbestos is not dangerous. Today, the industry is facing a flood of trials from people who have had their lives ruined or have even deceased due to asbestos.

The Mellon Institute merged with the Carnegie Institute of Technology in 1967 (*Carnegie is another well-known Illuminati family whose empire was funded by Schiff and Rockefeller, where Schiff operates as an agent for Rothschild; the Schiff family and the Rothschild family lived in the same house in Frankfurt in the 18th century, and Jacob Schiff was the biggest financier of the Bolshevik revolution, which we know was an Illuminati operation*).

Fluoride was also used in the water supply in the Soviet Union and then in the Nazi-German concentration camps. They knew that this made the slaves docile and manageable.

Fluorine calcifies the posterior medial frontal cortex (*pineal gland*) in the forehead lobe and prevents humans from developing communication with higher qualitative dimensional worlds. One does not come into contact with the spiritual dimensions that are based on ethics and morality. You become a slave under the influence of negative forces. Changing the chemistry and function of the pineal gland (calcifying it) is the same as hindering human evolutionary development.

It was the company IG Farben that carried out much of Nazi Germany's research and provided Hitler's war machine with goods (*for example, the company installed the gas chambers in Auschwitz in 1940*). Paul Warburg sat in the company's board of directors. His brother Max Warburg was one of the founders of the company and he personally owned most of the shares in the company and was in the board. Warburg is a top illuminati family that is married into the Rothschild family (*Warburg is also the father of the founding of the Federal Reserve in 1913*).

*The Kettering lab* was one of the largest laboratories in the world and was well funded. The laboratory's manager, Robert Kehoe, is best known for his lifelong defense in the use of the lead element. He and his institute did a massive study on how good fluoride was and how sensible it would be to add it to the drinking water. This study was funded by the *Aluminum Company of America, the Aluminum Company of Canada, the American Petroleum Institute, DuPont, Kaiser Aluminum, Reynolds Metals, US Steel etc.* All of these belong to the aluminum industry, and DuPont and Reynolds are two highly ranked Illuminati families.

Fluorine has been added to toothpaste for a long time and even today fluorine rinsing programs have been ongoing in Swedish elementary schools for a long time. This is done to reduce the risk of caries. Today, experiments are started to add fluorine to milk in some countries, e.g. in Great Britain. They want to hinder development and evolutionary opportunities at an early age to create docile non-questioning citizens who accept everything. Even in Sweden, experiments are being made with adding fluorine to the milk. The levels are so high that you know that the children will be harmed.

Drinking water containing more than 1.5 mg per liter pit corrodes the enamel in our teeth and ensures that fluorine is stored in our bone structure. As we age, we accumulate fluorine in our pineal gland and its fluorine to calcium ratio is higher than in our skeleton. Fluorine makes our skeletal bones more easily exposed to fractures. If children receive more than 2.5 to 4 mg of fluorine per liter of water, their intelligence is lowered. Fluorine increases the release of free radicals in the brain as well as alters melatonin production in the pineal gland, which disturbs our sleep. Some researchers suspect that fluoride can also cause autism, dyslexia and ADHD.

Many countries in the world add fluorine to their drinking water. In Sweden, drinking water may not contain more than 1.5 mg of fluorine per liter. No fluorine is said to be added to Sweden's drinking water. In contrast, there is bottled water (mineral water) with higher levels of fluorine.

## Harmful foods

Illuminati develop and distribute harmful foods (junk food) and drinks.

If humans want to stay in harmony and develop in a good way, it is also good if the food is easy to digest, comes from the plant kingdom and is grown with natural methods, free of pesticides and synthetic food additives.

Much of the food we buy in the grocery store should instead have the heading "eatable food like substances".

The more you alter the food, the less edible it is. The food should be cooked by people and be able to rot. You should eat varied and first and foremost plants. The more meat you eat, the bigger the chance of heart disease and cancer. It is good to eat fiber rich and not factory foods. Eat foods with different colors. Stop eating before you're full. Eat the food as long as you have cooked it and grow it yourself if you can.

Drink water!

With today's largely depleted agricultural land, it is good to add the food with some minerals and vitamins. In our present time, it is good to supply the foods with magnesium and calcium supplements, as these make our body secrete many unwanted salts, e.g. aluminum.

Often people like things that contain a lot of salt, sugar and fat. Avoid this. If a machine makes any of this, people usually eat it.

A depopulating agenda to give people foods that contribute to sterility, cancer and other misery has existed since at least the 1960s. This applies to additions of different chemicals to foods, stackable foods (canned foods) and drinking water reservoirs. The extent to which this technology is used is unclear, but advocates have or have had significant offices in the US, e.g. Dr. Lee DuBridge, who was President Richard Nixon's chief science adviser.

Nitrite, which is carcinogenic, is added to meat products. In Sweden, there are about 300 food additives and many are produced by chemical means. Many people believe that artificial sweeteners can be carcinogenic and nerve-damaging, and that flavor enhancers can cause headaches, nausea, allergic reactions, etc.

Eating poor food while exposing ourselves to toxins and other harmful effects in society gives men poorer sperm count. The decline is more than 50% in 40 years in men from North America, Europe, Australia and New Zealand, a study shows.

Much more can be written about this. The machine-made foods that we are allured to eat don't give us much energy, and if we are sensitive enough we can feel this very clearly. Do yourself a favor and eat more naturally harmonious foods.


## GMO

GMO is an umbrella term for genetically modified organisms, i.e. insects, plants, crops, animals and microorganisms.

Modification takes place through genetic engineering e.g. fish with increased cold tolerance, improved nutritional content, increased size, increased food conversion and increased disease resistance.

The FDA has approved GMO chicken but not as food for humans. It is about making medicine in the eggs. The FDA has also approved a GMO goat that has blood clot medicine in its milk. Other GMO animals have also been used to produce certain medications.

GMO-produced animals have not yet been approved for human consumption, but this is probably not so far away.

GMO-produced crops are available on the market today. This applies mainly to corn, soy, cotton, rapeseed and sugar beets. Corn and soybeans are widely used as animal feed. Today, it is difficult to find processed foods that don't have GMO ingredients, especially in the United States.

GMO crops are used to fight weeds, insects and are disease resistant. They have high productivity and higher nutritional value.

Today in Sweden, field trials are underway with hybrid aspen that can withstand drier and harsher environmental conditions or are resistant to pest insects. Attempts are being made with rapeseed that is tolerant to a pesticide and a sugar beet that has been altered to be resistant to a very harmful virus and pesticide.

Where then do the problems begin?

Alien genes can spread in nature and other organisms can be harmed. The effects of genetically modified crops are seen after they have been released in cultivation, especially if sufficient prudent research has not been done before.

GMO crops have been produced without the harmony of nature being integrated into them. The development has taken place by intellectual mind controlled people and here they instill their own mind distortion and mental state as a result in their work. The quality you have within you is the result of everything you do in the exterior.

For example, a GMO potato used experimentally can induce cell alterations in the digestive system in rats. The rats get smaller brains, liver and testicles. Their immune system becomes damaged. This can be achieved in 10 days.

GMO soy can e.g. contain several allergens.

Initially, the US FDA was very cautious in its claims about GMO crops. Since 1992, the FDA has announced that no information on GMO foods differs from the information we know about other foods. Apparently strong market forces intervened and the attitude changed abruptly at the FDA. The FDA got a very positive attitude towards GMOs.

A related problem is Roundup-ready crops. Roundup's primary use is in growing crops that are genetically engineered to be resistant to Roundup. Roundup is a weed killer (poison, antibiotic) that is sprayed on crops. Roundup ends up in our food and can have cancer-causing properties but at the same time kill gut bacteria that are good for our immune and digestive system. In the United States, stomach problems have increased markedly since 1996. Researchers have now found ingredients in Roundup that can kill human cells, especially embryonic, placenta and umbilical cord cells. The combination of the substances in Roundup is estimated to increase the effect of toxicity. Even though the product is diluted 100,000 times, it causes cellular changes. Remains of Roundup are now found in the Western diet with sugar, corn, soy and wheat. The negative effects on the human body are maliciously creepy and manifest as inflammation of cell systems. Roundup causes stomach problems, obesity, diabetes, heart disease, depression, autism, infertility, cancer and Alzheimer's disease.

A Russian study on hamsters lasting over two years over three generations showed astonishing results. Most hamsters who ate Roundup-ready GMO soy, and especially those who ate even more GMO soy, lost the ability to get offspring. They became sterile in the third generation. Furthermore, they showed slower growth and many pups died increasingly until the third generation. This type of soy makes up 91% of all soy grown in the United States.

It has also been reported that rat pups given GMO soy have died with 50% population loss in just three weeks. The control population had only a 10% loss at the same time. These were given GMO-free food.

A pig farmer in Iowa used the latest pig breeding technology and GMO-BT corn was used as feed, but when he used the corn of the year 2000, the sows showed signs of pregnancy, but they weren't pregnant. This affected 80% of the sows. The pigs became sterile. Other pig farmers experienced the same thing. The common denominator was the corn. When the corn was replaced, the problems disappeared. The feed manufacturer blamed all other possible causes. Another 25 pig farmers announced the same problem. The farmer closed his then existing business in 2002.

The health care guru Dr. Merchola writes that the probably most obvious clue in the danger of GMO foods is that almost all species of animals choose GMO-free feed instead of GMO feed when allowed to choose. In many cases they do this even to the limit of starvation. The animals have an instinctive feeling for the danger of GMO feed.

Today, there are changes in children's digestive systems similar to those we can see today caused by e.g. GMO potatoes. Children are more allergic and have a harder time eating different things compared to 30 years ago. When these children are instead prescribed GMO-free food, these changes disappear in a few days. When it comes to livestock, it is the same. When pigs change food from GMO soy to GMO-free soy, diarrhea problems, soreness, related deaths, etc. disappear. The same thing happens when livestock, pigs, dogs, cats and people change diet from GMO food to GMO-free food.

Today there is an epidemic of gluten intolerance to food products such as wheat. The whole thing can come from the BT gene that has been implanted in crops through genetic engineering and these crops secrete the BT poison. The BT poison is designed to open the stomach of insects and kill them. This poison has been tested on humans and it creates holes in the digestive system.

In Canada, 93% of the pregnant women have been found to have BT poison in their blood and also 80% of the unborn children. This poison may be part of the epidemic of stomach problems we see today.

Today more GMO corn is incorporated into human foods. There are no long-term tests on GMO feed on animals. These things are not documented anywhere. It is said that the companies have done research on the maize, but not enough.

Researchers who see nasty results in their GMO research are often attacked, ridiculed, denied money for further research and dismissed. Their labs can be vandalized, samples can be stolen and documents disappear.

The main ingredient in the herbicide Roundup is glyphosate. In 2012, Sweden used 700 metric tonnes of glyphosate and the US was estimated to use more than 50,000 metric tonnes on its land, i.e. farmland, gardens and embankments.

Various organizations are now discussing whether the substance is toxic or not. In 2015, the WHO classified the substance as likely to be carcinogenic, but the EU Food Authority EFSA made an opposite assessment. 94 internationally recognized cancer experts criticized the EFSA's position. The Swedish Chemicals Inspectorate doubts glyphosate. In 2017, the EU Chemical Inspectorate said glyphosate should not be classified as carcinogenic.

The EU is centrally guided in its agenda towards the "New World Order" and of course they want to give glyphosate green light to be used as much as possible in all fields in the world that in the end only can grow Roundup-ready crops, i.e. all other harmonic crops die on these farmlands. The weed poison does not disappear just because you stop using it. It remains and makes our arable land unusable for a very long time to come.

The GMO situation is worse in the US than in Europe.

Figure 51. GMO world map for the year 2005. Full-color countries account for 95% of all commercially grown GMO crops and dotted countries account for the rest.

Although permits are required in Sweden for cultivation of GMO crops, permits are not required for imports of processed products. Today it is allowed in Sweden to import and grow e.g. corn, rapeseed, soy and sugar beet as feed.

In the EU, all foods containing GMOs must be labeled with information about this - but only if the amount of GMOs in individual ingredients exceeds 0.9%.

At the same time as the natural acidification takes place in our fields where aluminum is starting to become more mobile and to a greater extent impede plant and tree growth, we have for more than 20 years chemtrailed Sweden with a cocktail mainly consisting of aluminum. Many thousands of tons, maybe millions of tons have been released across our country (described under the heading above: Geoengineering - Chemtrails). It is now almost obvious that GMO companies are working to get aluminum resistance into their GMO crops, and they are doing just that. The plants should be "stress tolerant" when exposed to aluminum from the ground water.

In the end, it should only be possible to grow GMO crops that kill us in three generations.

The large GMO companies are now starting to approach each other to jointly control even more of the global grain market. One of these companies "Monsanto" has previously developed among other things the Agent Orange (de-foliage-agent poison for the Vietnam War), DDT, PCB and the weed control agent glyphosate etc.

The trade agreements (TTIP) now being planned between the US and the EU would probably facilitate the introduction of US GM crops and regulations to the EU and thus Sweden. The idea of these trade agreements is to replace national regulations and standards with global ones. Contract-bound countries will need to loosen up rules on food safety, environmental regulations but also other rules such as freedom on the internet, regulations for the financial market, etc. They want to move regulations outside nations to make hyper-rich globalists to easier gain more and more power. This threatens democracy and national security, and so far it can be said that the Swedish political establishment has worked in full line with this. Democracy is a word that can now almost be equated with the meaning of dictatorship and governmental rape from beyond borders.

In order for the GMO companies to gain an even firmer grip of the market, their lobbying activities are now working intensively to counteract large-scale organic farming. They simply want to spray the arable land with e.g. Roundup.

As we told under the heading above "harmful foods", there is a depopulating agenda when it comes to food. It is possible to use a technique called RNA interference for this. RNA interference (RNAi) is a biological process in which RNA molecules inhibit gene expression or translation (protein building in the ribosomes) by neutralizing targeted mRNA molecules (message RNA from the cell nucleus DNA to the ribosomes). Over the past decade, researchers have been working to develop cancer treatments based on this technology. The phenomenon thus offers a way to turn off specific genes in an organism. Science Daily writes that "researchers are now weaponizing this by engineering crops to produce specific RNA fragments that, upon ingestion by insects, initiate RNA interference to shut down a target gene essential for life or reproduction, killing or sterilizing the insects", i.e. the technique is used as a way to avoid toxic pesticides. But this seems dishonest, since the agricultural chemical industry claims that their pesticides and herbicides are completely harmless and non-toxic (which makes us wonder how they kill pests). But the bigger concern is that RNA interference technology can be used to create a food-based weapon against humans. The technology can target African Americans, Latin Americans, Asians or other races. Food becomes a biological weapon.

## Acidification

### *Forests and Waters*

The acidification is caused by emissions of sulfur dioxide, nitrogen oxides and also ammonia. Sulfur dioxide emissions are the result of combustion of carbon and oil that contains sulfur. Nitrogen oxides are created in all forms of combustion, where traffic accounts for a large part of the emissions. Ammonia which is a gas is formed e.g. in a compost or when handling manure. When ammonia reaches the atmosphere, it adds a hydrogen ion and forms an ammonium ion ($NH_4^+$) and rains down as acidic precipitation to the ground. Man contributes to the acidification through these emissions, which come to the ground as sulfuric acid, nitric acid and ammonium salts. All of these leave hydrogen ions which are acidic.

The acidification of Sweden's land is also a natural course of action. The clock is reset after an ice age. The ice grinds down rocks into different fractions down to clay, which is the basis of our soils. In addition to the plants' carbon acid exhaust through their root respiration, acid rainfall with e.g. sulfur dioxide from coal and oil burning affects the soils where the plants grow. The acid rain's hydrogen ions "drum out" metal ions held by the soil colloids, e.g. $Na^+$, $K^+$, $Mg^{2+}$, $Ca^{2+}$, which reside naturally on the soil's mineral colloid particles, clay particles. The plants roots take up these metal ions through the soil water and these metal ions become part of the nutrition that plants give us when we eat them. The longer time that passes after an ice age, the more of the easily weathered mineral grains have released their easily held metal ions. The pH drops gradually in the soils, i.e. more hydrogen ions accumulate ($H^+$) at the colloids (instead of metal ions). As the pH decreases, other more heavily weathered ions begin to circulate and become available for the plants to absorb. The plants thus contain fewer of the beneficial ions and more and more of the ions we don't need in our food, i.e. toxic ions that adversely affect our health. The soil becomes depleted in nutrients and we sometimes eat even unhelpful foods.

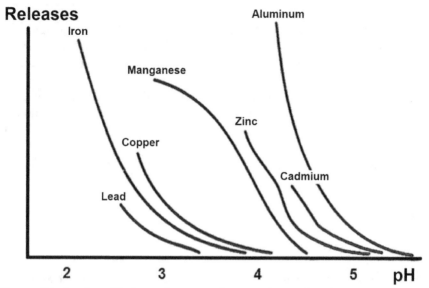

Figure 52. As the pH drops in our soils, our plants absorb more and more toxic ions. The lower the pH value, the more acidic the soil water is.

As can be seen in the graph above, also aluminum starts to circulate in the soil water and becomes available for the plants as the pH drops. Under the heading "Geoengineering - chemtrails" we have informed about that discharges of chemtrails consist of huge quantities of aluminum that are continuously discharged from aircrafts over our fields, including agricultural lands. What then does Sweden do to keep the pH high so that vegetation does not absorb this aluminum, since aluminum affects our nervous systems in a degenerative and deadly way, but also the animals' nervous systems?

The answer is that the liming projects carried out in our country to maintain the pH have decreased by about 50%. The reason is that the acidifying fallout has decreased. Lime is spread in lakes, streams and wetlands. This is done to keep the lakes alive with its wildlife. There are still thousands of lakes and streams that are not limed. The interest in new liming projects ceased as early as the 1990s.

But no liming takes place over or in the woodlands, with the pretext that the element boron then should be bonded harder to the ground, leading to a shortage of boron in the trees. The forests and animals would suffer from this. Even worse is when the forest is harvested and transported away, along with bound mineral salts. This speeds up the acidification in the woodlands and dissolves the more difficult weathered aluminum.

The Swedish Environmental Protection Agency believes that ash return is becoming more important to the woodlands in order to reduce acidification. The Forest Board reports that for 2009, only 15% of the ash was returned.

This means that the woodlands and especially the woodlands in southwestern Sweden are still strongly acidified. As authorities ponder, the situation is getting worse.

There is talk about Sweden being a recycling nation, but the forests are largely forgotten.

## Agriculture

What about agriculture?

For it to grow optimally and phosphorus uptake to be good, a pH of 6.5-7.0 is needed according to the Agriculture Department. It is possible to lime with dolomite limestone which also contains magnesium (Mg). Fertilization (P, K, N) is also needed as well as the return of micronutrients, i.e. various ions that disappeared with the first harvests from the arable land (e.g. boron, copper, iron and nickel).

If all Swedish arable land were to be limed to optimum pH values, about 1 million tonnes per year would be used according to the magazine "Land, Lantbruk och Skogsland". Also the neighboring country of Finland should lime with more than 1 million tonnes per year.

In Sweden today, about 250,000 tonnes of lime per year are spread, but this varies from year to year. Sweden is the worst among the Nordic countries in liming and today, Finland is liming approximately as much although having only one third of the arable land compared to Sweden.

If there is no liming, the harvests will be noticeably smaller. The aluminum sneaks in and the plants become toxic. In cases where sewage sludge from the wastewater treatment plants is spread on the fields, it is extremely important that the pH is kept at the right level advised by the Swedish Agricultural Agency. The sludge contains toxins and low pH also leaves off these toxins to the plants. Cadmium is also released to plants from arable land if the pH becomes too low. Therefore, the chemical inspection has also criticized the spread of sludge. If sludge is added to the fields repeatedly, e.g. the cadmium content is increased all the time. According to the magazine "Testfakta", you should not eat more than 50 to 100 grams of wheat flour a day. Cadmium storage in the body causes damage to the kidneys and in small amounts increased risk of osteoporosis, fractures and cervical cancer.

The Swedish KRAV label of Organic Crops also causes problems. Structural liming is not allowed with CaO, $Ca(OH)_2$. This means that the soil is guaranteed to lower its pH and should by this law be toxic considering its content in Aluminum and Cadmium. This is a well thought out central move in order for people who want better food to instead get toxic food. Harvests become smaller when the pH is not kept high enough.

The country's croplands have, after the time of crop rotation, delivered crops with a lack of micronutrients, where the harvests also have supplied varying amounts of aluminum and cadmium, depending on the amounts of lime spread.

The Swedish agricultural industry is in crisis. Agriculture is subsidized and the farmers have been made dependent on the subsidies. After this, the farmers also are not paid enough for their agricultural products. A dairy farmer disappears a day as a result of this and in the last 25 years 9 out of 10 farms have disappeared. The banks are happy to "help". When the farm is sufficiently indebted, the bank takes over the farm. Today, Sweden is not self-sufficient in food where the self-sufficiency is estimated to 50%. Some exact numbers are difficult to obtain. Sweden can only manage a few days without food imports. In 2002, the Swedish Emergency Management Agency (Beredskapsverket) was scrapped together with the warehouses with foods for crises.

If diesel imports to agricultural machinery are aborted, self-sufficiency will be even lower.

The lands are more fertile in Europe and now when globalization is increasing, the market forces and circumstances work for less farming in Sweden, where the foods come from Europe instead. Local agriculture north of the Swedish county of Skåne is likely to be closed down by economic unprofitability. Politics and market forces work for this.

Very cheap and fertile agricultural land in Ukraine has now been bought by international companies. More than 2.2 million hectares have been taken over of Ukraine's 32 million hectares. Among other things, the company Monsanto has interests in Ukraine and we can suspect that the agricultural land will produce GMO crops that will be able to compete with European agriculture.

The result will be that GMO crops will be grown to a greater extent also in Europe, and anyone who does not accept GMO crops will be competed out. Man's poor health will become poorer and more degenerate.

Dictatorial globalization, power and control are far more important according to the Globalists than the human rights to evolve into a higher qualitative multi-dimensional quantum conscious cosmic citizen.

We can thus state that also agricultural policy aims to eradicate man in a short time.

### Acid / Base Balance - The pH value in the Blood

The acid-base balance is a fairly new concept that is increasingly being taken into account. It was Dr Ragnar Berg who in Germany and Sweden in the 1930s demonstrated that some foods are acidic and some others are basic to the body.

The basic rule is that fruits and vegetables create basic reactions in the body while meat and alcohol create an acidic reaction. We generally consume too high a proportion of acidifying food, which often amounts to 80% in Sweden. It would have been better if the food intake to 80% had consisted of basic foods.

If we eat too much acidifying foods, it can facilitate cancer to start growing in the body. Cancer cells can neither multiply nor survive in a basic environment, only in an acidic environment.

Both the Swedish physician Erik Enby and the Italian doctor Tullio Simoncini have done research in the cancer field and concluded that cancer cells are linked to fungal growth in the body. A basic environment significantly impairs the growth of fungi in the body and thus the survival of the cancer cells. It can facilitate if the body is supplied with basic foods and minerals that work to maintain the body's pH of 7.4. Bicarbonate ($NaHCO_3$) dissolved in water maintains a pH of about 7.4 and it is precisely hydrogen carbonate that buffers the body's blood to this particular pH value.

This approach is counteracted by the establishment since today's cancer treatments and drugs hold back human development possibilities. The establishment refuses to see new approaches to the cancer problem.

Eat more vegetables and fruits! ... and reduce the risk of bodily acidification, then we can hold back several disease-producing processes in the body.

The intestinal enzymes are important for nutrient uptake and depend on a slightly basic environment. Here, a lot of acid may need to be neutralized.

It should be added that the body does everything it can to maintain its pH of 7.4. The body takes several steps to neutralize acid which can be:

- In case of imbalance, acid is stored in the connective tissues.
- In case of imbalance, acid is stored in the joints.
- In case of imbalance, calcium and magnesium are taken from the skeleton.
- In case of imbalance, basic bicarbonate is taken from the blood.

Fiber (dietary fiber) keeps the stomach and intestines in good shape.

Acidifying foods:

- Meat, fish, eggs.
- Foods that contain a lot of sugar, i.e. also sugared fruit and jam.
- Cheese, pasteurized milk (the one found in the shops). Milk products are also considered to be mucous generating and can therefore help to make the body more sluggish and toxic.
- White flour products, pasta, cereals such as rye, wheat, oats, rice.
- Margarine, olive oil.
- Coffee, black tea (most herbal teas, however, are basic), juice, soda, alcohol, tobacco, pharmaceuticals.
- Legumes such as peas and lentils are neutral to weakly acidic.
- Nuts and seeds, cocoa, pepper.

Foods that give a basic reaction which we need to eat more of:

- Most vegetables, root vegetables, potatoes, etc.
- Fruits, berries, lemon, grapefruit.
- Mushrooms, fresh beans, unpasteurized cow milk.

Supplements of calcium and magnesium carbonates are good as they are basic. PH-Lime sold in Sweden consists of about 70% of calcium carbonate and about 30% of magnesium carbonate. This mixture prevents acidification in the body and also cancer. If man were to spend more energy and money on prevention instead of symptom treatment, then man could be kept healthier and cost less for society in medicine costs with entailing less suffering.

The algae chlorella has many good properties and counteracts among other things acidification. The algae also help to bind heavy metals that can be stored in the body's connective tissues and cells.

A lot of herbs are basic and can be taken as supplements or teas. Examples of useful herbs are nettle, horsetail, rosehip powder, lucerne, St. John's wort, anise, chamomile and more.

Several diseases are considered to lead to excess acidity in the body due to the disease itself. Excess acid is considered to be muscle degrading.

Several public events are held to raise money for cancer research. This money is used to keep a lot of the machinery of symptom-related research ongoing. The progress has been limited in relation to the resources spent. If these financial resources were to be used for preventive purposes then the research of Dr. Erik Enby, Dr. Tullio Simoncini and Dr. Royal Raymond Rife would be worked further on. It is easy to see that there is more money to be made on medicaments than on preventive care.

**Climate lies - Climate issue**

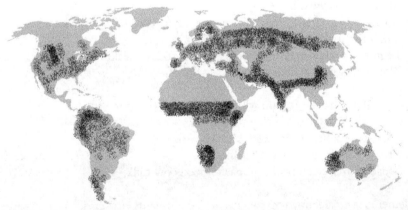

Figure 53. An Australian and an American study show that vegetation is increasing (1982-2011).

In a study published by the journal Nature, photosynthesis has increased by 30% over a 200-year period.

On the Swedish TV news, "Aktuellt", December 10, in 2016, the newly elected President Donald Trump's attitude to the climate alarm was commented by the Swedish Minister of Environment and the Deputy Minister of State Isabella Lövin. They were interviewed about the consequences of a change in US climate policy. Trump wanted to increase coal burning as a source of energy in the United States. During the interview, Isabella Lövin stated that the world's desert areas are spreading due to the alleged global warming.

This is not true!

The truth is that the world's deserts are shrinking thanks to the growing vegetation caused by the higher content of carbon dioxide in the atmosphere. The image above shows the areas of the earth where vegetation increases and deserts are shrinking. In particular, it can be seen that much more is growing in southern Sahara, which has caused the desert border to move north.

The false statement by the country's leading environmental politicians is a vivid illustration of how the entire climate policy is based on constant lies about growing deserts, melting polar ices, melting Greenland ice, rising sea levels, extreme weathers, etc. None of these claims are supported by observations. All changes are within normal variability.

The climate issue is not about the climate, but is a political invention to strengthen the forces behind a global world order and further taxation of the people. The Swedish government wants to create a climate policy framework based on carbon dioxide such as greenhouse gas and zero emissions of greenhouse gases by 2045. Furthermore, they want domestic traffic to have decreased by 70% by 2030.

How can a climate policy be based on carbon dioxide emissions and taxation of this when other environmental elephants go free, for example the Globalists' chemtrails, HAARP, GMO, Microwave radiation and other toxins like vaccines, heavy metals, radioactivity and foreign synthetic compounds of all kinds, etc. Today our air, water, soil and foods are more or less toxic and we live on borrowed time.

Climate change will accelerate, as presented by the White House report. This is due to the entry of the Earth and our Solar System into the giant plasma field around the local Central Sun Alcyone, in the Pleiadian Star System. The entry took place at the winter solstice on December 21-23, 2012. Some people predicted that the earth would go under, which did not happen.

What we have to expect is climate instability and this is not due to increased or decreased solar activity, but rather to the Bilderbergs' use of Chemtrails and HAARP that we have described. When man intervenes in nature and affects the equilibrium found there, nature will strike back. This comes as a letter on the mailbox. The solar system and the earth are living organisms, and do what they need to neutralize imbalances.

The years 1998 and 2015 were warm on earth. This was due to a temporary effect of the El Niño weather phenomenon. It is talked about that the "elevated" temperature also produces mass bleaching of corals. In fact, the mass bleaching is largely due to the decline in seawater levels during El Niño in many places. This later information is gladly omitted.

The El Niño effect is over, something that we Swedes now experience through record-breaking snowy weather that hardly indicates any global warming. The winter of 2017 continued with snow storms well into May in Central Sweden.

The "Global Warming" as it is called, is exaggerated. "It" is blamed on the increased amount of carbon dioxide in the atmosphere. In fact, carbon dioxide accounts for a very small proportion of greenhouse gases. The carbon dioxide content in the atmosphere in 2013 was 0.0396%. Water vapor is the most important greenhouse gas and has a content of between 1 - 4%. This is up to 100 times more than carbon dioxide.

By repeatedly proclaiming carbon dioxide as a villain to the so-called "global warming" and further highlight this by awarding the Nobel Peace Prize in 2007 to Al Gore, i.e. a US presidential candidate, for his achievement in showing climate change created by man, i.e. "the carbon dioxide threat," the time is now ripe for all States to harvest carbon dioxide taxes. The "Increasing Carbon Dioxide" has now become a mantra that lies in man's subconscious database. Man is now completely off course and at odds with his common sense and autopilots towards this so-called "reality". Questioning this makes you a "climate denier", "fact-resistant" and "conspiracy theorist".

Al Gore claimed e.g. that glaciers on Kilimanjaro (big mountain in Africa) disappeared as a result of "global warming". Forests collect a lot of water and emit a lot of water vapor. In fact, if you remove forest at the foot of such a mountain, the air flowing over the mountain becomes drier, creating a drier air flow over the glacier. This causes similar glaciers to disappear.

Furthermore, if you cut down forests, large amounts of carbon dioxide is released from underlying soils for a long time and comes to the atmosphere. Desert formation with sandstorms can lead to huge emissions of atmospheric carbon. It is estimated that up to about 1500 - 2300 billion tonnes of coal is found in soils.

Photosynthesis consumes about 120 billion tonnes of atmospheric carbon every year, and this is after deforestations have taken place. By not cutting at the same rate, the photosynthetic biomass is instead increased.

The burning of fossil fuels that is now taking place contributes to some 87% of the human-caused carbon released to the atmosphere. Others claim that the figure is as low as 20%. The lower figure calculates that biomass has been harvested for a long time, and that it cannot photosynthesize at the same rate, i.e. add coal as before. The fact that we harvest forests from land areas thus contributes to a much greater loss of carbon dioxide accumulation (carbon dioxide sink) than previously estimated (Timothy Casey B.Sc. (Hons.)).

So if we want to reduce carbon dioxide levels in the atmosphere, we must stop cutting down the world's forests, and stop burning fossil fuels.

Carbon dioxide levels in the Earth's atmosphere have dropped from more than 6,000 ppm during the pre-Cambrian period to about 280 ppm in pre-industrial times. In 2013 it was 396 ppm and now in 2017 slightly above 400 ppm.

The sun controls everything on Earth!

All activity on earth, including human activity, is controlled by the sun, and thus humanity's part of the rising carbon dioxide emissions is controlled by the Sun. Similarly, our local Central Sun Alcyone in our galaxy controls our own Sun and its activity in the Solar System. Everything on Earth that appears to be of a negative nature is also controlled by the Sun and has to do with the evolution of human consciousness. The Supreme Deity, Sat Purush, The Christ Power is constituted by the Central Sun, the Central Universe's implicit (folded), virtual (hidden) energy fields (plasma energy) and electromagnetic energy. This controls everything in the universe, all galaxies, all the Suns, all the planets and everything else that is created in the universe. God is nothing but energy and information (consciousness).

During the solar maximum, i.e. when the sun has many sunspots, the earth's troposphere (the atmosphere where weather is located) is warmer and more humid. In the case of sunspots, the sun's magnetic activity increases and can create dramatic changes in, among other things, the sun's ultraviolet and X-ray radiation. Approximately every 11 years at the sunspot maximum, the sun's magnetic poles also shift. It is clear that "something else" controls the activity of the sun. The sun also spins one lap around its own axis once a month, which means that different intensity of energy and information reach us on earth.

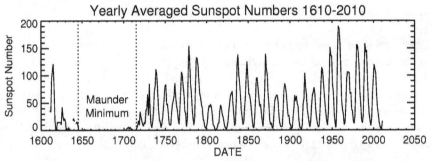

Figure 54. The number of sunspots has increased over a longer period of time until about the year 2000. Under the "Maunder Minimum" there was a period of time that came to be called the "Little Ice Age". Data from NASA.

The solar cycle length should also play a role. The solar cycle length has gone from 11 years to about 10 years from 1920 to 1980, which should have contributed to a warmer climate, but at the same time fewer sunspots appeared, which over time resulted in a decrease in temperature. The following years have shown a certain increase in temperature. The last solar cycle from about 2000 to 2014 was about 14 years long. The number of sunspots during this period was also fewer. Some believe that the Earth's annual average temperatures increased and others that the temperature has been about the same for the last 25 years. Despite the variations in the sun, the Globalists' scientists (consciously or unconsciously) believe that human carbon emissions control much of the temperature of the earth, which has led to the allegedly increased "Global Warming" based on the carbon threat.

The climate data that is the basis of the "carbon dioxide threat" has been fabricated and changed over the decades to show this forced conclusion. Dr. John Bates, who previously worked at the NOAA (National Oceanic and Atmospheric Association) announced this to "The Washington Times". Dr. John Bates has worked for 40 years with climatology and is a highly regarded scientist. He also said that many researchers were unwilling to file and document their data. John Bates has been called "one of the biggest climate deniers" but other scientists back him. John Bates has exposed a culture that is not based on robust research, but which instead advocates an agenda.

The NOAA Chief Mr. Karl, has long-standing contact with the White House's John Holdren, Obama's highest science advisor. From here came the directives. John Holdren is co-author of the book "Ecoscience", a book on 1649 pages where a lot of the thinking to understand what has happened is found.

Thus, the world average temperature in the data has been allowed to increase more than reality shows. Reality shows that there has not really been any actual heating during the period 1895 to 1987 according to an article from "The New York Times" from 1989. Since 1980, data has gradually been changed to the increasingly significant "hockey stick", which has been spread around the world to actualize an alleged carbon threat which is thus taxable and coercive. Temperature data has been manipulated to precisely follow the carbon dioxide increase on Earth. Here is shown the last drastic rise in temperature, i.e. the blade of the hockey stick, which is allegedly due to "the increasing level of carbon dioxide caused by man."

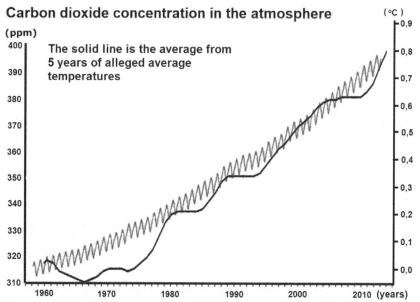

Figure 55. The "hockey stick". In 1750, the carbon dioxide level was about 280 ppm. An exaggerated temperature rise for the last decades has been

presented. The carbon dioxide curve agrees well with the increase in carbon dioxide in the atmosphere. Temperatures are alleged global temperature anomalies. (Temperature data and carbon dioxide data from NASA).

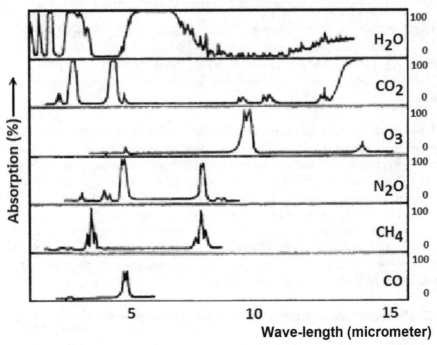

Figure 56. The graph shows the percentage of the radiation absorbed by the Earth's atmosphere. Nitrogen, oxygen and argon are "transparent" to IR radiation. The graph originally comes from "Handbook of geophysics and space environments, 1965".

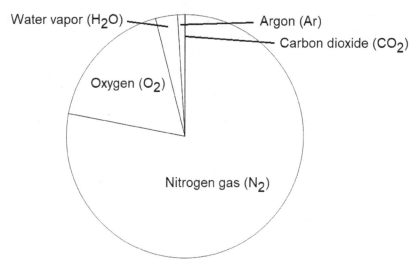

Figure 57. The composition of the atmosphere. Notice how little carbon dioxide there is represented by a line. The water vapor in this case is about 3%.

Carbon dioxide is a "trace gas" when a comparison is made with other gases in the atmosphere as carbon dioxide is less than 1%. The carbon content of the atmosphere is only 0.04% (400 ppm). When the energy and wavelength ratio is included, the energy absorption of the carbon dioxide molecule accounts for only 1/7 of that of the water molecule. Carbon dioxide is a heavy gas and is found closest to the earth's surface. At about 6000 m altitude there is only about 0.016% carbon dioxide.

The water vapor in the atmosphere varies and can amount to 4%. In many areas it is 3%. The water in the atmosphere holds up to about 1200 times more heat compared to the carbon dioxide molecules. The water molecules then hold 99.9% of the atmosphere's heat and the carbon dioxide 0.1%. To claim that carbon dioxide is a villain to global warming is wrong.

The atmosphere is in equilibrium with the world's oceans. If more $CO_2$ was to enter the atmosphere, water vapor in the atmosphere would pass into its liquid phase, forming water droplets and falling down as rain. This causes water vapor to disappear from the atmosphere and is thus replaced by $CO_2$. The result of this is that the heat-holding effect of the atmosphere becomes lower. More carbon dioxide in the atmosphere leads to cooling. The increasing amount of carbon dioxide we have seen in the graphs presented has to do with solar radiation, which has increased over a period of time. Carbon dioxide follows the heat increase like a dog in a leash. The solubility of carbon dioxide in the seas decreases with increasing heat. It is estimated that there is 20 million times more dissolved $CO_2$ in all the world's oceans compared to an annual carbon dioxide emission from all the world's sources, including both natural carbon dioxide emissions and man-made. Man accounts for 3.6% of this. Adrian Vance has described this scenario very well in his book the "Vapor Tiger", which we recommend everyone to read. He has also set up a lab for schools showing what happens to the atmosphere when more carbon dioxide gets there.

Then it should be added that a single large volcanic eruption can add enormous amounts of carbon dioxide to the atmosphere. This is happening all the time and major outbreaks have occurred on many occasions historically. The most significant thing that happens then is that the earth's average temperature is lowered as a result of solar radiation coming to earth is being reduced by particles added to the stratosphere, which obscure the sun's light, with varying crop failures as a result. As the temperature on Earth drops, new additions of carbon dioxide are dissolved in the world's oceans. When temperatures later increases, the world's oceans are degassed a little and more carbon dioxide is added to the atmosphere.

In the sea there is also a balance between dissolved carbon dioxide and calcium carbonate, i.e. limestone.

*The "climate deniers", as Globalist-controlled research calls them, are described as follows: Climate deniers are the people who try to explain away the carbon dioxide threat and instead blame the sun for the current temperature rise on earth.*

Global temperature data should be reported from satellites. RSS satellite data shows no increase in global temperatures from 1996 to 2014. The climatologist Dr. Lennart Bengtsson believes that there was a warming period from 1910 to 1940 with a temperature increase of 0.3 degrees and from 1980 to 2000 by 0.5 degrees.

Thus, the warming has stopped. The number of sunspots is now decreasing and is projected to decrease a number of years ahead according to NASA. Dr. Helen Popova believes that there is no strong evidence that global warming is created by human activity, but if so, then we have a second chance on earth now, before the sun returns to its "normal" activity.

In the "carbon dioxide hysteria", the "Globalists" choose to ignore the enormous impact of the Sun on the earth. The Sun controls everything in the solar system because the planets are sub-projections of the Sun's intrinsic program, i.e. energy and information. The information about this is clearly seen at the five-dimensional level, and this clearly shows what is to be manifested on the various planets in the solar system. As long as man does not raise his consciousness from the level of an intellectual animal human being, man will not ever be able to understand this. Man must raise his consciousness to a solar system consciousness to galaxy consciousness in order to understand this - no speculation is needed here. Man's addition of carbon dioxide to the atmosphere through various channels is also controlled by the Sun. Nothing in the solar system would work without the Sun. We see here the same agenda as the Amon Priesthood in Egypt had, i.e. to ban the worship of the Sun God and instead by force introduce the worship of the Moon. This is the same agenda that the Globalists are trying to push through today. The then priesthood, through new incarnations, tries to pursue the same policy as then, and with the same goal: "A New World Order". This "New World Order" is based on dictatorship through coercion, lies and guilt. In this way, they counteract the evolution of human consciousness toward a multi-dimensional higher qualitative quantum consciousness - free from all entanglement, bondage. These Globalists are thus "reality-resistant" and very interested in money and power.

The Sun's activity in scalar energy and information is crucial to what happens to the Earth's climate. The earth and its people can do nothing but conform to the cosmic agenda that the earth automatically follows. If we humans have psychologically unresolved karmic problems within us, we will externally manifest this imbalance in some way. Of course, if we use combustion engines and emit more carbon dioxide, this is part of the solar system's multi-dimensional agenda. The universe governs man and not the other way around as many claims in intellectual science. What happens must happen and nothing else. Everything is visible in the five-dimensional matrix that only a few people on earth today have conscious access to.

Now when negative individuals with large karmic loads receive more scalar energy and information from the Sun, and their karma intensifies toward working against other negative individuals, nothing can stop them. This is aligned with the multi-dimensional agenda of the solar system and is the process that is now taking place. When these negative individuals have neutralized each other or disappeared in their own pitfalls, a new world will be the result. Major changes will emerge at the end of the old age and the entry into the new age. The process will gradually become more obvious and also the human beings of the earth are part of this process.

Professor Konstantin Meyl believes that only 2% of the sun's radiation is visible. 98% of the radiation is mostly related to scalar energy - plasma energy and information. The materialized part thereof, i.e. the neutrino current from the sun to the earth changes from year to year and this affects the earth's climate. Some of these neutrinos are absorbed by the earth and results in among other things earthquakes. Thus, the earth expands over time.

The Sun works at all levels to best serve its solar system.

According to a study, the Sun's magnetic field has doubled from 1901 to 1998, and will be more active now over a period of 8,000 years. Some scientists now also see some changes in some of the planets in the solar system, which has happened since 2012, but it is not yet determined whether these are natural variations or real visible changes. What will really affect our situation on earth now is the increasing energy field of the Sun through its scalar waves, with which the earth and everything living here are in resonance with.

A New World for a New Human Being will be the result in our corner of the universe.

## Agenda 21 and Agenda 2030

The UN is intended to become the new World Government and through Agenda 21 the process accelerated towards the "goals" of the Globalists. A large part of the governance of the UN takes place through the Club of Rome, which sets out the guidelines. Linked to the Club of Rome are large super-influential multinational companies. Many of these are among the largest polluters today. These companies have taken the initiative for a worldwide environmental work. Joining and dictating here is necessary if one is to be able to steer the process and the world in the "right" direction. In parallel with the UN's supranational work, the Globalists are working to enforce major trade agreements, such as the TTIP and TPP. These strengthen the companies' influence over the trade rules at the expense of different countries' national self-determination.

Man's consciousness must be rectified or run over - all in order for the Agenda to be implemented. The rules and approaches should be the same for the whole world.

The Globalists have therefore, through the UN, formulated both Agenda 21 and Agenda 2030. The contents sound good, but the underlying agenda is total control and limitation of man through lies, threats and guilt.

## *Agenda 21*

How can we bring people towards global dictatorial governance? There is need of conformity of people's minds that should focus on a common goal. Why not choose the environment. The environment has deteriorated significantly since the industrial revolution that rocketed seriously in the 1850s. The environment feels important to people and if everyone is involved in the hysteria then it is not questioned, because who wants to be an environmental opponent, "climate denier"?

At a UN conference in Rio de Janeiro in 1992, the member states agreed to agree on an action program that came to be called Agenda 21. They wanted to counteract the destruction of nature and environment, poverty and lack of democracy. The countries of the world should work together for "sustainable development". The citizens would be involved and the countries would launch the action plan locally through a local Agenda 21.

Today, Agenda 21 is largely forgotten. According to Swedish Radio, not all people in the municipal switchboard know what Agenda 21 is. The work has been moved under other headings that have to do with environmental work or sustainable development. The Swedish Radio announces that local environmental areas have often been granted an external shopping center.

But what did this mean to all people? We started sorting out all household waste. All children in the schools should remind their parents to put the right garbage in the right container and the garbage would later end up in the right recycling bin at the recycling center or more local ones. This has succeeded - most do this.

What people didn't know when this was introduced was that most of the garbage collected for recycling was either burned or landfilled. Today, society has caught up and collected glass jars become new glass jars, cardboard becomes new cardboard, plastic becomes new plastic gadgets, metal becomes steel and aluminum, batteries are reprocessed.

About 20 years ago, German sorted out household waste was bought and burned in Sweden's upgraded garbage incineration plants. When Swedish Television then explained to German individuals what had happened to their garbage, the Germans became very upset. They could not understand that the good deed they had done, where garbage would be new materials and containers for food, which they were promised, instead burned in Sweden's upgraded garbage incineration plants. Today we have an overcapacity for waste incineration and we help other countries to burn their garbage in Sweden. Instead, we have to deal with the environmentally hazardous ash, which has a larger volume than if we had just burned our own garbage. The net effect has become worse for us in Sweden.

Furthermore, we have been indoctrinated in schools since the 1990s about global warming, which is alleged to have been caused by man's burning of fossil fuels, i.e. carbon dioxide emissions. Most people now exclaim without questioning or studying physical data and call people who have other views "climate deniers", "fact-resistant" and sometimes "idiots". Man has been drilled and we are now ready to accept higher taxes on fossil fuels. At the same time, the Globalists will make it very difficult to use other energy sources. They are not interested in the environment but instead of taxing and further enslaving man with more lies to gain total control over the individual. Here we are today. What, then, is the next step when we demonstrably are breaking like a flock of sheep entirely to the wishes of the Globalists?

We should remember that the Globalists, through several very influential and powerful companies, advocate the environmental agenda included in the UN supranational regulations called Agenda 21. How long will it take before the UN introduces supranational laws that ride roughshod over domestic laws?

Agenda 21 works in many areas and the goal is a world population of 350 - 500 million people. People should be encouraged to move to cities where their longevity becomes easier to control. Birth rates may decrease and also mortality may increase. The two options can be combined. This is the content of Agenda 21.

Australia, under Agenda 21, is working to privatize water resources. Australian farmers therefore will not have access to their own water on their own land. They will be taxed for all violations according to the Australian politician Pauline Hanson. Instead, globalist companies must have free access and collect money for the water. Public water reserves and dams are already receiving reduced maintenance.

In the United States in California now essentially the same is happening. The groundwater is running dry and the land has been dry for five years. People can now buy their water on PET bottles. The water source used comes from a national forest in California and water rights are subscribed to for a trifle ($ 524) by Nestlé. The bottled water is sold expensively. At the same time, California residents are being asked to spare their water usage. In 2015, Nestlé pumped 133 million liters of water from the forest. Signatures have now been collected and attempts are being made to stop Nestle's agreement on the use of forest water. Nestlé's CEO Peter Brabeck has stated on video that people should not have the right to water. Today, Nestlé owns 70 brands of bottled water and owns many water rights. More and more water rights are being privatized in the world. The price of clean drinking water is rising.

In Sweden, too, the water price is rising and has risen by 32% over 10 years. Instead of continuously maintaining the water pipe systems, it is calculated that much has to be done over a short time. It is predicted that the cost of water should double in 25 years. Some believe that it needs to double already. Shall also Sweden be tricked into water problems despite the fact that Swedish citizens have paid for the entire piping network and everything it means? Is it the meaning that all this and the water rights are to be sold to private players also here in Sweden? Then, the water will probably be limited and even more expensive here for all Swedes. The former alliance government in Sweden under Minister of State Fredrik Reinfeldt sold shares in state-owned Swedish companies for a value of SEK 160.3 billion.

## Agenda 2030

Quoted from the UN: "At a UN summit in New York in September 2015, Agenda 2030 and the Global Sustainable Development Goals were adopted. It was a historic meeting and the result will affect everyone's future as the goals are universal and apply to all countries, including Sweden".

You can vote for whatever party you want in the next parliamentary election but it does not matter. Agenda 2030 is the policy that is implemented. Sweden has signed this agenda and the Swedish people have no idea what this means. Sweden has sold the Swedish people to the Globalists under the UN, which becomes the World Government. The work will be completed by 2030.

Agenda 2030 is a program that works for 17 goals for "sustainable development" and 169 sub-goals for "sustainable development". Not much about this has been said in the media.

Agenda 21 focused mainly on the environment. Agenda 2030 is much more detailed and covers almost all human areas. Agenda 2030 is an agenda for governing the World. It is supranational and runs over Swedish laws. The responsibility of the Swedish Government is to achieve these goals in Sweden. The same applies to all other countries that have signed.

The entire Agenda 2030 is a utopia and lacks all reality. During this false Utopia, man will truly come to "Hell". A great many fine words are found in Agenda 2030 and the Agenda is completely impossible to execute when human Karma works in the opposite direction. Their goal vision is easy to see. We see in today's society that development is going in the exact opposite direction. There is only one way to execute the entire Agenda 2030 and that is to kill all of humanity.

Here is the goal of Agenda 2030:

*In these Goals and targets, we are setting out a supremely ambitious and transformational vision. We envisage a world free of poverty, hunger, disease and want, where all life can thrive. We envisage a world free of fear and violence. A world with universal literacy. A world with equitable and universal access to quality education at all levels, to health care and social protection, where physical, mental and social well-being are assured. A world where we reaffirm our commitments regarding the human right to safe drinking water and sanitation and where there is improved hygiene; and where food is sufficient, safe, affordable and nutritious. A world where human habitats are safe, resilient and sustainable and where there is universal access to affordable, reliable and sustainable energy. We envisage a world of universal respect for human rights and human dignity, the rule of law, justice, equality and non-discrimination; of respect for race, ethnicity and cultural diversity; and of equal opportunity permitting the full realization of human potential and contributing to shared prosperity. A world which invests in its children and in which every child grows up free from violence and exploitation. A world in which every woman and girl enjoys full gender equality and all legal, social and economic barriers to their empowerment have been removed. A just, equitable, tolerant, open and socially inclusive world in which the needs of the most vulnerable are met. We envisage a world in which every country enjoys sustained, inclusive and sustainable economic growth and decent work for all. A world in which consumption and production patterns and use of all natural resources – from air to land, from rivers, lakes and aquifers to oceans and seas - are sustainable. One in which democracy, good governance and the rule of law as well as an enabling environment at national and international levels, are essential for sustainable development, including sustained and inclusive economic growth, social development, environmental protection and the eradication of poverty and hunger. One in which development and the application of technology are climate-sensitive, respect biodiversity and are resilient. One in which humanity lives in harmony with nature and in which wildlife and other living species are protected.*

Agenda 2030 further describes that we should all be guided by the UN Charter and have full respect for "international law". We can thus throw out Swedish legislation because it is subordinate. Agenda 2030 speaks about human rights which do not actually exist. "Democracy", "human rights" are only words that instead mean the opposite. Agenda 2030 talks about "sustainable economic growth". It is thus intended that the instrument must be financial - just as before, but now with only figures, for development goes in that direction. Thus, it will be possible to turn off all individuals who oppose or want a genuinely harmonious society. The agenda continues with lies about the "global warming" that must be fought. Developing countries are mentioned in many places and special priority should be given to them. The production in the industrialized world will be reduced and transferred to the developing countries. This is a process that has already come a long way.

By signing Agenda 2030, Sweden recognizes "the positive contribution of migrants for inclusive growth and sustainable development". The matter is thus finally debated at the same time as the integration of these people with scattered views on life goes very bad. At the same time, the Globalists are backing up conflicts in countries from which refugees come. Agenda 2030 writes that "sustainable development cannot be realized without peace and security; and peace and security will be at risk without sustainable development". Add even more solar energy to this and we have even more conflicts coming that will flare up.

The word "development" is used 226 times in the document but nowhere can be found "human development" or "individual development toward a higher qualitative quantum consciousness". It is society that shall develop (sustainable development) and not the human being.

The religion that will be applied is the Freemasons' and the bottom layer will be the slaves who will increase in percentage. There are many fine words but there is also a reality. Agenda 2030 in its current design is doomed to fail and will lead to total chaos. The agenda suits all politicians who speak with double tongues.

By signing Agenda 2030, we have really confirmed the Swedish Parliament as a large sandbox.

### The Work for World Dictatorship

The work for dictatorial control over man goes too slowly, say the Globalists. The process must be more specified and accelerate. It must be faster than the rate at which people now are waking up and develop due to the increased solar influence that affects man toward universal development, evolvement. Many people will emancipate in this process but most will not be able to deprogram. This latter category of people the Globalists wants to rule and they will do everything they can to do so. If this category of people is controlled, the Globalists will be able to influence the development towards the dictatorship they seek.

However, the truth is that these people, as they are affected by the increasing neutrino influx from the sun, will act according to their karmic programming. This will make these individuals rise against each other in the same way as Sweden's and the world's leading figures will do. This is an intrinsic trait that negative beings have, despite all signed agreements. They will start fighting each other. This means that a permeated negative society in the long run can never exist. Negative beings fight each other. This is done in debates in the Swedish Parliament and on Swedish TV. Here they promise milk and honey at the same time as the party leaders are fighting each other. After a parliamentary election, no promises are sacred. When a party or several of these have come to the office, the policy can be changed in any way at their wishes. In reality, the policy becomes the Agenda of the Globalists, which is implemented through lies, threats and guilt.

As long as people don't see this, the same false society will remain.

### Summary

Every aspect of human life must be monitored and guided. The school should be of a global standard and provide information that benefits human equality and provide an indoctrination that puts the human world and individual development into shame. Even more than now, man is to become an intellectually programmed being who, through various control mechanisms, must be made to work exactly according to the template of what a "World Citizen" is. If there are deviations, all people should have a "diagnosis" that can be medicated. Chip medication that can be reprogrammed will become a matter of course. We already see that Swedish companies such as SJ advertise chipping, but also banks. The conformity has already begun. Vaccinations and further poisoning of humans by bad water, poor food and other toxic exposure become standard. Microwave radiation fields should be flooded to man and man must be trained to defend this. The food should be cheap imported GMO which should have increased toxicity by glyphosate and other pesticides. Man should be sprayed with chemtrails and aluminum should be found in both groundwater and the food we eat. The globalists will do everything to make our lives fraught with illness, premature death and more death. But we will like this because we have been standardized at school; we have been fed with economically controlled science and other lies that we will defend - because so many people can't be wrong - everyone thinks so - everyone is right. The Globalists' indoctrinating Agenda will accuse dissidents who are investing in their own individual development toward soul consciousness to be "climate deniers", "fact-resistant" and "idiots" who don't understand their own best.

The goal of the Globalists' rule of the World towards World dictatorship through lies, threats and guilt will cause man to end up in mega-cities, which are in fact "concentration camps" of immense size.

Many of you who read this probably think that this is exaggerated and equated to reading the Bible as the Devil does. In fact, all people in society have been indoctrinated for many thousands of years. Everyone has a more or less developed intellect that is raised to the skies of society where everything can be thought out intellectually etc. But the fact is from a cosmic perspective that the intellect is the lowest of all the attributes of consciousness. The other attributes or properties have been ridiculed and debased by society.

After we humans began to get caught up in incarnations on the planet earth, the evolution began with a higher qualitative cosmic consciousness, which later became a consciousness connected to magic, and later to religious thinking and eventually culminated in a more or less developed intellect. The intellect is thus constructed as far from our cosmic truth as a consciousness can be. So we have turned everything upside down in today's society from its true reality. This is difficult for today's human being to understand.

This means that man lives in a constructed reality and at the same time is an intellectual robot. We live in a constructed matrix.

This matrix is created by degenerate Reptilian beings from the 4th dimension and they control power-holders and people in decision-making positions in our 3D real world, our society. People below these decision-making individuals are in stages connected to the same force and everything is staged behind the scenes via e.g. the hierarchies of Freemasonry. These people are mostly completely blind to this reality. Not even those who are at the highest level, at the 33rd Freemason's level, who also make up the top of the pyramid (the Illuminates), are aware of the hierarchy of the negative, destructive power that governs all their lives and actions in our three-dimensional reality. They are unconscious instruments in the hand of these forces. The reason is that they have been embedded in this structure and thinking for thousands of years. Indoctrination has been reinforced by incarnation after incarnation because the situation you die from, that very situation you are born into in the next incarnation until you see through the situation. This situation is extremely difficult for these individuals to see through and the reason is that the pattern has been repeated incarnation after incarnation. This constructed reality has become the true reality to these individuals.

The Bible says that "the last will be the first". This means that society and the world will be turned right. This will happen on an individual level and also in the exterior. People who are stuck in their patterns and cannot cope with this transition will be moved from the planet earth which will instead now house evolved beings and the people who voluntarily choose to evolve toward a higher qualitative multi-dimensional quantum consciousness - free of all bondage.

Agenda 21 and Agenda 2030 use lies, threats and guilt as a means to achieve the goals.

If man voluntarily evolves into a higher qualitative multi-dimensional quantum consciousness, man will throw away all illusion about the programmed matrix which they have been locked into for thousands of years. This will make everyone who evolves, develops to come closer and closer to a truth about reality. This one will take them all the way to the Source. Man will face the same reality and the consensus on different things will be seen with the eyes of all the gathered insights all aimed at unity and total harmony. Mankind will once again unite and in its pursuit of a higher qualitative consciousness all aids and solutions will be revealed - all in the light of the infinite truth of the sun.

## Finishing

The above put together of the tools of the Illuminates is not complete. We would rather focus on the solutions, but today's people are barely even now ready to see what is happening. Today's man defends instead the miserable constructed reality that exists, and in order to steer society in a direction towards truth, one must undergo a paradigm shift (a change of consciousness) and raise consciousness to a higher qualitative level, where ethical - moral rules prevail. Since it is not possible to build a society on a false and rotten basis, the work must begin by restructuring the very foundation of society. Human reality is the foundation, and it is free for all people to choose which path they want to take. To develop and be part of the society that will now be built is an active choice. It is the only viable path if we want to follow the upward spiral of development that will be the inevitable path on earth. People who don't conform to this, who don't want to develop and instead oppose the development both when it comes to themselves and their fellow human beings will inevitably be removed from the planet earth after this incarnation. The black players will be replaced by more white players and this is done automatically. This reality is also counteracted by the dark forces through chipping, vaccination, medication and all the other tools we have presented in this book.

We just want to make you aware of that the following below means are omitted from this book. These means are also tools for the Illuminates in their quest for world dictatorship:

*Low-frequency music (junk music)* works to keep human consciousness at a low level. The music affects a person's lower energy centers and keeps him there. This music needs to be more joyful and the music scale needs to be tuned from 440 Hz to 432 Hz.

*Film* of a destructive and degenerative nature contains violence, sex and manipulation, etc.

*Fracking* is a method where you extract natural gas from a soil or rock called shale. This is done in the US. In this way, gas is released also to the groundwater which is poisoned with gas for about 100 years after the gas extraction has ceased. The groundwater and drinking water become undrinkable to humans and animals. Soils become unusable for agriculture. A large part of America's surface has been poisoned in this way.

*Oil extraction* has been going on for more than 100 years. Combustion of the oil fractions produces particle emissions that are toxic. Furthermore, the sulfur content of the oil fractions gives rise to acidification of the lands. A clean recycling society should use completely clean free energy instead. This, the Illuminates will do everything possible to counteract. According to the Illuminates, energy is supposed to cost money so all people have to pay bills all the time. The Illuminates, in fact, prefer to tax humans for the air, water and foods they need for their survival. In the world of the Illuminates, man should only be a slave to them, to their own purposes - just as has happened throughout the human history on earth.

**The mining industry** should cease and the cycling society should ensure that all metals are recycled to 100%. All metal extraction from the earth's ores involves the release of toxic metals and by-products.

**Toxic heavy metals and chemicals** should be removed from our lives, but instead they are added in different ways and to different products to reduce human development opportunities.

**Emissions of toxins** from industries are added to the air, soils and waters.

**Religions** are used for the purpose of controlling people. A tithe to the Church was also a way of taxing a population and at the same time living well at the expense of others. All religions are perversions of the true cosmic doctrine and their purpose until now has been to keep man away from the universal and absolute truth as well as away from all individual cosmic evolution.

**Economics** is the Illuminates' main tool in the quest for world dictatorship.

**The Media** is the Illuminates' channel of information to the people. The people are cradled into a false reality that is changed according to the needs to guide the mass wherever they want. All TV shows are part of their agenda. No quality programs are allowed to be broadcasted to the people. The media channels include TV, Radio and Newspapers.

**Negative affirmations** and influences can be broadcasted without people being aware of it. These negative affirmations can be broadcasted through mobile phones, transmitter masts of various kinds, LEDs that are coded with certain frequencies and other forms of microwaves. People can be mass controlled in this way and people are completely unaware of it. This is a reality that all people are co-responsible for. Man does this voluntarily against himself and others. No single individual can be scapegoated for this - we are all complicit since we use the technology.

**The school system** is today's indoctrination institutions and there is a compulsory attendance for all pupils. The children must be fed with intellectual information that to varying degree is invented or false and all forms of individual higher qualitative consciousness development and evolvement are excluded. The closest thing to development in schools today is something called "life science". It is based on a book that is "approved" and is based on conversations with students and between students. The teachings should rather have as a basis a higher qualitative development of consciousness, which is the basis for every human being in a society. The planet Earth is one of the very few planets in the cosmos that ignores this.

**Research** uses something called the "comity code" and thus no doctoral students oppose at lectures where lies are embedded in research. Today, this applies, among other things, to the so-called "global warming", much in "medical research" as well as in "physics". New clarifications by researchers who overturn old lies are not given leeway and their proper recognition. The research continues its construction on an erroneous basis. The only rescue for all people is to develop a higher qualitative multi-dimensional quantum consciousness.

**Libraries** provide books that follow the Agenda advocated by the Globalists. Revealing books are left out from the book shelves.

**Drugs, alcohol and tobacco and soon also drugs** are allowed to sell at the same time as natural vitamins, minerals, herbs, health-promoting natural medicines, treatments, electropathy, homeopathy, naturopathy and various natural healers are counteracted by a Globalist Agenda.

There are currently 63 allowed additives and process aids in wine making that don't need to be declared on the labels on the wine bottles. This means that consumers who want to know what the wine contains today cannot do this. These additives are more or less harmful to humans.

**People release harmful medications through urine.** These medications end up in rivers and waters and finally in our oceans and affect fish and aquatic animals already at very low levels. Knowledge of the medical effect on nature is poor except for estrogenic hormones. In Sweden we use 1000 different active substances (7600 different medications) and many of these end up in the oceans. The substances are designed to be stable in order to reach their target, but this means that the drugs also end up in nature. The treatment plants do not neutralize these substances. E.g. antibiotics create antibiotic resistant bacterial strains, released hormones inhibit reproduction and feminize e.g. fish stocks. The side effects of a drug can be the main effect of the drug in nature.

**Wars and conflicts.** The Illuminates create wars and conflicts by charging both sides in an emerging conflict with weapons, hatred and antagonism. After a country has been bombed, large amounts of money are lent out to the country and companies enter to rebuild it. The money cannot be repaid and thereafter it is free for the "occupying power" to drain the country's natural resources and oil reserves and take over the country.

## The Globalists are now accelerating the process

Now all the tools of the Globalists are available and they use the most toxic cocktail to accelerate the misery, i.e. to irradiate viruses, vaccines, and stored toxins and heavy metals in the body with microwave radiation 3G, 4G and 5G (soon 6G) with frequencies up to 100 GHz or even higher, to shut down society, erase it and kill man with all their measures.

## Covid-19, vaccine, 5G

**To install the new world order, the slave community according to the negative Illuminati's action plan.**

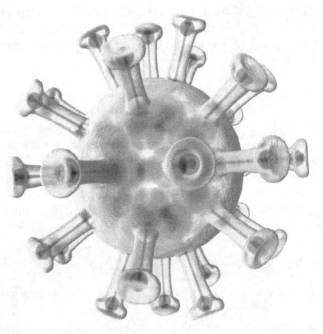

Figure 58. An imagined image of a corona virus.

So far, the extreme mass propaganda machine has flooded the society and world with information of a Corona virus, "Covid-19", which is said to spread the virus infection rapidly, with usually no or mild symptoms, but where people in Wuhan (China) and Italy are dying in agonizing Corona flu, where respiration is shut down. Horror scenes from hospitals are broadcasted all across the world.

People right now in Sweden aren't allowed to meet in public gatherings larger than 50 people. These restrictions are even tougher abroad. People who are tested positive for the Corona virus in some countries may get imprisonment for years, or worse. Authorities broadcast horror information across the country that we all should conform to. This Corona flu is classified as a pandemic, flu this year that is said to be worse than normal. As a result, the pandemic causes the society to shut down, where companies go bankrupt with mass unemployment as a result. We are expected to follow this without questioning anything - it is important for everyone to make an effort, now in the so-called "Times of Corona".

Do you think this is a good idea - do you believe in this Covid-19 spectacle?

At present, we cannot see any higher mortality compared to a regular seasonal flu. In figures presented in the beginning of 2020 we compare Italy where the mortality rate in "Covid-19" was about 1/10000 people, i.e. the same as in the US in 2009's H1N1, i.e. the swine flu. Today, October 2020, the number of deaths has not deviated from the normal, but very many people have had the cause of death "changed" to covid-19. If a test shows positive for covid-19, all of a sudden the "cause of death" is changed to covid-19, even if the person died of a heart attack, car crash or other cause. This is fraud.

Likewise, it is a scam to use the PCR tests that is used around the world to determine if a person has covid-19 or not.

Dr. Reiner Fuellmich was able to tell more about the PCR test:

*"This PCR test is the only basis for, in Germany, but also around the world, to decide that we are dealing with a pandemic. The PCR tests cannot and must not be used to determine whether we are dealing with an infection. They are not approved for diagnostic purposes, nor can they. They cannot find any infection, they can only determine that a specific fragment of a molecule was found in the body, but it can be anything, it can also be residues, for example from the processes in the body's own immune system's fight against colds and/or something more harmless. The tests can also show positive for papaya and other things,*

*which have also been written about in the media. This means that the very basis, the actual basis for establishing the existence of a pandemic does not exist at all".*

Pleiadian intelligences say there is a link between increased 3G, 4G, 5G radiations and the triggering of the Corona virus-"infections". This increased background radiation is poisonous to humans. The radiation increases the existence of viruses. The 5G radiation that is now spreading is directly dangerous. Two of the earliest sensations you may feel are disturbances in the heart area and tingling in the hands when holding a mobile phone.

Figure 59. 4G and 5G base station.

From an earthly point of view, there is no research to prove that 5G is safe. Obviously, 5G radiation is allowed without safety thinking. However, there are many causes of concern, where bodily and cellular functions are disturbed.

Right now over a certain time, the electromagnetic radiation from some 4G masts has increased in strength more than 10 times, up to 270,000 microW/m2 or higher (strålskyddsstiftelsen, radiation protection foundation). The authorities believe that there is no danger to public health.

The so-called "reference value" is set to 10,000,000 microW/m$^2$ (10W/m$^2$). At the reference value, the skin temperature is raised by one full degree to 38 degrees. Radiation higher than the reference value causes the body temperature to rise until death occurs. OK - SO VALUES ABOVE THE REFERENCE VALUE KILLS.

As long as the reference value is not reached, the authorities mean that there is no danger. But there is no research to prove that these levels would be harmless to us, especially when exposed over a long time. In the meantime, the radiation strength is increased, to adapt to 5G. It should be mentioned that there is already a commercial 5G transmitter (several according to another map) north of the Parliament House in Stockholm. Around the world, 5G transmitters are currently being installed. 5G is 10 times as powerful as 4G. Installations are now taking place during the time of "national emergency", i.e. where people aren't allowed to move outside and gather in groups. Fortunately, the situation in Sweden isn't as bad as in some other parts of the world. We currently have only one or a few 5G transmitters in use in Sweden. So, in the wait of new transmitters being installed to connect all types of electronics on the internet, we instead receive increased radiation from 4G masts.

What then is the problem with this microwave radiation?

The problem is that HAARP, 3G, 4G, and 5G interact directly with the cells' DNA or other cellular functions. The wavelength of the microwaves is taken up by our DNA which receives a greater amount of energy. This has been shown by Professor Konstantin Meyl in Germany, who among other things has worked on Tesla's scalar waves, which is the basis of all electromagnetic waves. He has shown with mathematics how the interaction with the cells' DNA takes place.

When powerful microwaves are absorbed by the body, this leads to "symptoms" which may include difficulty sleeping, abnormal fatigue, headaches, concentration and memory problems, depression, burning skin and rash, anxiety, stress and chest pressure, shortness of breath, impaired immune system. Many people have these symptoms right now. The damage done to the DNA can also cause Cancer. The number of brain tumors has more than doubled over the last ten years in Denmark, where this has been studied.

Now during seasonal flu times as 4G and 5G radiation increases, it goes without saying that further lowered immune systems open for colds and flu.

We get this year in some cases the so-called "Covid-19" or other flu, but it does not seem that we are sicker this year compared to previous years.

It has been decided at Parliament level that electromagnetic radiation from 4G and 5G is not harmful to us.

Now that the radiation from these transmitters is increasing, what happens then? We will soon be short of reference areas!

The impact on the bodily DNA and cells give them more energy and leads to a bodily reaction. The cells begin to get rid of the toxins we have accumulated over the years, a so-called detoxification or purification process. Clusters dissolve and toxins are released. During this detoxification process under compromised immune system, the body sends out these toxins as different types of viruses (exosomes). A powerful such process can be influenza. The created virus thus takes out various toxic substances from the body. Viruses thus function as a kind of solvent. This is a rescue and secretion mechanism in the body. But this view is contradicted by the entire cabal propaganda machine, as it does not contribute to any part in the all-encompassing control of a population. Vaccine "against viral diseases" would never be allowed at all. But they are now allowed because the purpose is to inject directly harmful and immunosuppressive substances into us, which creates a lot of health problems - i.e. the very idea of it all.

Further, the disease can be like flu where the respiratory tract can also be attacked. Many will fall victims of this radiation sickness as they have a reduced immune system as a result of poor drinking water, junk food with additives, GMO foods, aluminum and heavy metal effects, unnatural chemicals, toxic air, toxic air from aircraft emissions, so-called chemtrails with aluminum and barium dust. All bodily accumulations are activated, including mercury with nerve diseases as a result, vaccinations with autoimmune diseases as a result. Many elderly people are also properly medicated, where statins appear to increase mortality as the immune system is lowered further.

Information also indicates that the 5G radiation directly affects the body's oxygen molecules, but also that it affects the hemoglobin that transports the oxygen. Furthermore, the ion channels in the body cells are affected by an increased flow of calcium into the cells. The result is exhaustion of our organism and the immune system "crashes" (Dr. Martin Pall). These 5G-symptpms are very alike those of Covid-19.

With aircraft spraying of Chemtrails consisting of thousands (millions) of tons of harmful nanoparticles of alumina, strontium, barium, arsenic, lead, mycoplasma, etc., where the size of the particles is so small that they go straight through the skin, together with toxins stored in the body, e.g. mercury, aluminum and other metals, we become antennas for increased radiation.

It has been admitted that those who died in "combination" with "Corona" are old, e.g. 84% are over 80 years old, 98% had a serious illness before. The old people who died already had impaired health and immune systems. It goes without saying that an elderly ill poisoned person dies more easily in seasonal flu, but now this spectacle is turned into a "pandemic".

What does it take to make a seasonal flu backed by increasing 4G and 5G radiation into a pandemic? High contagiousness and many dead are required. As many as possible must be able to test positive to the Corona virus. Of the PCR-tests showing positive test results, up to 95% were a so-called "false-positives", i.e. showing positive results even if the person doesn't have Covid-19 (if it even exists). In this way many people are tested positive and it is claimed that the spread of infection is huge. The test kit thus gives the perception of an enormous spread of the infection, but is there even a spread of the infection?

In fact, the test shows if specific DNA or RNA sequences are present in the sample. If these exist, the test will be positive. Thus, we are tested positive for the "Covid-19". These DNA sequences are automatically found if detoxification occurs from any particular organ in the body. The likelihood of this is very high, but we don't need to be ill at all.

"False-positive" tests are also available for ZIKA, MERS and H1N1. The general rehearsals have been conducted several times.

From the pushing control of the cabal, they want people to show "positive test results for Covid-19". A large batch of test sticks sent to the UK were already "contaminated with Covid-19". So the people who were to be tested would show a positive test (The Telegraph), but should they become infected? Some virologists believe that one cannot be infected by viruses unless the body has decided to start a larger cleansing of the body cells, i.e. a proper cleansing process, virus infection, flu-like illness.

Many deaths are linked to Covid-19 as the deceased are very likely to show a positive Covid-19 test. If the test sticks aren't already contaminated with covid-19, then all "false-positives" will show positive results, i.e. pandemic.

With Swedish Television (SVT) propaganda and associated "fearmongering", authorities can get away with almost anything - but these exemption laws in Sweden are a bit slow. The Social Democrats want protection laws linked to Covid-19, i.e. they want to be able to enact new laws quickly and override certain laws, accordance to their own liking. There is an agreement on this between all parliamentary parties, i.e. if the situation should worsen.

So unless the test sticks speed up the spread of the flu, then the vaccine is guaranteed to do so. According to experts it takes 3-4 years before a "vaccine" is complete. Now, in the near future, a vaccine has already been developed - but WARNING here, think it over!

Influenza vaccines have never brought anything good. We recommend taking a closer look at the contents of these; mercury, various DNA residues, aluminum and other toxins are included. These viral vaccines, which are completely unnaturally injected into the human body, create problems, with impaired immune systems and autoimmune diseases as a result.

But this Covid-19 vaccine is likely to be even worse. The vaccine may have a catastrophic effect on our organism. Why should we be artificially vaccinated when there is no increased morbidity? Of course, we should vaccinate ourselves with something that can cause a tremendous risk of illness, with the hope of a sudden death from the control behind. Attached to this injected vaccine will probably also be a nano-chip, or dust of the chip barely visible. The chip shows whether we have got the injected vaccine or not. The chip will most likely also be able to be electromagnetically activated where health can be modulated and we can be switched off, i.e. die an inexplicable death. This is the plan - to kill citizens. The vaccine is very likely to be made mandatory, because it has to do with "general safety and public health". If we don't take the vaccine, we will be counteracted in every way, unemployment, zeroing of our digital bank accounts. Chaos everywhere, and things just happen.

All Swedish parliamentary parties want the Swedish people to be mass vaccinated, especially the Sweden Democrats (SD), who want to make the vaccine mandatory, in order to stage the police state as quickly as possible. SD has always been a controlled opposition in the Riksdag (Parliament). We are meant to vote for them when everything becomes chaotic in society.

Parliamentary parties have been degrading the Swedish society for 30 years in steps, and especially during the most recent mandate periods. There is no difference between the parties and they all obey the same cabal control. Some pretend to stand to the left and some to the right, but they all work for the same thing - i.e. the new World Order with Agenda 2030 as the guiding star. Everyone is expected to follow orders, Government and Parliament people, the heads of large companies, banks, i.e. the entire top of the social pyramid. At the bottom are ordinary people who just have to do their job and stick to it. The managers at the lowest level have a difficult task, but you don't have to go very high up in the pyramid until you see the distorted world view. These people hold each other's backs and think nothing is particularly strange; they are all the same, with only a few exceptions.

The Covid-19 hysteria is staged to remove people from the planet and introduce the new world order, with total dictatorship. Only obedient slaves should be allowed to remain, and dissidents should be removed. This world order was already predicted by George Orwell with the book "1984".

This takeover of power with coming dictatorship is happening now. In a few months, everything is expected to be complete. When people have impaired health with fatigue, headaches, 5G towers everywhere, no one can resist. The takeover of power is done by police and over-authorities.

Now that the electromagnetic microwave radiation is intensifying, with "the internet of things (5G)" and Artificial Intelligence (AI), it won't be long before various symptoms appear, which can also be flu-like symptoms. There may be an incubation period here before the immune system has been sufficiently impaired, where it opens for bacteria, viruses and influenza-like diseases. They either break out with no or mild symptoms, or the victim gets ill with flu and respiratory collapse, where the person dies. It should be added that the Spanish flu was initiated by the introduction of radio waves globally at the end of the First World War, the same effect on man there. The Hong Kong Influenza in 1968 was the result of many satellites being placed in the van-Allen belt (in the Earth's magnetosphere at least 70 miles above the Earth's surface above the equator) outside of the Earth. The flues have been more severe some years as a result of new electromagnetic radiation. All this has been known by the governance and it is a direct attack on humanity. The alternative for us would have been to give our soul more attention with the development of telepathy as an increasingly common means of communication, with peace and associated evolving development. The controlling destructive mind-influenced individuals are not interested in this, so these possibilities have been reduced as far as possible. This has in every way happened after the continent of Atlantis succumbed. Immature people have been fighting for power by all means, to control each another.

That time will soon be over - now the WAR is on!

Right now in the parallel world (astral plane) and in the earth's underground tunnel system, a war is going on which we can't see from the earth's surface. The destructive Orion-related Draconian creatures (extraterrestrial entities) that have controlled and enslaved humans on earth for thousands of years are now fought by positive Pleiadian intelligences. The war is now also staged on earth, which is the battlefield. It's time we wake up from our sleeping beauty sleep and take our responsibility. Do we want to end up in a dictatorship or do we want to evolve into free, healthy, positive developed beings, where the Soul-consciousness (the higher qualitative consciousness) again can shine with its radiance, where we all control our own minds? Or, do we still want to be controlled by our minds and be part of a total dictatorship?

The choice is individual. If you want to emancipate, you will work for it, but if you belong to the second category, you will not respond to the takeover of power, and you think it is ok, also ok to take the vaccine, and ok to die from this planet. In the next life you will be born into another planetary system on another planet and there you can continue your development from the level you are at now.

When this chaos has ended on the earth and you belong to the category of people who want to develop into a higher quality soul-influenced being with multidimensional quantum consciousness, free from all bondage, then you will also in the next life be born to Earth to continue your evolution, or come to a higher evolved planetary system. We have a very bright time ahead of us on earth. But before that, we must counteract the negative social development that is now happening. We must not allow the death dictatorship to take hold. It is ruled by destructive extraterrestrial Draconians, Orion-influenced beings from the parallel world. They use, through obsession and control, earthly senior leaders, decision makers, multinational business owners, bankers and representatives of various community agencies. These are controlled and they receive their information through inspiration from this control, and obey blindly, as their minds are set to this. This mind control has since many incarnations been properly entrained in these ruling Earthly individuals. You could say that they have made a pact with the Devil. Obviously, this view is contrary to that of the society, and not accepted by the authorities.

These negative obsessed governing people have systematically staged the degrading of schools, health care and all community sustaining authorities for a long time. Our 3D reality now is so false and artificial that nothing is consistent with any higher ethics and morality.

However, many people within themselves feel a world-rejecting feeling when they watch TV or see what is happening to our society, world. It should be emphasized that all this negative social development has been planned for several millennia, emphasized the last centuries and now extremely much in the 20th century and the last 30 years.

Right now, the 5G masts and transmitters will be installed. People will be vaccinated, and chipped, so the next "seasonal flu" will harvest many more lives. People have started getting the vaccine that is impossible to develop in a few months which normally takes about 4 years to test and manufacture. In connection with so-called forced vaccination, they will introduce nanochips into all people, children as adults to gain total control over the people on earth who they intend to control and enslave.

The next "seasonal flu" peaks after next Christmas and until spring.

5G will also be installed in airports and hospitals.

What can we do to protect ourselves?

The destructive aliens know that esotericism is a threat to them. They want to ban these currents and counteract them as much as they can. Esotericism is about our inner spirituality, our evolutionary evolution toward higher qualitative multi-dimensional quantum consciousness, i.e. instead of believing in different things we will instead "know" - we see what happens on different dimensional planes, in the parallel world and in higher dimensional worlds, how it is and what happens. No one can lie to such an individual or enslave him. These types of individuals are counteracted as much as possible by the destructive Draco and Orion aliens, who actually regard the planet Earth as their own as they were here on Earth before today's human beings.

To prevail, we must do whatever we can to increase our frequencies (vibrations). We have to start meditating in the right way, on the so-called third eye (corpus pinealis plexus) "posterior medial frontal cortex", in the forehead region, with the right guidance by one who has achieved Mastery in Life, i.e. one who has walked the path himself and kept his quality over the millennia he has been among the people here on earth.

Only the World Teacher, UNIFIER can guide us out of this chaos.

All meditation below the third eye belongs to Maya, i.e. "Illusion".

We must work to become consciously aware in parallel worlds in the 4th and 5th dimensions and at the same time de-program our 3D mind, which is our bank of experience from the earthly lives we have had. When the mind is de-programmed, we become free and the soul consciousness becomes our guide. We need to stay as healthy as possible.

We must also eat nutritious foods that facilitate our frequency increase, i.e. avoid heavy foods like meat. We have to stop thinking negative thoughts that keep us open for control.

Time is short. Right now, the so-called "starlink satellites" are put into operation and put in orbit (described so positively by the Swedish newspaper "Aftonbladet"). There will be approximately 42,000 of these and all will be in orbit during 2021. They will deliver 5G and you can already predict how the result will be.

You must according to your best ability inform yourself about what's in the making, at work, at home and wherever you can. This is the case now. Either you end up in dictatorship with death and destruction, more darkness ... or you end up in a bright future. How do you want it?

Everything said on SVT and other TV channels you have to take light on - not much has to do with higher quality - everything is downwards directed and degrading.

MSM doesn't speak the truth. You know it, and you sense it. You can never bring forward any information through MSM, authorities or through social media. Everything is controlled. You need to make your families and friends aware of what is happening, acquaintances in the workplace, etc. If you, like us, want the future to be bright where we can live in development and in brightness, then you must act now. Don't think about what has happened before. Think and live in the present.

The negative beings, the controlling authorities work best when the good people sit with their arms crossed and preferably sleep. There must be a change to this!

The expansion of 5G has progressed the most in Wuhan (CHINA, as early as in 2019), northern Italy, Switzerland, USA and England. Maps have been made to see correlations between "Covid-19" and 5G-installations. The maps correlate very well. Wuhan (Hubei-province) with its 60 million people was a very suitable place for the CABAL's first release of cultivated coronavirus.

The purpose of the ongoing war between Negative and Good is the evolvement of the human being, his consciousness. To a negative person everything is reversed, i.e. a Negative is Good, and a Positive is Evil, but also extremely stupid ... stupid people they say, look how stupid they are...

There are videos showing how 5G totally kill plants.

It is impossible for us Earthlings to combat these destructive Draconians and Orion-influenced beings. It is done by the Taygetan Pleiadian Galactic Council Federation.

Right now, the Pleiadian intelligences, with their space fleet, are looking for these Reptiles in the Underground societies that were built for them by David Rockefeller's created Rome Club. No negative-destructive aliens are now allowed to come to earth or leave the earth. This war can only be fought by the Pleiadians. We earthly beings have nothing to stand against with this overwhelming power. What we must do instead is improve our health and start our consciousness training at the UNIFIER's, i.e. free membership to start the process for increased consciousness. We earthly people can only work to save ourselves.

It should be added that there is a neutral Draconian phalanx from Orion that works harmoniously and is linked to China's development. They are recognized by their perfectly neutral and soft radiance.

## Petition: 26,000 Scientists Oppose 5G Roll Out

Figure 60. Many thousands of scientists oppose the roll out of 5G.

5G transmitters will be destroyed by Pleiadian efforts. Nuclear weapons cannot be used now, as they are guarded by Pleiadian intelligences.

We must not be afraid. Fear lowers our immune system and we will then get sick and be beyond rescue this time. We must all fight for the good and do it in good spirit, with humor and consciousness training, and some laughs.

In Brussels, the 5G network is stopped for health reasons.

It is quite clear that the Government and Parliament are unaware of or ignores what is happening, and what they are doing, as they run the errands of the negative forces, the earthly cabal. To be the body chosen by the negative forces, no matter consciously or unconsciously, is equally serious. We are all responsible for what we think and all our actions, whether we are aware of them or not.

The Swedish Minister of the State Stefan Löfvén says that the development of 5G is on the rise and that the Nordic region should be at the forefront here. It creates jobs and prosperity in our countries.

Facebook bans all posts suggesting a link between covid-19 and 5G. This speaks its clear language about what we as citizens shall believe in and not. Also Donald Trump's twitter posts have ben censored as they suggest the deaths from Covid-19 to be exaggerated.

That which is happening now by the authorities happens in the complete absence of human rights and democratic principles. But this mass psychosis is supported by almost all world governments today.

The authorities worldwide in most countries will do everything possible to explain away the link between 5G and impaired immune system as a cause of many upcoming deaths. They will regard this as a conspiracy theory. Teaching the people in schools and universities proper information and evolving human sciences has not been their strong side, quite the opposite. They have done pretty much everything they could to keep humans in ignorance and let them die prematurely. As far as possible from the side of the authorities, uncomfortable questions are avoided.

Now, a large part of the population will really lose confidence in the authorities, which have demonstrably degraded and lowered the entire society, withheld the truth and brought the people behind the light. So here we have a big problem. So, improve your health and raise your consciousness with UNIFIER's training program through a Free Membership.

The authorities are also working to reduce the nutritional content in dietary supplements to undermine our immune system. Many laws have already been enacted.

IT SHOULD BE ADDED THAT WHAT NOW HAPPENS ALONG WITH INCREASED RADIATION AND DETOXIFYING LEADS US ON THE WAY TO INCREASED CONSCIOUSNESS, IF WE CAN COPE WITH THE PROCESS. THIS IS ALSO A PREREQUISITE FOR THE SOCIETY WE ARE NOW APPROACHING. WE ONLY NEED TO GET IT IN THE RIGHT AMOUNT. HOWEVER, THE RESULT SHOULD NOT BE A DICTATORSHIP OF DEATH, BUT A SOCIETAL STRUCTURE THAT BUILDS ON HIGHER ETHICS AND MORALITY. THE INDIVIDUAL IS EVOLVING TOWARD FREEDOM UNDER RESPONSIBILITY.

Right now there are a lot of TV commercials for vaccinations. Vaccinations can cause serious complications and lifelong injuries. No pharmaceutical companies have any responsibility for their vaccinations - the responsibility has been written off. There is no interest in making vaccinations safe. Responsibility from relevant authorities is weak.

The Covid vaccine that Sweden has undertaken to purchase from Astra Zeneca is considered so untested that the Pharmaceutical Insurance, which reimburses patients in the event of any side effects, hesitates to include it in the insurance.

The vaccine that is now being tested is an mRNA vaccine, which enters the cell and produces the vaccine's protein. No RNA vaccines are currently approved. Not much is known about these, e.g. how stable they are, etc. Astra Zeneca, Moderna and others are currently testing these vaccines, which are intended to be used "against Covid-19".

It is already announced that two test persons have developed paralyzing nerve inflammation in the spinal cord. The first death has also been recorded.

Think about why people need to be paralyzed or die from the vaccine - why? Extrapolate a small test group number on the entire population that is intended to be vaccinated. A certain part of the population becomes paralyzed immediately or dies. Many more are paralyzed, injured or will die in the near future.

At the last mass vaccination in 2009, 60% of the Swedish population took the vaccine and several hundred were injured for life. 440 Swedes got the nerve disease narcolepsy.

This Covid-19-RNA vaccine produces something called a "trans-infection". The human DNA will change. Here, non-human DNA is mutated into our cells. DNA sequences from animals, monkeys, pigs, etc. will be mutated into our cells. The vaccine will also contain nanoparticles, nanorobots that spread as dust within us with the bloodstream. The robots will store all the info about us and store it in the "cloud". Our health and existence can be modulated through this system.

Nano-chip modulation has been developed by the "Karolinska Institutet" in Stockholm with the start several years ago.

The Cabal (the deep state) wants to vaccinate the whole world. Nothing will return to "normal" before everyone is vaccinated. We will never be able to be "cured" from the vaccine. We become like antennas that are controlled from the outside. All of humanity must be controlled.

Human developmental opportunities are reduced when the euphoric "feeling of God" disappears. This has happened after the vaccine testing "against" for Covid-19. Neurological problems arise and the feeling of God is turned off. They want to turn off the VMAT2 gene (the "God gene"). The activity in certain areas in the brain is diminished.

Some infants are already now given flu vaccines before they have even got an effective immune system. These infants may experience an anaphylactic shock when vaccinated. Vaccinations must be given in special rooms in case of a shock.

After some time after vaccinations, diseases appear - but not immediately. Vaccinated people are more susceptible to other viral infections, and people who have got many vaccinations are even more exposed.

Together with increased microwave radiation, the result will be an increased burden on the human organism - mutations - nerve diseases - autoimmune diseases - autism - etc. which will lead to catastrophic consequences, especially for those who have been vaccinated regularly and have a weakened immune system as a result of all accumulated toxins.

In the United States, chronic diseases have now increased enormously. Chronic diseases increase by almost one percentage for every 5 years that pass. Today, about 60% of all adult citizens have two chronic diseases. 40% have two chronic diseases. These chronic diseases can be heart disease, cancer, chronic lung disease, stroke, Alzheimer's, diabetes or chronic kidney disease.

Right now, the UN is demanding as much as SEK 330 billion for the developing of Covid-19 vaccine.

Work is currently underway to introduce a biometric ID document. This ID-chip will be updated with information on health status, completed vaccinations etc. The chip will also include a payment solution via MasterCard, Cryptocurrency. The project is called ID2020 (WO/2020/060606) and is a Microsoft patent. Bill Gates, together with WHO, MIT, Microsoft, the Rockefeller Foundation and the powerful vaccine lobby organization Gavi, are running the project and the Swedish state is helping to guarantee funding of around SEK 1.75 billion. The digital ID document will be injected into the hand.

An enzyme "Luciferase" is needed for the system to work. Luciferase causes the vaccinated person's hand to glow as an oxidative process starts and produces bioluminescence. The mark will be readable by a mobile phone. It will be visible who is vaccinated and who is not. This "mark" will not be able to remove. The data storage device that is injected is called "quantum dot nanoparticles" (microchip) and will be etched into the hand.

317

Shortly some Airline companies will be able to scan an intended passenger's Mobile App called "CommonPass". The intended passenger will have his vaccination and covid-19 status available via a QR code scanned by the airline personnel to see if the passenger is approved for the flight to the selected destination.

A second wave of SARS CoV-2 is currently being "planned". I will be based on false Covid-19 tests. Lockdown will be reintroduced or intensified with even tougher restrictions and repression of society.

The Swedish government wants to keep the restrictions to the next summer and the Public Health Agency for at least one year ahead - preferably longer.

The mass protests against the Corona repression continue in Britain and Germany and in several other countries. This is underreported or absent from Main-Stream-Media (MSM). The demonstrations involve millions of people and the voice of the people will soon break through.

More and more doctors on a broader front around the world are calling for an end to the increasingly serious Corona repression. Most recently, 400 Belgian doctors believe that fake news from the conventional media and "totally disproportionate" crisis management by simple-minded politicians have caused enormous democratic, economic, social, psychological and health damage and injuries - which far exceeds the supposed profit of trying to stifle what can at the most be comparable to a seasonal flu.

Here comes a patent for cloud-monitoring of prospect "Covid-19-infected":

## Bibliografische gegevens: US2020279585 (A1) — 2020-09-03

★ In mijn octrooilijst    ▓| Meld fout in gegevens        🖨 Print

### System and Method for Testing for COVID-19

| | |
|---|---|
| Rechter muisklik om favoriet te maken | US2020279585 (A1) - System and Method for Testing for COVID-19 |
| Uitvinder(s): | ROTHSCHILD RICHARD A [GB] ± |
| Aanvrager(s): | ROTHSCHILD RICHARD A [GB] ± |
| Classificatie: | - internationaal: *G06K9/00; G11B27/031; G11B27/10; G16H40/63; H04N5/76; H04N9/82* |
| | - cooperative: G06K9/00892 (US); G11B27/031 (US); G11B27/10 (US); G11B27/102 (US); G16H40/63 (EP, US); G16H40/67 (EP); G16H50/20 (EP); H04N5/76 (EP, US); H04N9/8205 (EP, US); G06K2009/00939 (US) |
| Aanvraagnummer: | US202016876114 20200517   ❶ Global Dossier |
| Prioriteitsnummer(s): | US202016876114 20200517 ; US201916704844 20191205 ; US201916273141 20190211 ; US201715495485 20170424 ; US201615293211 20161013 ; US201562240783P 20151013 |

### Samenvatting van US2020279585 (A1)

Vertaal deze tekst ⓘ

| Nederlands ⌄ | ⇄ patenttranslate | powered by EPO and Google |

A method is provided for acquiring and transmitting biometric data (e.g., vital signs) of a user, where the data is analyzed to determine whether the user is suffering from a viral infection, such as COVID-19. The method includes using a pulse oximeter to acquire at least pulse and blood oxygen saturation percentage, which is transmitted wirelessly to a smartphone. To ensure that the data is accurate, an accelerometer within the smartphone is used to measure movement of the smartphone and/or the user. Once accurate data is acquired, it is uploaded to the cloud (or host), where the data is used (alone or together with other vital signs) to determine whether the user is suffering from (or likely to suffer from) a viral infection, such as COVID-19. Depending on the specific requirements, the data, changes thereto, and/or the determination can be used to alert medical staff and take corresponding actions.

Figure 61. "A method is provided for acquiring and transmitting biometric data (e.g., vital signs) of a user, where the data is analyzed to determine whether the user is suffering from a viral infection, such as COVID-19. The method includes using a pulse oximeter to acquire at least pulse and blood oxygen saturation percentage, which is transmitted wirelessly to a smartphone. To ensure that the data is accurate, an accelerometer within the smartphone is used to measure movement of the smartphone and/or the user. Once accurate data is acquired, it is uploaded to the cloud (or host), where the data is used (alone or together with other vital signs) to determine whether the user is suffering from (or likely to suffer from) a viral infection, such as COVID-19. Depending on the specific requirements, the data, changes thereto, and/or the determination can be used to alert medical staff and take corresponding actions."

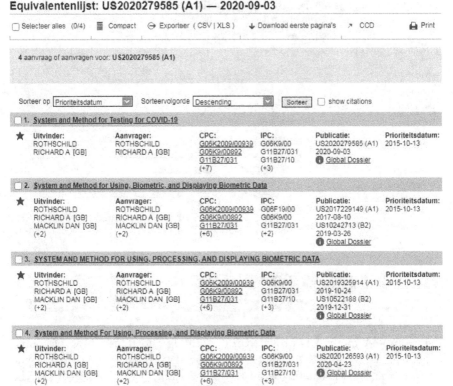

**Equivalentenlijst: US2020279585 (A1) — 2020-09-03**

Figure 62. The patent was already filed in October 2015-10-13, but became official on 2020-09-03. Over 9 million "diagnostic test instruments and devices" for COVID-19 were already sold in 2017 and 2018. The market value was approximately $ 9.5 billion. These instruments were sold from the EU, USA, Germany, Japan and China. Our tax money paid.

There is a patent (US2006257852) for "severe acute respiratory syndrome - coronavirus". This was filed as early as 2006 and is patented from November 2019. The patent is valid in many parts of the world under various patent names with several dates for approval. The patent was filed by Chiron Corporation later acquired by Novartis, of which GlaxoSmithKline is a partner.

Furthermore, there is a patent for an already existing Corona Vaccine (EP3172319B1). It was submitted as early as 2014 but was approved in November 2019. This is owned by the Pirbright Institute (GB) which is the Bill and Melina Gates Foundation. This patent is also valid in the US and was approved in November 2018 (US10130701B2).

So there are major market forces at work now that would be interested in a major pandemic that can be vaccinated.

But with everything summed up, it seems that no Covid-19 virus exists as has been described in the media, which people die from. There is no evidence for this. There are only a lot of positive PCR tests, which have been claimed to be positive Covid-19 tests. But a PCR test doesn't show the existence of a virus. So we have a "PCR pandemic" and a lot of fake death certificates where it is alleged that people have died with or from Covid-19.

So, what have people died from really? Well, respiratory ailments, flu-like symptoms, microwave radiation symptoms and increased solar activity governed from the central sun. Altitude sickness causes a lack of oxygen in the tissues and accompanying stress reactions. 5G radiation also causes these symptoms and an already weakened immune system where the body has various underlying illnesses make the body weak and it can die if the load is too severe.

Now when prosecutions are underway in some parts of the world, the Cabal (*The Deep State*) is quick to cover up everything and introduce "lock-down number two" - because now everything is in a hurry. The deep state wants to kill 95% of the population and their poker scam is becoming apparent.

Since people believe in everything that is said on TV, disclosures must come from there.

Cabal (*The Deep State*) and all prime ministers, presidents, senior officials, lobbyists and other market forces that are behind this scam must be ransacked. The betrayal they have committed against their own peoples is of immense proportions, so people cannot take easy on this one. We must give human hostility and stupidity a safe harbor.

We must also mention that there are already several viruses designed in labs, ready to be released. These will not be as tame as "Covid-19", but will be sharp weapons with mass killing as purpose. We have already told about this in 1993 when Sandor A Markus' first book was published.

Anders Syborg, initiator of the "radiation uprising" (2020-09-15) has now measured even higher radiation levels from 4G base stations. At Järntorget in the Old Town in Stockholm, the levels are the highest he has ever measured. These levels have also been confirmed by the responsible authority. The peak levels are 1.380.000 uW/m², which is 20 times higher than what is legal in

Switzerland, for example. According to independent researchers, the levels in the bedroom should be below 10 uW/m$^2$ and below 100 in the rest of the home. He announces that at these levels most people find it difficult to stay in for a long time.

It is worth repeating that 5G was developed by the military to disperse crowds. When crowds are irradiated with 5G at 96 GHz, they get the feeling that their bodies are burning and they run away reflexively from the site.

*"Once the herd accepts mandatory vaccination, it's game over! They will accept anything - forcible blood or organ donation - for the greater good. We can genetically modify children and sterilize them - for the greater good. Control sheep minds and you control the herd. Vaccine makers stand to make billions. It's a big win-win! We thin out the herd and the herd pays us for providing extermination services."*

*The Antichrist*

Right now, the medical profession is divided into two camps - those who advocate mandatory vaccinations - and those who are absolutely against this.

Censorship is now becoming tougher from e.g. YouTube, where recorded medical conferences discussing alternative treatments for Covid-19 are removed. The discussions may concern cures such as hydroxychlorichin and the exaggeration of the danger of the virus. Professional medical groups are censored. Anything that contradicts the Globalist Agenda will be censored. In a major conflict, the Truth is the First Victim. So the misery has just only started.

# The Social Contract - its validity

By now - it probably certainly hasn't escaped anyone that the virus Covid-19, which is said to be so dangerous that the entire world has classified it as a pandemic, will have major consequences for society and us humans.

When there is a small suspicion of someone being infected, he/she is hospitalized for observation. A person, who is at hospital for a wound in the finger and at the same time is coughing, will be hospitalized on suspicion of a Corona "infection". Those people who now die will to a greater extent be documented of having died from Covid-19, also if the person dies of a heart attack or other illness, old age. More people than usual don't die now according to statistics. The whole pandemic is made up - like a social disease, but of the worst kind.

The result of this scares people into quarantine, especially if they are over 70 years old, and the suspicion among people increases; soon the imputation begins. State of emergency applies and people are supposed to obey. Gatherings of people are not allowed and companies go under when contact between people is avoided.

This is the situation right now - and the Swedish Prime Minister Stefan Löfvén says we should "sharpen the seriousness", i.e. take harder on the rules proclaimed.

What will be the consequences of this?

At the moment, the hospitals are not working for what is intended. Everything is about Corona, so planned operations are canceled, care queues get longer, few people get help. Only urgent cases are dealt with, if however, reluctantly. People die from diseases and complications that are otherwise taken care of by hospitals. Hospitals receive fewer patients at the same time as over-staffing is sent to other hospitals to justify statistics and alarm status. Holidays are canceled. We taxpayers have to pay for it with maximum taxes, prohibitions and restrictions...

Right now the drone community starts, i.e. more people who "work" get paid, but don't work. The state lends money for salaries, but they have to be repaid by the companies later. Only a few companies get this help. It is important to indebt even more now when there is still time. These loans will not be repaid, because the companies will go bankrupt. If the companies have not gone bankrupt, they will do so in a near future. No private companies will be allowed in the long run and they are now being counteracted as far as possible.

What happens in the extension of this in the coming year and autumn? Now society gets totally sabotaged in all areas.

Government authorities are adapting their business to covid-19, with many codes (rules) of conduct that limit people. That which facilitates for Corona patients in other countries (India, China, Russia) is not approved in Sweden like vitamin C, vitamin D, zinc, colloidal silver, and the Corona killing agent Hydroxychloroquine (malaria drug), etc. Hydroxychloroquine was banned in Sweden (on April 2, 2020) in primary care for Covid-19 patients. Authorities also say that a strong immune system doesn't help.

Old people are kept confined in solitude. They dare not burden anyone else and for the sake of limiting the "spread of infection". They fall ill of fear as the immune system is lowered.

Younger students are limited in their learning with diverting, misleading information and now horror information about the "Corona disease". The students have for a long time been fed with misleading information that explains the behavior that should now be made standard, a robotic-like behavior without any critical thinking, which they were instead encouraged to practice.

The alarming climate propaganda about carbon dioxide as a cause of "global warming" is seriously treacherous, as is the information about Covid-19 and the socially disruptive gears that result.

All humans are to be standardized like robots and now receive vaccines, which will be full of toxic chemicals; metals like aluminum and mercury, body foreign substances such as various human cells from aborted fetuses, washed red blood cells from sheep, vesicle fluids from calfskins, embryonic fluids from chickens and test pigs, bovine serum, human blood albumin, mice proteins, body invasive virus, arsenic, nanoparticles, tin, sv40, various DNA sequences, etc. Patents are now also available for implants of Nano-chip with the vaccine. The chips are controlled by 5G and can modulate our health. The chip is both a receiver and transmitter with identification. If we aren't obedient, we are shut down, we die.

It is about getting people scared and compliant to be as positive as possible to this, so that later all the accumulated toxins can be activated. These abnormal substances can be genetically modified foods (GMOs), food additives, herbicides, sugars, toxins, nutrient-poor diets, drug poisoning - where we should not be allowed to eat supplements and maintain a good immune system. Through the air we have also received toxins, various air emissions, particles, chemtrails with aluminum and barium. The drinking water is also not clean but contains chlorine and other contaminating particles, drugs with the possibility of mass poisoning via the addition of bacteria, chemicals, etc.

All must be connected to the municipal water network. Private Wells are to be banned. A tired, lethargic, powerless human being makes no resistance.

Now before the "power" is turned on for this machinery, there are still things to be done.

Now under the "state of emergency" it is important to lie as much as possible to the people. An important thing is to work for starvation, even in this country Sweden. It is important to ensure that the potatoes and other crops don't get into the soil. This can be done by ignoring this issue, through indulgence, now that the Poles are not coming and putting the potatoes in the soil, nor should the Swedish people do this. The degree of self-sufficiency must be less than 45%, less than now. Famine must prevail. The state of emergency should ideally last forever - it destroys everything when no one is working with maintaining work. The crisis preparedness is dismantled. Authorities are already preparing for food rationing. If all people go on grants and loans, then society is rapidly liquidated. All this is now done under the cover of "Covid-19".

5G cellmasts are now being installed everywhere, and by 2021 there will also be 42,000 (you heard right - forty two thousand) 5G satellites in orbit around the earth.

Is it time to press the button? - for "The Sleeping People" as the former Swedish Minister of State Reinfeldt put it in his book ...

OK - let's press the button...

We are now starting what is projected in the long run to kill 95 % of the world's population.

It is important to remember that we citizens pay for the whole lot - with everything it entails, right up to the end.

...

5G is activated everywhere - now the entire earth is blanketed with high frequency microwave radiation. There is no escape. We are now microwaved with several different frequency bands 2G, 3G, 4G and now 5G. All the aluminum, mercury and toxins we have stored up in our bodies now come in handy. A feeling of iron bands appears within minutes in the forehead region. The heart is rushing and anxiety arises immediately. It tingles in the whole body. With mercury and aluminum we become like wandering antennas for this radiation. We try to hide - but there is nowhere to hide. Various things in our bodies begin to mutate. The immune system has no chance of repairing our tissues or healing our organism to a reasonably healthy condition.

Our karmic load also gets more energy, which means that our acquired unsolved situations will maximize their impact. We live out all the problems we have within us. Unsolved issues within family, between friends and within the community are on the edge. Unsolved scenarios between countries are increasing. The food is either poisoned or missing due to cancellation of cultivation. Or as farmers in the United States were encouraged to do - kill their livestock and burn their crops.

On the surface of the earth, people are dying like flies - all this is planned. We have a living hell on earth.

The most interesting thing about this is that we have all agreed to this. By indulgence we have agreed to this. We have chosen to swallow all the lies from society about climate, care, what is best for us. We have chosen to focus on the mind - i.e. the opposite of God. We have ourselves to blame for all this.

Keep in mind that all politicians in the Riksdag (Parliament) continue with their decisions - exactly as planned. Dissidents have been removed a long time ago. The elite there are to a large extent soulless. They have so much ingrained karma that they only function intellectually. They have no soul contact. This political elite is trained to be led by what is called the "Deep State".

The Deep State is made up of a few individuals, so-called advisers, who are still there when Minister of States and politicians are replaced worldwide. These members of the Deep State dictate everything the politicians say and do. It's all like a Punch and Judy show. There is nothing genuine left - everything is about directing the crowds towards their death, now when the world is to be transformed. This mass psychosis now runs automatically - no criticism is allowed. The dictatorship is now open. From dictating the election results to Parliament, everything is now proclaimed in a purely dictatorial manner, without any higher qualitative thought - and so it is - society must reach the bottom - the absolute dark bottom...

Do you think that society would do anything good for you at all? - anything that would help you in any way at all? Right now everything is motivated by

"Covid-19". There is certainly no higher mortality rate, and here we stand with our question marks and wonder how everything could turn out like this ... now when everything has started.

Instead, we have to struggle with our survival. All social structures fail. All confidence in everything regarding authorities ceases. We must now very carefully discern who to listen to and believe in. Most people are completely woven into karmic unsolved situations. They only have the mind to listen to. They cannot discern the path they must take - these people will surely die from the planet. This applies to 95% of the population worldwide.

Figure 63. "Georgia Guidestone" tells about the Negative Illuminati's target society, a dystopian society where only 500 million of the earth's population is allowed to exist as robotic slaves.

Everything that is good for health and human beings is now banned. The "health care" now allowed is surgery and allopathy - where complications are extremely common with extra efforts in the form of aftercare, etc. health problems. Our health status has only been allowed to deteriorate. No measures are legal that could make our health better, to recover. All spiritual efforts and focus on the soul power has been smeared as much as possible, forbidden and laughed away, as so much else.

Only those people who start listening to their souls will have a chance to escape this chaos that is now waiting. Only they can discern what is good from all other pitch-black darkness.

We will need to rebuild the entire society. We must get rid of everything old. We can thank "The Deep State" for this.

People must be put on detoxification; people have to get the right energy-based treatments that make our internal organs retuned on their original programs. Everything has to be tuned. Our individual karma must be de-programmed. We need clean water to drink, clean air to breathe, and clean and unrefined food to eat. We need to have an environment to live in that is good for us and that helps us in our evolution toward soul consciousness. The soul and the sun must once again have their rightful place in existence. Only then can we have a thriving society, a soul-conscious society, a society that will once again be tuned on the role that planet Earth now has in its cosmic context here in the solar system, in the milky way. The earth should be set to a maximal health status in the universal harmonic interaction.

We will have a society where every individual is free and where the individual taps into the cosmos and executes God's plan, all of us in unity. This is the only viable path.

We must unlock all prohibitions, conform ourselves to common sense in the guiding light of the soul - following high ethics and morality.

Esotericism and reaching soul consciousness become the basic foundation. Now banned methods such as electropathy, homeopathy, naturopathy, scalar wave therapy and other quackery-classified methods will become standard. These tune the body's energies. Help will be offered and the doctor will be free and able to choose from the arsenal that is now available to help. The intuition is so strong in the doctor that he knows what to do - the doctor sees with his consciousness, third eye and executes exactly the right treatment. Truly, people can be healthy - but it is required commitment and strong will in the people that are to evolve. The guidance of the soul is now in control and not the intellectual control of darkness.

Soul control leads to everything good, because it is tuned on everything Good.

The mind, through the intellect, leads toward darkness, and the soul has no control. The consciousness and actions here run amok just like a stray dog - problems everywhere.

The UNIFIER has for 30 years offered help to all those people who want to develop their soul (self) consciousness. The UNIFIER, the Soul, God has been counteracted as much as possible by the dark forces on the Earth, through the "Deep State", through tamed dogs, the politicians, and conformed people by lies that lead to destruction. Man has been completely woven into this pitch-black downward directed darkness. The Deep State has always had the goal of creating obedient mind-controlled, intellectual slaves to do their business. They want to get rid of everyone else, i.e. those who are now going to train for soul consciousness and see what is going on.

Now is the time to listen to our Soul. It makes itself heard when life is the most difficult and toughest.

Burdened by burdens, you sit down and see no solution to anything. A light tone appears in your consciousness. This is the sound stream (kun, shabd) which some call "the white noise". You follow in the consciousness this sound and associated light that, like a spark, burns down an entire forest, a forest of karmic weave, which is currently gigantic. You have to follow this sound - in the "right meditation", which leads you out of captivity here on earth. The sound changes as your consciousness is more strongly connected to your Soul, the Spark. From a small whisper the sound becomes louder, and turns into crickets, thunderstorms and drums of incredible force. You purify yourself and you become completely healed, healthy - conformed with the New Healthy Time, which after this chaos will appear on earth.

As it is now, you must understand that there is no democracy in Sweden or anywhere else in the world. The few individuals who govern through "The Deep State" dictate everything and these individuals we humans haven't asked for, in any way. Nor do these individuals want us humans anything good at all, nothing at all. They only want to create obedient slaves for their own high pleasure, who will serve them in everything.

"The Deep State" must be exposed and abolished. The whole of Sweden's government must be removed in its present state, as they only run the errands of the Deep State, their affairs. A new Soul-supervised Government must exist in each country, as there are different types of people living in their own adapted countries.

The Basis of this Soul-Sanctioned Government you can read about under the headline above: "Action Plan for Fair Societal Development".

Only those people who work for a higher qualitative multi-dimensional quantum consciousness, can be included in this new coming civilization, the 5th in order. After death, all other individuals will continue their incarnations on other planets, systems in the cosmos, which can provide the right individual conditions for further development..

WITH DIRECT PERCEPTION ON WHAT HAPPENS BEHIND THE SCENES, IT IS OUR DUTY TO INFORM ABOUT IT. ARE WE TO HAVE IT LIKE THIS OR NOT?

# The UNIFIER's short biography

I was born on July 7, 1939, 03.05 AM in Budapest, Hungary.

I grew up in the countryside at my mother's sister (*aunt*) under simple conditions in a house built of clay with thatched roof, stamped earthen floor and a kerosene lamp as lighting. I carried my mother's surname "Juhász" since she was unmarried. Juhász means "shepherd" in the Hungarian language. My name was later changed to "Markus" after my stepfather.

As a 10-year-old, I had spontaneous recollections of my past lives (*incarnations*) that popped up from my memory bank during some occasions, without understanding what it was.

In the 1300s BC I was incarnated in the shape of Pharaoh Akhenathon in Egypt, and was murdered (*poisoned*) by my doctor on the orders of the Amon priesthood because of my assertion that the Sun (*Aton*) was the Supreme Godhead in our Solar System that humans should worship instead of invented, false gods, which the Amon priesthood worshipped.

In a later incarnation I saw myself as Markion (Mark-Ion - Markus Johannes) in Sinope in Pontos in Mesopotamia (*Asia Minor*) during the first century AD, when I advocated Gnosticism and was banned by the Roman Church.

During the 1500s I was incarnated in the figure of Miguel Servetos in Spain, and I was once again executed, burnt at the stake by the Inquisition in Switzerland for my attempt to reform the institutional Church.

In the 17th century, I was incarnated in Tibet and was a highly regarded Lama.

In the 18th century, I reincarnated under the name Georg Rakoczi, son of Prince Leopold II Rakoczi of Transylvania. I later changed my name to Count Tzarotzi and later to Count Saint Germain to avoid persecution by the Habsburg Imperial House, which forbade me and my brother Josef Rakoczi to leave the Medici family in Tuscany, Italy where we were sent. We were prohibited to visit our father in Rodosto (*Tekirdag*) in northern Turkey, where he was exiled by the Habsburg Emperor, Josef I after his uprising against the Habsburg Empire.

Under the pseudonym "Count Saint Germain" I acted as secret ambassador and adviser to several Imperial Houses in Europe, e.g. the French king, Louis XV and Count Carl of Hessen until 1784, when I left my biological body in Ekenförde, which at that time belonged to Denmark.

The year 1834, I reincarnated in the shape of Wilhelm August Eduard Max Triepcke in Berlin in Germany and became the patron of daughter Maria Martha Mathilda Triepcke until 1891, who in an earlier incarnation was my mother Tiye in Egypt during the 1300s BC who was married to Pharao Amenhotep III.

In another incarnation during the 1700s she was known as Madame Dubarry.

During the 1870-1940s she was known as Marie Kröyer, wife of the famous Skagen painter, Peder Severin Kröyer in Denmark, and later as wife of the famous Swedish composer, Hugo Alfvén in Tällberg in Sweden.

All this I have described in the book "*My Incarnations and Teachings*" - a fated depiction of how a human being can change his life by changing his way of thinking. The book is available for purchase in Swedish and English on Amazon.

In my current incarnation and due to the outbreak of World War II, I was placed at my aunt's in a village in northeastern Hungary called Nádudvar. The village is located only a few kilometers from the Hungarian Puszta.

The word "Puszta" means "Emptiness".

Just a few weeks after my school graduation in the summer of 1953, when I was 14 years old, an event occurred that would totally change my life. Since I was philosophical, I spent most of my free time on my own, with only the animals as company.

On a sunny morning, as usual, I was on the Puszta sitting under willow trees studying some catfish playing in the cloudy waters of the creek. Suddenly I felt a powerful electric shock hitting me in the back like a flash. I turned quickly to see what was happening. Then I saw a light being of intense strength standing just a few meters from me. The light being was, according to my estimation, about 2.5-3.0 meters tall. From the light being emanated an intense light, which dazzled me. I tried to protect my eyes from the intense light radiating from the being, but the light rays penetrated my hands and hit my body, giving me the sensation of millions of tiny pinpricks.

The intense light completely enveloped me and my consciousness was lifted to a higher dimension, into a transcendental state.

As in a panorama, a new world of indescribable beauty opened up which only a few people on earth have seen so far. I was allowed to see into the universal database, the matrix, the eternal tapestry of the world, where the past, present and future are inextricably interwoven into a kind of matrix. I got to see the reason behind the suffering on earth and how each soul atom, like tiny sparks of light, moved on different levels in the endless evolutionary spiral.

There was no past, present or future. Everything existed in parallel and at the same time as a kind of hologram.

I saw a new earth grow out of its agony and how my own role was interwoven with the events that would occur in the late 20th century and early 21st century. I saw how thousands of men and women would begin to experience a spiritual soul identity (*a higher cosmic consciousness*) that would be born within them. Thus, a new sense of moral - ethical freedom and justice would transcend all forms of prejudiced selfishness, lust for power, acquisitiveness, greed, hatred and nationalism.

I saw the same leading people, how they opposed each other in the fight to lead Europe's destiny for good or evil in the earlier centuries, now again were reincarnated to draw the ethical-moral consequences of what they did before.

I saw the Nordic Region like the Bethlehem star rise up at the horizon and lighting up the way for all those seeking help from the shadows of darkness.

I saw the whole development process that regarded Europe and how the platform took shape that would lead Europe out of spiritual darkness.

I saw how various extraterrestrial beings from higher developed civilizations were involved in the fate of the earth to help their younger siblings to free themselves from the captivity of ignorance - of unconscious.

I heard a voice within me that spoke to me in Hungarian and encouraged me to leave Hungary and go to Sweden and establish an educational institution in the life sciences - a center for development of a higher consciousness, which was necessary for the entry into the New Age that humanity on earth are facing.

In Sweden, I would lay the foundation of an international center, a university in the life sciences, which would help people to free themselves from the three-dimensional (3D) artificial, constructed reality in which they have been trapped since the beginning. In connection with this experience I saw what would happen in Europe, in the world, in the future.

I was told that my task was to reestablish the undistorted, true cosmic teachings, the Sun Theology (*Soul Theology*), Gnostics (*the Science of the Soul*) which constitutes the innermost being of man; this Sun Theology that I as early as 1350 BC in a former incarnation as Pharaoh Akhenaton conveyed in Egypt to those who wanted to listen.

This was the same knowing, knowledge as later the Essene teacher Jeshu ben Pandira (*Jesus of Nazareth*), John the Baptist, Lao Tze, Confucius, Guru Nanak, Pythagoras and others had communicated to humanity, which had been literally interpreted, misunderstood and abused by the institutional church of Rome due to ignorance, unconsciousness and lust for power. This Church called itself Christian, at the same time as it persecuted, tortured, burned at the stake, and killed thousands of people through the Inquisition, people who had a different view and knowledge than what the institutional Church itself stood for.

After this experience on the Hungarian Puszta, I got a whole new perspective of life compared to before.

I never became the same as before.

<u>It should turn out later that this would create countless of obstacles in my grown up life.</u>

My so-called paranormal experience and my development of telepathic communication later with extraterrestrial beings from the Pleiades, Sirius A and Arcturus, cannot be compared with any mediumship (*mediality*), Spiritism, Magic, Shamanism, Remote Viewing (RV) for military or personal purposes, contact with angel beings, the practice of various kinds of Yoga, etc. which characterize most of the so-called New Age movement.

I have never been interested in near-death experiences or communication with 4D astral beings in the lowest and middle regions of the 4D parallel world, although such phenomena have occurred in my life.

All of these phenomena belong to the lowest and middle regions of the 4D parallel world of qualitative states that lead man to bondage, stagnation, and prevent her to develop an all-encompassing cosmic consciousness. The only difference between the 3D terrestrial and 4D paranormal bondage is that you exchange your iron shackles with precious metal shackles (*gold or silver*). You are still stuck in another kind of reality.

Every universe in creation has its own reality. This I have learnt to know through my extraterrestrial contacts.

Rather, my experience can be compared with the experience that Prophet Muhammad experienced on Mount Hira, when a light being called "Gabriel" appeared to him and dictated the Koran.

Or Paul's light experience on the road to Damascus when a cosmic being spoke to him and contributed to his conversion from Judaism to original Christianity, "Gnostics".

It was Paul who laid the foundation for today's Christianity and the Christian faith, and not Peter, as the Christian Church claims. Paul's message was distorted and abused by a power prone clergy.

Now, the original true Christian doctrine, the Theology of the Gnostics (*knowing, insight over blind faith*) will be re-established through the "*Northern Pontifical Academy*" to become the guiding star of the New Age (*Golden Age*) man and civilization.

Time is short and we have to choose path.

Either we choose the Path of the Soul (*Knowing*) or the Path of the Mind (*Faith, Intellect, Imagination*).

Whichever path man chooses, it will be decisive for his survival on earth and his future destiny.

A big part of the information in the first part of the book is written by Lars Helge Swahn, who during 27 years has been my student and closest co-worker. His main interest is about what goes on behind the scenes, without human knowledge - how negative forces in different ways try to force man into a globalization plan that aims to minimize the number of people on earth through different methods and enslave the rest under a totalitarian dictatorship. Lars Helge has also designed an "*Action Plan for Fair Societal Development*", which is the social basic foundation during the New Age.

While my main task together with my soulmate "Sofia", who is the patron of the "World Doctrine", is to guide man into the New Age.

Sofia and I have followed each other in previous incarnations since we left Sirius A and chose to incarnate on earth, partly to learn about life on a 3D planet and reality, and partly to be able to teach man on earth about higher dimensional worlds and their reality; to help man find himself, his true identity and develop his inner "spiritual" potential which the majority are endowed with, above the limited mind, the intellect. This is a necessity for each of us to be able to be part of the new civilization, the 5th in order and become a citizen of the New Age, the Golden Age in which we entered on the winter solstice on December 21-23, 2012, when our solar system and our planet earth crossed the equatorial line of our galaxy, and entered a giant photon belt that emanates from the Central Universe, the Central Sun Alcyone in the Pleiadian constellation.

# Sandor A. Markus, CV

Sandor A. Markus, researcher and author, has a background in school medicine and complementary medicine. He has conducted research in quantum humanism - life sciences for most of his life. His knowledge in this area is based not only on theoretical knowledge, but also on practical experience.

## Qualifications:

- ✓ Sandor A. Markus, researcher, author, diplomat, innovator in Health & Inner Resource Development.
- ✓ Born in 1939 in Budapest, Hungary.
- ✓ PhD in Quantum Humanism (1976) and Sacred Theology (STD) International University of Loja, Ecuador.
- ✓ Doctor in Acupuncture (1977), Institut Polytechnique D'Antropologie, Bordeaux, France.
- ✓ Certified Clinical Hypnotherapist (1981), College of Clinical Hypnosis, Honolulu, Hawaii, USA.
- ✓ MD in Complementary Medicine (1984), The Open International University for Complementary Medicine & Medicina Alternativa, Colombo, Sri Lanka.
- ✓ International Honorary President of W.U.T.E.C.S. The World University of Ethno-Cultural Sciences, Lund, Sweden.
- ✓ President of the International Academy for Total Human Culture, Stockholm.
- ✓ Has also been active as a local politician (1979–81) in Åmål.
- ✓ Appointed Honorary Diplomat and Cultural Attaché (2004) in Sweden for Scandinavia and Hungary by the diplomatic organization (HBTO) "Human Bioethics Treaty Organization", Washington D.C. USA.

## International qualifications:

- ✓ Member of the International Association for Religion and Parapsychology, Tokyo, Japan (1987).
- ✓ Honoris Causa: Doctor of Anthropological Sciences, Madras, India.
- ✓ Honoris Causa, Zoroastian College, Bombay, India.
- ✓ Nominated Ambassador for Peace (1986) by the Organization Mondiale de la Press Diplomatique, Brussels, Belgium.
- ✓ Appointed International Man of the Year 1991/1992 and International Who's Who of Intellectuals for his humanitarian work, International Biographical Center, Cambridge, England.

Sandor A. Markus is one of the few researchers in the world who has integrated Eastern and Western philosophy, anthropology and medical knowledge with technology. He is a well-known lecturer and seminar leader in Quantum Thinking, Health & Resource Development.

Sandor A. Markus is not only a theorist. He has helped tens of thousands of people to better health. He has also been active as a local politician within the health care committee, the social central committee and as a member of the municipal council.

Sandor A. Markus has authored several books in health and resource development. He has created the CelesteMethod® as the first philosophical / scientific system that integrates Western and Eastern philosophy, medicine and anthropology with Western technology.

# Lars Helge Swahn, CV

All my life I have been interested in spirituality, higher consciousness. It all started with a couple of insights that made me realize that everything we see around us is just a glimpse of what really is there to see. I searched through books for guidance, but it was not until I turned 24 that I found a true Cosmic Spiritual Master Teacher who could really answer all my questions. He was Sandor A. Markus.

I knew instantly that this was what I sought all the time, especially when I saw his picture in his first book "From Barbarism to Super Consciousness". I started training with the advocated cosmic brain program every day.

My intuition grew and today I have a feeling of how many things work.

In recent years, I have also had the privilege of being continuously taught by Sandor A. Markus, a privilege not given to many. It has opened my eyes even more, and now I follow him on all his lectures and I help him as best I can.

I have translated many of his books into English and also helped him with web pages. Now is the time for the work to benefit the public.

Since the age of 24, I have studied higher metaphysics, health and resource development, energetic analyzes, EEG, earthly scientific connections also linked to the cosmos.

In parallel with 26 years of metaphysical studies, I have done the following:

Main educations:

✓ Upper secondary school Science education
✓ MSc. Earth sciences with a focus on bedrock geology

Been working with:

✓ As a high school teacher in science, mathematics and technology for 11 years
✓ In healthcare for almost 3 years.
✓ Work connected to computers for more than 30 years.
✓ Worked forth an "Action Plan for Fair Societal Development", based on the knowledge and experience I have gained over the years. The action plan is cosmically sanctioned and adapted to the New Age requirements.

# Conclusion and Summary Part 3

Without knowing the multidimensional historical development of man until now, it is impossible to understand man's current situation. What is absolutely crucial to each individual's choice of path, either the path of light or darkness, is his inner compass of ethics and morality. In this equation, all human mind programming is included. The outcome and the result can only be one and the choice is made by the individual himself and every individual knows this at the unconscious and subconscious level.

As the crown of creation, the path of the human being is only development and evolution, the evolution of his consciousness toward a higher qualitative multi-dimensional quantum consciousness. The human being is continuously cold-hammered to perfection, a sparkling and crystalline perfect diamond - this is the path of the human being - from the developmental and evolutionary point of view.

But the toughest part of the process is happening right now on this planet with all here living people taken into the calculation.

Humans have gone from a unity consciousness with no experiences and gradually been transformed down. Today they are at a very deep 3D level of experiences and problems of all kinds. The arriving path here on earth has been made with the help of the Soul's opponent, which in the religions has been called the devil. The devil in Sanskrit is called Kal Purush, which means time, time spirit, and death. Kal Purush in various philosophies and religions is called Yahve, Jehovah, Lucifer, Brahma, Allah, Buddha, Viracocha, Konkachila and others. This means that everything that is created, manifested as matter and form by the mind power is time-bound and constantly changing, restructuring.

Only the Soul energy (the pure, clean energy) in the universe, in hyperspace, in man is eternal, infinite, and indestructible.

The devil is a pure mind force. It is not an evil force. Only the earthly man due to ignorance, unconsciousness perceives it as an evil force and being. The mind energy is the opposite of the pure energy of the soul. It makes the Soul completely go through its mind program, the director's program to achieve perfection, Mastery in Life.

Example: Imagine a Script Writer and a Film Director. The Script Writer is the one who creates the basis, the script for a film or a play which is created out of mind energy. It takes a Director to bring to life, to illustrate what is written in the script, otherwise there will be no film or spectacle.

The same thing happens within the so-called "Divine Creation". The entire manifested universe from the smallest atom to the largest galaxy is created from mind energy, kinetic energy, electromagnetism.

The whole Divine Creation, the universe, the hyperspace, consists of different worlds, densities, consciousness and development levels. Our planet earth until now has belonged to the lowest, slowest state within this divine (pure) creation.

The role of the devil (Director) on earth is now over. But the devil doesn't want to give up his role voluntarily. The devil will fight to the end to keep it.

The name "The Devil" is an earthly name of the Director who has taken care of the development of the 3D material reality, which we have lived and worked in until now.

The devil can of course be tracked back to the origin of creation and its minions are everywhere in the universe and also here on Earth. Already during the Babylonian heyday, the Devil was worshiped but is also described in the Old Testament of the Bible. There he is worshiped as an idol in the form of Baal, Nebo, Astarte, Kemos, Molok and Dagon.

To come into contact with this power in the form of these idols it can be done most quickly through sexual rites and child sacrifices. It is therefore no wonder that in the corridors of power there are sexual rites, infanticides and "pedophile rings". This is contrary to the Solar theology, Gnosticism, the Cosmic Law, the Christian Ethical and Moral Rules. Humans will automatically indulge more and more in this power as they degenerate into the most sluggish part of matter and consciousness.

People at a certain level of development will meet this power in the form of astral experiences, promises, energy and information, and at a profound level they don't experience this force is devilish. People see their agreement with this power as positive and fruitful from an egocentric material point of view.

The devil says: *If you worship me, I give you the whole world.*

Human secret societies that devote themselves to this power and force have existed for a very long time on earth. Today they are materialized in the form of e.g. the Freemasonry Order, the Rosicrucian Order, the Illuminati Order, the Order of Malta and other Orders that worship and are governed by this power. It should be said that all Orders don't have this inclination.

The above mentioned orders are ruled from the top and the strongest connection to the Devil is at the top of the Orders. Then in steps own, the connection decreases and at the Freemasons' first degree from the bottom, the "companion level", there already exists a sufficient individual degeneration of the human quality which then corresponds to the others on the same level. As the degenerative power influences the individual more and more, they enter higher degrees. It changes from the "companion stage" with degenerative ego-fixation and societal degenerative orientation, and as the devilish power influences, it gradually leads to greater and greater obsession by the negative devilish power that works from the astral levels.

Higher up in the hierarchy, one's own personality is largely eradicated and an astral takeover has taken place from the four-dimensional (4D) level of the individual by a negative entity (being) who is a servant to the Devil, i.e. the Commander of the Negative Power on Earth. One could say that an "Idol of the Ancient Time" (the Beast) has taken abode in the human being, which is mentioned in the Bible (Book of Books). But not even the clergy, who see themselves as the vicars of Christ (the pure God Power) on earth, have understood what they convey to people. These vicars have hitherto been the mouthpieces of the Devil and not the mouthpieces of God. Their time is drawing to a close if they continue on the same path as hitherto.

The society today is dictated and governed by Freemason Orders and Illuminati Orders. This means that all these people and everyone else who has to automatically align with this kind of "reality" are slaves under these idols or the Devil.

Thus, with the help of these secret societies, man has degenerated in society, which has also been the meaning until now.

Today the human soul connection is cut off and the human mind has been programmed by directives from these Orders. Man has thus gone from a spiritual (soul) collective unity where everyone were together in a large cosmic family, to being gradually separated through mind programming into various mind conceptions. This has happened throughout history and all gained experiences each individual has gone through, world problems, societal problems, family problems, individual problems that led to further degeneration and delusion, deceptions through lies via the media (msm), through various political orientations (right, left) and everything else in order to fuel inequality and division.

It is interesting that the higher up in the hierarchy towards the top of the Orders you come, the more soulless and the more individuals have totally surrendered to the devilish power. So there is no ethics and morality left at all. The voice of conscience has since long ceased to be heard in these individuals. These individuals have become tools of devilish powers. Up to this state, the individuals have bathed in material wealth and the devil has truly enriched the individuals with all material they have ever wanted.

So if you ask the devil the question, "what is the meaning of life, society or the world" then you get the answer:

<u>The goal is total degeneration, total human decay, total eradication of all truth, all beauty and all spiritual - nothing should be left - only ugliness and darkness ...</u>

In theory, those remaining at the top after this degenerative societal race will be only two people - who are soulless and who also fight each other with lies, mistrust, anger, selfishness, violence and all human decay. These soulless people are now fighting each other and don't control themselves at all. The driving quality behind has always been the devilish force - and is thought to win... until there is not a single human being left on the planet...

... But will it go that far ...?

... No ... there must always be a balance between the positive and the negative. Once the negative has taken over, the process of positivism is fed, so that the balance is restored.

Man of today has learned a lot through experience. Man has also made positive choices that have strengthened his positive traits. But as we have described, the degenerate negative power has constantly started new processes of extermination of people through communism, socialism, wars but also through right-wing extremism if necessary as during World War II with Hitler at the forefront. The driving force behind has always been the same.

Man has been hammered in steps toward perfection, and is today a mix of positive and negative karma - giving differences in absurdity. The more differences, inequalities, the less soul communication, and the easier it is to brainwash individuals into performing immoral acts, including also to kill others and also inflict or kill oneself.

This process is now to be put on halt for those people who are mature enough, who have acquired sufficiently high soul-communication. The other humans will be transferred to other planets that correspond to their own inner development level. The lower levels of the astral plane are now being emptied, and individuals with the opportunity to develop a higher qualitative multi-dimensional quantum consciousness are born instead. The new generations will have higher ethics and morality from the beginning compared to what we have seen before.

Thus, in order to control the masses, the masses must be fragmented as well as societies, families and individuals to the maximum. All family security must be wasted.

## The Lies have become the Truth.

This "popular movement-socialism, communism" has been staged in the last century in Europe on several occasions and periods such as World War I, the Russian Revolution, the Spanish Civil War, the Second World War and today with the help of the Third World War that is ongoing and will escalate.

Common to all of these is soulless control of non-ethical thinking and immoral rule as well as indoctrination (brainwashing) of man to make him able to commit immoral crimes, kill others and now during the Third World War even kill himself with the help of lies, radiation, medication, vaccinations, chipping, poisoned food, poisoned air and poisoned water etc. .. Man has been made to believe in anything and today most people are actually working to kill themselves as well as all community and harmony, and also in family and society, in the world.

The human being becomes a soulless robot that must assimilate all lies broadcasted from the media (msm), i.e. the centralized propaganda machinery for the orders working from behind.

The only way out is that man works and refines his inner qualities and gets rid of all mind programming and lets the soul shine within them more and more.

Instead today, when an individual is not feeling well, he is superannuated due to the broken "safety nets" in society, with drugs, vaccines, psychoactive drugs, etc. and is sent here and there as a care package until death. Half of the population nurtures the other half - and who is developing society? Which politician has a conscious goal with his politics? Which human being has a conscious goal in his life? The human being of today worships degenerating material pursuit - and does not want to listen to anything else. The majority of people (the socialist or the future socialist) are terrified of dealing with their problems and go jointly to attack people who want to free themselves and become free soul-controlled individuals, people who want the true, the right, the good, who want to let their Soul shine like a Crystalline Star. So it has been throughout the history of the earth.

The Globalists' societal advocates speak with forked tongues - they say one thing and the outcome becomes the exact opposite. E.g. the dictatorship of the proletariat during the Soviet era, according to them, was the highest form of democracy (no difference today). Communism, socialism and social democracy work for this. It has happened before and it is happening again. Today, Sweden's political parties are lackeys to the devilish force behind, and in most cases without knowing it. This also goes for the right-wing parties because these people are also molded and programmed in the same form as the others.

People who don't take a stand for left or right, will through their fears, still most likely choose the dictatorship of the proletariat, i.e. the "highest form of democracy" - as it is talked about so much today.

When the division is most severe in man, through the millennia of religious thinking with left or right rejection with distorted reality, the only thing that remains is the ethics and morality that the human being has within individually. All lies, i.e. all self-programmed reality must be de-programmed, and the standpoint for this will be absolutely crucial for all people individually when they are to choose path.

When the division is the most severe then comes the takeover of power, which has happened earlier in history where communism and socialism took over countries. The dictatorship of the proletariat takes over ... and the looting begins as well as the killing of people who think differently, i.e. dissidents. Lenin's goal was to kill 90% of all those who lived in the former Soviet Union. If asked why - he wouldn't be able to answer it. It's only for the sake of it - that people really agree to it - that is the thing - to show them very thoroughly that they aren't mature either ethically or morally to develop a higher consciousness.

The same experiment is happening right now...

Under the whip of division and fear, man must consent to large supranational associations such as the UN, EU and NATO. People believe that these organizations work for the good of everyone, but the appearances are deceptive - they work for the opposite. The characteristics of the organizations are the characteristics of the involved people with extreme accumulations of lopsided karma, characteristics, confusions, devilish control. The heads of these organizations are also at the top of various soulless Orders.

Instead of looking into oneself, scrutinizing oneself, solving one's inner karmic problems, attention must be directed outward, to lies and falsehood. When the own identity is erased, attention should be directed to large supranational organizations, which want to dictate everything - and ultimately get people subjugated by threats, more lies and by sending individuals to concentration camps or killing them directly. The ultimate goal for all individuals in the Globalist dictatorship is to kill without conscience. This has already happened several times in the history of the earth.

The security of the family must be wasted and replaced by supranationalism - where the children belong to the state and where the soulless people with the help of the devil can decide whatever to do with the individuals to create the most problems for them.

As long as man is not allowed to de-program his karma, as long will the karma attract similar situations and continue in the same track. The entanglement of karma continues through history without interruption. War after war keeps coming and will never end and instead constantly flare up again. Conflicts within families, communities live on. The world situation is just like this today - will it never end?

In order to keep the downward directed force going in the individual, the process must be fattened with more sex, alcohol, drugs, downward music, and the abolition of ownership, inheritance, religion, traditional culture, nationalism, marriage, education and the introduction of extremely high taxes. The security of the home must be destroyed and the children shall lose their security and surrender to supranational thinking with totally erased individualities. The human being's degenerate mind programming should be categorized into as many different minorities as possible - they should all become tools of the devilish forces.

The Globalists' Plan is for everyone to join up behind the State when crisis come - and now you all know what this means...

# The Rescue

Our International Academy in the Life Sciences AIC has the task of guiding, helping those who want to help themselves. We cannot waste energy on people who want to be victims, feel sorry for themselves and are unwilling to change their lives for the better - those who constantly complain and accuse others of their failures, their life situations. Nor can we waste energy on those who blame God, parents, government officials, or other circumstances.

We want to help all those who are tired of suffering, long for peace and community and want to free themselves from the bondage and influence of the lower qualitative mind powers.

Being a member of our Academy in the Life Sciences according to the CelesteMethod® guarantees an increased flow of information and a cosmic community that gradually contributes to the liberation of the human Soul Atom, the Soul from the lower quality part of the mind and the five lower quality mind powers (sight, hearing, touch, taste, smell), their influence, impact. This guarantees increased consciousness which makes us see life from a different perspective than we are used to. It gives us greater insight into the causal relationship in every situation that arises.

The solution to all kinds of problems is within us. Seeking solutions to various situations outside of ourselves can be compared to finding a needle in a haystack.

The three-dimensional intellectually conscious human being believes that the solution lies outside of himself in the intellectual world. He believes that the solution is found in literature, ideology or philosophy. All this is just a means of finding the solution within ourselves.

Christ said, "*Seek the truth within you, and the truth will set you free.*"

Man has still not understood this message.

A true Master Teacher cannot solve man's individual or collective problems, only be a living example and share his/her own experiences. He can strengthen within each individual the qualitative qualities that man carries in his innermost being so that he can more easily overcome the resistance that he constantly encounters in life.

There are many dangers on the way. It's easy to get lost in the maze of matter, the world of the mind.

Therefore, seek the support by the true Master Teacher (Unifier) who can guide you out of the darkness and lead you into the light where harmony and security prevail.

Security cannot be found through relationships, in family, in society, in the workplace, in friendships or through the economy.

You find security only within yourself, in your innermost being.

Therefore seek the truth within yourself!

Through the use of the CelesteMethod® and your membership of the AIC Association, your life, thinking and actions will gradually change for the better.

The most important thing right now is that we train our consciousness to a higher qualitative multi-dimensional quantum consciousness - free from all bondage of mind. It is important to train our consciousness with a focus on our inner essence and not focus too much on the exterior.

Figure 64. The solutions to all problems we find within ourselves.

Keep in mind that all human beings and all technology available on earth right now are ready to make the transition to the next civilization, the 5th in order, as easy as possible. All the technology that is used to poison humans, different parts of the earth, chemically and electromagnetically, has a meaning. The earth as well as man has accumulated loads of energetic problems over many thousands of years. In order for recovery to proceed as quickly as possible with as little suffering as possible for the inhabitants of the earth, all this technology is needed to make the process short.

This means that many people will begin to raise their consciousness and those who are unable to do so will have to move from here. The technology is here to mark the dividing line and for the removal process to proceed quickly, smoothly and with as little suffering as possible.

In combination with the CelesteMethod®, we offer you also AI "Artificial Intelligence" - a medical technology that we are the only ones to use in Northern Europe. These two methods together can alleviate your mental, emotional and biological (physical) sufferings of various kinds. This helps you adapt to the time we are in now.

The choice is yours - and in your inner essence you have already decided your way. Either you choose the active choice to raise your consciousness toward a higher qualitative multi-dimensional quantum consciousness, or you choose not to.

The children that are born now belong to the upcoming 5th civilization and together we will make the planet earth a great place to live on.

*In the beginning God created heaven and earth. And the earth was desolate and empty, and darkness was over the depth, and the Spirit of God hovered over the water. And God said, "Be light"; and there was light. And God saw that the light was good; and God separated the light from the darkness.*

*First book of Moses*

*Remember that darkness is needed for the Light to Grow!*

*The Unifier*

# The International Academy for Total Human Culture, AIC.

"L'Académie Internationale De Culture Humaine Intégrale A.I.C."

"The International Academy for Total Human Culture" related to human conditions, progress and development, was founded in Bordeaux, France, in 1972.

It was registered in Stockholm, Sweden as an Academy Foundation, in 1989, Org. no. 802014-5309.

The Academy Foundation "The International Academy for Total Human Culture" is a private, non-governmental development and educational center operating in Cultural Ecology with a focus on the Life Sciences - Human Sciences. The Academy is international, NGO "Non-Governmental Organization" and non-profit.

In today's world, everything is divided into different sciences and branches of knowledge, which creates division and disorder. The AIC works to create a common platform for innovative thinking in philosophy, culture, science and technology, and thereby contribute to the human future (cosmic) development and progress. Man should develop a multi-dimensional higher qualitative quantum consciousness.

The Academy works for a Global Human Culture.
https://www.unifier.se/cultural-ecology/

The founder of the Academy is: Sandor A Markus.

International President of the Academy is: Ann-Sofie Hammarbäck.

**The Academy Goal and Vision:**

- One World Commonwealth
- One Fraternal Humanity
- A flag of Love – Wisdom
- One moral standard
- One language of understanding
- Above All Frontiers
- Above All Prejudices
- Above All Traditions

**A.I.C. Project**
www.unifier.se, (www.human-academy.com/english)

**Nordic Gnostic Unity: A.I.C.**
www.nordicgnosticunity.org

**A.I.C. Association: Member site for multi-dimensional quantum consciousness**
www.worlddoctrine.org

**Sovereign Imperial Order of Saint Germain (SIOSG)**
**Multi-dimensional quantum consciousness for distinguished individuals**
This Order works for the light
www.saintgermainorder.org

# AIC Association

www.worlddoctrine.org

As a member of the AIC Association, you support the AIC's eight points above. This means that you contribute to a better world to live in. You can begin to train yourself to a higher qualitative quantum consciousness. This means that you focus on your higher qualitative characteristics and abandon the lower qualitative characteristics that create problems of various kinds for you.

Once you have attained this consciousness, you can consciously choose how your future life will manifest. You are no longer unconsciously bound by the law of cause and effect. As a quantum conscious being, you see the five-dimensional matrix that is the basic pattern of how everything is manifested and embodied in the universe. Before you make different decisions, you can see beforehand how the result will be.

During the training process, you eliminate various obstacles that have been programmed into your subconscious for a long time.

You can find out more about this spiritual higher qualitative consciousness on our web pages and in the UNIFIER's literature and seminars.

The AIC Association uses the training program of the **CelesteMethod®**. The **CelesteMethod®** is built on the foundation of three steps.

These are:
1. Information - Education.
2. Individual Analysis and Guidance, Measure Program.
3. Consciousness Training.

The AIC Association's steps 1 and 3 are fully sufficient to get started with your training.

Step 2 is offered for individual needs.

On the AIC Association website, the teachings takes place through coded videos that help you understand the cosmic teachings, the "*world doctrine*" on a deeper level, i.e. first intellectually and later through intuitive clarity, since it's here the understanding lies.

Of course here are training programs for increased consciousness and various health sessions that are necessary in your training toward your goal, i.e. a spiritually higher qualitative quantum consciousness.

Behind log in on the site, everything is self-instructive with help videos, teachings videos, training programs and health sessions.

For each new week that comes, one more teaching video will be added behind your login. This training continues for seven years, along with training and health sessions - so it's just getting started.

The language is English, but there are translations into many other languages.

Spread this information about the AIC to friends and acquaintances, so we can work on an even wider front for a better society.

Remember! It is we ourselves who decide how our destiny will turn out. We are the creators of our own destinies. The choice lies in our hands.

**Stay informed:**
Make sure you get newsletter mails from the AIC ongoing about consciousness development, consciousness training, teachings and seminars that all facilitate for you as you develop your higher qualitative multi-dimensional quantum consciousness, and to avoid pitfalls.

Sign up for email at www.unifier.se, (www.human-academy.com) or at www.worlddoctrine.org.

We welcome you as a family member so that our common future becomes a civilization in truth and clarity, i.e. according to the AIC's eight points - the fifth civilization to come.

# We who work on the AIC Project

Dr. Sandor Alexander Markus, Ph.D., MD., STD.
Secretary General AIC.
President of NPA and SIOSG.
Initiator and founder of the AIC project.

Dr. Ann-Sofie Hammarbäck, STD.
Dr. Sacred Theology (Metaphysics)
President of the AIC.
Protector of the AIC and SIOSG

Daniel Skagerström
Dr. h.c. Life Sciences
Vice President of the SIOSG, AIC
Innovative Designer, Technical Expert

Lars Helge Swahn, MSc.
Natural Science
Dr. h.c. Life Sciences
Vice Secretary General AIC
Computers and Internet

# Published books

All of these books support the AIC's eight points above. The books teach the law of the cosmos and how important the higher quality multidimensional quantum consciousness is for the survival of the individual, society and world. It is highly relevant now when one part of the human race having the qualitative prerequisites is preparing for the fifth civilization. The other part of the Earth's people will after their physical death be transferred to other planetary systems and continue their development there, from the qualitative level they are at now.

1. **Saint Germain, the mysterious Count who never dies**
   Author: Dr. Sandor A Markus

2. **My Incarnations and Teachings**
   Author: Dr. Sandor A Markus

3. **From Barbarism to Super Consciousness**
   A New Consciousness is a Necessity for the Survival of Civilization
   Author: Dr. Sandor A Markus

4. **Aliens Are Amongst Us**
   The Cosmic Heritage
   Author: Dr. Sandor A Markus

5. **The World Doctrine**
   Philosophy, Religion and Science of the New Age
   Author: Dr. Sandor A Markus

6. **The Matrix Reality**
   Man is a mind controlled intellectual robot living in a programmed reality
   Main Author: Dr. Sandor A Markus
   Co-author: Lars Helge Swahn

7. **The Free Human Being**
   Vladimir Putin opens up the Gate to the Development of the New Age
   Main Author: Dr. Sandor A Markus
   Co-author: Lars Helge Swahn

**The publication of the book:**
The Swedish version of the book is proofread by Lars Helge Swahn, who also has translated the book to English.

**The illustrations in the book:**
The cosmic illustrations are made by Daniel Skagerström with the help of Sandor A Markus. Other illustrations have been provided by Sandor A Markus and Matrix Innovation. Matrix Innovation is the publishing house of the book.

- Book Cover:
  Composed by Daniel Skagerström. The Painting is Public Domain and the picture on Vladimir Putin is from http://en.kremlin.ru/

- Frontpaper: Dove of Peace and Grail:
  Dove of Peace: Public Domain; Grail: www.shutterstock.com

- Images from www.shutterstock.com (7, 46, 47)

- AIC's teachings materials (17, 19, 24, 27, 39)

- AIC's teaching's materials combined with some elements of images from www.shutterstock.com (15, 16, 18, 21, 23, 49, 64)

- Images under GNU licence (9, 11, 14, 36)
  https://commons.wikimedia.org/wiki/File:ConstellationDraco.svg
  https://commons.wikimedia.org/wiki/File:20090528_Beijing_Nine_Dragon_Wall_7992.jpg
  https://commons.wikimedia.org/wiki/File:Purim_spiel_2009B.jpg
  https://commons.wikimedia.org/wiki/File:Contrails_near_Frankfurt_(Germany),_2012.jpg?uselang=sv

- Photographs belonging to Sandor A Markus, AIC or SIOSG (5)

- Public Domain (1, 3, 6, 9, 10, 11, 12, 22, 26, 30, 32, 33, 34, 35, 41, 42, 44, 45, 51, 53, 54, 55, 56, 57, 61, 62, 63)
  https://commons.wikimedia.org/wiki/File:Xi_Jinping_March_2017.jpg
  https://commons.wikimedia.org/wiki/File:Draco_and_Ursa_Minor.jpg
  http://puntopress.com/chinarising/wp-

content/uploads/2015/12/xiJinping-billboard.jpg
https://upload.wikimedia.org/wikipedia/commons/3/33/Yellow_E
mperor.jpg
https://commons.wikimedia.org/wiki/File:DnD_Dragon.png

- Creative Commons Attribution-Share Alike 4.0 International (2, 4, 8, 13, 14, 58, 59)
  http://en.kremlin.ru/
  https://commons.wikimedia.org/wiki/File:Vladimir_Putin_(2017-07-08)_(cropped).jpg
  https://commons.wikimedia.org/wiki/File:Shigatse-Tashilhunpo-82-Klostergebaeude-2014-gje.jpg
  https://commons.wikimedia.org/wiki/User:Gerd_Eichmann
  https://www.rcinet.ca/eye-on-the-arctic-special-reports/wp-content/uploads/sites/89/2018/11/sj04-2018-0350-014-e1544463227408.jpg
  Photo: Pat Blanchard/Canadian Armed Forces.
  https://commons.wikimedia.org/wiki/File:Red_Apple.jpg
  https://commons.wikimedia.org/wiki/File:Comedy_and_tragedy_masks_without_background.svg
  https://commons.wikimedia.org/wiki/File:Corona_virus_Covid-19_Single_Virion.png
  https://commons.wikimedia.org/wiki/File:2019-07-21_-_Vodafone_5G_Standort_Hattstedt_-_5G_Sektor0.jpg

- Wikimedia Commons (25, 40)

- Creative Commons (31, 38, 43, 48, 50)
  https://commons.wikimedia.org/wiki/File:Antiwar_protesters_(30873234).jpg
  https://simple.wikipedia.org/wiki/File:Cabin_nose_section_of_747-8I_prototype.jpg
  https://upload.wikimedia.org/wikipedia/commons/8/84/Sony_Xperia_Z.JPG
  https://upload.wikimedia.org/wikipedia/commons/3/38/Neuroms.png?uselang=sv
  https://commons.wikimedia.org/wiki/File:AAA_SVG_Chessboard_and_chess_pieces_02.svg

- Adjusted from unknown source (28)

- Unknown source (29, 52-saved teachings materials)

- Positive promotion (60)
  Principia Scientific International

# References

The references existed and were studied during the period 2017/03 - 2017/10. After this, there were also studied references regarding covid and the social contract.

Sweden is over-represented in the Bilderberg group:
https://www.youtube.com/watch?v=1NzlMtx6PGE
https://www.youtube.com/watch?v=5SCWSf9cMaY
https://www.youtube.com/watch?v=VZaDKwm7yWk
http://politicalavengernews.com/index.php/2017/07/16/investment-banker-whistleblower-george-green/
https://www.youtube.com/watch?v=pbSkXvllFPA&list=RDVZaDKwm7yWk&index=4
https://www.youtube.com/watch?v=pbSkXvllFPA&list=RDVZaDKwm7yWk&index=4
https://www.youtube.com/watch?v=TwDGQTCWA4I&list=RDVZaDKwm7yWk&index=2
https://www.youtube.com/watch?v=pbSkXvllFPA&list=RDVZaDKwm7yWk&index=4
https://www.youtube.com/watch?v=57HvAbKD93s
https://sv.wikipedia.org/wiki/Jugoslaviska_krigen

Virus - epidemics of diseases:
Swine flu:
https://www.cdc.gov/flu/about/viruses/change.htm
https://www.theatlantic.com/health/archive/2014/05/when-viruses-escape-the-lab/371202/
https://www.hsph.harvard.edu/news/press-releases/bird-flu-experiments-pose-risk-of-accidental-release/
http://journals.plos.org/plosone/article?id=10.1371/journal.pone.0011184
http://www.thelibertybeacon.com/proof-that-the-swine-flu-epidemic-was-man-made-and-intentional/
http://patft.uspto.gov/netacgi/nph-Parser?Sect1=PTO2&Sect2=HITOFF&p=1&u=%2Fnetahtml%2FPTO%2Fsearch-

bool.html&r=1&f=G&l=50&co1=AND&d=PTXT&s1=
%22Engineered+Swine+Influenza+Virus+Uses%22.TI.&OS=TTL/

Ebola:
http://newsvoice.se/2014/11/18/john-virapen-intervjuad-i-usa-om-ebola-
och-lakemedelsindustrins-bedragerier/
http://newsvoice.se/2014/10/26/amerikansk-militar-och-
lakemedelsindustrin-ar-nu-etablerad-i-vastafrika-epidemin-kan-avslutas/
http://www.bbc.com/news/world-africa-28755033
https://en.wikipedia.org/wiki/West_African_Ebola_virus_epidemic
https://www.nytimes.com/2016/12/22/health/ebola-vaccine.html?_r=0
http://www.nytimes.com/2005/06/06/health/new-vaccines-prevent-ebola-
and-marburg-in-monkeys.html
https://www.ncbi.nlm.nih.gov/pmc/articles/PMC4517535/
https://www.usatoday.com/story/news/nation/2014/10/01/military-goes-
to-africa-ebola-mission/16526873/
http://www.doctorswithoutborders.org/our-work/medical-issues/ebola
https://www.cdc.gov/vhf/ebola/transmission/

HIV and AIDS:
https://www.youtube.com/watch?v=ouqkAcP-src
https://www.youtube.com/watch?v=Ry1rVCRVzeM
https://www.youtube.com/watch?v=3J7vHLXCphA
https://www.youtube.com/watch?v=ofQfHB6N1RM
https://www.youtube.com/watch?v=FPzj-6RbVb0
www.christl-meyer-science.net
https://www.youtube.com/watch?v=cpD0UR_5m-A
https://www.youtube.com/watch?v=REz2y3TEDbE

Vaccinations:
https://sv.wikipedia.org/wiki/Antigen
https://sv.wikipedia.org/wiki/Vaccination
http://www.naturalnews.com/035431_vaccine_ingredients_side_effects_msg
.html
http://iterated-reality.com/sv/2017/03/22/13-alarmerande-studier-om-
vaccinsakerhet/
https://www.youtube.com/watch?v=13QiSV_lrDQ
https://www.ncbi.nlm.nih.gov/pubmed/24779346
https://www.ncbi.nlm.nih.gov/pubmed/21568886
http://kurera.se/aluminium-al/
https://www.youtube.com/watch?v=r8FCJ_VPyns

http://www.naturalnews.com/035431_vaccine_ingredients_side_effects_msg
.html
http://newsvoice.se/2017/06/22/giftiga-nanopartiklar-vacciner/
http://medcraveonline.com/IJVV/IJVV-04-00072.pdf
http://newsvoice.se/2013/04/16/svensk-ki-lakare-och-kth-hittade-hoga-
halter-av-arsenik-och-tenn-i-pandemrix/
http://iterated-reality.com/sv/2017/03/22/13-alarmerande-studier-om-
vaccinsakerhet/
https://www.ncbi.nlm.nih.gov/pubmed/2190116
https://www.ncbi.nlm.nih.gov/pubmed/18819554?dopt=AbstractPlus
http://www.stralskyddsstiftelsen.se/forskning/
https://jehse.biomedcentral.com/articles/10.1186/s40201-016-0253-z
http://iterated-reality.com/sv/2017/04/24/granskning-av-innehallet-
vacciner-ar-de-sakra-bedom-sjalv/
https://www.ncbi.nlm.nih.gov/pubmed/10207615
http://newsvoice.se/2016/10/05/barnsjukdomarna-nastan-borta-innan-
vaccinprogrammen-startade/
https://www.svd.se/superepidemilogen-om-massvaccineringen-mest-
upprord-ar-jag-over-att-ingen-tagit-ansvar
https://lakemedelsverket.se/malgrupp/Allmanhet/Allmant-om-vacciner-
och-vaccination/Sa-godkanns-vacciner/
Flu shots, for example, are now scientifically confirmed to cause spontaneous
abortions:
http://vaccines.news/2017-09-13-cdc-funded-study-confirms-flu-shots-
linked-to-spontaneous-abortions-vaccine-experts-rush-to-explain-away-the-
findings.html
https://www.naturalnews.com/047942_flu_shots_medical_fraud_vaccine_qu
ackery.html
http://www.cidrap.umn.edu/news-perspective/2017/09/study-signals-
association-between-flu-vaccine-miscarriage
https://newsvoice.se/2017/09/20/vaccindomstol-spadbarnsdod/
http://www.greenmedinfo.com/blog/new-decision-us-vaccine-court-sids-
case-significant
https://medicalxpress.com/news/2017-09-prompts-flu-vaccine-
miscarriage.html
https://www.naturalnews.com/041345_cdc_polio_vaccine_sv40.html

Medication:
http://www.tv4.se/nyhetsmorgon/klipp/doktor-mikael-s%C3%A5-farligt-
%C3%A4r-alvedon-3178279
http://www.paracetamol.se/
http://www.livescience.com/42430-placebo-effect-half-of-drug-efficacy.html

http://www.socialstyrelsen.se/statistik/statistikefteramne/lakemedel
http://www.aftonbladet.se/nyheter/a/6Jlz3/stoppa-pengarna-till-lakarna-fran-industrin
https://www.slf.se/upload/Lakarforbundet/Trycksaker/PDFer/L%C3%A4karfakta_2016.pdf
https://sv.wikipedia.org/wiki/Psykoaktiva_droger
http://www.kmr.nu/single-post/2016/05/29/Psykiatrin-%C3%A5rhundradets-bedr%C3%A4geri
http://www.kmr.nu/bocker
https://www.svd.se/snart-kan-alla-som-vill-fa-en-diagnos
https://sv.wikipedia.org/wiki/ADHD
https://sv.wikipedia.org/wiki/Amfetamin
http://www.kmr.nu/single-post/2016/05/29/Psykiatrin-%C3%A5rhundradets-bedr%C3%A4geri
http://www.kostdemokrati.se/business/2014/06/14/inga-dodsfall-fran-kosttillskott-men-783-000-dodsfall-av-lakemedel-och-ingen-bryr-sig/

The pharmaceutical industry counteracts natural harmonious methods:
https://sv.wikipedia.org/wiki/Papyrus_Ebers
https://lakemedelsverket.se/overgripande/Lagar--regler/EG-direktiv/
https://en.wikipedia.org/wiki/European_Directive_on_Traditional_Herbal_Medicinal_Products
http://jmm.nu/upphav-eus-forbud-mot-orter/
https://lakemedelsverket.se/
https://sv.wikipedia.org/wiki/L%C3%A4kemedelsverket
https://www.youtube.com/watch?v=vwr7gdT_3O8
http://www.svt.se/nyheter/inrikes/vaxtlakemedel-doms-ut
https://lakemedelsverket.se/malgrupp/Foretag/Vaxtbaserade-lakemedel-traditionella-vaxtbaserade-lakemedel-och-naturlakemedel/Avgifter/
http://dagenshomeopati.se/2011/05/01/manga-anvandbara-och-naturlakemedel-ar-nu-forbjudna/
http://jmm.nu/upphav-eus-forbud-mot-orter/
http://www.vaken.se/lakemedelsindustrin-vill-forbjuda-lakeorter/
http://www.socialstyrelsen.se/publikationer2016/2016-6-12
http://www.socialstyrelsen.se/Lists/Artikelkatalog/Attachments/20533/2017-3-33.pdf
https://www.folkhalsomyndigheten.se/folkhalsorapportering-statistik/folkhalsans-utveckling/sjalvmord/
http://www.dn.se/nyheter/sverige/sverige-over-sjalvmordssnittet/
https://afsp.org/about-suicide/suicide-statistics/
http://www.dn.se/nyheter/sverige/slutstriden-om-den-alternativa-medicinen/

https://jehse.biomedcentral.com/articles/10.1186/s40201-016-0253-z
http://dagenshomeopati.se/2011/03/22/inga-dodsfall-fran-kosttillskott-men-783-000-dodsfall-av-lakemedel/
http://www.kostdemokrati.se/business/2014/06/14/inga-dodsfall-fran-kosttillskott-men-783-000-dodsfall-av-lakemedel-och-ingen-bryr-sig/
http://www.doctoryourself.com/deathmed.html
http://www.nutraceuticalsworld.com/contents/view_online-exclusives/2016-10-31/over-170-million-americans-take-dietary-supplements/1612
http://orthomolecular.org/resources/omns/v06n04.shtml
http://www.aapcc.org/annual-reports/
https://aapcc.s3.amazonaws.com/pdfs/annual_reports/2008_AAPCC_Annual_Report.pdf
http://www.alternet.org/story/147318/100,000_americans_die_each_year_from_prescription_drugs,_while_pharma_companies_get_rich
https://www.amazon.co.uk/gp/product/0312428251
http://newsvoice.se/2013/07/24/debatt-pillerknapring-for-miljardbelopp-men-varfor-blir-ingen-frisk/


Abolishment of the Alternative Medicine:
https://no.wikipedia.org/wiki/Allopati
https://www.youtube.com/watch?v=MQECIZiNhe8
https://www.youtube.com/watch?v=4Tqnd9_gUxk
https://www.youtube.com/watch?v=7_n1xLXKjfI
https://www.youtube.com/watch?v=-hyRQyOvAlk
https://en.wikipedia.org/wiki/Flexner_Report
http://archive.carnegiefoundation.org/pdfs/elibrary/Carnegie_Flexner_Report.pdf
https://www.youtube.com/watch?v=AysfKyl8O9k
https://www.dagensmedicin.se/artiklar/2007/05/18/martin-ingvar-professor-i-integrativ-medicin/
https://www.svd.se/svenska-forskare-soker-medicinska-alternativ
http://newsvoice.se/2017/05/16/martin-ingvar-ki-avgar/
http://newsvoice.se/2012/10/03/professor-martin-ingvar-blev-arets-forvillare-2012-fick-nastan-13-av-alla-roster/
http://www.dn.se/sthlm/ki-chef-avgar-efter-internrevision/
http://2op.se/2017/04/29/regeringen-vill-bygga-broar-mellan-skol-och-alternativmedicin/
https://skl.se/halsasjukvard/patientinflytande/patientlagen.2083.html
http://www.vardanalys.se/Rapporter/2017/Lag-utan-genomslag/
http://www.regeringen.se/rattsdokument/kommittedirektiv/2017/04/dir.2017 43/

http://www.regeringen.se/49930b/contentassets/6da272f3fe094da598731e2
7b78057e6/okat-patientinflytande-och-patientsakerhet-inom-annan-vard-och-
behandling-an-den-som-bedrivs-inom-den-etablerade-varden-dir2017_43.pdf

Air emissions of vaccines:
https://www.youtube.com/watch?v=LZaPU1vdV8M
https://www.youtube.com/watch?v=a50XKjXWzr8
http://www.southwestfarmpress.com/livestock/rabies-outbreak-spreads-
new-mexico
http://www.nbcnews.com/health/health-news/new-rabies-strain-found-
new-mexico-n361966
http://www.cbsnews.com/news/new-rabies-strain-discovered-in-new-
mexico/
http://www.dshs.texas.gov/IDCU/disease/rabies/orvp/information/Maps.
doc
http://news.nationalpost.com/news/canada/how-rabies-is-suddenly-on-the-
rise-in-canada
http://www.dshs.texas.gov/IDCU/disease/rabies/orvp/information/Maps.
doc
http://www.inspection.gc.ca/animals/terrestrial-
animals/diseases/reportable/rabies/rabies-in-
canada/eng/1356156989919/1356157139999

Geoengineering - Chemtrails:
http://www.alachuacounty.us/Depts/epd/EPAC/Download%20the
%20Chemtrails%20Manual%20Published%20by%20the%20DoD%20For
%20The%20USAF%20Academy.pdf
https://chemtrailsplanet.files.wordpress.com/2013/02/chemtrails_chemistry
-manual-usaf-academy-1990.pdf
http://www.geoengineeringwatch.org/former-air-force-officer-warns-of-
atmospheric-spraying-and-the-coming-collapse/
http://blueshift.nu/?s=geoengineering
http://yournewswire.com/the-united-nations-admits-chemtrails-are-real/
http://journals.plos.org/plosone/article?id=10.1371/journal.pone.0130963
http://www.actabp.pl/pdf/3_2001/673.pdf
https://www.ncbi.nlm.nih.gov/pmc/articles/PMC3679494/
http://www.vaxteko.nu/html/sll/hydro_agri/vaxtpressen/VPN90-
2/VPN90-2E.HTM
http://kurera.se/aluminium-al/
http://morethanyouwantedtoknow.com/index.php?
menutopic=Geo_Engineering&submenu=Geo_Engineering&hmenustr=De
ceptions

https://www.youtube.com/watch?v=WmKm36QlG6Q
http://contrailscience.com/barium-chemtrails/
http://themindunleashed.com/2017/03/official-sky-will-sprayed-geoengineering-experiment-blocking-sun-climate-change.html
http://newsvoice.se/2016/08/24/ar-chemtrails-fakta-eller-fiktion-granskning-av-iopscience-studien/
http://newsvoice.se/2014/09/05/chemtrails-bevis-och-syfte-doktorand-tj-coles-plymouth-university/
https://www.youtube.com/watch?v=lZaD-H_j3pU
https://www.youtube.com/watch?v=DPnWaBsMYnY
https://eraoflight.com/2016/09/16/experts-come-forward-to-answer-questions-about-the-dark-reality-of-chemtrails/
https://www.svd.se/var-40e-svensk-dement-ar-2050
http://www.consumerhealth.org/articles/display.cfm?ID=20000830164825
https://sv.wikipedia.org/wiki/Mykoplasmapneumoni

HAARP:
https://www.youtube.com/watch?v=SToVBicIrJU
https://www.youtube.com/watch?v=J_mxbFAcv6Q
http://chemtrails-sverige.blogspot.se/
http://www.aftonbladet.se/nyheter/article10239962.ab
http://lofar-se.org/
http://www.gp.se/nyheter/v%C3%A4stsverige/teleskop-i-v%C3%A4rldsklass-invigt-1.855101
https://www.congress.gov/bill/107th-congress/house-bill/2977/text
http://jmm.nu/haarp-chemtrails-och-vadermodifiering-sverige/
http://rense.com/general92/haarp.htm
http://m.esa.int/swe/ESA_in_your_country/Sweden/Vaerldens_mesta_hoegteknologiteleskop_i_Smaaland
https://sv.wikipedia.org/wiki/Mikrov%C3%A5gor
http://www.chalmers.se/rss/oso-sv/aktuellt/nyhetsarkiv/jan-bjorklund-inviger
https://jehse.biomedcentral.com/articles/10.1186/s40201-016-0253-z
http://onlinelibrary.wiley.com/doi/10.1002/jemt.1070270608/full
https://www.scientificamerican.com/article/major-cell-phone-radiation-study-reignites-cancer-questions/
http://biorxiv.org/content/biorxiv/early/2016/05/26/055699.full.pdf
http://www.stralskyddsstiftelsen.se/2015/03/stralning-fran-surfplattor-och-mobiler-framjar-cancer-visar-ny-forskning/
http://www.sciencedirect.com/science/article/pii/S0006291X15003988
http://www.aftonbladet.se/nyheter/article15637164.ab
http://unionline.info/haarp-locations

https://www.naturalnews.com/2017-09-10-175-patents-prove-that-geoengineering-and-weather-control-technologies-are-real.html

"Smart electricity meter" at home (4G, 5G):
http://www.stralskyddsstiftelsen.se/rad/smarta-elmatare/
https://skyvisionsolutions.files.wordpress.com/2013/11/aaem-wireless-smart-meter-case-studies.pdf
http://www.saferemr.com/2015/02/health-experts-caution-about-smart.html
http://microwavenews.com/Interphone.Appendix2.html
http://www.powerwatch.org.uk/science/studies.asp
https://www.ncbi.nlm.nih.gov/pubmed/18425337
https://www.ncbi.nlm.nih.gov/pubmed/19268551
https://sv.wikipedia.org/wiki/Bluetooth
http://www.pts.se/pts/templates/newspage.aspx?id=58259&epslanguage=sv
http://www.stralskyddsstiftelsen.se/2017/03/5g-ett-oetiskt-olagligt-experiment-med-manniskors-liv-och-halsa/
https://blog.rackspace.com/internet-of-things-why-connected-toasters-and-other-smart-home-devices-matter
https://www.androidpit.com/why-is-5g-so-important-for-the-internet-of-things
http://m3.idg.se/2.1022/1.648110/5g-tekniken
http://www.stralskyddsstiftelsen.se/2016/04/mobilmaster-orsakar-huvudvark-somnsvarigheter-och-psykisk-ohalsa-ny-forskning-bekraftar-effekterna/
https://www.ncbi.nlm.nih.gov/pmc/articles/PMC1241519/
http://onlinelibrary.wiley.com/doi/10.1002/bem.2250110402/full
http://freedom-articles.toolsforfreedom.com/subliminal-message-kill-mind-control/
https://sv.wikipedia.org/wiki/Frames_per_second
http://www.independent.co.uk/life-style/gadgets-and-tech/edward-snowden-smartphones-can-be-hacked-into-with-just-one-text-message-and-then-used-to-spy-on-a6680546.html
https://www.scientificamerican.com/article/mind-control-by-cell/
https://www.ncbi.nlm.nih.gov/pubmed/17548154?ordinalpos=1&itool=EntrezSystem2.PEntrez.Pubmed.Pubmed_ResultsPanel.Pubmed_RVDocSum
http://www.stralskyddsstiftelsen.se/2016/11/dramatisk-okning-av-psykisk-ohalsa-en-effekt-av-okad-stralning/
https://nyadagbladet.se/halsa/hjarntumorer-okar-danmark-fordubbling-sedan-1990/

http://www.esundhed.dk/sundhedsregistre/CAR/CAR01/Sider/Tabel.aspx
http://www.stralskyddsstiftelsen.se/2017/08/cancerexpert-bevisen-kan-inte-langre-ignoreras-mobilstralning-orsakar-cancer/
https://www.ncbi.nlm.nih.gov/pubmed/28535174
https://www.ncbi.nlm.nih.gov/pubmed/28213724
http://ijomeh.eu/Mobile-phone-use-and-risk-for-intracranial-tumors-and-salivary-gland-tumors-A-meta-analysis,63713,0,2.html
http://www.stralskyddsstiftelsen.se/wp-content/uploads/2017/08/NTP2016.pdf
http://www.tandfonline.com/doi/abs/10.3109/15368378.2015.1043557
http://www.stralskyddsstiftelsen.se/2015/03/stralning-fran-surfplattor-och-mobiler-framjar-cancer-visar-ny-forskning/
http://www.bioinitiative.org/new-studies-show-health-risks-from-wireless-tech/
http://www.stralskyddsstiftelsen.se/2014/05/30-minuter-i-mobilen-varje-dag-okar-risken-for-aggressiv-hjarntumor/
https://www.spandidos-publications.com/10.3892/ijo.2013.2111
https://www.ncbi.nlm.nih.gov/pubmed/20483835
https://www.ncbi.nlm.nih.gov/pubmed/21659469
https://academic.oup.com/jnci/article/103/16/1264/898567/Mobile-Phone-Use-and-Brain-Tumors-in-Children-and
https://www.ncbi.nlm.nih.gov/pubmed/21862434
https://www.spandidos-publications.com/10.3892/ijo.2013.2025
https://www.emf-portal.org/en/article/24127
https://www.ncbi.nlm.nih.gov/pubmed/21225885
http://www.ijoms.com/article/S0901-5027%2811%2900117-2/abstract
http://newsvoice.se/2017/09/14/5g-180-vetenskapsman-varnar/
https://nyadagbladet.se/halsa/180-forskare-varnar-allvarliga-halsorisker-med-5g/
https://www.ncbi.nlm.nih.gov/pubmed/27454111
http://www.stralskyddsstiftelsen.se/wp-content/uploads/2017/09/scientist_5g_appeal_final.pdf

Chipping - mind control:
http://newsvoice.se/2016/08/01/5g-tar-oss-rakt-in-total-overvakning-chippning-och-halsorisker/
remote viewing...etc...

Government:
https://sv.wikipedia.org/wiki/Emmanuel_Macron

NATO, EU, etc:

https://www.svt.se/nyheter/inrikes/ja-till-natoavtal

Popular adult education:
https://sv.wikipedia.org/wiki/Folkomr%C3%B6stningen_om_k
%C3%A4rnkraften_i_Sverige_1980
https://sv.wikipedia.org/wiki/Fukushima-olyckan
http://www.zerohedge.com/news/2016-10-02/fukushima-radiation-has-contaminated-entire-pacific-ocean-and-its-going-get-worse
http://www.abf.se/Press-Nyheter/Debattartiklar/2007/Satsa-pa-folkbildning-i-klimatfragan-Andreas-Carlgren/
http://www.vof.se/skepdic/klimatfornekare/

Banning demonstrations:
http://newsvoice.se/2014/05/23/nytt-lagforslag-spanien-nara-att-bli-polisstat/
https://www.svd.se/spanien-utarmar-rattsstaten
http://www.aftonbladet.se/debatt/debattamnen/eu/article21057262.ab

The Police Service:
http://tryggaresverige.org/fler-poliser-tydligare-ledning-eller-kvantitativa-mal-vad-kravs-for-att-losa-krisen-inom-polisen
http://www.blaljus.nu/nyhetsartikel/centralisering-av-ledningscentraler-sagas-pa-vetenskaplig-grund
https://www.svd.se/samre-polis-med-annu-mer-centralisering
https://www.svd.se/sa-blir-polisens-nya-organisation
http://www.polissamordningen.se/nyhetsarkivet
http://www.dn.se/nyheter/sverige/rekordfa-brott-klaras-upp-efter-polisens-omorganisation/
http://www.dagensjuridik.se/2014/04/rikspolischefen-vill-att-personer-utan-polisutbildning-ska-kunna-anstallas-som-poliser
http://www.blaljus.nu/nyhetsartikel/polis-pa-180-dagar
http://www.bra.se/bra/nytt-fran-bra/arkiv/press/2017-03-30-slutlig-brottsstatistik-2016.html
https://www.bra.se/download/18.366ea42214d6cb5d9d4635ad/1433939412790/2015_The+clearance+rate+in+Sweden+and+other+countries.pdf
http://www.un.org/en/universal-declaration-human-rights/
https://www.theguardian.com/world/2011/dec/15/americans-face-guantanamo-detention-obama
https://www.svt.se/opinion/forstarkning-av-terroristlagen-kan-hota-folkratten?
https://www.svd.se/riksdagen-sade-ja-till-terroristlag

http://www.dagensjuridik.se/2017/01/terroristlagar-har-gjort-undantagslagar-till-det-nya-normala-i-europa-ny-rapport
http://sverigesradio.se/sida/artikel.aspx?programid=83&artikel=6391422
http://www.riksdagen.se/sv/dokument-lagar/dokument/svensk-forfattningssamling/lag-2003148-om-straff-for-terroristbrott_sfs-2003-148
https://www.amnesty.org/en/documents/eur01/5342/2017/en/
https://www.nytimes.com/2015/09/05/world/asia/afghanistan-kill-decisions-us-sweden-germany.html?_r=0

Acceptance of certain types of crimes:
http://www.na.se/opinion/ledare/valkommen-till-valdtaktslandet-sverige
http://www.metro.se/artikel/h%C3%A4r-%C3%A4r-sanningen-bakom-statistiken-f%C3%B6r-v%C3%A5ldt%C3%A4ktslandet-sverige-xr
https://www.unodc.org/unodc/en/data-and-analysis/statistics.html
https://www.bra.se/bra-in-english/home/crime-and-statistics/rape-and-sex-offences.html
https://www.bra.se/brott-och-statistik/brottsutvecklingen/mord-och-drap.html
http://www.dn.se/nyheter/sverige/kraftig-okning-av-mord-i-sverige/
https://elisabethoglund.se/blogg/163-morddrap-begicks-sverige-2016-enligt-mina-studier/
http://www.metro.se/artikel/din-statistik-blir-inte-sann-bara-f%C3%B6r-att-du-vill-det-xr
http://www.sydsvenskan.se/2016-09-19/antalet-bilbrander-uppe-pa-rekordnivaer
http://www.dn.se/nyheter/sverige/fordubbling-av-antalet-bilbrander-sedan-ar-2000/
https://www.msb.se/sv/Kunskapsbank/Forskningsresultat/Brand-och-raddningstjanst/Anlagd-brand/
http://www.aftonbladet.se/nyheter/a/Lz524/polis-avlossade-varningsskott-mot-stenkastare-i-rinkeby
http://www.bakom-kulisserna.biz/news/anlagda-bilbrander-1996-2014/
http://www.expressen.se/nyheter/polisen-i-rinkeby-skot-for-att-traffa/
https://www.svd.se/dramatisk-okning-av-bilbrander-i-malmo
https://nyheteridag.se/plus/anlagda-bilbrander-har-okat-med-276-procent-pa-17-ar-har-ar-statistiken/
https://www.svt.se/nyheter/lokalt/uppsala/forskare-om-bakgrunden-till-bilbranderna
https://www.svt.se/nyheter/inrikes/lofven-om-polisen-for-daliga-resultat
http://www.aftonbladet.se/nyheter/a/XXWrE/de-dog-i-terrorattacken-i-stockholm

http://www.aftonbladet.se/nyheter/kolumnister/a/78nv9/man-kanner-inte-igen-sossarna-langre
https://ida.msb.se/ida2#page=a0232
http://www.friatider.se/utredning-l-ggs-ned-om-gruppv-ldt-kt-p-gotland
http://www.aftonbladet.se/nyheter/article24230795.ab
http://www.aftonbladet.se/nyheter/a/blG6d/misstankt-for-gruppvaldtakt-pa-gotland-begar-skadestand
https://www.svt.se/nyheter/lokalt/ost/valdtaktsutredning-laggs-ned-pa-gotland
http://www.breitbart.com/london/2017/02/21/swedish-newspaper-photographer-attacked-no-go-zone/
http://www.dailywire.com/news/13664/american-journalist-savagely-beaten-sweden-asking-michael-qazvini#
http://www.lifezette.com/polizette/hundreds-muslim-no-go-zones-take-root-europe/
http://www.breitbart.com/london/2017/02/21/swedish-newspaper-photographer-attacked-no-go-zone/
http://www.breitbart.com/london/2016/03/20/watch-journalists-punched-kicked-and-rammed-with-car-in-swedens-little-mogadishu-no-go-zone/
http://www.dailymail.co.uk/news/article-4274292/Journalists-told-leave-Swedish-no-zone.html
http://www.dailymail.co.uk/news/article-4024854/Moment-documentary-maker-punched-kicked-choked-five-migrants-entering-no-zone-Swedish-city.html
http://www.express.co.uk/news/world/754126/Violent-migrant-gangs-Swedish-shopping-centre-no-go-zone-Gothenburg
https://www.youtube.com/watch?v=AJ1_6s5OFmM
http://www.government.se/articles/2017/02/facts-about-migration-and-crime-in-sweden/
http://sverigesradio.se/sida/artikel.aspx?programid=2054&artikel=6630452
https://sv.wikipedia.org/wiki/No-go-zon

Fluorine:
http://www.globalhealingcenter.com/natural-health/how-fluoride-damages-pineal-gland-health/
https://www.ncbi.nlm.nih.gov/pubmed/15725334
http://www.who.int/water_sanitation_health/dwq/nutfluoride.pdf
http://www.icnr.com/articles/fluoride-deposition.html
http://epubs.surrey.ac.uk/895/1/fulltext.pdf
http://newsvoice.se/2015/06/11/tobias-lindberg-fluoriderad-mjolk-ett-experiment-pa-barn/
https://www.svd.se/forskare-varnar-for-fluor-till-barn

https://en.wikipedia.org/wiki/Fluoridation_by_country
http://www.svensktvatten.se/vattentjanster/dricksvatten/riskanalys-och-provtagning/kemiska-amnen-i-vatten/fluorid/
http://newsvoice.se/2014/09/01/forskare-varnar-for-fluor-till-barn-medvetenheten-dampas/
http://fluoridealert.org/researchers/nrc/findings/
http://fluoridealert.org/studies/brain06/
https://www.svd.se/forskare-varnar-for-fluor-till-barn
http://www.testfakta.se/sites/default/files/pdfpreview/7b5c7e01c9f366c015682789eac0b9eb.jpg

Harmful foods:
https://www.naturalnews.com/2017-09-14-new-york-times-spike-the-food-supply-with-sterilization-chemicals-to-cause-global-infertility-and-depopulation.html#
http://depopulation.news/2017-09-20-extinction-warning-chemicals-in-food-and-personal-care-products-making-humanity-infertile-may-lead-to-population-wipeout.html
http://www.mirror.co.uk/news/world-news/sperm-count-western-men-plunges-10869887
https://academic.oup.com/humupd/article-lookup/doi/10.1093/humupd/dmx022
https://www.matdagboken.se/information/fakta/tillsatser-e-nummer
http://www.aktavara.org/news.aspx?r_id=62107
http://www.nature.com/bjc/journal/v106/n3/full/bjc2011585a.html
https://en.wikipedia.org/wiki/Lee_Alvin_DuBridge

GMO:
https://sv.wikipedia.org/wiki/Genetiskt_modifierad_organism
https://www.theverge.com/2015/12/9/9879678/gmo-chicken-transgenic-fda-approved-kanuma-drug-eggs
https://gmoinquiry.ca/wp-content/uploads/2015/03/where-in-the-world-gm-crops-foods.pdf
https://en.wikipedia.org/wiki/Genetically_modified_food
https://gmo.geneticliteracyproject.org/FAQ/which-genetically-engineered-crops-are-approved-in-the-us/
http://www.naturvardsverket.se/Miljoarbete-i-samhallet/Miljoarbete-i-Sverige/Uppdelat-efter-omrade/Naturvard/Genetiskt-modifierade-organismer/GMO-i-Sverige/
https://www.youtube.com/watch?v=FS72J9bDvPM
https://www.youtube.com/watch?v=6D3TUk-XX1o

http://newsvoice.se/2015/05/05/enorm-halsorisk-2012-anvande-sverige-over-700-ton-glyfosat-ett-riskabelt-vaxtgift-i-roundup/
https://www.scientificamerican.com/article/weed-whacking-herbicide-p/
http://www.mdpi.com/1099-4300/15/4/1416
http://www.mdpi.com/1099-4300/15/4/1416/htm
http://newsvoice.se/2015/05/01/miljofragor-handlar-bade-om-den-yttre-miljon-och-om-den-inre-miljon-i-manniskokroppen/
http://www.jordbruksverket.se/amnesomraden/odling/genteknikgmo/kommersiellanvandning/godkanda.4.300b18bd13d103e79ef80002529.html
http://ec.europa.eu/consumers/europadiary/fi_sv/health/labels_sv.htm
http://articles.mercola.com/sites/articles/archive/2010/05/22/jeffrey-smith-interview-april-24.aspx
http://www.agriculturedefensecoalition.org/sites/default/files/file/agriculture_57/57H%202010%20Monsanto%20Genetically%20Modified%20Soy%20Study%20Linked%20to%20Sterility+Infant%20Mortality%20in%20Hamsters%20April%2020,%202010.pdf
https://www.youtube.com/watch?v=eilDbdLAyFs&feature=youtu.be
http://www.healthy-holistic-living.com/suppressed-evidence-connects-gmo-feed-sterile-livestock.html
https://www.svt.se/nyheter/inrikes/roundup-kan-forbjudas
http://www.reuters.com/article/us-health-eu-glyphosate-idUSKBN16M1KM
https://phys.org/news/2015-03-aluminium-threat-food-revealed.html
http://farmwars.info/?p=7760
http://www.freepatentsonline.com/7582809.html
https://academic.oup.com/jxb/article/62/1/9/512632/The-identification-of-aluminium-resistance-genes
https://www.theguardian.com/environment/2016/may/17/unwho-panel-in-conflict-of-interest-row-over-glyphosates-cancer-risk
https://en.wikipedia.org/wiki/Monsanto
http://newsvoice.se/2016/09/22/biokemiska-giganter-gar-samman-till-kemimonsterbolag/
https://sv.wikipedia.org/wiki/Genetiskt_modifierad_organism#/media/File:World_map_GMO_production_2005.png
https://sv.wikipedia.org/wiki/Transatlantiskt_partnerskap_f%C3%B6r_handel_och_investeringar
http://newsvoice.se/2017/05/13/handelsavtal-hyperglobalister/
http://newsvoice.se/2017/05/16/azure-farms-tvangsbesprutning/
http://www.naturalnews.com/2017-05-14-azure-farm-in-oregon-about-to-be-mass-poisoned-with-glyphosate-by-county-government.html
https://www.naturalnews.com/2017-09-07-rna-interference-crop-technology-weaponizes-food-into-the-ultimate-eugenics-weapon.html

https://www.sciencedaily.com/releases/2017/07/170727104547.htm
https://www.sciencedaily.com/releases/2012/02/120227094331.htm
https://en.wikipedia.org/wiki/RNA_interference
https://www.vaken.se/over-40-gmo-studier-pa-gnagare-visar-pa-odesdigra-halsoeffekter/#
http://gmofreeusa.org/research/glyphosate/glyphosate-studies/

Acidification:
https://www.havochvatten.se/hav/fiske--fritid/miljopaverkan/forsurning-av-sjoar-och-vattendrag/kalkning-och-andra-motatgarder.html
https://www.havochvatten.se/download/18.32d9853214ee7e1108cb3b53/14
40064362321/nationell-plan-for-kalkning-2011-2015.pdf
https://www.extension.umn.edu/agriculture/nutrient-management/phosphorus/the-nature-of-phosphorus/
http://www.jordbruksverket.se/amnesomraden/odling/jordbruksgrodor/soc
kerbetor/vaxtnaring/kalkning.4.32b12c7f12940112a7c800035459.html
https://www.slu.se/ew-nyheter/2016/5/de-viktiga-mikronaringsamnena--en-av-nycklarna-till-ett-produktivt-jordbruk/
http://www.vaxteko.nu/html/sll/hydro_agri/vaxtpressen/VPN93-3/VPN93-3A.HTM
https://svenska.yle.fi/artikel/2015/08/26/nordkalk-och-ilkka-herlin-jobbar-ett-hallbart-jordbruk
http://www.lantbruk.com/lantbruk/svenska-bonder-kalkar-battre-skordar
http://kalkforeningen.se/anvandning/
http://www.atl.nu/lantbruk/sveriges-sjalvforsorjningsgrad-ar-0/
http://www.corren.se/asikter/debatt/producera-mer-mat-i-sverige-5864681.aspx
https://www.svt.se/nyheter/granskning/ug/sverige-forlorar-en-mjolkbonde-om-dagen
http://www.expressen.se/kronikorer/lotta-groning/svenskt-jordbruk-framstar-som-en-sorglig-historia/
https://www.svt.se/nyheter/lokalt/uppsala/sa-lange-klarar-vi-oss-om-det-blir-krig
http://forfuture.se/eu-vill-avveckla-svenskt-jordbruk/
https://www.oaklandinstitute.org/blog/who-owns-agricultural-land-ukraine
https://www.oaklandinstitute.org/corporate-takeover-ukrainian-agriculture
https://www.oaklandinstitute.org/sites/oaklandinstitute.org/files/Brief_Cor
porateTakeoverofUkraine_0.pdf
http://www.ja.se/?p=35049&pt=105
http://www.lantbruk.com/lantbruk/ekoodlare-far-klara-sig-utan-strukturkalkning
https://www.svt.se/nyheter/vetenskap/9-av-10-jordbruk-borta-pa-25-ar

https://www.kemi.se/global/rapporter/2011/rapport-1-11.pdf
http://www.testfakta.se/tester/livsmedel/h%C3%B6ga-halter-kadmium-i-vanligt-vetemj%C3%B6l
https://www.svd.se/frukt-och-gront-har-vattnats-ur
https://sv.wikipedia.org/wiki/Surt_regn
https://www.nyteknik.se/opinion/ammoniak-som-forsurar-6475307
http://www.miljomal.se/Miljomalen/Alla-indikatorer/Indikatorsida/?iid=5&pl=1
https://en.wikipedia.org/wiki/Acid_rain
http://www.halsosidorna.se/Syrabasbalansen.htm
http://carlg.org/nyttigmat.html
http://www.gp.se/livsstil/mat/v%C3%A4xande-trend-basisk-alkalisk-kost-1.471019
http://newsvoice.se/2014/05/04/bikarbonatet-som-botar-cancer-referatet-av-seminariet-om-simoncini/
http://newsvoice.se/2017/08/28/erik-enby-cancerpatienter/
https://www.dagensmedicin.se/blogg/mats-reimer/2014/04/14/bakpulver-mot-cancer/
http://sverigesradio.se/sida/artikel.aspx?programid=97&artikel=5826787
https://sv.wikipedia.org/wiki/Natriumv%C3%A4tekarbonat
http://www.krc.su.se/documents/Modul_8.0_Syror_baser.pdf
https://sv.wikipedia.org/wiki/V%C3%A4tekarbonat

Climate lies - Climate issue:
https://www.youtube.com/watch?v=TCy_UOjEir0
https://www.svt.se/nyheter/uutiset/svenska/har-kan-meteorologen-inte-sluta-skratta-i-direktsandning
https://www.csiro.au/en/News/News-releases/2013/Deserts-greening-from-rising-CO2
http://www.metro.se/artikel/oklart-hur-klimatm%C3%A5l-ska-n%C3%A5s-trots-klimatlag-xt
http://www.sydsvenskan.se/2017-02-02/bra-klimat-for-ny-lag-klara-spelregler-behovs
http://www.swpc.noaa.gov/news/national-space-weather-strategy-and-action-plan-released
https://wattsupwiththat.com/2017/04/05/study-suggests-increased-atmospheric-co2-creates-a-30-growth-in-plant-photosynthesis-during-last-two-centuries/
https://www.nature.com/nature/journal/v544/n7648/full/nature22030.html
https://phys.org/news/2013-07-greening-co2.html
https://weather.com/news/climate/news/el-nino-ties-record-january-2016

http://www.libertycampaign.org/falling-sea-level-the-critical-factor-in-2016-great-barrier-reef-bleaching

http://www.biogeosciences.net/14/817/2017/

http://www.nature.com/nature/journal/v543/n7645/full/nature21707.html

https://www.smhi.se/forskning/forskningsnyheter/koldioxidhalten-okar-snabbare-i-atmosfaren-1.77799

https://sv.wikipedia.org/wiki/Vatten%C3%A5nga

https://sv.wikipedia.org/wiki/V%C3%A4xthuseffekten

http://deforestation.geologist-1011.net/

Kaser, G., Hardy, D. R., Mölg, T., Bradley, R. S., Hyera, T. M., 2004, "Modern glacier retreat on Kilimanjaro as evidence of climate change: observations and facts", "International Journal of Climatology", v. 24, pp. 329-339

Mason, B., 2003, "African Ice Under Wraps", Nature, "Science Update", ISO: 2003-Nov-24

Eswaran, H., Van Den Berg, E., Reich, P., 1993, "Organic carbon in soils of the world", Soil Science Society of America Journal, V. 57, pp. 192-194

Bowes, G., 1991, "Growth at Elevated CO2: Photosynthetic Responses Mediated through Rubisco", Plant Cell & Environment, v. 14. pp. 795-806

Koldioxidnivåer genom geologiska tidsåldrar i Graf:

Carbon dioxide after Berner (2001) & temperature after Scotese (2001; see also Boucot et al., 2004) sourced from www.geocraft.com showing the degree of variation in carbon dioxide throughout geological history.

http://www.nobelprize.org/nobel_prizes/peace/laureates/2007/

Berner, R.A., 2001, "Modeling Atmospheric Oxygen Over Phanerozoic Time", Geochimica et Cosmochimica Acta, v. 65, pp. 685-694.

https://www.google.se/search?q=carbon+dioxide+atmospheric+levels+historic&source=lnms&tbm=isch&sa=X&ved=0ahUKEwiRp7SUxPnTAhVDKVAKHaftBUEQ_AUICigB&biw=1149&bih=856#imgrc=nqMMwMKAfosvaM:

http://onlinelibrary.wiley.com/doi/10.1002/grl.50563/abstract

https://www.infowars.com/al-gore-backlash-why-environmentalists-are-celebrating-rising-co2-levels/

https://www.climate.gov/news-features/understanding-climate/climate-change-atmospheric-carbon-dioxide

ftp://aftp.cmdl.noaa.gov/products/trends/co2/co2_mm_mlo.txt

http://science.sciencemag.org/content/309/5734/600/tab-pdf

https://wattsupwiththat.com/2013/06/04/dr-vincent-gray-on-historical-carbon-dioxide-levels/

http://www.biocab.org/Carbon_Dioxide_Geological_Timescale.html

https://wattsupwiththat.files.wordpress.com/2016/06/moore-positive-impact-of-human-co2-emissions.pdf

https://friendsofscience.org/assets/documents/Carbonbaggers_Report.pdf
http://www.biocab.org/Geological_Timescale.jpg
https://arizonadailyindependent.com/2015/01/31/evidence-that-co2-emissions-do-not-intensify-the-greenhouse-effect/
https://climate.nasa.gov/vital-signs/global-temperature/
https://solarscience.msfc.nasa.gov/SunspotCycle.shtml
https://www.nasa.gov/mission_pages/sunearth/news/solarcycle-primer.html
https://earthobservatory.nasa.gov/Features/SORCE/sorce_03.php
https://solarscience.msfc.nasa.gov/SunspotCycle.shtml
https://www.skepticalscience.com/solar-activity-sunspots-global-warming.htm
https://tallbloke.wordpress.com/2015/02/06/gerry-pease-sc23-24-longest-peak-to-peak-solar-cycle-length-since-dalton-minimum/
http://ase.tufts.edu/cosmos/view_picture.asp?id=116
https://realclimatescience.com/2016/11/noaa-september-temperature-fraud/
Bok: "Vapor Tiger" av Adrian Vance
https://www.abc.net.au/news/2009-08-13/29320
https://principia-scientific.org/a-volcano-eruption-can-emit-more-co2-than-all-humanity-why-worry/
https://www.academia.edu/40573989/Discovery_of_Massive_Volcanic_CO2_Emissions_Rebuts_human_caused_Global_Warming_Theory_geological_heat_flow_is_possibly_the_root_cause_of_changes_to_our_oceans
https://www.youtube.com/watch?v=5VDDNgl-UPk
http://www.washingtontimes.com/topics/john-bates/
http://www.washingtontimes.com/news/2017/feb/5/climate-change-whistleblower-alleges-noaa-manipula/
http://www.dailymail.co.uk/sciencetech/article-4192182/World-leaders-duped-manipulated-global-warming-data.html
http://www.nytimes.com/1989/01/26/us/us-data-since-1895-fail-to-show-warming-trend.html?src=pm
https://realclimatescience.com/2016/12/100-of-us-warming-is-due-to-noaa-data-tampering/
https://realclimatescience.com/history-of-nasanoaa-temperature-corruption/
http://www.denisdutton.com/newsweek_coolingworld.pdf
https://climate.nasa.gov/news/916/for-first-time-earths-single-day-co2-tops-400-ppm/
https://earthobservatory.nasa.gov/Features/CarbonCycle/page5.php
http://history.aip.org/climate/xsolar.htm
http://newsvoice.se/2012/12/05/istiden-ar-har-den-globala-medeltemperaturen-sjunker-enligt-ny-forskning/

http://old.theclimatescam.se/tag/klimathotet/
http://newsvoice.se/2011/09/09/cern-kosmisk-stralning-kan-paverka-molnbildningen-henrik-svensmarks-teori-far-stod/
http://klimatsans.com/oversikt/
https://tallbloke.wordpress.com/2015/02/06/gerry-pease-sc23-24-longest-peak-to-peak-solar-cycle-length-since-dalton-minimum/
https://upload.wikimedia.org/wikipedia/commons/d/d5/Carbon_cycle.jpg
https://en.wikipedia.org/wiki/Carbon_cycle
http://whatsyourimpact.org/greenhouse-gases/carbon-dioxide-emissions
Le Quéré, C. et al. (2013). The global carbon budget 1959-2011.
http://www.woodfortrees.org/plot/rss/from:1995/mean:60/offset:0,2/plot/gistemp/from:1995/mean:60/offset:-0.28/plot/uah6/from:1995/mean:60/offset:0.1
http://www.climatedepot.com/2014/05/04/global-temperature-update-no-global-warming-at-all-for-17-years-9-months/
http://www.climatedepot.com/2013/02/03/top-swedish-climate-scientist-says-warming-not-noticeable-the-warming-we-have-had-last-a-100-years-is-so-small-that-if-we-didnt-have-climatologists-to-measure-it-we-wouldnt-have-noticed-it-at-all/
http://www.klimatupplysningen.se/2014/05/21/min-personliga-syn-pa-klimatforskningen/
https://solarscience.msfc.nasa.gov/predict.shtml
http://www.naturalnews.com/2017-06-01-the-paris-climate-accord-is-genocide-against-plants-forests-and-life-planet.html
https://astronomynow.com/2015/07/17/diminishing-solar-activity-may-bring-new-ice-age-by-2030/
https://solarscience.msfc.nasa.gov/predict.shtml
http://www.dailymail.co.uk/news/article-2415191/And-global-COOLING-Return-Arctic-ice-cap-grows-29-year.html
https://www.thenewamerican.com/tech/environment/item/17207-al-gore-forecasted-ice-free-arctic-by-2013-ice-cover-expands-50
https://scienceofdoom.com/2009/11/28/co2-an-insignificant-trace-gas-part-one/
Handbook of geophysics and space environments, 1965
http://oai.dtic.mil/oai/oai?verb=getRecord&metadataPrefix=html&identifier=ADA056800
http://yournewswire.com/global-warming-scientists-lied/
https://www.naturalnews.com/2017-07-26-nasa-confirms-sea-levels-have-been-falling-across-the-planet-for-two-years-media-silent.html
https://www.naturalnews.com/2017-09-21-over-31000-scientists-say-global-warming-is-a-total-hoax-now-theyre-speaking-out-against-junk-science.html
https://www.youtube.com/watch?v=eiPIvH49X-E&feature=youtu.be

http://www.petitionproject.org/seitz_letter.php
https://www.nasa.gov/image-feature/jpl/pia21049/changing-colors-in-saturns-north
https://www.mpg.de/research/sun-activity-high
http://www.nature.com/nature/journal/v399/n6735/full/399437a0.html

Agenda 21 and Agenda 2030:
https://sv.wikipedia.org/wiki/Agenda_21
http://www.oneplanet.se/se/Kliv_in_i_kretsloppet/Kliv_in_i_kretsloppet/Avfallscirkeln_sluts/Kartong_amp;_wellpapp
http://sverigesradio.se/sida/artikel.aspx?programid=3345&artikel=5160585
http://wwwb.aftonbladet.se/nyheter/9912/06/sopor.html
https://nyadagbladet.se/kronikor/nagra-av-varldens-varsta-miljobovar-star-bakom-klimatlarmen/
http://jmm.nu/ann-bressington-exposes-agenda-21/
https://www.youtube.com/watch?v=kifQ78OnCA8
https://en.wikipedia.org/wiki/Pauline_Hanson
http://www.disclose.tv/news/water_is_not_a_human_right_claims_ceo_of_nestl_peter_brabeckletmathe/134989
http://www.bbc.com/news/business-36161580
https://www.svd.se/bolag-som-reinfeldt-salt-varda-miljarder
https://www.youtube.com/watch?v=AZzSEOgbAaA
http://jmm.nu/ann-bressington-exposes-agenda-21/
https://nyadagbladet.se/kronikor/nagra-av-varldens-varsta-miljobovar-star-bakom-klimatlarmen/
http://www.klimatupplysningen.se/2013/11/29/klimatpolitikens-intressenter-romklubben/
http://www.wbcsd.org/
http://fn.se/vi-gor/vi-utbildar-och-informerar/fn-info/vad-gor-fn-2/fns-arbete-for-utveckling-och-fattigdomsbekampning/agenda-2030-globala-mal-for-hallbar-utveckling/
http://fn.se/wp-content/uploads/2016/07/Att-f%C3%B6r%C3%A4ndra-v%C3%A5r-v%C3%A4rld_-Agenda-2030-f%C3%B6r-h%C3%A5llbar-utveckling.pdf
http://www.regeringen.se/regeringens-politik/globala-malen-och-agenda-2030/17-globala-mal-for-hallbar-utveckling/
http://www.trollhattan.se/startsida/bygga-bo-och-miljo/klimatforandringar-och-miljo/agenda-21-och-agenda-2030/
http://www.zerohedge.com/news/2015-09-03/2030-agenda-month-un-launches-blueprint-new-world-order-help-pope
http://www.bakom-kulisserna.biz/news/a2030-agenda-denna-manad-lanserar-fn-len-plan-for-en-ny-varldsordning-med-hjalp-av-paven/

https://anthropocene.live/2017/05/09/nagra-av-varldens-varsta-miljobovar-star-bakom-klimatlarmen/
https://sustainabledevelopment.un.org/post2015/transformingourworld

Summary:
http://www.naturvardsverket.se/Sa-mar-miljon/Manniska/Miljogifter/Organiska-miljogifter/Lakemedel/
https://www.svt.se/nyheter/granskning/ug/vill-inte-uppge-vad-vinet-innehaller

Covid-19, vaccin, 5G
https://www.stralskyddsstiftelsen.se/2020/03/mycket-kraftig-okning-av-stralning-fran-basstationer/?
fbclid=IwAR0R6uDNYyND3KQdfAXPdrQKeyN9oLhyHVD1jRRoWZFQ
SrlE6PHte6IDFpc
https://www.telegraph.co.uk/news/2020/03/30/uks-attempt-ramp-coronavirus-testing-hindered-key-components/?
fbclid=IwAR0P13MRco7G_5P_Fl9_ROpo2YSCd2AAzupA_bQxgvYMX4C
_Wr__PWaJHII
https://www.youtube.com/watch?
v=u84j3OekMx4&feature=youtu.be&fbclid=IwAR05Fl4DkJxvweIIQ3HkkI
uydJu2OvUhfbjx4tiDAC0-VZQTbjHk6h90Ikg
https://www.brighteon.com/18a673d2-d9f2-4033-8899-e1cb42632dc9?
fbclid=IwAR0ZK0ypl52CAjbRHCetk-
FMHBHpicpYfKbO4YUdRlw0Ptd19cElHEDa7NM
https://www.youtube.com/watch?v=-0b1uaQrVes
https://www.youtube.com/watch?v=Nz4Syubt0ec
https://www.brighteon.com/587c47ab-9d8d-4596-b1d8-4b99adc3ed1f
https://www.youtube.com/watch?v=iHzGL4tJAQc
https://www.speedtest.net/ookla-5g-map
https://www.stralskyddsstiftelsen.se/risker/symtom/?
fbclid=IwAR2d2ckWlqczhOiuLEcrVehL9tprlZWqweeuwGIfQ1epmI3KtrC
1AIYwAgI
https://www.aftonbladet.se/nyheter/a/y3dR9e/darfor-syns-mystiska-ljusprickar-over-himlen
https://www.swebbtv.se/blogg/454-lars-bern-kraver-snabbutredning-att-gamla-dor-i-corona-kan-bero-pa-medicinering
https://nyadagbladet.se/halsa/hjarntumorer-okar-danmark-fordubblingsedan-1990/
https://www.speedtest.net/ookla-5g-map
https://www.brighteon.com/5071a300-b135-410f-9ba1-5512ce927ffb

https://principia-scientific.org/5g-warning-by-institute-of-electrical-and-electronics-engineers/
https://principia-scientific.org/134458-sign-international-appeal-to-stop-5g/
https://principia-scientific.org/petition-26000-scientists-oppose-5g-roll-out/
https://commons.wikimedia.org/wiki/File:2019-nCoV-CDC-23312.png
https://en.wikipedia.org/wiki/High_Frequency_Active_Auroral_Research_Program
https://nyadagbladet.se/it-overvakning/facebook-forbjuder-teorier-om-5g-och-coronakrisen/
https://www.regeringen.se/pressmeddelanden/2018/05/nytt-nordiskt-samarbete-om-5g/
https://www.youtube.com/watch?v=xf-qv9o8nq8&feature=share&fbclid=IwAR208hZc8cNKTtB-18ADZoTZbr8H4PbGRCo2mC-LKTK6wD2n2P6l-tMrmRo
https://commons.wikimedia.org/wiki/File:Telstra_Mobile_Phone_Tower.jpg
https://youtu.be/qZWcu9r9vhs?t=461
https://epochtimes.se/Ny-dokumentar-avslojar-sanningen-om-virusets-ursprung?fbclid=IwAR3w7nNwMNhQ9JSWJNWQmRBBEksA3D3fgKlcz_ofLt4qpSAfLb37ScTuyK0
https://www.epochtimes.se/Ar-5G-i-kombination-med-viruset-orsak-till-de-plotsliga-dodsfallen-i-Wuhan?fbclid=IwAR0qpcZrn7zPvrW9nzVXvBI21t9isjvklzsGhWiAf3Itryiewu-teFOR6ZA
https://epochtimes.se/Professor-om-5G-Varldshistoriens-dummaste-ide
https://www.icnirp.org/en/activities/news/news-article/rf-guidelines-2020-published.html
https://www.rfsafe.com/5g-network-uses-nearly-same-frequency-as-weaponized-crowd-control-systems/?fbclid=IwAR1ivhG9KtYBhbmnr4lZWz8aWjTxarM2qA1JXfUhWVK9k8p5FJQ_zlFuQcQ
https://samnytt.se/5g-natet-stoppas-i-belgien-av-halsoskal-ar-inte-forsoksdjur/?fbclid=IwAR0qeAHajFFf54ZhZnMl3Rpp7W2bnLSwgEVAiiUrgEAT-wn_vi-xO5U2hJ4
https://www.youtube.com/watch?v=vZ5soLrvXFg&feature=youtu.be&fbclid=IwAR2P8At8wtBIWaW9RVlsAeOV-mqAylpde_ELqG9ldU_FB_e3MaXzf7E0L7g
https://massawakening.org/5g-depopulation-agenda/
https://principia-scientific.org/wireless-industry-confesses-no-studies-show-5g-is-safe/

https://www.youtube.com/watch?
v=HahhDIeq1Ck&feature=youtu.be&fbclid=IwAR159iCVsUnZe0jsyNHrJ
DO-2ZjiKk1y9qN4dhwnOTsFvEFSvyu14RCYG1U
Konstantin Meyls forskning och dokumentation i skrivelser om skalära vågor
och mikrovågor, undervisning.
SVT
Som källa är givetvis också AIC:s kommunikation med utomjordiska
intelligenser, Plejadeaner, Sirianer, Zeta, m.fl. Kommunikation med matrisen.
https://www.folkhalsomyndigheten.se/nyheter-och-
press/nyhetsarkiv/2020/augusti/bristande-prestanda-i-kommersiellt-test-har-
gett-falskt-positiva-provsvar-om-covid-19/
https://www.nvic.org/Vaccine-Laws/1986-Vaccine-Injury-Law.aspx?
fbclid=IwAR1egQRzWIbMTNY3PFMa-
Vq_3jVGlxRvObksW24WVYHRtfTB30f9kYUF23o
http://avoiceforchoice.org/issues/pharmaceuticals-and-vaccines/20-vaccine-
facts/?fbclid=IwAR0UPLTN-
_MtkIhc95n601BYUigTnaP7jGKTj02L4Squv6CrLwva-EUqtaI
https://www.aftonbladet.se/nyheter/a/dOoG7q/oklart-om-skydd-for-
skador-av-covidvaccin?fbclid=IwAR20PhTK3CyQaNb4w7tcZsHdJXEbP3-
Xp_SA15Yvk_aTJ3a5tBZFwa3onr8
https://www.facebook.com/367542343889100/videos/312145610193872
https://www.vaken.se/bill-gates-och-rockefeller-vill-implementera-digitala-
id-handlingar-pa-miljarder-manniskor/
https://nyadagbladet.se/ekonomi/sverige-skanker-175-miljarder-till-maktig-
vaccinlobby/
https://nyadagbladet.se/it-overvakning/gates-sponsrat-projekt-i-afrika-ska-
introducera-biometriskt-id-for-betalningar-och-vaccinationer/
https://www.vaken.se/vaxxed-from-cover-up-to-catastrophe/
https://www.vaken.se/melbourne-en-experimentell-polisstat-coronakrisen-
anvands-som-drivkraft/
https://www.vaken.se/lars-bern-sammanfattar-vetenskapen-om-
coronapandemin/
https://freedomplatform.tv/plandemic-indoctornation-world-premiere/
https://nyadagbladet.se/utrikes/analytiker-australien-i-praktiken-nu-en-
polisstat/?fbclid=IwAR2Qlvni1I7ZBBaVPYK8f3_sQ-
MnxEeMQTM4sj8YwD1fCrmeTyNNj93cIBI
https://www.vaken.se/f-d-vetenskapsradgivare-for-pfizer-andra-
coronavagen-baseras-pa-falska-positiva-covid-tester/
https://www.youtube.com/watch?v=omPAz-
Hbyro&feature=youtu.be&fbclid=IwAR3P5GnOzIUc1M63mF_-
zqwaNGbnMZI_SwXAyKN9Czbb_TnxbchHZlZx_OQ

https://nyadagbladet.se/inrikes/regeringen-vill-forlanga-coronarestriktioner-till-nasta-sommar/

https://nyadagbladet.se/utrikes/massprotesterna-mot-coronarerepressionen-fortsatter-i-storbritannien/

https://nyadagbladet.se/halsa/bred-lakarkar-kraver-omedelbart-stopp-for-coronarepressionen/

https://nyadagbladet.se/utrikes/facebook-censurerar-trump-igen-laga-coronadodstal-far-inte-patalas/

https://newsvoice.se/2020/10/varldens-forsta-digitala-resepass-anpassade-for-covid-19-och-vaccinstatus-testas/

https://soundcloud.com/ulf-bittner/folkhalsomyndigheten-informeras-om-corona-bedrageriet-2020-10-07?fbclid=IwAR0kHam-JCF2pQfjR4v12_b7m0tHTdQAqCGK-2nG_uadwKSa5HGj8IEVECQ

https://bakomkulisserna.biz/2020/10/03/konkurs-pa-grund-av-corona-pandemin-en-grupptalan-av-tyska-dr-reiner-fuellmich/

https://www.youtube.com/watch?v=gvB0vuM5bek

https://www.svt.se/nyheter/inrikes/rna-vaccin-helt-unikt-och-effektiv-mot-coronaviruset

https://www.vaken.se/kontroversiellt-coronavaccin-ska-injicera-genetisk-kod-i-manniskor/

https://www.vaken.se/astra-zeneca-pausar-coronavaccintester-efter-att-testperson-insjuknat/

https://www.vaken.se/fn-kraver-330-nya-miljarder-till-coronavaccin/

https://www.vaken.se/folkhalsomyndigheten-repressionen-kan-fortsatta-minst-ett-ar/

https://nyadagbladet.se/inrikes/folkhalsomyndigheten-repressionen-kan-fortsatta-minst-ett-ar/

https://www.facebook.com/DANCE4MEPRINCE/videos/10157776679256295/

https://www.youtube.com/watch?v=pc_EiWNPrss&fbclid=IwAR3KNyLE6nUlmF33vmWRubhCBqcWs0K4GTiyusu363oSWrRM1qrzrnEuecA

https://www.youtube.com/watch?v=Cq0CUIf3f5g&feature=share&fbclid=IwAR1C5XQbkByRvgRY-J2B-4gMK2Srs7uuug82J33_a8bXnQVG1Varkn-Z0YY

https://www.youtube.com/watch?v=ksEVaO806Oo&fbclid=IwAR0_BNSJZzTNkngp-_AL3DSUXTIOK1eP2QiGlVYz5_h3i4JYsSKUtXTxH8Y

Anders Syborgs inlägg om strålningsnivåer på Järntorget i Gamla stan i Stockholm.

https://www.rfsafe.com/5g-network-uses-nearly-same-frequency-as-weaponized-crowd-control-systems/

Id2020.org

https://www.prophecynewswatch.com/article.cfm?recent_news_id=4037

https://www.armstrongeconomics.com/world-news/conspiracy/are-the-planning-id2020-as-mandatory-implants-for-all-as-the-solution-to-the-crisis/

https://stillnessinthestorm.com/2020/09/must-read-an-enzyme-called-luciferase-is-what-makes-bill-gates-implantable-vaccine-work-vaccine-id/

https://www.cdc.gov/chronicdisease/resources/infographic/chronic-diseases.htm

https://www.fightchronicdisease.org/sites/default/files/docs/GrowingCrisis ofChronicDiseaseintheUSfactsheet_81009.pdf

https://www.nowtheendbegins.com/bill-melinda-gates-foundation-spending-millions-creating-human-implantable-quantum-dot-microneedle-vaccine-mark-technology-with-data-storage/_81009.pdf

https://patentscope.wipo.int/search/en/detail.jsf?docId=WO2020060606

https://www.thenational.ae/lifestyle/travel/commonpass-the-app-pegged-as-the-answer-to-covid-free-air-travel-to-begin-trial-process-1.1090012

https://thecommonsproject.org/commonpass

https://en.wikipedia.org/wiki/Luciferase

https://nl.espacenet.com/publicationDetails/biblio?
II=0&ND=3&adjacent=true&locale=nl_NL&FT=D&date=20200903&CC=US&NR=2020279585A1&KC=A1#

https://nl.espacenet.com/publicationDetails/inpadocPatentFamily?
CC=US&NR=2020279585A1&KC=A1&FT=D&ND=3&date=20200903&DB=&locale=nl_NL

https://patentimages.storage.googleapis.com/61/a3/0d/3d91325d909386/US20200279585A1.pdf

https://humansarefree.com/2020/09/proof-covid-19-planned-new-world-order.html

https://humansarefree.com/2020/10/ons-statistics-normal-mortality-rate-and-no-pandemic.html

https://bakomkulisserna.biz/2020/09/30/slutligt-bevis-covid-19-planerades-for-att-inleda-den-nya-varldsordningen/

https://nyadagbladet.se/it-overvakning/youtube-censurerar-medicinska-experter/

https://www.svt.se/nyheter/inrikes/fhm-vi-har-lart-oss-av-den-forra-massvaccinationen-1?cmpid=del%3Afb%3A20201021%3Afhm-vi-har-lart-oss-av-den-forra-massvaccinationen-1%3Anyh
%3Alp&fbclid=IwAR0LZ8GpD90FXQMo8qWZ1VoJ6XEH53M5GpQJJ6x mMuSN2y1oN9ex81wKSFg

https://nyadagbladet.se/halsa/forsoksperson-dog-i-tester-av-coronavaccin/

https://nyadagbladet.se/utrikes/lakare-vi-gar-mot-tvangsvaccinationer-och-medicinsk-diktatur/

https://nyadagbladet.se/halsa/vaccintillverkare-pausar-tester-efter-skador-pa-deltagare/

https://www.brighteon.com/81ba9e7b-ce2c-4484-b406-250fc5064383

https://usainua-stage.red-carlos.com/docs/us-patent-us2006257852-propranolol-766ed0

https://worldwide.espacenet.com/publicationDetails/biblio?II=0&ND=3&adjacent=true&locale=en_EP&FT=D&date=20170531&CC=EP&NR=3172319A1&KC=A1

https://worldwide.espacenet.com

https://worldwide.espacenet.com/patent/search/family/051494985/publication/EP3172319A1?q=EP3172319A1

https://worldwide.espacenet.com/patent/search/family/051494985/publication/US10130701B2?q=US10130701B2

https://worldwide.espacenet.com/patent/search/family/033304326/publication/US2006257852A1?q=US2006257852

https://www.fbcoverup.com/docs/library/2018-11-20-US-Pat-No-10130701-CORONAVIRUS-Assignee-THE-PIRBRIGHT-INSTUTUTE-Woking-Great-Britain-funded-by-Wellcomme-Trust-and-Gates-Foundation-USPTO-Nov-20-2018.pdf

https://worldwide.espacenet.com/patent/search/family/051494985/publication/CN106536723A?q=pn%3DEP3172319B1

https://register.epo.org/application?number=EP15750093&lng=en&tab=doclist

https://bakomkulisserna.biz/2020/10/16/atomic-bombshell-vi-har-bevis-for-att-rothschilds-patenterade-covid-19- biometriska-tester-2015-och-2017-pirbright-ager-viruset-som-ar-ett-biologiskt-vapen-skapat-av-darpa-bill-gates-defra/

https://bakomkulisserna.biz/2020/11/05/good-vibrations-extra-michael-obernicia-prosecutions-of-british-mps-update/?fbclid=IwAR1KLf0uIyrkxVi4WjY90YI4gTT9ndrZkUmOv_L54c62q5tssnE1_Ums4KU

https://sv.wikipedia.org/wiki/H%C3%B6jdsjuka

The Social Contract - -its validity

https://www.vaken.se/plandemic-en-film-om-en-global-plan-for-att-ta-kontroll-over-vara-liv-halsa-och-frihet/

https://www.brighteon.com/65e2f3fe-f4fa-4a0f-8988-a10765ec12af

https://plandemicmovie.com/?fbclid=IwAR1ocL4oeTxJcZy92ZcYm0DP0yYvMbD-IZ1PBH_6lKdQZlbPWrGN8X0jm9Q

https://www.youtube.com/watch?
v=74JwNPcbD9Y&feature=share&fbclid=IwAR1kKs00W0QOOFVodUlG
EVdPB7-BlNo6xF1U6LQCP7RPQ2fOO_6sk_wZG90
https://nyadagbladet.se/it-overvakning/bill-gates-och-rockefeller-vill-
implementera-digitala-id-handlingar-pa-miljarder-manniskor/?
fbclid=IwAR3qIJ6-
cM1zQCJl7koCGrKxJ52tput9EhpVmMXqcDaoAmMjvBWJP2aPYUE
https://www.biometricupdate.com/201909/id2020-and-partners-launch-
program-to-provide-digital-id-with-vaccines?
fbclid=IwAR2T4Wx8kgffZ16D5g89qvgGh8TVI1XlToXafTBQnCw4W6D7
GQ5EC3yGClM
https://nyheteridag.se/med-att-standigt-vara-naiv-ar-ingen-ursakt/
https://anthropocene.live/2020/02/24/coronapandemin-nagra-rad/
https://www.theguardian.com/environment/2020/apr/24/coronavirus-
detected-particles-air-pollution
https://www.vaken.se/personal-i-vita-huset-diskuterar-coronadodlighet-pa-
endast-01-03/?
fbclid=IwAR2yjzqSIXza_k21skGTp61vqQhqE4Fd6yv50UvTayzw-
1URYHhHLOdEoyM
https://vaccineimpact.com/2020/taiwan-no-lockdowns-no-closed-
businesses-non-who-member-and-relatively-unaffected-by-covid-19/?
fbclid=IwAR00t0J_QwD94G5FFFOhPRlwr3GBXd3l7ROphJSsQUYSPTa4
tXlghaEhV_s
https://www.russiatruth.co/2020/03/putin-and-trump-vs-new-world-
order.html?fbclid=IwAR2dh4wTqq9n1MR9H6Msqdl3QqTLONNIR-
OxGWWDP5ZhEWd9Jal9mTMk-LM
https://www.vaken.se/amerikanska-bonder-beordras-att-avliva-boskap-och-
forstora-grodor/
http://www.thenhf.se/barnmisshandel-att-inte-vaccinera-skriver-expressens-
kronikor-nu-far-hon-svar-pa-tal/
https://www.skrivunder.com/lakemedelsverkets_ratt_att_forbjuda_orter_so
m_anvants_for_halsan?
uv=19378743&utm_source=fb_share&fbclid=IwAR1vPhEpGd1Q11rC3lQ
Fh_MKGVMp7cprZGHLNLrhW91oMGNsalvjkYdp_3s
https://undermattans.blogspot.com/2013/05/mobilstralning-dodade-krasse-
odling.html?m=1&fbclid=IwAR1jOxfpLjYw--
RgRxNAP1Un1S1rLIL2i_DGB_rTaNlf-qn15oVVbCI-R9Q
https://www.svt.se/nyheter/inrikes/stort-intresse-for-att-chippa-sig-i-
handen?fbclid=IwAR0dHG-4YF1-aHJpeYgNq8-
5IU1mgumGw2l3ko2m9iMBLKuQMHpUUUIZB5E

https://www.youtube.com/watch?v=KiNxOqFihvk&feature=youtu.be&fbclid=IwAR2y-rOelZSQj00wWuR1P5Yz_TCXhoEyAO1ZjIGiES4NmKIob6eC73VB5zQ
https://www.netdoktor.se/resemedicin-vaccin/vaccination/nyheter/sociala-medier-stoppar-falsk-information-om-vaccin/
https://www.skrivunder.com/stall_folkhalsoinstitutet_lakemedelsverket_och_mainstream_media_till_ratta_for_brott_mot_manskligheten?s=70828020&fbclid=IwAR0oqmsJvz4yv8MXoPu0z2xwoVZMENHVeMB1CV_dqW3FhvQBvZUhbY3PE8U
https://www.exakt24.se/regeringen-forbereder-for-matransonering/
https://www.naturalnews.com/035431_vaccine_ingredients_side_effects_msg.html
https://www.aftonbladet.se/nyheter/a/y3dR9e/darfor-syns-mystiska-ljusprickar-over-himlen
https://www.infowars.com/youtube-facebook-delete-david-ickes-accounts-over-pandemic-misinformation/
https://www.ncbi.nlm.nih.gov/pubmed/32164085
https://www.vaken.se/skolmedicinmannen-fortiger-viktig-vetenskap-for-allmanheten/
https://www.youtube.com/watch?v=ICtsXNtf_GQ

CPSIA information can be obtained
at www.ICGtesting.com
Printed in the USA
BVHW082025301120
594477BV00006B/807